Risk Allocation and Distributive Justice in the Energy Industry

To Joy, Chimasirim, Chimeka, and Chimkarila

Risk Allocation and Distributive Justice in the Energy Industry

Law, Policy and Practice

Smith I. Azubuike

EDINBURGH
University Press

Edinburgh University Press is one of the leading university presses in the UK. We publish academic books and journals in our selected subject areas across the humanities and social sciences, combining cutting-edge scholarship with high editorial and production values to produce academic works of lasting importance. For more information visit our website: edinburghuniversitypress.com

Edinburgh University Press Ltd
13 Infirmary Street
Edinburgh EH1 1LT

Typeset in 10/12 Goudy Old Style by
IDSUK (DataConnection) Ltd, and
printed and bound in Great Britain

A CIP record for this book is available from the British Library

ISBN 978 1 3995 1770 6 (hardback)
ISBN 978 1 3995 1772 0 (webready PDF)
ISBN 978 1 3995 1773 7 (epub)

FSC www.fsc.org
MIX
Paper | Supporting responsible forestry
FSC® C013604

Contents

Acknowledgments

I am immensely grateful to God, the giver of strength and wisdom, for the successful completion of this book.

My profound gratitude goes to my family for their love and support while writing this book. Thank you, Stephen Ross Dow, for helping me shape the idea in this book.

Preface

Petroleum operations enhance energy security in resource-rich nations and contribute to the global energy mix. However, they contribute to environmental pollution and global warming. Most petroleum resources are found offshore, thus accounting for increased offshore drilling operations. The drilling operations are preceded by a contract between the operator and the contractor, who share the risk associated with offshore drilling operations using mutual indemnity clauses and other risk allocation tools. The industry practice is for operators and contractors to accept liability for injury or death, property damage or pollution damage without regard to the negligence or gross negligence of the parties. This industry practice is based on the operators and contractors having custody, care and control over the activity that led to the harm.

The House of Lords in *Caledonia North Sea Ltd v London Bridge Engineering Ltd* (*London Bridge* case) describes the industry risk allocation practice as market practice, and the freedom of contract doctrine supports the liberty of parties to contract based on agreed terms. As such, the freedom of contract makes the risk allocation practice absolute and not qualified. Hence, parties usually apply mutual indemnity clauses as a shield against liability arising from gross negligence. The risky nature of offshore petroleum drilling operations provides a ground to allow liability arising from negligence. However, the oil industry applies the same underpinning when a downside occurs from gross negligence. This absolutism in the freedom to contract on liability arising from gross negligence contradicts public policy, which seeks to protect the interest of non-contracting third parties from harm. The reason is that allocating risk without regard to liability arising from gross negligence is akin to encouraging moral hazard, which can lead to offshore pollution damage impacting the public when offshore pollution occurs. Again, liability arising from gross negligence results in higher fines in most jurisdictions like the United States of America.

Post-Macondo risk allocation has seen a growing tendency to dilute established mutual indemnity provisions through contractual mechanisms such as carve-outs, especially for liabilities arising from gross negligence, breach of warranties and safety regulations. There is also evidence that operators are pushing for contractors to be liable to a specific minimum amount for contractors' pollution negligence, even if the pollution arises from the reservoir. Operators believe this minimum liability will incentivise contractors to avoid incidents. However, contractors are opposed to the idea.

Solving this challenge requires a repurposing of the contractual risk allocation practice of the oil industry, especially in gross negligence cases. Rethinking the practice would require understanding, defining and mainstreaming a standard of proof for gross negligence to allow its broad application as a term of art in the oil industry.

A comparative analysis and assessment of risk allocation from a public policy perspective have not received an exhaustive and rigorous book-length exposition. Although earlier scholarship has focused on risk allocation in the oil and gas industry, little attention (from articles) has been paid to the risk of gross negligence risk, specifically the need to allocate this risk with consideration of public policy. This book is an attempt to fill that gap.

This book provides an authoritative exposition of the legal, policy and institutional frameworks necessary to mainstream the practice of risk allocation in gross negligence cases in the offshore oil industry. It explores how mutual indemnity can be qualified before applying as a shield in gross negligence when pollution damage occurs during offshore petroleum operations. The book explores the assumptions and guiding principles underpinning risk allocation, and how to solve the challenges that gross negligence presents when parties insert it into their contract. Most importantly, this book advances a distributive justice perspective on how liability arising from gross negligence can be shared between the parties to the agreement. It emphasises the proportionality principle to achieve this objective.

Overall, the book aims to enhance an understanding of the nature and scope of risk and risk allocation in gross negligence cases in the offshore petroleum industry, assess its application by participants in selected jurisdictions in the oil industry, and explore the concepts of freedom of contract and public policy and their interplay with gross negligence.

The book is organised in a user-friendly style to enhance its utility among operators and contractors, resource-rich countries, policymakers, courts, insurance companies, practitioners, scholars and academics interested in offshore drilling operations and the risk allocation process in the energy industry. It interweaves descriptive materials on risk allocation and drilling contracts in the offshore energy industry with analytical evaluations of how public policy and distributive justice could influence and repurpose risk allocation for environmental sustainability in the offshore energy industry.

Smith I Azubuike, PhD
Durham Law School
Durham University, UK
August 2024

Foreword

A curious feature of the ongoing transition to a less carbon-intensive global economy is the resilience of the oil and gas industry, even in the expensive, high-risk and complex operations that are required in offshore waters. As Dr Azubuike notes, since the Russia-Ukraine conflict, governments in many countries have supported the expansion of oil and gas activity in the interests of 'energy security'. While such policies appear inconsistent with Net Zero commitments, their impacts also include an increased probability of offshore pollution accidents and wider risks to environmental sustainability and human rights, particularly from petroleum operations in offshore areas.

In this innovative book, Dr Azubuike focuses on the public interest element in offshore petroleum activities but takes us away from the realm of government and industry to the less well-travelled realm of company operators and their contractors, where contractual risk management leads to the inclusion of mutual indemnity, exclusion or limitation of liability clauses. This is an area where standard industry forms, originating in associations or private templates, prevail. However, this book presents pathways that should be considered when allocating risk.

An event farther back in time acts as a driver behind Dr Azubuike's concern about risk management practices and the public interest: the Macondo oil spill in the Gulf of Mexico in 2010. The litigation between the operating company and the drilling company subcontractor informs this book. It revealed a great deal about industry practices and raised questions about the public interest that Dr Azubuike is not afraid to tackle. It appeared after the Macondo incident that mutual indemnity agreements could be used as a shield against liability for gross negligence so that a wrongdoer would be protected even when harm impacts non-consenting third parties. To address this, he explains the industry practice of risk management in a straightforward and helpful manner and critically assesses it to identify ways of 'mainstreaming public interest more efficiently and equitably' especially in such gross negligence cases.

In his response to this worrying outcome of Macondo, Dr Azubuike offers a version of risk allocation that incentivises pollution prevention during offshore drilling operations and, at the same time, contributes to protecting the public interest and the contracting parties' interests. To do so, he proposes an 'integrative framework that incentivises pollution prevention in offshore drilling', while still upholding the risk and reward system typically used by the industry. It benefits from notions of distributive justice in its proposals for how liability arising from gross negligence can be shared between the parties to an agreement in ways that respect environmental sustainability and public safety.

In offering us a new framework, Dr Azubuike hopes to stimulate our thinking about the allocation of risk in future offshore drilling contracts, especially gross negligence risk, and to encourage the parties to make greater provision for the public interest in designing and concluding them. If such contracts are to play an important part in our energy future, and recent actions by governments suggest they will, at least in some parts of the world, then his argument for greater consideration of the public interest in their usage is timely and an important call for attention from both scholars and, of course, the parties themselves.

Peter D Cameron
Professor of International Energy Law and Policy
Director, Centre for Energy, Petroleum and Mineral Law and Policy
University of Dundee, UK
December 2023

Table of Cases

Table of Instruments

Abbreviations

AI	additional insured
AIEN	Association of International Energy Negotiators
AIPN	Association of International Petroleum Negotiators
ANI	American Nuclear Insurers
API	American Petroleum Institute
BP	British Petroleum
CAT	catastrophe
CLEE	Convention on Civil Liberty for Oil Pollution Damage Resulting from Exploration for and Exploitation of Seabed Mineral Resources 1977
CO_2	carbon dioxide
DESNZ	Department for Energy Security and Net Zero
E&P	exploration and production
ESG	environmental, social and governance perspectives
ETPS	economic, technical, political and social
FDP	field development plan
FIDIC	International Association of Consulting enginees
HS	host state
IADC	International Association of Drilling Contractors
ILS	insurance-linked securities
IMHH	Industry Mutual Hold Harmless Agreement
IOCs	international oil companies
ISO	Insurance Services Office Inc
JOA	joint operating agreement
JOC	joint operating committee
JV	joint venture
LOAIA	Louisiana Oilfield Anti-Indemnity Act
LOGIC	Leading Oil and Gas Industry Competitiveness
MER	maximising economic recovery
MNCs	multinational oil companies
MODUs	mobile offshore drilling units
MPH	miles per hour
NESS	necessary element of a sufficient set
NNPC	Nigerian National Petroleum Corporation
NOC	national oil company
NPFC	National Pollution Funds Center (US)

NSTA	North Sea Transition Authority (UK)
OCIL	Oil Casualty Insurance Limited
OECD	Organisation for Economic Co-Operation and Development
OEE	Operators' Extra Expense
OGA	Oil and Gas Authority (UK)
OIL	Oil Insurance Limited
OPA	Oil Pollution Act (US)
OPOL	Offshore Pollution Liability Agreement
P&I	protection and indemnity
PESTLEO	political, economic, social, technology, legal, environmental and operational
PSC	production sharing contract
SDGs	Sustainable Development Goals (United Nations)
SEPE	social, economic, political and ecological
SLO	social license to operate
SPV	special-purpose vehicle
STEEPLED	social, technological, economic, environmental, political, legal, educational and demographic
TBL	triple bottom line
TOAIA	Texas Oilfield Anti-Indemnity Act
UCTA	Unfair Contract Terms Act (UK)
UK	United Kingdom
UKCS	United Kingdom Continental Shelf
US	United States of America

Chapter 1

Risk Allocation in the Offshore Energy Industry: An Overview

1.0 GENERAL INTRODUCTION AND BACKGROUND

The Russia-Ukraine crisis and the sudden increase in energy prices in 2022 reinforced the emphasis on energy security and increased petroleum development in resource-rich countries.[1] Oil and gas play a major role in energy security, arguably due to their affordability, reliability and accessibility in the global hydrocarbon market. As several petroleum-rich countries grapple with energy security, they are looking to develop more offshore petroleum fields by issuing new licences.[2] For example, the United Kingdom has launched its thirty-third offshore licensing round, which attracted 115 bids across 258 blocks from seventy-six companies.[3] The implication is that drilling activities will continue in the North Sea for two or three more decades. New licences will increase the likelihood of offshore pollution accidents, which can impact environmental sustainability. However, strong petroleum laws and contractual practices can mitigate possible environmental impacts during offshore petroleum drilling operations.

Drilling for oil and gas offshore is complex and risky, hence the need to allocate risk associated with offshore drilling operations. Risk allocation is usually between an operator and a drilling contractor, and the agreement covers mainly the operator's groups and the drilling contractor's group. The agreement also covers various other issues, and parties usually negotiate their responsibilities. The practice is for both parties to execute a mutual indemnity agreement and assume liability for injury, death, property damage or pollution damage based on custody, care and control. The allocation of risk is not based on fault but on contract and the party who is best able to control the risk. Therefore, the negligence or gross negligence of the party at fault does not result in their liability. Instead, liability is based on the responsibility that has been accepted under the contract. The rationale advanced for this practice is to ensure certainty of responsibility, avoid double insurance, prevent lengthy litigation and so on.

1 Victor C Azubuike, 'The Energy Transition and Energy Security Nexus: An Outlook for the United Kingdom' (2023) Journal of Energy and Natural Resources Law, 503.

2 Alex Lawson, 'UK offers new North Sea oil and gas licences despite climate concerns' *The Guardian* (London, 7 October 2022) <www.theguardian.com/business/2022/oct/07/uk-offers-new-north-sea-oil-and-gas-licences-despite-climate-concerns> accessed 02 March 2023.

3 Melisa Cavcic, 'UK's First Licensing Round Since 2019 Brings 115 Bids from 76 Oil & Gas Firms' (OFFSHORE ENERGY, 17 January 2023) <www.offshore-energy.biz/uks-first-licensing-round-since-2019-brings-115-bids-from-76-oil-gas-firms> accessed 02 March 2023.

Risk allocation plays a crucial role in managing risk in petroleum drilling operations that entail substantial capital investment and high levels of risk. However, allocating risk in the manner adopted by the oil and gas industry raises concerns about public safety and environmental protection, and the role that public policy and distributive justice can play in ensuring a higher level of care during offshore petroleum drilling operations. Because the risk allocation is not fault based, the relevant parties bear all losses arising from death or injury to personnel, property or pollution damage, whether occurring on the surface of the water or from the well. In other words, mutual indemnity clauses are used as a shield in risk allocation. However, they should apply as a sword or a carve-out when liability arises from gross negligence. Therefore, recalibrating the practice of risk allocation from the point of view of public policy, distributive justice and the need for environmental sustainability serves as an analytical mechanism for shedding some light on the use of mutual indemnity clauses as a shield for liability arising from gross negligence during offshore petroleum operations.

This oil industry practice has mostly remained uncontested. However, the Macondo accident in 2010, which raised issues about contractors' liability for gross negligence, and the litigation that followed raised a new legal issue regarding liability for gross negligence in offshore drilling operations. Evidence from risk allocation negotiations between operators and contractors suggests that operators seek to modify the traditional risk allocation method. One of the contentious issues is the liability for gross negligence.[4] This changing perception of risk allocation, especially by operators, puts the practice of risk allocation in the spotlight. Ideally, the manner of risk allocation should encourage parties to exercise care to avoid harm and losses during a drilling operation. Therefore, exploring risk allocation in the context of how harm and damage can be mitigated or prevented through contractual clauses in petroleum operations is essential for environmental sustainability and public interest.

In all petroleum regimes, some laws regulate offshore petroleum activities and specify fines for pollution damage, but most of these laws do not act as a disincentive for wrongful drilling operations, especially for well pollution damage during drilling activities. The reason is that the operator is responsible for well pollution and is directly liable to the government, irrespective of the drilling contractor's gross negligence. However, public policy is against contracts that protect a wrongdoer from gross negligence, especially when the harm can impact non-consenting third parties. Therefore, if offshore drilling contracts continue without allocating fault in gross negligence cases, more offshore accidents are likely to occur, despite regulations to protect the environment. A potential solution to this dilemma is to adopt a distributive approach to risk allocation in gross negligence cases. The rationale for this approach is that it would place responsibility for pollution damage

4 Torgeir Willumsen and Terje Holte, 'Contractors' Pollution Risk Gets Dirty' (*Offshore Engineer*, 14April2015) <www.oedigital.com/news/452942-contractors-pollution-risk-gets-dirty> accessed 9 October 2023.

on both parties, thereby fostering mutual oversight and discouraging moral hazards. As such, this book recommends a practice where a party at fault bears liability for its gross negligence up to a specified limit, to balance the risk and reward system and the different statuses of the parties in the oil industry. The proportionality element of distributive justice, adapted in this book, can be achieved using a liability cap. Mechanically, it means that where there is gross negligence, the party at fault cannot rely on a mutual indemnity agreement as a shield against liability. To ensure compliance with the practice, oil and gas laws, model clauses or model production sharing contracts (PSCs) could make indemnity agreements subject to gross negligence. In this way, legal operatorship remains unchanged, but a different set of incentives for accident prevention is mainstreamed into the practice of risk allocation to achieve public policy objectives.

In this regard, this book evaluates the use of gross negligence in offshore drilling contracts through the public policy lens and determines how gross negligence can apply to drilling operations. The purpose is to advance a contractual practice in risk allocation where gross negligence will constitute grounds for a party to assume liability when a downside occurs in a drilling operation. The book also promotes using distributive justice as the basis for determining how liability for gross negligence should be assigned, taking into account the benefit that each party derives from the petroleum operation.

This book offers a multi-jurisdictional and systemic examination of the practice of risk allocation, in standard forms and private contracts, from both PSCs and Concession regimes such as Nigeria, Indonesia, the United Kingdom (UK) and the United States of America (US). It also explores the concepts of risk, mutual indemnity agreements and other tools for allocating risk, and the rationale for the oil and gas industry practice. In achieving its objective of mainstreaming a risk allocation practice that discourages harm, this book first discusses the concept of risk and its various approaches. Then, it highlights risk allocation practice, especially in gross negligence cases, and examines it in light of public policy, considering the extent to which it supports environmental sustainability. It discusses freedom of contract and examines the extent to which parties in the oil and gas industry are free to utilise mutual indemnity clauses as a defence for gross negligence when a downside occurs in a drilling operation.

The book further identifies gross negligence as a *sui generis* risk and unpacks the challenges confronting risk allocation in gross negligence cases in the petroleum industry. It also discusses guiding principles essential to address the difficulties identified in ensuring environmental sustainability and public safety in risk allocation. These guiding principles include public policy, human rights, sustainability and distributive justice. It advances the principle of distributive justice as a crucial element in risk allocation and highlights an adaptable legal framework for its implementation in the oil and gas industry. It also identifies practical institutional and financial frameworks that can assist in allocating risk in gross negligence cases, and provides a summary for stakeholders to consider in gross negligence risk allocation.

1.1 UNDERSTANDING THE CONCEPTS OF RISK AND RISK ALLOCATION

The concept of risk can be viewed from various perspectives (decision-making in business, insurance, construction, oil and gas, social life and so on).[5] Risk relates to the impact that uncertain outcomes might have on achieving a particular set objective.[6] In simple terms, risk could be described as exposure to danger. Some scholars view risk as the probability surrounding an event. The reason is that risk is an indispensable and unavoidable part of an event or business.[7] To others, it is a 'hazard, an exposure to misfortune or chances of negative consequences' or the 'possibility of an event happening, accompanied with consequences if it does happen'.[8] Risks may be categorised in several ways, such as dynamic and static risks, speculative and pure risks, fundamental and particular risks, and so on.[9] The categorisation of risk most closely linked to this study is that into fundamental and particular risks. The former relates to losses affecting many people, while the latter is associated with a specific cause in cases such as oil pollution and fire. Risk is a negative concept in a project that requires proper management, and the level of risk involved in a project determines the parties involved and the value of the contract.[10]

While risk can be managed, diminished, transferred or accepted, it cannot be ignored,[11] because all projects involve risk. As such, allocating risk to manage economic outcomes is essential. Some scholars note that risk allocation involves defining and assigning possible future losses and gains for various hypothetical situations should a downside occur.[12] As part of a risk management strategy, risks

[5] Risk has been referred to as involving two essential dimensions: possible consequences and associated uncertainties (see Terje Aven and Vidar Kristensen, 'Perspectives on Risk: Review and Discussion of the Basis for Establishing a Unified and Holistic Approach' (2005) 90(1) Reliability Engineering & System Safety 1). Risk has also been seen as involving core elements such as possible outcomes, uncertainty and methods of measuring possible outcomes. See Terje Aven and Ortwin Renn, 'Risk Perspectives' in Terje Aven and Ortwin Renn (eds) *Risk Management and Governance Concepts, Guidelines and Applications*, (Springer 2010). See also Terje Aven and Bodil S Krohn, 'A New Perspective on How to Understand, Assess and Manage Risk and the Unforeseen' (2014) 121 Reliability Engineering & System Safety 1; Ortwin Renn and others, 'Systemic Risks from Different Perspectives' [2020] Risk Analysis 1.

[6] David Hillson and Peter Simon, *Practical Project Risk Management: The ATOM Methodology* (2nd edn, Berret-Koehler Publishers 2012).

[7] Eric Banks, *Catastrophic Risk: Analysis and Management* (John Wiley & Sons Ltd 2005) 3.

[8] Peter Megens, 'Different Perspective of Construction Risk – How Should It Be Allocated?' (1996) 15(4) AMPLA Bulletin 179.

[9] Emmett J Vaughan and Therese Vaughan, *Fundamentals of Risk and Insurance* (10th edn, John Wiley & Sons 2007) 2.

[10] Patson Wilbroad Arinaitwe, *Risk Allocation in Oil and Gas Service Contracts: A Comparative Analysis of US and UK Continental Shelves* (Lap Lambert Academic Publishing 2014).

[11] Michael Latham, *Constructing the Team: Joint Review of Procurement and Continental Arrangement in the United Kingdom Construction Industry* (Final Report, July 1994) <constructingexcellence.org.uk/wp-content/uploads/2014/10/Constructing-the-team-The-Latham-Report.pdf> accessed 12 October 2023.

[12] Chi K Lam and others, 'Modelling Risk Allocation Decision in Construction Contracts' (2007) 25(5) International Journal of Project Management 485.

are allocated to the parties involved in a contract. The contractual document, which regulates their rights and obligation, sets out the extent of parties' liabilities regarding each risk. In other words, a contract can be considered 'a trade-off between the contractor's price for undertaking the work and his willingness to accept controllable and uncontrollable risks'.[13] The exchange should conform to the law and policy considerations as parties freely contract.

Insurance theorists view the concept of risk from different perspectives.[14] They see risk as the likelihood or chance of loss that a party can mitigate through preventive measures, the division of the actual from the expected result, or the possibility of having an outcome distinct from the desired outcome. Loss and indeterminacy are common elements that exist in most of these definitions.

1.2 RISK AND RELATED CONCEPTS

1.2.1 Risk and Uncertainty

Risk and uncertainty are interrelated, as a connection exists between the concepts, primarily as the former arises from the latter. The nexus between risk and uncertainty has been considered in terms of the quantum of measurability,[15] the possibility of the occurrence of a probable state of nature[16] and how uncertain events affect goals.[17] However, the latter aspect highlights that the two concepts are not theoretically identical. In a business context, a risk is a common state in decision-making where a person has incomplete information concerning a possible outcome, whereas uncertainty typifies an uncommon situation where a piece of information relating to the desired result is missing.[18]

Risk and uncertainty are closely linked, but a distinction exists between them. Some scholars note that uncertainty involves an exposure that cannot be measured or quantified, given the absence of predictability of the future outcome.[19] Such uncertainty exists where multiple alternatives could result in a particular outcome, but the possibility of the outcome is unknown[20] because of insufficient information or knowledge about the current condition. In other words, it is difficult to foresee the future outcome of an activity given people's incomplete understanding of the world and, hence, their limited knowledge of what might transpire in future. Consequently, uncertainty cannot apply to an outcome because the

13 ibid 485.

14 ibid.

15 Frank H Knight, *Risk, Uncertainty and Profit* (Dover Publications 2006) 233.

16 Mauro Maldonato and Silvia Dell'Orco, *Natural Logic: Exploring Decision & Intuition* (Sussex Academic Press 2011).

17 Hillson and Simon (n 6).

18 Fiona Macmillan, 'Risk, Uncertainty and Investment Decision-Making in the Upstream Oil and Gas Industry' (PhD Thesis, University of Aberdeen 2000).

19 Sareen Surbhi, 'Difference between Risk and Uncertainty' (*Key Differences*, 15 June 2017) <key-differences.com/difference-between-risk-and-uncertainty.html> accessed 12 October 2023.

20 John M Keynes, A *Treatise on Probability, The Collected Writings of John Maynard Keynes, Vol VIII* (Macmillan 1921); Knight (n 15) 233.

probabilities are not precise. Therefore, we cannot control, mitigate or assign uncertainty because the possible outcomes are unknown. In contract law, uncertainty is used to describe the absence of a basis for determining whether an agreement has been kept or breached.[21] Uncertainty exists when there is no basis to determine if an outcome will be adverse or favourable (loss or gain).

On the other hand, risk may result in loss or gain. Knowing the result of a risk usually arises from being able to measure the possible outcome of the risk or the chance that the outcomes are known. It provides a basis for risk management, cost–benefit analysis, budget planning and so on, whereas there is no objective basis for risk management, cost–benefit analysis and other control techniques in uncertainty.[22] Unlike uncertainty, we can control risk, mitigate it and assign it, if we put the proper measures in place and take the necessary precautions. Frank Knight notes that risk provides a basis for seeking insurance, whereas a person cannot insure against uncertainty.[23] The difference between risk and uncertainty is vital in accident insurance, as unpredictability results in uncertainty when calculating the exposure to loss.[24] Concerning offshore petroleum operations, the concept of risk involves situations where loss exposure exists during drilling operations.

1.2.2 Risk and Probability

Some scholars[25] have used the term 'probability' when referring to risk, but theoretically, the two concepts are distinguishable. Probability is often used to explain the likelihood that something may occur. It also describes the degree of assurance someone places on an uncertain event, which is determined by their knowledge.[26] The latter view is obviously subjective and has received the support of Melvin Eisenberg, who notes that 'probability' relates to how a person ascribes the likelihood of an event as against the objective possibility that the event will happen.[27] However, some scholars have looked at probability from an objective point of view, noting that the term involves a tangible property.[28] This perspective presents

21 Alex Y Seita, 'Uncertainty and Contract Law' (1984) 46 University of Pittsburgh Law Review 75.

22 Future Learn, 'Decision Making in a Complex and Uncertain World: Risk and Uncertainty' (University of Groningen) <https://www.futurelearn.com/courses/complexity-and-uncertainty/0/steps/1824> accessed 12 October 2023.

23 Knight (n 15).

24 ibid.

25 Barry F Anderson and others, *Concepts in Judgement and Decision Research: Definitions, Sources, Interrelations, Comments* (Praeger 1981); Frank E Harrison, *The Managerial Decision-Making Process* (5th edn, South-Western College 1998); Philip Holmes, *Investment Appraisal* (International Thomson Business Press 1998).

26 Jacob Bernoulli, *Ars Conjectandi* (Thurnheysen 1731).

27 Melvin Aron Eisenberg, 'Probability and Chance in Contract Law' (1997) 45 UCLA Law Review 1005.

28 Mark R Crovelli, 'Why the Definition of Probability Matters (Mises Institute, 26 January 2011) <mises.org/library/why-definition-probability-matters> accessed 12 October 2023. See also Charles Yablon, 'The Meaning of Probability Judgments: An Essay on the Use and Misuse of Behavioral Economics' (2004) University of Illinois Law Review 899.

probability as something that can be measured, recorded and evaluated like other physical things. Nevertheless, what is unknown cannot be predicted, measured or managed. Again, since probability involves the likelihood of a risk event occurring, the factors for assessing it may be objective or subjective.

In allocating risk during offshore petroleum operations, parties anticipate risks within the context of petroleum activities. For example, there is the risk that someone may be injured or die, or that pollution damage may occur, arising from the operator's or drilling contractor's fault. Participants then allocate these risks among themselves, following oil industry practice. The essence is to identify someone who will bear the economic responsibility in the event of a downside. As such, we understand the probability element as the likelihood that an adverse event may occur and that a given party would be responsible for the economic burden of the downside.

1.3 RISK CATEGORISATION

Risk has several classifications that have been adopted over the years,[29] yet the PESTLEO[30] classification appears to be a nuanced way of classifying risk due to its broad coverage of common issues in petroleum operations. The first element in the PESTLEO acronym is political risk. This risk relates to government interference with the operations of a business or activity, which usually affects both public and organisational interests.[31] Sometimes, this risk arises from political decisions, expropriation of company assets, contract cancellation or change of leadership in the host state (HS). These situations affect the contractual relationship between the HS and the company, and impact the latter's investment.[32] As such, multinational oil companies (MNCs) usually aim to use stabilisation or force majeure clauses to protect their businesses from the HS's political interference. Most drilling contracts typically leave these risks to the operator to handle.

The second element is economic risk. This risk arises when critical adjustments in an HS's economy could affect the projected investment return. This adjustment could arise from a country's change in economic policy which can affect the exchange rate and some extant legislation. This risk may also be due to a country's political challenges, which may impact economic growth and investor confidence in the HS. The economic risk could be about the commercial viability of a petroleum

29 Some scholars have discussed risk using methods such as ETPS ('economic, technical, political and social'). Other methods include SEPE analysis ('social, economic, political and ecological' risks) and STEEPLED ('social, technological, economic, environmental, political, legal, educational and demographic' risks). For details, see Francis J Aguilar, *Scanning the Business Environment* (Macmillan 1967).

30 PESTLEO is an acronym that represents 'political, economic, social, technology, legal, environmental and operational' risks.

31 Abdullah A Faruque, *Petroleum Contracts: Stability and Risk Management in Developing Countries* (Bangladesh Institute of Law and International Affairs 2011) 64.

32 John C Kinna, 'Investing in Developing Countries: Minimisation of Political Risk' (1983) 1(2) Journal of Energy & Natural Resources Law 89.

operation, especially regarding operating costs and return on investment. It also relates to a company's capacity to access foreign exchange in an HS and deal with repatriation issues without undue constraints. The structure of petroleum operations puts the operator in a position to deal with these issues.

The third element is social risk. This risk arises from the operations and interactions of a company with its stakeholders. Oil and gas companies often encounter tension within their value chain as they pursue their corporate goal. The tension is mostly with oil-bearing communities, sometimes resulting in disruptive outcomes to a company's activities or reputation. The typical organisational response is to commit to a socially responsible operation and attempt to balance profitability and sustainable operation. One way of managing this type of risk is through inclusive engagement of all stakeholders in a transparent manner that earns the trust of the stakeholders. This engagement can result in a social licence to operate. Adverse publicity and related tension can result from improper engagement with stakeholders. In petroleum operations, the operator is responsible for engaging with oil-bearing communities to avoid disruptive activities. Most times, the operator engages in community development projects as part of its corporate social responsibility and community relations mechanism, to improve life in the community and reduce the possibility of local tension.[33]

The fourth element is technology risk, which relates to how technological challenges impact a company's operation, typically through the unavailability of service for business, lack of skilled personnel to engage with the evolving world, data usage challenges and cybersecurity issues.[34] Technology supports business operations; enables innovation, growth and market penetration; and reduces costs when applied correctly. However, when a business is affected by technological issues, such as hacking, it can have a detrimental impact on the company. Addressing this challenge requires implementing risk management strategies to mitigate the impact of a possible downside. This same reasoning applies in the oil and gas industry, as parties to a drilling agreement usually insert provisions regarding confidentiality and prohibition of unlawful information access to safeguard against technology risk. It will amount to a breach of contract should any party not abide by the clause.

The fifth element is the legal risk arising from a company's exposure to regulations that affect its procedures and activities, or due to the company not being aware of specific laws or information regarding applicable regulations. Legal risk sometimes emanates from changes in law, legal claims in court, failed business

33 Dima Jamali and Mirshak Ramez, 'Corporate Social Responsibility (CSR): Theory and Practice in a Developing Country Context' (2007) 72(3) Journal of Business Ethics 243.

34 Kelechi Ofoegbu, 'How Contractual Risk Allocation Provisions of Oil and Gas Contracts Have Been or May Be interpreted by an English Court – A Case Study of Some Model Offshore Drilling Rig Contracts Developed in the United Kingdom, Canada and the United States of America' (PhD Thesis, University of Dundee 2018).

transactions with other companies and so on.[35] A common legal risk arises from claims for environmental degradation and human rights violations against MNCs operating in an area. Some court actions against MNCs have been successful, leading to the payment of millions of dollars as compensation. These claims sometimes give MNCs negative publicity, which affects their share price. Litigation could also arise from other contractual parties regarding breach of contract, property damage or the general risk allocation method. Similarly, certain unclear clauses may result in litigation for parties to get clarity on the nature and extent of their responsibilities in the contract.

The sixth element is environmental risk. It involves a possible or actual threat of adverse effects on the environment and living organisms, caused by a company's activities, such as those of an MNC engaged in petroleum operations. These activities occur when, for instance, carbon is emitted into the atmosphere, or waste and effluents are discharged into the marine ecosystem, thus exposing the ecosystem and marine life, soil, air and water quality to harm or danger.[36] There is a possibility that MNCs may not be able to comply with all the environmental regulations of the HS, thus exposing them to environmental risk, which has implications for a company's reputation. There are also global environmental laws, both hard and soft, that these companies need to comply with, as non-compliance may result in negative publicity. Environmental compliance is an essential aspect of petroleum operations, involving huge costs, and non-compliance usually attracts huge penalties. As will be seen later, parties in a drilling contract usually allocate the risk of pollution damage among themselves, with the operator assuming responsibility for subsurface pollution while the contractor takes responsibility for surface damage.

The final element is operational risk, and it arises from the possibility of loss due to human or system error, flawed internal processes or external events. Operational risk cuts across the value chain of a company. Every drilling contract anticipates a downside during operations, hence the practice of risk allocation to manage the economic consequence of a risk. A company can mitigate most operational risks since they arise mainly due to human factors. In the context of drilling operations, operational risks abound. After the Macondo accident, the US National Commission on the BP Deepwater Horizon Oil Spill and Offshore Drilling found several human errors that resulted in the disaster. The Commission also noted that the desire to finish the drilling of the Macondo well in a hurry led to several safety issues being neglected, and that these errors were attributable to the operator and contractor.[37]

[35] Roger McCormick, *Legal Risk in the Financial Markets* (OUP on Demand 2010).

[36] Ofoegbu (n 34).

[37] National Commission on the BP Deepwater Horizon Oil Spill and Offshore Drilling, *Deep Water: The Gulf Oil Disaster and the Future of Offshore Drilling* (Report to the President of the United States of America 2011).

1.4 SCHOLASTIC PERSPECTIVES ON RISK

Scholars have different views about the classifications of and approaches to risk. In this regard, Ortwin Renn has identified the existence of positivist and social constructionist schools of thought.[38] He notes that the positivist perspective stems from an objective view of an activity or event, which can be assessed using the likelihood of clear adverse outcomes. This categorisation combines approaches that look at risk as objective measures of probability and degree of harm, and positions them in like manner to allocate resources according to their degree of seriousness. Scholars such as Barry Anderson[39] and Knight[40] belong to this class. On the other hand, the social constructionist perspective sees risk in terms of social or cultural constructions, which should be examined using different criteria.[41] This school of thought applies subjective approaches, such as those of lifestyle preferences and values, in prioritising risk, in contrast with the positivist school of thought, which uses objective criteria. Scholars like James Short[42] are known to belong to this school.

There is another classification, in which three basic groups are identified: realist, weak constructionist and strong constructionist.[43] Deborah Lupton notes that the realist sees risk as an objective hazard or danger that exists and can be evaluated separately outside of cultural and social processes. This categorisation is theoretically akin to the positivist school of thought highlighted above. The weak constructionist group theorises risk as an objective hazard or danger that is manifestly facilitated through cultural and social processes and does not exist in isolation from the process. The last group is the strong constructionist class, which identifies that nothing is literally a risk on its own, yet what we see as a hazard or danger results from socially, historically and politically conditioned ways of seeing risk.[44]

Constructionists advance that what we know about risk is unavoidably tied to our daily experiences and that it is a contradiction to see risk from an objective point of view. The divergence of opinion regarding the concept of risk supports this latter view. Scholars see risk from their point of view, which may have been impacted by cultural and social experiences. The weak and the strong constructionists are alike except for how they see the hazard element objectively. The former class recognises that risk could be based on an objective fact expressed, understood and applied within a social and cultural context.

[38] Ortwin Renn, 'Concepts of Risk: A Classification' in Sheldon Krimsky and Dominic Golding (eds), *Social Theories of Risk* (Praeger Publishers 1992).

[39] Anderson and others (n 25).

[40] Knight (n 15).

[41] Ofoegbu (n 34).

[42] James F Short Jr, 'The Social Fabric at Risk – Towards the Social Transformation of Risk Analysis' (1984) 49(6), American Sociological Review 711.

[43] Deborah Lupton, *Risk* (2nd edn, Routledge 2013).

[44] ibid.

The latter group accepts the cultural and social influence but questions the objective nature of risk.

Another classification is that of Catherine Althaus,[45] who notes that various fields of study apply specific forms of knowledge to uncertainty to organise its unpredictability and transform it into something predictable – risk. Althaus does not classify the disciplines, but she considers the form of knowledge that each discipline applies to uncertainty, in order to understand the concept of risk. From Althaus's perspective, one can deduce that sociology and anthropology apply culture and social theories to uncertainty and view risk as a cultural experience, theoretically belonging to the constructionist school of thought. Despite Althaus's non-classification of risk per se, we can align specific approaches with the groupings discussed above.

There is also the economic perception which strengthens Althaus's perspective about disciplines. Althaus notes that the discipline of economics sees risk as merely another resource that must be allocated. Economics proponents advance that this perception of risk centres around incentive and reward, and is linked to utility and monetary value.[46] Renn agrees with the economic perception that risk analysis is integral to a more extensive cost–benefit consideration, especially as risks are the likely utility losses resulting from an activity or event. The essence is to distribute resources for society to maximise their utility.

Some scholars have extended the cost and benefit analysis by linking probabilities, decision-making and uncertainty.[47] They note that probabilities are essentially uncertainties about things in the present and in the future, and that both cost-and-benefit analysis and decision analysis are founded on probabilities. The point of difference is that cost-and-benefit analysis utilises objective criteria, whereas probabilities are subjective expressions of the personal beliefs and judgements of the decision maker.

The economics perception of risk presents a picture of the risk allocation practice in the oil and gas industry. The conceptualisation of risk as losses/resources capable of being distributed shows that the risk allocation practice centres around the economic consequences of a negative event, not on the event itself. The events are not viewed as resources. Undeniably, the occurence of the event prompts the actual resource allocation. When a party in an offshore petroleum operation estimates its potential liability in the event of a downside, such a party is ultimately assessing the *expected value* of the outcome of the downside occurring.[48] Several assumptions are made in the context of petroleum drilling operations, which form the basis for allocating risk to the party that can manage it. The aversion to risk comes into play during risk allocation. This aversion is a function of quantitative

[45] Catherine E Althaus, 'A Disciplinary Perspective on the Epistemological Status of Risk' (2005) 25(3) Risk Analysis: An International Journal 567.

[46] Ofoegbu (n 34).

[47] Baruch Fischhoff and others, *Acceptable Risk* (CUP 1984).

[48] MA Mian, *Project Economics and Decision Analysis: Deterministic Models* (Pennwell Books 2011) 181.

and qualitative factors that parties utilise to realise their preferred level of risk exposure, leveraging the economic approach. As such, since the economics perspective theorises risk as a resource that can be distributed, contracting parties are involved in this process when negotiating a drilling contract. The process is also theorised when parties allocate risks to their advantage, expecting their strategies to produce the anticipated result.

1.5 OTHER APPROACHES TO RISK

1.5.1 The Judicial Approach

The judicial perception of risk arises from how most courts interpret the law to arrive at a decision. It means that the law forms the basis of judges' views about risk. In this regard, a scholar has highlighted that risk is conceptualised as an actual or possible event that creates chaos of a damaging kind. where a recognisable perpetrator and victim exist.[49] This fault-based perception of risk enables a court to concentrate on responsibility for wrongful conduct, resulting in the award of damages, fines or other penalties against the perpetrator. The task before any court in presiding over risk-related cases is to decipher the lawmaker's intention and arrive at judgments by using the law as a mechanism of social engineering to protect the public from risk.

In risk allocation, courts often consider the need to protect public safety, health and the public good. However, courts are guided by the law in interpreting risk events, public policy considerations and the need to influence society's perception toward risk.[50] Again, courts sometimes assess how parties allocate risk and whether this promotes harm prevention, rather than whether a party is liable for being involved in risky behaviour. This practice is akin to using the law as a tool for social engineering.

In risk allocation, courts often consider the need to protect public safety, health and the public good. However, courts are guided by the law in interpreting risk events, public policy considerations and the need to influence society's perception toward risk.[50] Again, courts sometimes assess how parties allocate risk and whether this promotes harm prevention, rather than whether a party is liable for being involved in risky behaviour. This practice is akin to using the law as a tool for social engineering.

1.5.2 The Legislative Approach

Judicial interpretation of risk is based on what the lawmaker set out in the law. Most regulation aims to protect society from risk and harm, as reinforced by the

[49] Francois Ewald, 'Insurance and Risk' in Graham Burchell, Colin Gordon and Peter Miller (eds) *The Foucault Effect: Studies in Governmentality* (University of Chicago Press 1991)

[50] Kip W Viscusi, 'How Do Judges Think about Risk? 1(1) American Law and Economics Review 26.

utilitarian philosophy and underpinned by cost–benefit analysis.[51] Within this context, every regulation seeks to identify and mitigate the possible causes of harm before they occur. As highlighted, the utilitarian philosophy of regulation has not been without opposition from the pragmatist, who advances that pragmatism is the motive that propels risk regulation.[52] Daniel Farber identified pragmatism as a better justification for regulation, as it integrates innovation with respect for the legal tradition. In the context of drilling contracts, several laws regulate drilling activities to mitigate the risk of an accident. The essence is public safety and protecting life and properties during offshore drilling operations. These laws usually attach fines and penalties as deterrents for wrongful conduct.

1.5.3 The Economic Approach

The economic approach to risk differs from the previous two. It looks at the undesirable outcome and tries to link resource allocation, market behaviour and the legal system by conceptualising risk from a cost-and-utility perspective.[53] This perception of risk arises from a transactional cost perspective, and from the utility and disutility that result from a particular event. The goal is to achieve efficiency in a transaction by defining which party can best bear a given risk[54] and, ultimately, bear it at the cheapest cost. Scholars have highlighted that the ability to bear risk hinges on the ownership of, or access to, the resources to manage risk, should a downside occur.[55] This ability involves having the required authority, level of expertise and resources to execute risk management plans to realise the objective of the contract. Another writer sees this as the party that can ensure that the risky event does not occur.[56] Thus, determining the party that can bear the risk is a practical aspect of risk allocation.

In minimising transactional cost (including risk), it is crucial for parties to share information, simplify the transaction and use incentives to achieve the desired objectives. In this regard, information sharing is essential for cost efficiency in the risk allocation process. Although information exchange is critical for efficiency purposes, a party may be unwilling to disclose a piece of information that is against its interest, thus resulting in inefficiencies due to information asymmetry. One way around this would be to use standard term contracts to obtain relevant information to maximise the effectiveness of the risk allocation process.

[51] Sidney Shapiro and Robert Glicksman, *Risk Regulation at Risk: Restoring a Pragmatic Approach* (Stanford University Press 2002).

[52] Daniel A Farber, 'Legal Pragmatism and the Constitution' (1987) 72 Minnesota Law Review 1331.

[53] Richard A Posner, *Economic Analysis of Law* (3rd edn, Little Brown & Co 1986).

[54] Peter A Diamond, 'Posner's Economic Analysis of Law' (1974) 5(1) Bell Journal of Economics and Management Science 294.

[55] Martin Loosemore and CS McCarthy, 'Perceptions of Contractual Risk Allocation in Construction Supply Chains' (2008) 134(1) Journal of Professional Issues in Engineering Education and Practice 95.

[56] Patrick Selim Atiyah, *Essays on Contract* (OUP 2012).

Although the ability to bear risk is crucial, the deterrence aspect, which prevents a downside, should also be considered in the risk allocation practice. This practice will ensure that a party is responsible for the economic consequence of its action and will facilitate harm prevention. How parties achieve risk allocation is essential, especially as parties need to cooperate and share information transparently about risk aversion, risk profile and insurance, to support the allocation process.

1.6 ESSENTIAL CONCEPTS IN THE DISCUSSION ABOUT RISKS

1.6.1 Risk Management

Risk management is a concept that describes how a company can handle risk to achieve its goal. Several definitions of this concept exist. Risk management has been seen as a tool for identifying, appraising, managing and administering risks that challenge the growth of a business.[57] It is about putting preventive measures in place to avoid the occurrence or escalation of a risk event. In the context of public policy, risk management is the method for calculating an event's risks and assessing its likely benefits.[58] Within project management, risk management involves planning, identifying, analysing and controlling risk in a particular project.[59] The essence of managing risk is to enhance the prospect of favourable outcomes while mitigating adverse consequences. In the context of drilling operations, risk management relates to how parties to a drilling contract put mechanisms in place to prevent or handle any undesirable outcome. Putting safety measures in place, taking out insurance and ensuring responsible drilling operation is a risk management strategy. Ultimately, the risk management process seeks to reduce the possibility of a downside, which will make a party responsible for bearing the economic consequence of a risk that has been allocated to it.

1.6.2 Risk Aversion

People, by their nature, are risk averse. In decision-making, people often prefer low-risk transactions, even when they could make sacrifices that result in positive outcomes.[60] Scholars have recognised that people instinctively avoid risk whenever possible, and they distinguish between between risk neutrality and risk aversion.[61] They recognise that those who are risk-averse would typically agree to relinquish something valuable if it would protect them from a greater risk of

[57] Douglas Masham, 'What Are Risk Management and Insurance?' in John E Besant-Wones and Lori Hyln (eds) *Managing Risks of Investments in Developing Countries* (World Bank 1992).

[58] The Royal Society, *Risk: Analysis, Perception and Management* (The Royal Society 1992).

[59] Ofoegbu (n 34).

[60] James G March and Zur Shapira, 'Managerial Perspectives on Risk and Risk Taking' (1987) 33(11) Management Science 1404.

[61] Russell Cooper and Andrew A John, *Theory and Applications of Microeconomics* (McGraw-Hill Education 2012).

loss when a downside occurs. Insurance is one option that risk-averse individuals use, as it provides greater risk diversification and economic protection should a negative event occur. In the context of risk allocation, parties tend to accept the risk they can get cover for or bear. This attitude exemplifies an aversion to risk as it demonstrates that parties are unwilling to accept risks beyond their control. Aversion to risk evolves with time, especially as market participants respond to the dynamic nature of the market by accepting or avoiding risk.[62] This response is not a reflection of risk appetite, as risk aversion can increase even when risk appetite remains unchanged.

1.6.3 Risk Allocation

Risk allocation involves the distribution of the economic consequences that may arise from the business relationship of two or more parties. In commercial contracts, such as drilling operations, risk allocation includes how parties distribute possible downsides to achieve certainty of responsibility, contractual efficiency and reduction in the level of responsibility they may face. Essentially, oil and gas industry participants allocate risk among themselves to avoid the fault-based tort law system, lengthy litigation to identify the responsible party, and double insurance. Risk allocation is a risk management strategy that enables parties to assume responsibility for what they can bear and what they exercise custody, care and control over. The oil and gas industry uses exclusion and limitation of liability and indemnity clauses to allocate risk through a standard or private contract.

Apart from parties allocating risk among themselves, a court can also assign risk among parties, either by legislative intervention or by operation of law.[63] Risk allocation can occur for several reasons. For example, it could be due to an increase in contract cost or factors that make the performance of the contract difficult,[64] or because of inaccurate or misleading information from a party or client.[65] It has been highlighted that risk allocation should be looked at from the perspective of a specific sociobehavioural setting to understand its application in that context.[66] This means that risk allocation can operate differently in various situations, and the rationale will also depend on the circumstances. In contractual risk allocation, as a rule of thumb, parties are required to take out insurance to enable them to fulfil their economic obligation in the contract should a downside occur. Where a party fails to take out insurance, they may be in breach of the contract. Further discussion about risk allocation is set out later in this book.

62 Jean-Pierre Zigrand, Hyun Song Shin and Jon Danielsson, *Risk Appetite and Endogenous Risk* (Financial Markets Group AXA Working Paper Series No 2 Discussion Paper No 647, 2010).

63 Ofoegbu (n 34).

64 John Cibinic, Ralph C Nash and James F Nagle, *Administration of Government Contracts* (5th edn, Wolters Kluwer 2016).

65 Brian M Cole, 'Misrepresentation in Public Contracts: Allocating the Risk of Loss' (1970) 21 Syracuse Law Review 1004.

66 Loosemore and McCarthy (n 55) 95.

A related term to risk allocation is risk transfer. Risk transfer is an instrument of economic risk reduction and motivation for parties to a contract. It has been described as a risk management mechanism that involves a contractual party shifting the economic consequence of a specific risk to another party.[67] One way of doing this is by obtaining insurance, which effectively passes the economic outcome of the risk to the insurance company, should a downside occur. Other means of risk transfer include 'hold harmless' provisions and a requirement to provide insurance cover for the benefit of another party. This practice provides a basis for a party to accept the economic consequence of another party's fault pursuant to a mutual indemnity agreement. In this regard, a scholar notes that risk transfer is about the deliberate exchange of the likely outcome of an event by moving risk from one party to another, and that the procurement of insurance facilitates risk transfer.[68]

1.6.4 Risk Mitigation

In contractual agreements, parties take steps to prevent or reduce the effect of a risk event, should a downside occur. The essence of taking this step is to mitigate risk. Risk mitigation involves developing options and actions to improve opportunities and reduce threats to a project goal.[69] Measures such as risk avoidance, transfer, control, acceptance and monitoring are risk mitigation processes. It has also been highlighted that risk mitigation involves reducing the likelihood of a risk event or reducing the outcomes if it happens.[70] In risk mitigation, a common understanding must exist and an ideal strategy must be designed to suit the specific situation of the business, especially regarding the use of insurance.

1.6.5 Contractual Risk Allocation in the Oil Industry

Contractual risk allocation in the oil and gas industry is a risk management technique[71] that uses mutual indemnity and exclusion or limitation of liability clauses in the upstream hydrocarbon industry. It is essential in forming an efficient contract between an operator and a contractor.[72] An efficient contract is a contract that improves the position of both parties, or improves the position of one party without

[67] CNA, 'Risk Transfer: A Strategy to Help Protect Your Business' (CNA Risk Control, 2006) <www.cna.com/web/wcm/connect/b7bacbf0-b432-4e0c-97fa-ce8730b329d5/RC_Guide_RiskTransferStrategytoHelpProtectYou+Business_CNA.pdf> accessed 12 October 2023.

[68] James Lam, *Enterprise Risk Management: From Incentives to Controls* (2nd edn, John Wiley & Sons 2014).

[69] Ofoegbu (n 34).

[70] ibid.

[71] Mustafa S Syahrir, 'Liability and Risk Control through Effective Clauses in Oil and Gas Service Contracts' [2004] Oil Gas and Energy Law 2.

[72] Kirsten Bindemann, 'Production Sharing Agreements: An Economic Analysis' (Oxford Institute for Energy Study WPM, October 1999) <ora.ox.ac.uk/objects/uuid:3ba0589f-8c3a-43b9-b034-24f7dae7e0c5> accessed 12 October 2023, 30.

making the other party worse off.[73] It considers the risk involved in addressing the challenges of the unique operating environment and the huge costs that may result from negligible acts or omissions.[74] In this book, risk refers to various exposures that operators and contractors face during offshore drilling operations.

The inherent risks, substantial financial cost and multiple parties involved in an offshore petroleum operation are significant drivers for allocating risk. There are several industry forms and private templates used to allocate risk. Notable among them are the AIEN (Association of International Energy Negotiators, formerly the AIPN, Association of International Petroleum Negotiators) Well Service Contract, IADC (International Association of Drilling Contractors) forms and LOGIC (Leading Oil and Gas Industry Competitiveness) model contracts, among others.

1.7 CONCEPTUAL UNDERSTANDING AND USAGE OF TERMS

1.7.1 Negligence and Gross Negligence

Negligence is a flexible term that is not subject to strict limits. It is relative to person, place and circumstance, and is established through proof. Negligence has been defined as the 'omission to do something which a reasonable man, guided upon those considerations which ordinarily regulate the conduct of human affairs, would do, or doing something which a prudent and reasonable man would not do'.[75] It also 'connotes the complex concept of duty, breach and damage suffered by the person to whom the duty was owing'.[76] The implication is that a person is negligent when that person fails to conform to a prudent person's required standard of behaviour in a particular circumstance. The behaviour must result from conduct, not a state of mind, as the former differs from intent.[77] Some courts associate negligence with inflicting injury,[78] and this judicial perception suggests that negligence is conduct.

In some jurisdictions, efforts have been made to set up several pointers of liability by adopting three degrees of care, or degrees of negligence: slight negligence, ordinary negligence and gross negligence.[79] This categorisation attempts to show

[73] ibid 29.

[74] Sharon Wilson, 'Contractual Allocation of Risk in Upstream Oil and Gas Projects' (2008) 3 Energy Source 3.

[75] Bryan ME McMahon and William Binchy, *Law of Torts* (3rd edn, Butterworths 2000) 145.

[76] ibid.

[77] Daniel O Howard, 'An Analysis of Gross Negligence' (1954) 37(4) Marquette Law Review 333.

[78] *Donnelly v Southern Pacific Co* 118 P 2d 465 (Cal 1941); *Altman v Aronson* 231 Mass. 588 (1919).

[79] 'Slight negligence' has been defined as 'an absence of that degree of care and vigilance which persons of extraordinary prudence and foresight are accustomed to use.' 'Ordinary negligence', though variously defined, is fundamentally a failure to exercise such care as the great mass of mankind exercise under the same or similar circumstances. 'Gross negligence' has been defined as a want of even slight care, failure to exercise reasonable care, and very great negligence. See Howard (n 77) 334.

the extent to which a course of conduct can be negligent for establishing liability. Certain essential elements must exist to prove the tort of negligence. These elements include a duty of care or a legal obligation, which requires a person to conform to a certain standard of conduct to protect others against unreasonable risks. Negligence also involves a failure by a person to conform to the required standard of care, an actual loss or damage suffered by the plaintiff arising from the defendant's conduct, and a reasonably close connection between the defendant's conduct and the plaintiff's injury.[80] These elements are general and do not prove the case. Rather, they point to issues and set the terms in which cases are argued. They are established through proof. To establish negligence, the plaintiff is not legally required to prove the intention or predetermined act of the defendant to cause harm. In law, it is enough for the plaintiff to show that the defendant's conduct was negligent.[81] The plaintiff also does not need to show the degree of negligence or the existence of a different standard of care.

In the law of torts, various standards of care or degrees of negligence are not recognised in different classes of actions.[82] The reason is that degrees of negligence do not increase or decrease liability, as the defendant will still be liable to pay damages if found negligent. Thus, the egregiousness of the defendant's conduct does not matter since it results in liability for the defendant. This position is different in contract law, where the degree of negligence may be classified as gross negligence. The recognised standard in tort is the care a prudent person would exercise in a specific circumstance.[83] The question always is: What care would a reasonable person exercise if found in the same circumstances as the defendant, or what would a reasonable person do in these circumstances? In answering this question, the test applied is an objective test from a reasonable person's perspective; not a subjective test from the defendant's perspective, with the defendant's morality or personal sense of right or wrong.[84]

Regarding gross negligence, the concept is traceable to the Roman legal system.[85] There existed two degrees of negligence in the Justinian time: *culpa lata* and *culpa levis*.[86] The former degree of negligence resulted when a person failed to use the care of an ordinary person of rational intellect. *Culpa lata* referred to contract law sometimes, but was used more often in the context of criminal law and quasi-contracts. It applied the reasonable person's standard and included acts in which a person of unrefined intelligence would not be involved. On the other hand,

[80] Page Keeton and William L Prosser, *Prosser and Keeton on the Law of Torts* (5th edn, West Publishing Co 1984) 165; Dan B Dobbs, *The Law of Torts: Practitioner Treatise Series* (vol 1, West Group 2001) 269.

[81] RFV Heuston and RA Buckley, *Salmond and Heuston on the Law of Torts* (21st edn, Sweet & Maxwell 1996) 194.

[82] ibid 223.

[83] *Brown v Kendal* 60 Mass 292 (1850).

[84] Keeton and Prosser (n 81) 169.

[85] Melville M Bigelow, *The Law of Torts* (8th edn, Little, Brown and Company 1907) 118.

[86] Sheldon D Elliot, 'Degrees of Negligence' (1933) 6(2) Southern California Law Review 99.

culpa levis, or ordinary fault, referred to the failure to conform to the conduct of a careful businessman.[87] Roman law of negligence dealt primarily with contractual duties arising from agreements such as bailments. It did not apply to wrongs in torts that were independent of contracts. In England, the concept is associated with Henry de Bracton's *De Legibus et Consuetudinibus Angliae*, which incorporated much of the Roman theory of degrees of negligence.[88] Bracton's treatise contributed to the field of bailments, where the courts used degrees of negligence in settling disputes.[89] Lord Holt, handing down his opinion in *Coggs v Bernard*, reviewed the degrees of negligence based on Bracton's treatise and outlined the liability and degree of care attached to each situation.[90]

Gross negligence, unlike negligence, is not a term of art. Its meaning in commercial transactions is usually deduced from a court's evaluation of the parties' agreement regarding the nature and extent of a party's liability. In this regard, the court in *Sommer v Federal Signal Corporation*[91] considered whether the term could apply to pierce a limitation of liability clause in a commercial agreement. It identified that gross negligence must 'smack of intentional wrongdoing or demonstrate a reckless indifference to the rights of others' for a court to exclude it as a defence to liability. The court, in its decision, highlighted the element of intention. However, as we shall see in Chapter 4, where a detailed discussion is presented, gross negligence is a conduct, not an intention. Despite the unclear description of the concept, the court's decision suggests that gross negligence applies in a contract to prevent a party from relying on a limitation of liability or exclusion clause where egregious conduct results in a downside. It also shows that courts focus mostly on the conduct of the party at fault and the outcome of the wrong, especially as the extent of negligence and scale of risk are closely linked.[92]

1.7.2 Human Rights and Environment

Oil and gas operations often result in pollution, which affects the environment and human rights. Human rights are rights that are attached to a person arising from their existence on earth. These rights include, but are not limited to, the rights to

[87] ibid.

[88] Frederick Green, 'High Care and Gross Negligence' (1928) 23(1) Illinois Law Review 12.

[89] Ben McFarlane, 'Bailment', in Peter Cane and Joanne Conaghan (eds), *The New Oxford Companion of Law* (OUP 2008). Bailment arises when a bailee takes possession of goods owned by a bailor.

[90] [1703] 2 Ld Raym 909. The defendant in this case undertook to transport some casks of brandy from one cellar to another without compensation. The defendant was negligent in handling the casks, and one of them broke and poured on the ground. The plaintiff sought to hold the gratuitous bailee (defendant) liable for the loss. The court then set out the liability and degree of care attached to each situation. See also Green (n 89) 12; and 'The Three Degrees of Negligence' (1874) 8 American Law Review 652.

[91] 79 NY 2d 540 (NY 1992).

[92] Patrick H Martin, 'The BP Spill and the Meaning of Gross Negligence or Willful Misconduct' (2011) 71(3) Louisiana Law Review 957.

life, a healthy environment, food and to earn a living. The right to a healthy and sustainable environment was further strengthened in 2022 by the United Nations General Assembly Resolution.[93] Oil pollution's socioeconomic and environmental impacts include loss of biodiversity, damage to aquatic ecosystems, air and water pollution, groundwater contamination, destruction of wildlife and degradation of farmland. Biodiversity constitutes a significant source of economic existence and social connection for oil-bearing communities.[94] As such, when an oil spill occurs, it impacts the right to a healthy environment, which is a basic human right.

Excluding indemnity or limitation of liability clauses as a defence in gross negligence cases advances the public's interest and protects human rights and the environment. The term 'human rights and environment' in this book is related to the right to an environment with minimal pollution impact. This right is enhanced by practices that discourage environmental harm during oil and gas operations, such as not allowing a party in an oil and gas drilling operation to rely on an exclusion or limitation of liability clause when involved in a wrongful act of gross negligence.

1.7.3 *Sustainability*

Sustainability in a broad sense involves a situation where natural and man-made resources remain at least constant for the near future so that the well-being of future generations does not decrease.[95] This entails utilising resources to meet the present generation's needs without impacting on the future generation's ability to meet their needs. Thus, sustainability expresses what public policy ought to achieve based on the principle that the well-being and survival of people depend on the natural environment.

The risk of pollution to the environment is apparent in oil and gas activities, as gas emission, waste water and oil pollution dominate the hydrocarbon operation process, thus impacting the ecosystem and affecting the health and livelihoods of people. British Petroleum's (BP) health, safety and environment policy of 'no accidents, no harm to people, and no damage to the environment'[96] underlines the need for sustainability and emphasises people and the planet in petroleum operations.[97]

93 United Nations General Assembly Resolution 76/300, The Human Right to a Clean, Healthy and Sustainable Environment (UNGA, July 2022).

94 Smith I Azubuike and Ondotimi Songi, 'A Rights-Based Approach to Oil Spill Investigations: A Case Study of the Bodo Community Oil Spill in Nigeria' (2020) 1(1) Global Energy Law and Sustainability 28.

95 Tom Kuhlman and John Farrington, 'What is Sustainability' (2010) 2 Sustainability 3436.

96 British Petroleum, 'BP ANZ Health and Safety Policy' (BP, 29 July 2019) <www.bp.com/content/dam/bp/country-sites/en_au/australia/home/products-services/fuels/health-safety-policy.pdf> accessed 12 October 2023.

97 Mohamad Danish Anis and Tauseef Zia Siddiqui, 'Issues Impacting Sustainability in the Oil and Gas Industry' (2015) 5(4) Journal of Management and Sustainability 115.

The need to ensure sustainability in petroleum operations has been heightened due to environmental concerns and the level of negligence reported in the BP Macondo disaster of 2010. As global oil and gas companies deliver on energy security, they have a responsibility to protect the environment, lower emissions and reduce the risks of climate change and environmental damage. Delivering on this responsibility requires continuous improvement and innovation to advance sustainability, especially on environmental issues. It also requires focusing operations in ways that can support progress toward achieving the United Nations Sustainable Development Goals (SDGs), mitigating risks of pollution or contamination by applying environmental management systems and contractual strategies, and embedding the sustainability reporting practice for oil and gas companies.[98] Sustainability is necessary for every aspect of petroleum operation, particularly in drilling activities. As such, there is a need for companies to incorporate sustainability into the design of their activities, to allow for a transition from old practices to sustainable operational approaches.[99]

1.7.4 *Distributive Justice*

Distributive justice concerns itself with the fair apportionment of benefits and burdens amongst members of a given community. Fair distribution considers the amount of what is to be distributed, the procedure of distribution and the resulting allocation pattern.[100] Its principles tell how some specific benefit or burden ought to be shared. Distributive justice is not limited to only economic issues; it is also a normative principle that assists in apportioning benefits and burdens of economic activities,[101] such as allocating the responsibilities associated with hydrocarbon operations.

While some philosophers' discussions about distributive justice have centred on benefits and resources, John Finnis's discussion includes 'burdens'.[102] Other scholars posit that distributive justice is concerned with sharing benefits and burdens that are 'communal' in some respect or, from a narrow perspective, the division by the state of benefits and burdens.[103]

98 IPIECA, 'Sustainability Reporting Guidance for the Oil and Gas Industry' (IPIECA, March 2020) <www.ipieca.org/resources/sustainability-reporting-guidance> accessed 12 October 2023.

99 Bruno S Silvestre, Felipe Augusto P Gimenes and Romeue Silva Neto, 'A Sustainability Paradox? Sustainable Operations in the Offshore Oil and Gas Industry: The Case of Petrobras' (2017) 142 Journal of Cleaner Production 360.

100 Michelle Maiese, 'Distributive Justice', *Beyond Intractability* (June 2013) <www.beyondintractability.org/essay/distributive_justice> accessed 12 October 2023. See also Chris Armstrong, *Global Distributive Justice: An Introduction* (CUP 2012) 16.

101 Julian Lamont and Christi Favor, 'Distributive Justice' (Stanford Encyclopaedia of Philosophy 1996) <plato.stanford.edu/entries/justice-distributive> accessed 12 October 2023.

102 Peter Cane, 'Distributive Justice and Tort Law' (2001) (4) New Zealand Law Review 404.

103 David Bostock, *Aristotle's Ethics* (OUP 2000) 58.

Gregory Keating[104] advances that distributive justice relates to the fair allocation of benefits and the burden of risky but valuable activities – and, on a secondary note, that it is a matter of corrective justice.[105] Keating premises his concept of distributive justice on the argument that the benefits and burdens of harmful but mutually beneficial activities should be designed so that those who benefit from the activity also bear its burdens. Thus, bearing the burden of harm created is also in line with corrective justice.

1.7.5 Freedom of Contract

The term 'freedom of contract' relates to the right of parties to provide for the terms and conditions that will define their relationship,[106] albeit within the confines of law and policy. Freedom of contract is essential in building a functional market-based economy as it enables parties to determine the nature of their engagement as they pursue their economic activities. The court in *Printing and Numerical Registering Co v Sampson* recognised this freedom when it stated that '[p]ublic policy requires that men of full age and competent understanding shall have the utmost liberty of contracting and that their contracts . . . shall be held sacred'.[107] Freedom of contract is based on the perspective that people can agree on terms that suit them. However, the limit of law makes freedom of contract a qualified and not an absolute right.[108] The limit to the freedom to contract is also recognised under the principles of European contract law, which provide that contractual freedom depends on the conditions of fairness and good faith, and the rules established under the principles.[109] Ultimately, the limit placed by law exists to guide contracting parties regarding the terms of their contract to balance unequal bargaining power and protect the public.

Participants in the oil and gas industry exercise their freedom of contract when allocating risks. Scholars believe that transferring liability for negligence caused by one party to another is in line with the nature of oil and gas operations. However, doing the same for grossly negligent conduct is contrary to public policy, which seeks to protect the public's interest.[110] Thus, public interest is a ground on which the law has limited the freedom of contract. In a more critical examination of the concept, Holmes J noted thus: 'I confess that I think that the

[104] Gregory C Keating, 'Distributive and Corrective Justice in the Tort Law of Accidents' (2000) 74 Southern California Law Review 192.

[105] To Keating, corrective justice is derived from the conception of justice which sees the tort law of accidents as being in line with the ordinary notions of harm and reparation, agency and responsibility, rectification of losses for wrongful actions and so on.

[106] Niall O'Connor, 'Whose Autonomy is it Anyway? Freedom of Contract, the Right to Work and the General Principles of EU Law' (2020) 49(3) Industrial Law Journal 285.

[107] [1875] LRCh. 19 Eq 462, 465.

[108] David P Weber, 'Restricting the Freedom of Contract: A Fundamental Prohibition' (2013) 16(1) Yale Human Rights and Development Law Journal 51.

[109] O'Connor (n 106).

[110] Smith I Azubuike, 'Rethinking Operator-Contractor Risk Allocation in a Post-Macondo Era' (PhD Thesis, University of Dundee 2019).

right to make contracts at will that has been derived from the word "liberty" in the [constitutional] amendments has been stretched to its extreme by [these] decisions'.[111] In this regard, freedom of contract should involve the right to contract within the limits of law and policy in the public's interest.

1.7.6 *Public Policy*

Thomas Dye offered a simple definition of public policy, stating that public policy involves 'anything a government chooses to do or not to do'.[112] This definition identifies that government is the primary agent of public policy and that policy-making is an essential duty exercised to protect its citizens from harm by mainstreaming the relevant legislation or policy to prevent or discourage conduct that could result in harm. Public policy is dynamic, primarily as its meaning depends on the time and needs of the society. However, the conservative view of most courts is that public policy is determined by legislation and judicial decisions, and not people's opinion. Because the meaning of public policy is dynamic, it has been described as 'an unruly horse',[113] especially in interpreting contractual clauses. An agreement or conduct is adjudged contrary to public policy if it results in harm to a person or the state, or results in a breach of law. Although the traditional role of a court is to enforce contracts, agreements contrary to public policy provide an exception to the conventional function of a court. Thus, a court has a duty to hold that such a contract is contrary to public policy and invalid due to being against the public good.

From a normative perspective, public policy can be viewed as the principles, primarily unwritten, on which social laws are established, or the principle that injury to the public good is a basis for refusing to enforce the legality of an agreement or transaction.[114] Farshad Ghadoosi categorised public policy into three aspects: public interest, public morality and public security.[115] This categorisation indicates that public policy seeks to achieve that which is for the public's good. As such, this study refers to public policy as a practice, law or conduct that promotes the public's good and discourages harm against society.

1.8 ESSENTIAL TERMS IN A CONTRACT MATRIX

1.8.1 *Co-Venturers*

A co-venture arises from a joint operating agreement (JOA). The oil and gas industry practice is for co-venturers to enter into an unincorporated contractual joint venture agreement where participants covenant to be individually or severally

111 *Lochner v New York* 198 US 45 (1905), 45.

112 Thomas Dye, *Understanding Public Policy* (15th edn, Pearson 2016).

113 David A Friedman, 'Bringing Order to Contracts Against Public Policy' (2012) 39 Florida State University Law Review 563.

114 Oxford Lexico, 'Public Policy' (*Oxford Lexico*) <www.dictionary.com/browse/public-policy> accessed 12 October 2023.

115 Farshad Ghodoosi, 'The Concept of Public Policy in Law: Revisiting the Role of the Public Policy Doctrine in the Enforcement of Private Legal Arrangements' (2016) 94(3) Nebraska Law Review 685.

liable according to their percentage holding capacity under the relevant licence. They also agree to pay indemnity according to the extent of their shareholding when a downside occurs during petroleum operations.[116] The percentage holding of the co-venturers in the Macondo disaster was the following: BP (65%), Anadarko (25%) and Mitsui MOEX (10%).[117] This represents the extent of individual shares of equity or costs and liabilities in the event of a downside.

Under a JOA, the party with the highest shareholding capacity is appointed the operator of the venture and is responsible for the everyday activities of the joint venture. However, the operator's activities are subject to the control and supervision of the joint operating committee (JOC),[118] which consists of all participating co-venturers. The JOC meets periodically to review jobs done by the operator and give approval or authorisation for future operations.[119] Typically, an operator is appointed under a 'no gain, no loss' principle. This appointment means that the operator does not get extra benefits and does not bear additional risk by acting as an operator. Co-venturers own assets purchased for the joint venture as tenants in common, and share the hydrocarbon produced from the operations according to their shareholding capacities.[120]

Fundamentally, in a JOA, the 'no gain, no loss' principle presupposes that the operator's liability is restricted except for gross negligence. JOA partners will, therefore, indemnify the operator for liabilities or costs incurred by the operator that did not arise from gross negligence.[121] In addition to gross negligence, the operator will not be indemnified where the loss or liability resulting from a non-consent by a participant(s), or a sole risk operation by the operator.[122] A sole risk occurs when a participant vetoes a programme but is overruled by most of the participants, and the participant still proceeds to carry out the programme as wished.[123] Sometimes the JOA will exclude the operator's liability for consequential loss[124] or anything done or omitted by the operator's affiliates in the conduct of the joint venture operations.[125] The operator's duties in the joint venture are essentially contractual.

[116] Douglas A Holdway, 'The Acute and Chronic Effect of Waste associated with Offshore Oil and Gas Production in Temperate Marine Ecological Process' (2002) 44(3) Marine Pollution Bulletin 185.

[117] Natural Gas Intelligence, 'Anadarko: BP-Mitsui Settlement a Positive Step' (*Natural Gas Intelligence*, 23 May 2011) <www.naturalgasintel.com/anadarko-bp-mitsui-settlement-a-positive-step-2> accessed 12 October 2023.

[118] Junaidu B Marshall, 'Joint Operating Agreements in the Oil and Gas Industry: The Consequence of Sole Risk and Non-Consent Clauses to Joint Operations' (2016) 6(10) Journal of Asian Business Strategy 251.

[119] PW O'Regan and TW Taylor, 'Joint Ventures and Operating Agreements' (1984) 14(1) Victoria University of Wellington Law Review 85.

[120] ibid.

[121] Charles D Marshal Jr, 'Liability for Oil and Gas Operations: An Operator's Perspective' (1993) 39 Annual Institute on Mineral Law 211, 214.

[122] ibid 218.

[123] Mary S Peters and Manu Kumar, 'Why International Oil Companies Choose to Enter into Joint Operating Agreement' (2012) 53(2) Acta Juridica Hungarica 179.

[124] Holdway (n 116) 245.

[125] Toby Hewitt, 'Who Is to Blame? Allocating Liability in Upstream Project Contracts' (2008) 26(2) Journal of Energy and Natural Resources Law 177, 204.

Regarding pollution damage, the responsibility is on the joint venture partners, who are joint licensees for the petroleum operation but are represented by the operator. While multiple persons may hold a licence, legally there is only one licensee, the other holders notwithstanding.[126] It is the licensee's obligation, among other things, to ensure that adequate provision has been made to cover liabilities that may arise from the petroleum operation. The licensee is also expected to maintain the required financial capacity to meet its obligation in case of any liability arising from the petroleum operations carried out by the operator it appointed or worked for.[127] Finally, as the licence holder, the licensee is directly responsible to the government for the petroleum operations in the area awarded.

1.8.2 Operator

The operator is the party appointed by participants in the joint venture to carry out petroleum operations on their behalf. The operator usually holds the highest shareholding capacity amongst the co-venturers. It oversees the day-to-day running of the operations, and has attendant rights, duties and obligations. The operator's activities are supervised, controlled, reviewed and approved by the JOC composed of participating representatives from the joint venture. Benefits (joint venture account property, hydrocarbon produced from the operation) and burdens (joint venture liability) incurred by the operator while carrying out its day-to-day activities for the venture are the responsibility of the venture except for sole-risk non-consent and gross negligence.

The operator functions as the controller of the petroleum operations for the venture. The operator has to ensure that all petroleum activities are carried out in 'good workmanlike manner' and with good oilfield practice to avoid loss or accident while complying with health, safety and environmental regulations during petroleum operations. The operator has a duty to keep books, records and accounts of the venture, provide production statements and reports, pay the relevant taxes and maintain the title documents of the venture. It also has a fiduciary duty to other participants in the venture, and must disclose any relevant conflict or likely conflict of interest.[128]

The operator is the contact person for the joint venture. It manages the venture and designs the well programme, with approval from the operating committee. It represents the interests of the joint venture and is the first person to contact when a downside occurs. As part of its operational function, the operator pays royalties, rentals and shut-in payments; complies with regulatory filings and laws; accounts for the cost of operations and production; and fulfils contractual obligations towards third-party service providers. The operator also ensures the

[126] Philip Mace and others, 'Oil and Gas Regulation in the UK: Overview' (*Thomson Reuters Practical Law*, 1 October 2017 <uk.practicallaw.thomsonreuters.com/5-524-5349?transitionType=Default&contextData=(sc.Default)&firstPage=true&bhcp=1> accessed 12 October 2023.

[127] Offshore Petroleum Licensing (Offshore Safety Directive) Regulations 2015, s 9.

[128] Douglas G Mills and others, 'Exploring the Balance of Power in the Operator/Non-Operator Relationship under the CAPL Operating Procedure' (2010) 48(2) Alberta Law Review 378.

implementation of exploration and production activities; carries out contractual obligations to lessors regarding the property; and responds to third parties' claims for personal injury, property damage or pollution damage.[129]

Concerning liability arising from the operations, the operator takes responsibility for other JOA partners, or solely bears the responsibility if there are no co-venturers. It is also interesting to note that there are different types of operators. Some operators are international oil companies (IOCs), while others are national oil companies. They vary in terms of their size and resources. Their capacity to manage risk also determines their willingness and ability to take responsibility for specific risks.[130] Small operators mostly carry out petroleum operations in shallow waters, rather than in the deep waters and the Arctic, where there is greater financial involvement and pollution risk.

1.8.3 Contractor

The operator engages a contractor to carry out a specific task during hydrocarbon exploration. The contractor, sometimes an independent contractor, possesses the requisite skill in the service area, hence its involvement in the activity. The list of contractors includes companies specialising in drilling, cementing, wire logging or any other service required for drilling operations. Other subcontractors are usually found in an offshore platform providing one support service or another.

Given its role in the drilling operations, the drilling contractor is a crucial player in the contract matrix. Offshore drilling contracts are provided on a day rate, turnkey or footage basis.[131] The market for drilling contracts is driven by interconnected factors: day rates, utilisation and fleet size. The daily rental fee charged by the rig owner is the day rate. It covers the use of the rig and labour costs but excludes costs related to well construction (for example, equipment rental, chemicals and casing).[132] Demand and supply conditions drive the day rate. Thus, when the rig demand exceeds supply, the day rate increases. The capital spending pattern of oil companies informs the need for drilling contracts. The capital expenditure of oil companies is based on the future expectation of the price of oil and gas, and the associated exploration and development risks of offshore hydrocarbons.[133]

[129] Marshal (n 121) 211.

[130] Peter Cameron, 'Liability for Catastrophic Risk in the Oil and Gas Industry' (2012) 6 International Energy Law Review 207.

[131] Owen L Anderson, *Drilling for Black Gold under the Model Form Drilling Contracts* (White Paper, Energy and Mineral Law Foundation 1994) <emlf.org/product/drilling-for-black-gold-under-the-model-form-drilling-contracts> accessed 12 October 2023.

[132] Mark J Kaiser and Brian Snyder, 'A Primer on the Offshore Drilling Industry' (2013) 44(3) Ocean Development and International Law 287.

[133] JC Cole, 'Replacement Cost Economics of Offshore Drilling Rigs' (SPE/IADC Drilling Conference Paper, 28 February–2 March 1995) <onepetro.org/SPEDC/proceedings-abstract/95DC/All-95DC/SPE-28197-MS/57115> accessed 12 October 2023.

Utilisation is a measure put in place by the industry to determine the proportion of rigs working to the available fleet at a particular place and time. Thus, utilisation evaluates the drilling market's spare capacity. A high utilisation rate signals low spare capacity in the market, and oil companies compete to secure drilling services, increasing prices. However, it also indicates that operators can absorb more market capacity. Within a region, higher utilisation rates lead to the repositioning of fleets by drilling contractors, while higher utilisation rates around the globe encourage investment in rig construction.[134] Fleet size is the aggregate number of rigs of a specific water depth or class. The region or firm determines the fleet size and indicates the aggregate capacity in the drilling rig market.

Operators and contractors commonly use day rates in offshore drilling operations, and contractors generally provide drilling services under a 'contract of service', as against a 'contract for service'. The difference is the legal implication for certain liabilities which may arise during offshore drilling operations. A contract of service is more like an employer-and-employee contract. In contrast, a contract for service involves hiring an independent contractor for a certain fee to provide specialised services. In the oil and gas industry, although a drilling contractor is hired for a particular amount as an independent contractor, the legal implications of a contract for service do not extend to him under a day rate contract except under a turnkey.[135] The contractor under a contract for service is legally responsible for its actions.

1.8.4 Subcontractor

Subcontractors assist the drilling contractor in providing vital services related to a drilling operation. For example, they assist with wire logging, cementing, catering and other well-related activities. They also execute a similar indemnity contract like the operator and the contractor, under no liability or hold harmless regime, notwithstanding fault. They agree to take responsibility for their staff and property in the event of any damage, while the main contractor does the same. It is worth noting that some drilling contractors in the UK have neglected to sign up for the hold harmless regime as they consider their property (such as a drilling rig) of greater worth than that of a subcontractor under an indemnity agreement.[136] An example of a subcontractor is Halliburton, which carried out cementing works on the Macondo 252 well in the Gulf of Mexico.

[134] Kaiser and Snyder (n 132).

[135] Owen L Anderson, 'The Anatomy of an Oil and Gas Drilling Contract' (1990) 25(3) Tulsa Law Review 359.

[136] Greg Gordon, 'Risk Allocation in Oil and Gas Service Contracts' in Greg Gordon, John Paterson and Emre Usenmez (eds), *Oil and Gas Law: Current Practice and Emerging Trends: Volume II: Commercial and Contract Issues* (3rd edn, Edinburgh University Press 2018).

1.9 PURPOSE AND OBJECTIVE OF THE BOOK

Increasingly, the need to prevent loss/damage in resource extraction has become crucial for global petroleum operations, energy generation, building and construction activities and so on. As such, petroleum operations, particularly drilling, must be done sustainably to enhance community livelihood and preserve the ecosystem. This book attempts to reconcile public interest and the oil industry practice of risk allocation by investigating methods of mainstreaming public interest more efficiently and equitably, mostly in gross negligence cases in the oil industry, drilling contracts and general contract law.

After the Macondo accident, a clear need exists for ways to deal with conduct and approaches that could encourage offshore pollution in drilling operations, such as using mutual indemnity agreements as a shield against liability for gross negligence. At the same time, it is necessary to balance the risk-and-reward system and the financial positions of the well operator and the drilling contractor. Therefore, a risk allocation practice that incentivises pollution prevention during offshore drilling operations, and contributes to protecting the interests of both the public and the contracting parties, requires innovative shifts from the normative thinking and approach. That is what this book aims to offer.

The overall objective of this book is to contribute to the energy industry practice of risk allocation by proposing an integrative framework that incentives pollution prevention in offshore drilling. It aims to foster an understanding of the perspective of public interest in contractual risk allocation by leveraging doctrines and theories such as freedom of contract, distributive justice, the duty to prevent harm and public policy. The insights gained feed into the construction of a framework that aspires to incentivise pollution prevention in the design of risk allocation for offshore drilling contracts.

The public policy perspective is original in several aspects. First, the framework comprises. and leverages. contract and justice theories. and establishes a link between private contracts and the public's interest. Second, it aims to contribute significantly to the analysis and discussion of risk allocation by suggesting a legal direction regarding 'gross negligence' and harm prevention in petroleum operations. Third, as the concluding chapter demonstrates, the framework will stimulate the consideration of public interest in future offshore drilling contracts. Finally, this book gathers and deepens understanding of the opportunities for making risk allocation more effective, equitable and coherent through applying public policy and distributive justice perspectives.

1.10 METHODOLOGY AND STRUCTURE OF THE BOOK

This book utilises a comparative methodology to examine the practice of risk allocation in four essential jurisdictions, and to understand how gross negligence is represented in the various contracts and standard forms to exclude or limit liability in petroleum operations. Two jurisdictions (US and UK) apply the licensing system to award exploration rights, while the others (Nigeria and Indonesia) use a PSC form. The reason for selecting these four countries is that they are resource-rich countries with enormous oil and gas activities in their territories. The comparison focuses on the private and model form contracts used in these jurisdictions to allocate risks between a well operator and a drilling contractor.

The concept of 'public policy' provides the foundation for the comparative analysis, while distributive justice is used to demonstrate why a party at fault should bear the burden of its gross negligence and the extent of the liability that should apply. In addition, this book uses a doctrinal approach to analyse the basis for developing and applying mutual indemnity agreements in the oil industry, and whether risk allocation should evolve as events change in the oil industry. Finally, this book also utilises existing literature concerning risk allocation to achieve its goal.

This book has seven chapters, with an introduction that provides insights about the book and its relevance to the oil and gas industry and broad contractual arrangement. Chapter 1 examines the concept of risk and how it relates to uncertainty and probability. It highlights the various risk categories and perspectives, and discusses essential terms such as risk management, risk aversion and allocation. The essence is to provide a foundation for discussing risk allocation, and equip readers with the knowledge necessary to understand the book.

Chapter 2 discusses offshore petroleum operations and their various stages, from appraisal to post-decommissioning. It also examines drilling contracts in the oil and gas industry. The chapter further examines how risk is allocated in both of the standard forms and all the selected jurisdictions (USA, UK, Nigeria and Indonesia) to understand the difference in practice in the selected countries. It considers the tools used in allocating risks, such as indemnity, exclusion and limitation of liability clauses, and the rationale for allocating risk in the manner adopted by the oil and gas industry. Finally, the chapter presents some regulatory interventions regarding risk allocation and how these interventions place restrictions on industry practice.

Chapter 3 discusses essential considerations, such as freedom of contract, public policy, sustainability and distributive justice, in risk allocation. It examines the extent to which parties are free to contract, especially in gross negligence cases, and highlights the public policy and sustainability implications for risk allocation practice. The chapter discusses distributive justice as a basis for parties to assume liability for their wrongful conduct and notes that a cap on liability should apply to gross negligence cases between the operator, drilling contractor and subcontractors according to the benefit reaped from the activity. This chapter also highlights the elements of distributive justice and how they relate and apply to private contracts. Chapter 4 discusses gross negligence as a *sui generis* risk and considers how its standard can apply to risk allocation. It also examines corporate responsibility for gross negligence and the challenges of managing and allocating gross negligence in offshore petroleum operations. Chapter 5 advances the principles that will assist in allocating the risk of gross negligence, and the legal framework that should guide the allocation process. Chapter 6 considers the institutional framework necessary to facilitate the allocation of risk in gross negligence cases, and the role of insurance and other financial assurance tools. Chapter 7, the final chapter, provides a summary for stakeholders to reflect on and advance strategies to overcome the limitations of the allocation practice in the oil and gas industry.

Chapter 2

The Context of Offshore Petroleum Drilling Operations and Risk Allocation

2.0 INTRODUCTION

This chapter aims to offer insight into offshore petroleum operations and the stages of petroleum exploration and production. It focuses on the various types of drilling contracts, considers how risks are allocated in selected jurisdictions (Nigeria, Indonesia, the UK, and the US), and explores the changing perception of risk allocation in the offshore oil industry. Finally, it highlights that the risk allocation practice is underpinned by the industry perception of business benefit, and is implemented using risk allocation tools like mutual indemnity clauses in private contracts or industry standard forms.

2.1 OFFSHORE PETROLEUM EXPLORATION

Offshore petroleum drilling operations follow clearly defined work programmes that determine the required level of work and the length of time in the operations. In the early 1930s, there was evidence of petroleum exploration around the coastal areas of California and Louisiana and in places like Venezuela, Lake Maracaibo and the Baku area of the Caspian Sea. Most of these explorations were shallow-water developments, albeit commercially substantial ones. However, exploration moved into marginally deeper waters following the introduction of offshore mobile drilling rigs, replacing the previous practice of drilling from fixed wooden trestles.[1] Over time, offshore drilling improved through the use of submersible barges that could be moved to a drilling site, with the drilling rig attached to the back deck above water. However, the limitation with submersibles was that they were only suitable for drilling in the bays and marginally coastal waters up to forty feet of water depth. Given this constraint and the knowledge that deeper portions of the sloping continental shelves were rich in petroleum deposits, it became necessary to innovate drilling to access depths of 100 feet or more.

By the 1950s, the need for a new offshore drilling technology resulted in the emergence of the mobile jack-up drilling barge. The logic behind the jack-up barge was that the legs could be installed on the barge and lowered into the seabed using a jacking mechanism on the drilling deck. The jack-up is usually towed to the drilling site and then towed off to another location when the drilling ends.

[1] David W Sharp, A *Brief Introduction to Energy Insurance* (Amazon Marketing Hub 2022).

The jack-up barge has stood the test of time and is fondly regarded as the offshore drilling industry's workhorse. However, new technologies like floating structures are necessary to drill in deeper waters due to the height constraints of jack-up barges. The 1960s witnessed the entry of semi-submersible mobile drilling rigs to solve the challenge of drilling in deep waters. It proved successful in deep water drilling and could drill up to 5,000 feet.

After the HS has granted the licensee the right to access the hydrocarbon resources in a specified field, offshore petroleum exploration and exploitation usually follow. The permit to explore and exploit oil and gas is granted to a company later known as the contractor/licensee or operator of the licenced area. The licensee is a contractor to the HS, and its operations are carried out according to the terms and conditions set out in the petroleum regime, the model clause agreement or the model PSC agreement. Under the PSC or the Concession, the operating company/licensee is responsible to the HS where an accident or pollution damage occurs. It is also the responsibility of the operator/licensee to implement the work programme and ensure compliance with the HS's policies and regulations. The operator engages a drilling company to conduct drilling operations after seismic data have revealed the availability of hydrocarbon in commercial quantity. Activities like wire logging, cementing and certain technical aspects follow the drilling operation.

Generally, offshore petroleum operations involve several stages, such as exploring petroleum, appraising, developing, decommissioning offshore installations and post-decommissioning activities. The exploration process sets in after petroleum authorisation has been granted to the operator by the relevant authority. This authorisation enables geologists to search for possible petroleum deposits below sea level. Basically, exploration involves carrying out geophysical surveys in the authorised area using seismic instruments. The operator may drill an exploratory well depending on the petroleum data obtained in situ. The drilling of an exploratory well validates the findings of the seismic survey, thus requiring the services of a drilling contractor, and a drilling contract.

The appraisal stage focuses on determining the feasibility of efficiently exploiting the discovered petroleum, including identifying the best way to achieve this through various technical options. The essence of this segment is contentious, especially when the exploration stage shows evidence of petroleum deposits. In the oil and gas industry, certain operators may venture into production from this stage, in order to start making returns on their investments. This strategy, however, could be replete with several risks, primarily due to an assessment of the actual quantity of the discovery and the sizing of the production facilities.[2] As a result, there may be a need to drill additional wells to establish the actual volume of the reserves, and ascertain the opportunities and challenges surrounding the economic production of petroleum and the technical requirements necessary for the operation.

2 Ken Mildwaters, 'Oil and Gas: Commercial Contracts Matrix' (unpublished, University of Dundee 2016).

A feasibility study follows an appraisal analysis after the commercial viability of the resources has been determined. The essence is to ascertain the economic and technical strategy for producing petroleum, including information regarding budget implementation, resource requirements, surface and subsurface facilities, operation, maintenance culture and so on. This information is contained in the field development plan, a vital document that identifies the various stakeholders and participants in the operation and their roles in implementing the development plan. The relevant regulatory authority usually approves the field development plan. This approval enables the operator to commence the facility design process and initiate other procurement procedures to get the project up and running for production.

The next critical stage is the production phase. This stage involves the exploitation of the petroleum resource in commercial quantity for sale or distribution among the relevant host country and operator, depending on the nature of the petroleum agreement – PSC, Concession, Risk Service Agreement and so on. A production well is necessary for this stage, and a drilling contract follows to complete the process in line with the field development plan. The production phase consists of substages. The first is the build-up period, which puts the production wells on stream in a planned pattern, focusing on wells with better results. It requires constant observation and juggling to ensure optimal production is achieved with a combination of diverse wells. This process is known as production optimisation. The second is the plateau period, where well optimisation has been completed, and production is aligned with expectations and technical projections. The duration of this phase depends on the specific field under consideration. The third phase is the decline period, during which the well's productive lifespan starts to diminish. This can occur because the well has reached its reserve limit, or due to technical challenges that render further production from the well impractical or excessively expensive. The operator may use strategies to enhance or optimise the well, including workover intervention[3] or artificial lift,[4] before shutting it. The appropriate intervention depends on the work to be carried out in the well.

The final stages of a petroleum operation are the decommissioning of the platform and post-decommissioning activities. The former stage arises when the well no longer produces at its optimal capacity and continuing production has become uneconomic, returning a negative cash flow. The production installations are removed at this stage, and the well is plugged and abandoned.[5] The latter stage involves the removal of any

[3] Workover intervention is the process of performing major maintenance or remedial treatments on an oil or gas well. In some instances, workover involves the removal and replacement of the production tubing string after the well has been killed and a workover rig has been placed on location. See Tomas Elander Solli, 'Workover/Well Intervention and Regulatory Challenges', (*OnePetro*, 4 October 2011) <onepetro.org/OTCBRASIL/proceedings-abstract/11OBRA/All-11OBRA/OTC-22586-MS/37021> accessed 12 October 2023.

[4] Daniel I O'Reilly and others, 'Productivity Determination for Cyclic Production Using Steady State Harmonic Theory – Application to Artificial Lift Wells' [2019[Journal of Petroleum Science and Engineering 172.

[5] Mark J Kaiser, *Decommissioning Forecasting and Operating Cost Estimation: Gulf of Mexico Well Trends, Structure Inventory and Forecast Models* (Gulf Professional Publishing 2019).

remaining production infrastructure after the well has been abandoned. The aim is to restore the environment to a state closely resembling its condition before petroleum activities commenced. However, achieving near complete environmental restoration is challenging in practice. Other issues that could arise at this stage relate to residual liability after decommissioning. Post-decommissioning residual liability is determined by national governments in accordance with their domestic laws, as international and regional rules in this area are still evolving.[6] Again, global regulation exists for the decommissioning and disposal of offshore installations, although each country exercises the right to enact legislation to enhance the decommissioning of offshore petroleum structures.

Aside from the stages of petroleum operations highlighted, the offshore petroleum community is broadly divided into oil companies and service contractors. However, these companies have several subcontractors, manufacturers and suppliers who provide specialised services and equipment. The HS usually owns the hydrocarbon reserves but permits the contractor to develop and produce petroleum under a production sharing contract.

A primary activity identified in the stages of petroleum operations discussed above is drilling operations. Drilling exploratory, appraisal and production wells is essential to every offshore petroleum operation. Before drilling activities commence, parties, especially the well operator and the drilling contractor, enter into agreements to manage likely damages that may arise during petroleum operations. This agreement bypasses the application of tort law in determining fault. This process is done through a private contract between the operator and the contractor due to risk and capital involvement.[7] As already identified, petroleum operations involve operators, contractors, and subcontractors[8] who specialise in seismic acquisition and processing, drilling, cementing and wire logging. They

[6] Tim Martin, 'Decommissioning of International Petroleum Facilities: Evolving Standards and Key Issues' [2003] Oil, Gas & Energy Law Journal 5. The UK has provided some guidelines in this regard. See the guidelines by the UK Government's Department of Business, Energy and Industrial Strategy on the subject: <www.gov.uk/guidance/oil-and-gas-decommissioning-of-offshore-installations-andpipelines> accessed 12 October 2023.

[7] Toby Hewitt, 'Who Is to Blame? Allocating Liability in Upstream Project Contracts' (2008) 26(2) Journal of Energy and Natural Resources Law 177.

[8] In the oil and gas industry, an operator is the holder of a petroleum licence or lease for a particular petroleum operation. A contractor is the party that provides services for the operator of the lease or licence. The service could be well drilling services, well maintenance services, facility hire or maintenance. The allocation of parties' liabilities follows a standard industry contract which reflects the practice of risk allocation in the oil industry. The industry's allocation of liability is not tort-based. It follows the business convenience ideology that avoids long causal determination. The court in *Chesapeake Operating Inc v Nabors Drilling USA Inc* 94 SW 3d 163 [Tex App 2002] at 168 explained the challenges in drilling thus:

> Drilling sites, of course, can be hazardous places. When injuries occur, it is often difficult to tell who is at fault due to the complex nature of the enterprise, the large number of subcontractors usually involved, difficult questions regarding the right to control, and the intersection of premises liability and agency law in drilling operations. As a result, there are usually two disputes to resolve-one pitting the injured party against all those potentially responsible, and another among the defendants to allocate fault and the resulting burden of any settlement or judgment.

provide numerous operational equipment and tools, such as drill pipes, compressors, drill bits and other completion equipment.[9] Depending on the nature of the agreement between the operator and the drilling contractor, they could agree to a daywork, turnkey or footage drilling contract.

2.2 DRILLING CONTRACTS

As earlier stated, an oil and gas drilling contract outlines the rights/benefits and duties/burden a drilling contractor has regarding the provision of a drilling rig and personnel as required by an operating company. The drilling contract could be for offshore or onshore petroleum operations and cover an array of rig structures. In addition, it provides compensation to the contractor on a day rate, footage rate or lump sum payment for meeting specific targets. The following contracts are the predominant drilling contracts in the oil and gas industry, and they provide compensation to the drilling contractor for their services.

2.2.1 Daywork/Day Rate Contract

Daywork contracts are standard in the oil and gas industry. They are calculated based on the amount of time the drilling contractor puts into the daily drilling operations.[10] Under this type of contract, the drilling contractor provides the drilling crew and equipment, and is paid an agreed amount for each day spent in drilling, irrespective of the number of days involved or the depth drilled.[11] The contractor receives instruction from the operator consistent with a contract of service, and assumes the risks set out in the drilling contract. The operator assumes other risks not assigned to the contractor in the agreement. This arrangement is due to the structure of the compensation and command-and-control method, making it unavoidable for the operator to bear a significant amount of risk regarding the contract.

2.2.2 Footage Contract

A footage contract is an agreement that requires the operator to pay the contractor based on the depth of the hole drilled.[12] A specific amount is paid per foot of hole drilled, and as with daywork contracts, the drilling contractor provides the drilling crew and equipment and receives payment per foot of hole drilled. Footage contracts are not common practice in offshore drilling.

9 Ernest Smith and others, *International Petroleum Transactions* (3rd edn, Rocky Mountain Mineral Law Foundation 2010).

10 Timothy A Martin, 'Model Contracts: A Survey of the Global Petroleum Industry' (2004) 22(3) Journal of Energy & Natural Resources Law 281.

11 Mary Shaddock Jones, 'Offshore and Onshore Drilling Contracts' (Energy Symposium, 27 July 2011) <cdn.ymaws.com/www.iiah.org/resource/resmgr/imported/Offshore%20%20and%20Onshore%20 Drilling-%20Part%201%20Contr.pdf> accessed 12 October 2023.

12 Petter Osmundsen, Terje Sørenes and Anders Toft, 'Drilling Contracts and Incentives' (2008) 36(8) Energy Policy 3138.

2.2.3 Turnkey Contract

A turnkey contract entails paying a lump sum to the drilling contractor for meeting a preset target. The drilling contractor drills the oil well, establishes production and turns the completed job over to the operator for the amount agreed between the parties in the contract. Under this contract type, the contractor oversees the drilling and well completion for productions. The contractor assumes greater responsibility for the economic consequences of a downside while performing the contract.[13] Upon completion of the drilling, the contractor hands over the well to the operator. Turnkeys are primarily used in exploratory offshore drilling operations in the Gulf of Mexico, where the contracting parties agree to a particular drilling depth or reservoir formation in return for the payment of a specified amount.[14] The low utilisation of turnkey contracts could be because it focuses on one performance indicator: a specified drill depth.

2.3 ALLOCATING RISKS IN THE OIL AND GAS INDUSTRY

Due to the nature and risk of offshore oil and gas operations, operators and drilling contractors have designed several contracting practices, such as mutual indemnity agreements, to allocate risks and manage physical exposures to suit their business benefit – a typical example of the doctrine of freedom of contract. The practice in the oil industry is that risks are allocated based on ownership of property and personnel, and control of polluting activity. It means that parties bear the liability arising from the injury or death of their staff and damage to their property during drilling activities.[15] This liability is without regard to fault, whether resulting from negligence or gross negligence. Concerning pollution damage,[16] the drilling contractor assumes responsibility for surface pollution, while the well operator is responsible for subsurface pollution, notwithstanding the fault of the party that caused it.[17]

[13] In *Total Drilling Company v Abraham* 328 P 2d 1083 (NM 1958), the court identified that by accepting the agreed lump-sum consideration for the project, the drilling contractor would become responsible for any cost increase, whether arising from weather or a wild well. Note, however, that risks such as drilling a dry hole will still be borne by the operator.

[14] Petter Osmundsen, Terje Sørenes and Anders Toft, 'Offshore Oil Service Contracts New Incentive Schemes to Promote Drilling Efficiency' (2010) 72(3) Journal of Petroleum Science and Engineering 220.

[15] Injury or death of staff and property damage fall under the first limb of the rule in *Hadley v Baxendale* (1854) 9 Ex 341 as direct losses. These are losses that flow naturally from any conduct that occasions harm in drilling operations. People may either die or be injured or property will be destroyed in the event of an accident.

[16] Pollution damage could result in direct or indirect loss. Under the rule in *Hadley v Baxendale*, losses which may fairly and reasonably be considered as arising naturally from the breach of contract, which were reasonably foreseeable in the ordinary course of events, are direct losses; whereas damages that may reasonably be supposed to have been in the contemplation of both the parties at the time the contract was made are indirect losses. Regulatory fines for pollution at sea (physical damage) may be classified as direct losses, whereas loss of fishing and other economic rights, depletion of shrimp and other forms of consequential loss, may be regarded as indirect losses arising from the pollution.

[17] Peter Cameron, 'Liability for Catastrophic Risk in the Oil and Gas Industry' (2012) 6 International Energy Law Review 207.

The table below highlights the schematics of risk allocation in a typical standard-form contract in the petroleum industry.

Table 1: Schematics of risk allocation in a typical standard form contract in the petroleum industry

Adapted from Egbochue (2013)[18]

Standard form	Death/personal injury & loss/ damage KK indemnities	Pollution KK indemnities	Extension to party's group	Consequential loss
LOGIC Construction Ed, 2 October 2003	The company also indemnifies the contractor group in respect of loss/damage to permanent third-party oil and gas facilities and consequential losses (as defined) therefrom. Expressly stated that all of these indemnities and pollution indemnities apply irrespective of cause and notwithstanding negligence or breach of duty by indemnified party.	Contractor indemnifies company group against claims in respect of pollution occurring on or emanating from the contractor group's premises, property or equipment. Company indemnifies contractor group against claims in respect of pollution emanating from the reservoir or company group's property.	Company group does not include the company's other contractors.	Each party indemnifies the other against claims consequential loss (as defined) from its party group.
AIPN Model Well Services Contracts 2002	Operator also indemnifies contractor in respect of contractor group equipment, loss or damaged downhole. Indemnities do not apply to death, personal injuries, loss or damage caused by gross negligence or wilful misconduct of the other party.	Operator indemnifies contractor against claims arising from a worksite fire or explosion or blowout, cratering or uncontrolled well condition regardless of the cause.	Company group includes company other contractors.	Neither party is responsible to the other for consequential damages (as defined). Alternative two also adds an indemnity in respect of each party's group consequential damages claims. Another alternative carves out gross negligence.

(Continued)

[18] Chidi Egbochue, 'Reviewing Knock for Knock Indemnities Following the Macondo Well Blowout' (2013) 7(4) Construction Law International 9.

Standard form	Death/personal injury & loss/ damage KK indemnities	Pollution KK indemnities	Extension to party's group	Consequential loss
BIMCO Time Charter Party for Offshore Service Vessels 2005	Expressly stated that indemnity applies even if caused by the act, neglect or default of other party group or unseaworthiness of any vessel.	Owners indemnify charter against claims for pollution damage arising from acts or omissions of owners or their personnel which cause discharge, spill or leaks from a vessel other than emanating from cargo thereon. Charter indemnifies owners against claims in respect of all other pollution damage even if caused by the act, neglect or default of Owners Group or unseaworthiness of any vessel.	Charterer Group includes Charterer's contractor.	Each party indemnifies the other against claims for consequential damages (as defined) from its party Group.
International Association of Drilling Contractors Daywork Drilling Contract – US 2003	Operator shall release Contractor of any liability for, and shall protect, defend and indemnify contractor from and against all claims, demands and causes of action of every kind and character, without limit and without regard to the cause or causes thereof or the negligence of any party or parties . . . on account of body injury, death or damage to property.	Operator shall assume all responsibility for, and indemnify Contractor and its suppliers, from and against all claims, demands and causes of action arising directly or indirectly from all other pollution or contamination which may occur during the conduct of operations hereunder, including, but not limited to; that which may result from fire, blowout, cratering, seepage or any other uncontrolled flow of oil or gas.	Contractor includes its suppliers, contractors and subcontractors.	Each party shall be responsible for and hold harmless and indemnify the other party from and against its own special, indirect or consequential damages.

Generally, these model contracts are called ‘model forms’, ‘contract templates’, ‘model agreements’ and so on.[19] They are developed and endorsed by practitioners in the hydrocarbon industry on a mutual understanding for full acceptance.[20] Industry practitioners in the UK use the LOGIC model form contracts, while in the US, they use the AIPN and IADC model contracts. Petroleum regimes that use PSCs adopt elements from both systems of model contracts.[21]

2.4 CONTRACTUAL RISK ALLOCATION IN SPECIFIC JURISDICTIONS

This subsection considers how risk is allocated in the UK, US, Nigeria and Indonesia, and the similarities and differences in these jurisdictions.

2.4.1 *United Kingdom*

The UK hydrocarbon industry is based on a concession system administrated by the Oil and Gas Authority (OGA), now the North Sea Transition Authority (NSTA).[22] Concessions are akin to contracts in their setup but have some regulatory components. The rights, duties and obligations regulating the relationship between the government and a private party (licensee) are defined in the licence and are also set out in the model clauses.[23] The UK Petroleum Act requires that such regulatory conditions – model clauses – be first published in secondary legislation, which is then incorporated by reference into new licences.[24]

The legal framework for offshore petroleum activities in the UK includes acts and regulations covering various aspects of petroleum operations. However, no specific legislation comprehensively deals with liability for injury, property damage or pollution damage. Liability could be based on the Offshore Pollution Liability Agreement (OPOL), a strict liability regime, statutes and model clauses, or tort.[25]

19 Martin, ‘Model Contracts’ (n 10) 282.

20 ibid.

21 Notable associations that provide model form contracts for oilfield and construction services are as follows: the International Association of Energy Negotiators (AIEN), Leading Oil & Gas Industry Competitiveness (LOGIC), the International Association of Drilling Contractors (IADC) and the International Association of Consulting Engineers (FIDIC). Some major international companies in the hydrocarbon and construction industry have their own types of model form contract, which may not be immediately available to the public but which are widely applied in their contracts.

22 North Sea Transition Authority, ‘Types of Licence’ <www.nstauthority.co.uk/regulatory-information/licensing-and-consents/types-of-licence> accessed 12 October 2023.

23 See for instance, the Petroleum Licensing (Production) (Seaward Areas) Regulations 2008, and its 2017 amendment.

24 North Sea Transition Authority, ‘Licensing and Consents: Overview’ <www.nstauthority.co.uk/regulatory-information/licensing-and-consents> andhttps://www.ogauthority.co.uk/licensing-consents/overview/<www.ogauthority.co.uk/licensing-consents/overview> accessed 12 October 2023.

25 Cameron (n 17) 211–212.

Model clauses obligate licensees to use methods customary to good oilfield practices and employ steps to prevent harm in the area they are licensed to operate.[26] No limit on liability exists under tort, as an operator is liable for all costs so long as the damage is reasonably foreseeable. However, a party cannot recover purely economic losses as the damage must relate to property or persons to recover this type of loss.[27]

2.4.1.1 United Kingdom Model Contracts

Industry practitioners in the UK adopt the LOGIC model form of contract to allocate risk among themselves contrary to the fault-based position of harm and liability. This practice is well established in the UK.[28] This practice sets aside the traditional tort system of fault liability in favour of a risk allocation system based on the contract between parties. The risk allocation focuses on property damage, injury or death of personnel and pollution contamination. The provisions sometimes extend to group members under a mutual indemnity clause[29] or a 'knock-for-knock' scheme, regardless of cause.

Under the mutual indemnity arrangement in LOGIC model contracts, the operator (company) indemnifies contractors (and a contractor group) for third-party facility damage, personal injury or death of the operator's personnel without regard to fault.[30] However, there are qualifications applied, especially for non-pollution damage provisions.[31] The application of the knock-for-knock principle in contracts is founded on the principle of freedom of contract and the need for courts to give effect to the contract of parties when the vitiating elements of a contract are absent.[32] English courts have also echoed this position, for instance, in the *London Bridge* and *Orbit Valve* cases.[33] It is worth noting that not all indemnities are enforceable, as a court will look at the wording of the agreement.[34]

[26] Environmental Damage (Prevention and Remediation) Regulations 2009, schedule to para 23(1).

[27] Cameron (n 17) 211.

[28] Reference to model contracts here means the LOGIC and CRINE model contracts used to allocate risk between operators and contractors in the UK North Sea operations.

[29] Greg Gordon, 'Risk Allocation in Oil and Gas Service Contracts' in Greg Gordon, John Paterson and Emre Usenmez (eds), *Oil and Gas Law: Current Practice and Emerging Trends: Volume II: Commercial and Contract Issues* (3rd edn, Edinburgh University Press 2018) 447.

[30] Smith and others (n 9).

[31] LOGIC, *General Conditions of Contract for Supply of Major items of Plant and Equipment* (2nd edn, LOGIC 2005) <jimdo-storage.global.ssl.fastly.net/file/8adbb68e-23e7-44c2-9f53-c0e9ee20cc67/SCA%20T&C.pdf> accessed 12 October 2023.

[32] Vitiating elements of a contracts are duress, undue influence, fraud, misrepresentation and incapacity to contract.

[33] *Caledonian North Sea Ltd v London Bridge Engineering Ltd* [2002] UKHL 4; *EE Caledonia Ltd v Orbit Valve Co Plc* [1994] 1 WLR 1515.

[34] *Orbit Valve* (n 33).

The relevant section of the LOGIC form is reproduced below for easy understanding.

19. Indemnities

19.1 The CONTRACTOR shall be responsible for and shall save, indemnify, defend and hold harmless the COMPANY GROUP from and against all claims, losses, damages, costs (including legal costs) expenses and liabilities in respect of:

(a) loss of or damage to property of the CONTRACTOR GROUP whether owned, hired, leased or otherwise provided by the CONTRACTOR GROUP arising from, relating to or in connection with the performance or non-performance of the CONTRACT; and

(b) personal injury including death or disease to any person employed by the CONTRACTOR GROUP arising from, relating to or in connection with the performance or non-performance of the CONTRACT; and

(c) subject to any other express provisions of the CONTRACT, personal injury including death or disease or loss of or damage to the property of any third party to the extent that any such injury, loss or damage is caused by the negligence or breach of duty (whether statutory or otherwise) of the CONTRACTOR GROUP. For the purposes of this Clause 19.1(c) 'third party' shall mean any party which is not a member of the COMPANY GROUP or CONTRACTOR GROUP.

19.2 The COMPANY shall be responsible for and shall save, indemnify, defend and hold harmless the CONTRACTOR GROUP from and against all claims, losses, damages, costs (including legal costs) expenses and liabilities in respect of:

(a) loss of or damage to property of the COMPANY GROUP, whether:

(i) owned by the COMPANY GROUP, or

(ii) leased or otherwise obtained under arrangements with financial institutions by the COMPANY GROUP which is located at the WORKSITE arising from, relating to or in connection with the performance or non-performance of the CONTRACT; and

(b) personal injury including death or disease to any person employed by the COMPANY GROUP arising from, relating to or in connection with the performance or non-performance of the CONTRACT; and

(c) subject to any other express provisions of the CONTRACT, personal injury including death or disease or loss of or damage to the property of any third party to the extent that any such injury, loss or damage is caused by the negligence or breach of duty (whether statutory or otherwise) of the COMPANY GROUP. For the purposes of this Clause 19.2(c) 'third party' shall mean any party which is not a member of the CONTRACTOR GROUP or COMPANY GROUP.

(d) loss of or damage to such permanent third-party oil and gas production facilities and pipelines and consequential losses arising therefrom, as specified and defined in and in accordance with Appendix 1 to Section I – Form of Agreement where such loss or damage is arising from, relating to or in connection with the performance or non-performance of the CONTRACT. The provisions of this Clause 19.2(d) shall apply notwithstanding the provisions of Clause 19.1(c).

19.3 Except as provided by Clause 19.1(a), Clause 19.1(b), and Clause 19.4, the **COMPANY** shall save, indemnify, defend and hold harmless the CONTRACTOR GROUP from and against any claim of whatsoever nature **arising from pollution emanating from the reservoir** or from the property of the COMPANY GROUP arising from, relating to or in connection with the performance or non-performance of the CONTRACT.

19.4 Except as provided by Clause 19.2(a) and Clause 19.2(b) the **CONTRACTOR** shall save, indemnify, defend and hold harmless the COMPANY GROUP from and against any claim of whatsoever nature **arising from pollution occurring on the premises of the CONTRACTOR GROUP or emanating from the property and equipment of the CONTRACTOR GROUP** (including but not limited to marine vessels) arising from, relating to or in connection with the performance or non-performance of the CONTRACT.

19.5 All exclusions and indemnities given under this Clause (save for those under Clauses 19.1(c) and 19.2(c)) and Clause 21 **shall apply irrespective of cause and notwithstanding the negligence or breach of duty (whether statutory or otherwise) of the indemnified party or any other entity or party and shall apply irrespective of any claim in tort, under contract or otherwise at law.**

19.6 If either party becomes aware of any incident likely to give rise to a claim under the above indemnities, it shall notify the other and both parties shall co-operate fully in Investigating the incident

19.7 The indemnity given by the PARTIES under this CONTRACT are full and primary, and shall apply irrespective of whether the indemnified PARTY has, or has not, insurance in place relating to any claim, losses, damages or cost in respect of the subject matter of any indemnity given under this CONTRACT.

19.8 EACH PARTY expressly agrees that the indemnities set out in this clause do not extent to criminal sanctions imposed upon it, arising from, relating to or in connection with the performance or non-performance of the CONTRACT.[35]

It is evident from the above clauses that liability for injury, property or pollution damage is without regard to fault, howsoever caused and notwithstanding any breach of duty. The mutual indemnity scheme in the UK is established under LOGIC module contracts and further strengthened by the Industry Mutual Hold Harmless Agreement (IMHH). The IMHH has as its purpose the provision of practical and efficient means of bringing into being a set of hold harmless indemnities between parties.[36] This purpose is achieved through the core indemnity provisions that cover personal injury, disease, sickness or death of workers known as 'personnel', loss or damage to property, and consequential loss. The relevant hold harmless section is set out below.

[35] 'Standard Contracts for UK Offshore Oil and Gas Industry: General Conditions of Contracts for Service On- and Off-shore' *LOGIC Edition* 4, 2019, <app.logic-energy.org/standard-contracts/documents/view/services-on--and-offshore-edition-4---february-2019> accessed 2 February 2024.

[36] Gordon (n 29) 470. The IMHH applies to the United Kingdom Continental Shelf (UKCS), with the intention of underpinning offshore hydrocarbon operations. The IMHH scheme is designed to help participants manage risks in a comprehensive manner.

2. Indemnity by the Signatories

2.1 Subject to Clauses 2.3 and 2.4 each of the Signatories shall be solely responsible for and shall defend, indemnify and hold harmless the other Signatories and the other members of their respective Groups against all Claims arising from, out of, or relating to the Services in connection with:

(i) personal injury to or sickness, disease or death of Personnel of the Indemnifying Signatory or any other members of its Group; and

(ii) loss of, recovery of, or damage to any Property of the Indemnifying Signatory or any other members of its Group; and

(iii) Consequential Loss suffered by the Indemnifying Signatory or any members of its Group.

2.2 The indemnities given pursuant to this Deed shall be full and primary and shall apply irrespective of cause and notwithstanding the negligence or breach of duty (whether statutory or otherwise) of the Indemnified Party and shall apply irrespective of any claim in tort, under contract or otherwise at law. For the avoidance of doubt and to the extent permitted by law each Signatory agrees that it shall not rely upon the provisions of any statute, treaty or convention for the purpose of avoiding or limiting its obligations to any other Signatory under Clause 2.1.

2.3 The indemnities in Clause 2.1 (i), (ii) and (iii) shall not apply and are not given either in favour of or against, and shall not be enforceable either by or against, any Signatory in respect of any Claims arising out of events occurring prior to the date on which that Signatory became a Signatory (either on the date on which this Deed came into force or on the date of the Deed of Adherence which it executed, as the case may be).[37]

It is essential to note that the IMHH does not provide for or cover indemnity for pollution damage. Greg Gordon notes that the industry favours indemnity for injury, death, sickness or disease of personnel, property damage or loss, and a defined class of loss called 'Consequential Loss', but not pollution damage.[38] Again, while losses from the death of personnel, damage or loss of property and consequential loss are insurable, risk/loss arising from pollution are regarded as 'less quantifiable', hence the likelihood of creating complication to the IMHH clauses.[39] The perceived less quantifiable nature of pollution has informed the absence of pollution clauses in the IMHH.

Another vital aspect of the IMHH agreement is its application between or among contractors, not between operators and contractors.[40] However, some contractors, particularly drilling contractors, do not support the IMHH Deed as they

[37] See Clause 2 of LOGIC's '2022 Mutual Indemnity and Hold Harmless Deed' (21 October 2021) <app.logic-energy.org/imhh/documents/download/3> accessed 12 October 2023.

[38] Gordon (n 29) 471.

[39] LOGIC, 'IMHH General Guidance' <logic-energy.org/imhh/guidance> accessed 12 October 2023.

[40] Operators give consent to the agreement because it covers contractors working for operators in the project. This is so that the contractor to an operator will be captured under the group definition as an agent of the operator. The contracts usually state that signatories will indemnify, defend and hold each other harmless in the event of losses, damage or injury of personnel.

consider the value of their drilling equipment and the number of staff on a given offshore platform to be of crucial concern to them.[41] Some contractors have even withdrawn their signatories from the IMHH Deed. Between 31 December 2014 and 31 December 2017, eight signatories had withdrawn from the scheme.[42]

The IMHH agreement does not preclude parties from entering a different liability scheme if they so desire.[43] The indemnities provided under the Deed are considered as 'Full and Primary'. They apply irrespective of cause and regardless of the negligence or breach of duty (whether statutory or in other forms) of the party to be indemnified. Its application is also without regard to any claim under the contract, in tort or at law.[44]

Apart from the IMHH agreement, broad indemnity contracts between operators and contractors in the United Kingdom Continental Shelf (UKCS) also cover vital aspects of offshore hydrocarbon risk allocation. The practice in the UKCS is analogous to that in other jurisdictions where the operator provides indemnity for pollution damage arising from the well, occasioned by the sole or joint negligence of a drilling contractor. Usually, the drilling contractor exercises actual or constructive control in well drilling operations while the operator oversees the work programme.[45]

2.4.1.2 Analysis of the United Kingdom Mutual Indemnification Practice

An examination of the knock-for-knock principle in the UKCS reveals that indemnity clauses are used to allocate risks that may arise from offshore drilling operations, regardless of fault. The indemnity clauses cover the death of personnel, injury, property damage (hired, owned or leased) and consequential loss. Parties sometimes agree not to apply indemnification in the event of wilful misconduct or gross negligence. A party at fault can still claim indemnity regardless of their role in causing the damage. The party with the contractual responsibility is left to bear the burden.

Although 'gross negligence' is not a term of art in the UK, there is no prohibition on its use in drilling contracts. The absence of a statutory prohibition of mutual indemnity as a cover against liability for gross negligence leaves room for

[41] Gordon (n 29) 476. Some drilling contractors in the UKCS hold the view that other contractors on the platform have small numbers of staff and less valuable equipment compared to drilling contractors. This explains the non-adherence to the Deed or signatories to the IMHH Deed.

[42] LOGIC, 'Signatory Withdrawals – IMHH 2012 Scheme' (LOGIC 2018) <logic-energy.org/imhh/2012-2/signatory-withdrawals> accessed 12 October 2023. This may be because some contractors would not like to bear the liability of another party who was negligent. Under the IMHH scheme, a signatory is not held liable for their misconduct, howsoever caused. This could disincentivise the exercise of care during petroleum operations.

[43] Gordon (n 29) 472.

[44] IMHH Deed, clause 2.2.

[45] With respect to drilling operations, the role of the operator may be regarded as administrative and merely supervisory, especially as the drilling contractor is an independent contractor under a contract for service.

complacency and a negative incentive to prevent harm to the public. Risks are allocated based on business benefit and ability to bear the risk, but not behind an imaginary veil of ignorance that could facilitate public interest and fairness from a Rawlsian perspective. The absence of liability induces a want of care when no liability attaches to grossly negligent actions. An obligation arising from gross negligence serves as an incentive to exercise greater care as the awareness of potential liability encourages careful behaviour. In accident law, a sense of liability influences both parties to adopt socially optimal levels of precaution.[46]

The UK's risk allocation practice is not compatible with public policy considerations. It enables a party to use mutual indemnity as a cover against liability for severely wrongful oilfield practices. Public policy discourages practices that could cause harm to society. Allowing a party's severely wrongful conduct to go without liability encourages practices that could harm society. The model form creates room for moral hazard as there is no obligation in the risk allocation practice for a party to take care of a risk not allocated to them. Furthermore, the drilling contract does not make the party at fault have 'skin in the game' in the event of a downside.

2.4.2 United States of America

The US is a dominant player in the hydrocarbon industry, with huge reserves in the Gulf of Mexico. Hydrocarbon rights in US offshore waters are either federal or state owned (depending on the distance from the shore) and leased to oil companies. Unlike the UK, the US has different laws applicable in various states,[47] and some states have, through legislation, restricted the application of indemnity for negligent acts on the grounds of public policy.[48] However, federal legislation is essential in regulating petroleum operations for consistent practice. As a developed player in the hydrocarbon industry, the US has used the Concession system for many years. However, private ownership of hydrocarbon rights[49] also influenced the US regime in the development of its hydrocarbon law and formed the necessary foundation of business concepts in the petroleum industry.

Most of the petroleum activities carried out in the US take place in offshore waters and are subject to federal laws such as the Oil Pollution Act (OPA) 1990 and the Clean Water Act, with limited regulatory involvement on the part of

[46] Astha Srivastava and Ankur Srivastava, 'Economic Analysis of Accident Law: A New Liability Rule that Induces Socially Optimal Behaviour in Case of Limited Information' (2021) 17(1) Review of Law & Economics 119.

[47] For instance, Anti-Indemnity Acts exist in Texas and Louisiana. They preclude a party from benefiting from a wrong/negligence they have committed.

[48] The grounds for the restriction is to avoid a situation where a party with strong bargaining power passes some liabilities to another with weak bargaining power. Our focus here is on how public policy seeks to prevent a party from using mutual indemnity as a shield for gross negligence during oilfield activities.

[49] The 'rule of capture', as practiced then in the US.

states. Under the OPA, the general framework for risk allocation through indemnities is not provided, but the OPA acknowledges its use in contracts. Section 1010 of the OPA provides that the Act does not prohibit any agreement that holds harmless or indemnifies another party for liability arising under the Act. It also states that where liability is imposed, a party cannot transfer its liability to another party who is not responsible. It means that a responsible party cannot transfer his statutory liability to another party under the Act. The rationale is to enable the government to hold a party legally responsible or proceed against the party. However, parties could contract to limit, hold harmless or reduce the liability burden. A party is also not precluded from bringing an action against another who may be liable for the harm/damage under any agreement between them.[50]

2.4.2.1 Model Contract for Risk Allocation in the United States

In the US, standard form contracts exist, such as the AIEN and IADC model forms. The AIEN model form has assumed a place of pride in the US offshore drilling contract. It is used to allocate risk and determine parties' rights and liabilities in a contract. It provides a platform for negotiating, amending, adjusting and drafting offshore drilling contracts. In the AIEN Well Service model contract, pertinent sections of the model form set out in detail the nature and extent of the parties' rights and obligation in a drilling contract. Article 13 of the 2002 AIPN Well Services form addresses risk liabilities and indemnification for well services. The Article is set out below for ease of understanding.

13. Liabilities and Indemnification

13.1 General

To avoid the time and expense of protracted litigation between the Parties and to allow each Party to arrange for insurance or self-insurance as deemed appropriate to address the relevant risks, the responsibility for certain Claims shall be allocated between the Parties in accordance with the further provisions of this Article 13.

13.1.1 **Contractor's indemnity of Company Group.** Regardless of Cause, Contractor shall be liable for and indemnify Company Group from Claims arising out of personal injury, illness, death, or property loss or damage suffered by any member of Contractor Group.

13.1.2 **Rented or consigned property.** Property that has been rented to or consigned to Company by Contractor and (1) is specifically identified as part of Schedule 2 or, (2) is not being operated or maintained by Contractor Group shall be considered property of Company for purposes of this Article 13.

Alternative 1

13.1.3 **Company's indemnity of Contractor Group.** Regardless of Cause, Company shall be liable for and indemnify Contractor Group from

50 See 33 USC 2710, as amended through PL 108–201, 24 February 2004.

claims arising out of personal injury, illness, death, or property loss or damage suffered by Company, Company's Affiliates, Joint Interest Owners and Company's Invitees, and its and their shareholders, officers, directors, employees, agents, consultants, servants and insurers of all of the foregoing.

Alternative 2

13.1.3 **Company's indemnity of Contractor Group.** Regardless of Cause, Company shall be liable for and indemnify Contractor Group from Claims arising out of personal injury, illness, death, or property loss or damage suffered by any member of Company Group. . . .

13.2 **Special Risk and Indemnity Provisions**

To the extent of conflict, the following indemnity provisions control over the provisions of Article 13.1.

13.2.1 **Down Hole Equipment and Fishing**

13.2.1.1 Regardless of Cause, Company shall perform all fishing to recover Down Hole equipment at Company's expense.

13.2.1.2 Regardless of Cause, Company, at Company's sole option, shall either reimburse Contractor as provided in Article 13.2.4.2 or for the costs of repair of any equipment of any member of Contractor Group that is lost or damaged Down Hole, whichever is less.

Optional

13.2.2 **Surface Equipment**

Except to the extent of fair wear and tear, if Contractor can demonstrate that any equipment (other than that located Down Hole) of any member of Contractor Group has been subject to abnormal damage (meaning damage which could not be reasonably expected) resulting directly from corrosion, erosion or abrasion caused by the nature of the well effluent, Contractor shall be reimbursed as provided in Article 13.2.4.2 or for the cost of repair, whichever is less, except to the extent that such damage is caused by the Negligence of any member of Contractor Group. . . .

13.2.5 **Wild Well**

Alternative 1

Regardless of Cause, Company Shall Be Liable For And Indemnify Contractor Group from Claims arising from a Work Site fire or explosion or blowout, cratering or any uncontrolled well condition, including, without limitation, the cost of controlling a wild well, underground or above the surface, and the removal of debris, save and except Claims arising out of personal injury, illness, death, or property loss or damage suffered by any member of Contractor Group.

Optional (to Alternative 1)

In this regard, Company Shall Be Liable For And Indemnify Contractor Group for such Claims arising out of the Gross Negligence of any member of Contractor Group in excess of ________________ per occurrence.

Alternative 2

Regardless of Cause, Company Shall Be Liable For And Indemnify Contractor Group for the reasonable costs of controlling a wild well, underground or above the surface, and the removal of debris. . . .

13.2.10 Pollution

13.2.10.1 Regardless of Cause, Company Shall Be Liable For And Indemnify Contractor Group from Claims of pollution arising out of spills emanating from the equipment of any member of Company Group provided such equipment is in the care, custody and control of any member of Company Group.

13.2.10.2 Regardless of Cause, Contractor Shall Be Liable For And Indemnify Company Group from Claims of pollution arising out of spills emanating from the equipment of any member of Contractor Group provided such equipment is in the care, custody and control of any member of Contractor Group.

13.2.10.3 Regardless of Cause, Company Shall Be Liable For And Indemnify Contractor Group from Claims of pollution arising out of spills of material provided by any member of Contractor Group to Company for use by any member of Company Group once the material is delivered to the location and during transit on conveyance arranged by any member of Company Group.

13.2.10.4 Regardless of Cause, Contractor Shall Be Liable For And Indemnify Company Group from Claims of pollution arising out of spills of material to be provided by any member of Contractor Group to any member of Company Group during transit on conveyance arranged by any member of Contractor Group.

Alternative 1

13.2.10.5 Notwithstanding this Article 13.2.10.1, Regardless of Cause (including Gross Negligence), Company Shall Be Liable For And Indemnify Contractor Group from Claims of pollution arising out of a blowout, seepage of sub-surface origin or uncontrolled well flow.

Alternative 2

13.2.10.5 Notwithstanding Article 13.2.10.1, Regardless of Cause, (including Gross Negligence) Company Shall Be Liable For And Indemnify Contractor Group from Claims of pollution arising out of a blowout, seepage of sub-surface origin or uncontrolled well flow, unless due to the Gross Negligence of any member of Contractor Group up to a cap of ________________ and Company Shall Be Liable For And Indemnify Contractor Group for such Claims to the extent in excess of such amount.

Alternative 3

13.2.10.5 Notwithstanding Article 13.2.10.1, Regardless of Cause, except to the extent of the Negligence of any member of Contractor Group up to a cap of __________, Company Shall Be Liable For And Indemnify Contractor Group from Claims of pollution arising out of a blowout, seepage of sub-surface origin or uncontrolled well flow.[51]

[51] Association of International Petroleum Negotiators (now AIEN) Well Services Model Form 2002, Article 13.

Article 13 clearly explains the purpose of the allocation of risk between parties. It reiterates the standard mutual indemnity clause and includes some carve-outs for special circumstances. For instance, while parties may be indemnified for death, personal injury and damage or loss to property notwithstanding their cause, this may not apply if the damage resulted from the gross negligence of the party at fault. We must note that parties may agree otherwise in their contract, subject to the relevant anti-indemnity statute. Again, the term 'company group' in a mutual indemnity contract means contractors that work for the company. This differs from the LOGIC version, which excludes other contractors working for the company.[52]

Under Article 13.2.10 of the AIPN model form, an operator shall be held liable, regardless of cause, and shall indemnify the contractor/contractor group from pollution claims arising from an oil spill that emanates from the operator's equipment. Such equipment must be under the operator's custody, control and care. The same situation applies to the contractor. It is essential to state that a contractor usually bears the cost of claims or losses arising from its equipment, which always results in surface pollution during offshore drilling. The same position applies to an operator who bears the liabilities arising from well pollution since the operator controls the well programme. However, the operator is not the owner of the drilling equipment.

An interesting aspect of Article 13 of the AIPN Well Services model is the alternative clauses provided for drafting considerations. Alternative 1 includes gross negligence in the 'no liability, howsoever caused' category under which an indemnitee can still be indemnified. However, Alternative 2 carves out gross negligence as grounds that will trigger a stated monetary liability before the operator indemnifies the contractor where the amount exceeds the cap. Alternative 3 carves out negligence up to a stated financial cap.

The main provision of Article 13.2.10 is not compatible with public policy and does not promote the proportionality element of distributive justice.[53] This conclusion is reached because the Article does not give the party at fault an obligation to bear responsibility. However, Alternatives 2 and 3 align with public policy and distributive justice, providing for liability subject to a cap. The Alternatives provide room for a party to bear responsibility for their wrongful conduct, even when such risk was not allocated to them. Adopting Alternatives 2 and 3 can incentivise good oilfield practices that could prevent harm and discourage moral hazard. These Alternatives also assigns liability to a party at fault following the benefit derived from the risky activity. This is because they establish a cap on liability and do not assign liability for the entirety of the well pollution. The cap on liability conforms to the proportionality element in distributive justice and the Rawlsian idea of allocating risk behind a veil of ignorance.

The Alternatives present a modified mutual indemnification agreement and put measures in place to deter parties from seriously wrongful conduct that could

[52] Egbochue (n 18) 11.

[53] See Chapter 3 for a detailed discussion of distributive justice and its elements.

lead to bad oilfield practices and cause injury to others. In line with public policy, liability attaches to the Alternatives, albeit in conformity with the benefit reaped in the activity. The provision presents an underpinning based on a distributive outcome when the action of a party results in pollution damage. It becomes a harm-deterring and hazard-discouraging measure to protect society and the other contracting party from conduct likely to cause harm or injury.

2.4.3 Nigeria

The petroleum regime in Nigeria mainly uses PSCs when contracting with IOCs. A PSC is the most common means of engaging IOCs in the exploration and production (E&P) of hydrocarbons in developing countries. The PSC is often called the 'Host Government Contract', and it grants a licensee the legal rights to conduct hydrocarbon operations.[54] The terms in a PSC depend on the regime and the parties involved, especially as every contract is negotiated on separate terms and conditions.[55]

Nigeria is one of the leading producers of hydrocarbons in Africa and among the top ten producers in the world.[56] Its economy is dependent on oil revenue. The

54 Zhiguo Gao posits that a PSC is an

> agreement under which a foreign company, serving as a contractor to the host country/its national oil company, recovers its costs each year from production and is further entitled to receive a certain share of the remaining production as payment in kind for the exploration risks assumed and the development service performed if there is a commercial discovery.

International Petroleum Contracts: Current Trends and New Directions (Graham & Trotman Ltd 1994) 72. The PSC is one part of the regime that governs resource extraction and sets out the rights, duties and conditions that are necessary for an IOC to explore and exploit hydrocarbon in a given country. Before a particular PSC is signed, the IOC must win the contract through a competitive bidding process, ad hoc negotiation, or first-come-first-served mechanism. It is worth noting that for the PSC, an IOC is referred to as the 'contractor', whereas under a JOA with the host government it is called the 'operator'.

55 Taiwo A Ogunleye, 'A Legal Analysis of Production Sharing Contract Arrangements in the Nigerian Petroleum Industry' (2015) 5(8) Journal of Energy Technologies and Policy 2. Ogunleye – quoting Claude Duval and others, *International Petroleum Exploration and Exploitation Agreements: Legal, Economic and Policy Aspects* (Barrows 2009) – summarises the key features of PSC, to wit:

> The International Oil Company (IOC) is appointed by the Host Country (HC), directly or through its national oil company (NOC), as the exclusive 'contractor' (and not as a concessionaire) to undertake petroleum operations in certain area during specified time periods; The IOC operates at its sole risk, its own expense, and under the control of the HC; If petroleum is produced, it belongs to the HC, with the exception of a share of production that can be taken in kind by the IOC for cost recovery and for profit sharing; The IOC is entitled to recover its eligible cost under the PSC from a portion of the production from the area subject to the contract; After cost recovery, the balance of the production is shared, based on a predetermined percentage split between the HC and the IOC; The net income of the IOC is taxable, unless the PSC provides otherwise; The title to the equipment and installations purchased by the contractor pass to the HC either immediately or overtime, in accordance with the cost recovery schedules.

(Ogunleye 2.)

56 Julia Faria, 'Leading Oil Producing Countries in Africa 2020' (*Statista*, 29 July 2021) <www.statista.com/statistics/1178514/main-oil-producing-countries-in-africa> accessed 12 October 2023.

petroleum industry in Nigeria operates a business model using PSCs, joint ventures (JVs) and Risk Service Contracts.[57] However, PSCs play a critical role.[58] Nigeria has a national oil company (NOC) called the Nigerian National Petroleum Corporation (NNPC). The NNPC facilitates the government's PSC and JV activities and drives the hydrocarbon plan. As a significant player in the industry, Nigeria engages in deepwater hydrocarbon E&P in the Bonga, Erha and Agbami oil fields.[59] Under the PSC approach, a funding obligation is borne by the respective IOC as a contractor. Sometimes, there may be counterpart funding from the government. The IOC is solely responsible for providing investment and fulfilling technical requirements for day-to-day operations. The IOC bears all attendant risks, although it can recover the cost through the 'cost oil' provision.[60] PSCs are long-term arrangements concluded for thirty years, covering ten years of exploration and twenty years of production, with a relinquishment clause for part of the contract area.[61]

NOCs are often involved in PSC arrangements. The NOC, in this case, exercises control and management over petroleum operations, while the contractor, an IOC, is responsible for the work programme which is the basis of the drilling contract between the operator and the contractor. Although the well operator supervises the drilling operations, the HS retains the ownership right over the petroleum resources through the NOC. Arguably, such an arrangement represents a viable option for resource-rich developing countries.[62] Essentially, the PSC breaks ownership from operatorship, thus leaving the host government with the right to approve field agreements which may influence the allocation of risk between the operator and the drilling contractor.[63] In other words, the host government can use the right to regulate field agreements to check certain practices, such as using mutual indemnity clauses as a shield against liability for gross negligence during petroleum operations.

The NNPC is Nigeria's NOC. It contracts with IOCs on behalf of the government and executes a PSC for a particular block on specified terms as agreed by the parties. In some PSCs, reference is made to indemnity, negligence or gross negligence. In other PSCs, the indemnity clause is used to protect the government against third-party claims linked to the contract. Sometimes, indemnity

[57] Joseph Nwaokoro, 'Beyond Legislation: A Contractual Alternative to Legislating Local Content in Nigeria' (2009) 18 Current International Trade Law Journal 42.

[58] Yinka Omorogbe, 'The Legal Framework for the Production of Petroleum in Nigeria' (1987) 5(4) Journal of Energy and Natural Resources 273. This position has not changed: Nigeria still operates a mono-economy driven by oil, with little attempt to venture into other means of economic sustenance.

[59] Olajumoke Akinjide-Balogun, 'Nigeria: Legal Framework of the Nigerian Petroleum Industry' (*Mondaq*, 3 April 2001) <www.mondaq.com/nigeria/corporatecommercial-law/10726/legal-framework-of-the-nigerian-petroleum-industry> accessed 12 October 2023.

[60] Sola Adepetun, 'Production Sharing Contracts: The Nigerian Experience' (1995) 13(1) Journal of Energy and Natural Resources Law 21. ibid 23.

[61] ibid 23.

[62] ibid 28.

[63] See Chapter 6.

clauses are not mentioned. For example, there was no reference to indemnity and risk allocation in one of the PSCs between NNPC and IDEAL Oil and Gas and two others, covering OPL No 905 block, Anambra Basin, Nigeria. However, the PSC uses the terms 'gross negligence' and 'wilful misconduct' in the case of an accident. Gross negligence was defined as

> any act or failure to act of any senior supervisory personnel (whether sole, joint or concurrent) which was intended to cause, or which was in reckless disregard of or wanton indifference to the harmful consequences such act or failure to act would have on (a) the safety of personnel or property or (b) petroleum operations or (c) books and accounts and oil industry accounting standards and procedures.[64]

The definition of gross negligence, as provided above, only refers to the actions of senior supervisory personnel to establish whether there was an intention to cause harm. Nevertheless, gross negligence is not limited to a specific action, it is open to a broad interpretation. Corporate conduct could arise from company employees who did not receive adequate supervision or who followed the culture of complacency practised by the company.[65] Where an employee acted within the scope of their employment and for their employer's benefit, the company would be liable for the employee's acts of gross negligence resulting from their scope of work.[66] Most PSC forms signed by the NNPC and IOCs refer to gross negligence, and a definition of the term is provided in the petroleum contract. However, the description still fails to cover the concept of gross negligence. This book, in Chapter 4, provides a definition of gross negligence that will operate as a term of art. It identifies gross negligence as any conduct that *falls far below* the standard of a reasonable person (reasonable oilfield practice). The emphasis on *far below* distinguishes mere negligence from gross negligence. The standard for what is far below is that of a reasonable person (objective standard) instead of an individual's perspective (subjective standard).

Generally, PSCs assume that the operator and contractor are vertically integrated companies where the drilling service is part of the operator's company and not contracted out. However, the well operator and the drilling contractor's relationship is a non-vertical integration in a drilling operation. The difference lies in the fact that for vertical integration, the contractor will be an equity holder, while in non-vertical integration, the drilling contractor has no stake in the operator's company. The contractor is only paid for its services. Under a PSC, the practice of risk allocation entails that the gross negligence of the drilling contractor would be

64 Although there is no statutory or judicial definition of gross negligence, except for in individual contracts, gross negligence can prevent the contractor from applying the cost as 'petroleum cost or qualifying cost' under the agreement.

65 *United States v BP Exploration and Production Inc (Re Oil Spill by the Oil Rig 'Deepwater Horizon' in the Gulf of Mexico, on April 20, 2010)* 21 F Supp 3d 657 (ED LA 2014), findings of facts and conclusions of law, Phase I trial. Barbier J noted that it is irrelevant whether the conduct was by managerial personnel or not. It is sufficient that the employee work for the company.

66 ibid.

borne by the operator, who may not be able to recover the loss, notwithstanding the fault of the drilling contractor. Within the Nigerian context, the IOC (well operator) hires the driller, who is eventually discharged at the end of the drilling operations. Drillers are independent contractors hired on a contract for service, albeit the well operator plays a supervisory role. Their agreement is private and based on the parties' negotiations. It stands to reason that the IOC, which is a contractor to the host government and an operator of the oilfield, is the responsible party under a PSC arrangement. As such, an IOC must prevent, control and mitigate pollution in Nigerian waters during petroleum operations.

2.4.3.1 Standard Form Contracts for Drilling in Nigeria

The petroleum industry in Nigeria has no industry-wide accepted classic model. Instead, it adopts a patchwork of contractual templates for drilling operations from the UK and the US.[67] There is a chapter of the IADC in Nigeria,[68] established in 2012 with four members initially, but it had grown to twenty-six members by 2014.[69]

2.4.3.2 Risk Allocation in Drilling Contracts in Nigeria

In Nigeria, the allocation of risk between the operator and contractor follows the pattern of risk allocation under the Concession regimes examined earlier, albeit with some peculiarities. The contracts discussed in this book are not in the public domain; therefore, they have been anonymised. Nevertheless, it is worth mentioning that Shell, Agip, ExxonMobil, Chevron, Total, Elf and so on[70] are the principal operators in the Nigerian hydrocarbon industry, while Schlumberger, Halliburton, Transocean, Noble Drilling and other foreign companies are the most prominent drilling contractors.

In the private contracts examined below, negligence and gross negligence were treated as negligent conduct, which would not result in liability for the party at fault. The extracts below are from a private agreement between an operator and a contractor in Nigeria.

> **ARTICLE V – CONTRACTOR'S GENERAL OBLIGATIONS**
> **501. CONTRACTOR'S STANDARD OF PERFORMANCE**
> . . . Except for such obligations and liabilities specifically assumed by the Contractor, the Operator shall be solely responsible and assumes liability for all consequences of operations by both parties while on a daywork basis, including results and all other risks

[67] Some of the templates adapted in Nigeria include the AIEN model, the IADC model and the LOGIC model forms. This could present some challenges in the future as the adaptations mirror these models and do not provide that gross negligence should be a liability trigger.

[68] IADC, 'Nigeria Chapter' <www.iadc.org/chapters/nigeria> accessed 12 October 2023.

[69] Drilling Contractor, 'Nurturing Growth in Africa' <www.drillingcontractor.org/nurturing-growth-in-africa-30580> accessed 12 October 2023. As at October 2023, there are twenty-four members in Nigeria. See <iadc.org/chapters/nigeria/#nigeria-members> accessed 7 October 2023.

[70] Around 2016, the super-majors started divesting from shallow water to deep offshore, leaving indigenous companies to venture into shallow water operations.

or liabilities incurred in or incident to such operations, notwithstanding any breach of representation or warranty, either expressed or implied, or the negligence or fault of the Contractor, its employees, agents or servants, including sole, concurrent and gross negligence, either active or passive, latent defects and any liability based on any theory of tort, breach of contract or strict liability, including defect or ruin of premises, either latent or patent. . . .

ARTICLE IX – LIABILITY
901. EQUIPMENT OR PROPERTY
Excepts as specifically provided herein to the contrary, each party hereto shall at all times be responsible for and shall hold harmless and indemnify the other party from and against damage to or loss of its own equipment or property, regardless of the cause of loss, including the negligence of such party, and despite the fact that a party's items may be under the control of the other party, except that:

(a) The Operator shall, to the extent the Contractor's Insurance does not compensate the Contractor therefore, be responsible at all times for damage to or destruction of the Contractor's equipment or property caused by exposure to unusually corrosive or otherwise destructive elements, including those which are introduced into the drilling fluid from subsurface formations or the use of corrosive additives in the fluid.
(b) The Operator shall, to the extent the Contractor's Insurance does not compensate the Contractor therefore, be responsible for damage to or loss of the Contractor's drill string, and shall reimburse the Contractor for such damage or loss at the depreciated value of the item so lost or damaged; with the understanding, however, that the indemnity granted in this Clause 1001 shall not indemnify either party for liabilities incurred by it as a result of obligations undertaken in a contract with a third party. . . .

904. CONTRACTOR'S PERSONNEL
The Contractor agrees to protect, defend, indemnify, and save harmless the Operator, its officers, directors, employees and joint owners from and against all claims, demands and causes of action of every kind and character, without limit and without regard to the cause or causes thereof or the negligence of any party or parties, arising in connection herewith in favour of the Contractor's employees or of the Contractor's subcontractors or their employees, or the Contractor's invitees, on account of bodily injury, death or damage to property . . .

905. OPERATOR'S PERSONNEL
The Operator agrees to protect, defend, indemnify, and save harmless the Contractor, its officers, directors and employees from and against all claims, demands, and causes of action of every kind and character, without limit and without regard to the cause or causes thereof or the negligence of any party or parties, arising in connection herewith in favour of the Operator's employees or the Operator's contractors or their employees, or the Operator's invitees, other than those parties identified in paragraph 1004 on account of bodily injury, death or damage to property . . .

906. POLLUTION AND CONTAMINATION
Notwithstanding anything to the contrary contained herein, it is understood and agreed by and between the Contractor and the Operator that the responsibility for pollution or contamination shall be as follows:

(a) The Contractor will use its best efforts to assure that all operations undertaken on the drill site meet the environmental standards established by the Government of Nigeria, particularly with regard to maintaining zero discharge levels on drilling fluids and formation cuttings.
(b) The Contractor shall assume all responsibility for cleaning up and containing pollution or contamination which originates above the surface from improper care or disposition of items wholly in the Contractor's possession and control and directly associated with the Contractor's equipment and facilities.
(c) The Operator shall assume all responsibility for (including control and removal of the pollutant involved) and shall protect, defend, indemnify and save harmless the Contractor from and against all claims, demands, and causes of action of every kind and character arising directly or indirectly from all pollution or contamination, other than that described in subclause (b) above, which may occur from the negligence of the Contractor or otherwise during the term of this Contract or as a result of operations hereunder, including, but not limited to, that which may result from fire, blowout, cratering, seepage or any other controlled flow of oil, gas, water or other substance, as well as the use or disposition of oil emulsion, oil base or chemically treated drilling fluids, contaminated cuttings or cavings, lost circulation and fish recovery materials and fluids.
(d) In the event a third party commits an act or omission which results in pollution or contamination for which either the Contractor or the Operator for whom such party is performing work is held to be legally liable, the responsibility therefore shall be considered, as between the Contractor and the Operator, to be the same as if the party for whom the work was performed had performed the same and all of the obligations respecting defense, indemnity holding harmless and limitation of responsibility and liability, as set forth in (b) and (c) above, shall be specifically applied. . . .

910. INDEMNITY OBLIGATION
Except as otherwise expressly limited herein, it is the intent of parties hereto that all indemnity obligations and/or liabilities assumed by such parties under terms of this Contract, including, without limitation, clauses 1001 through 1009 hereof, be without limit and regard to the cause or causes thereof (including pre-existing conditions), strict liability, or the negligence of any party or parties, whether such negligence be sole, joint or concurrent, active or passive.

This extract represents the industry practice. There is no obligation in the contract for a party that does not have legal responsibility for risk to take measures to prevent harm. No provision makes the party at fault responsible for severely wrongful oilfield practices. As a result, it is incompatible with public policy and the burden aspect of distributive justice. It is worth noting that some of these contracts refer to specific terminologies as used in the IADC forms, a pointer that parties drafted these drilling contracts based on the IADC drilling forms, subject to minor modifications. IADC drilling contracts contain mutual indemnities that operate as a defence against liability for gross negligence in the event of a downside.[71]

[71] IADC, 'IADC International Daywork Drilling Contract Offshore' (*IADC*, revised 2007) <store.iadc.org/product/iadc-international-daywork-drilling-contract-offshore> accessed 12 October 2023.

Examining another operator and contractor drilling contract obtained for this study is appropriate. Its provisions regarding indemnity for property damage, injury or death of personnel, sickness and disease are similar to those above.

11.2 COMPANY Property and Personnel

11.2.1 General

Subject to Article 11.1.5 COMPANY shall be responsible for and shall defend and indemnify CONTRACTOR and all Subcontractors against:

(i) all loss or damage to the COMPANY Items and to the property of COMPANY, Other CONTRACTORs and their respective personnel at the Site, and

(ii) any personal injury, including fatal injury and disease, to the respective personnel of COMPANY and Other CONTRACTORs attributable to the Site however caused that arises out of or is connected with performance of the Work regardless of whether the negligence or breach of duty of CONTRACTOR or Subcontractors caused or contributed to such loss, damage or personal injury.

11.3 CONTRACTOR Property and Personnel

11.3.1 General

Subject to Article 11.1.5 CONTRACTOR shall be responsible for and shall defend and indemnify COMPANY and all other CONTRACTORs against:

(i) all loss or damage to the CONTRACTOR Items and to the property of CONTRACTOR, Subcontractors and their respective personnel at the Site, and

(ii) any personal injury, including fatal injury and disease, to the respective personnel of CONTRACTOR and Subcontractors attributable to the Site however caused that arises out of or is connected with performance of the Work or the provision of medical assistance under Article 6.8 regardless of whether the negligence of COMPANY or Other CONTRACTORs caused or contributed to such loss, damage or personal injury. . . .

11.5 Third Parties

Subject to Article 11.1.5 and without prejudice to any other express liability or indemnity provision of this Contract, each party shall be responsible and liable for any and all claims resulting from:

(a) personal injury, including fatal injury and disease, to Third Parties and/or;

(b) loss of or damage to property of Third Parties to the extent it is liable in accordance with applicable law

The liability assumed herein by CONTRACTOR shall be limited to **US $10,000,000 (ten million US Dollars)** for any one accident or series of accidents arising out of any one occurrence and in excess of such level liability shall be assumed by COMPANY but only to the extent that such liability arises out of or is connected with performance of the Work.

11.6 COMPANY/CONTRACTOR and Pollution . . .

11.6.2 COMPANY shall defend and indemnify CONTRACTOR against all claims for loss, damage or expense (including cost of control and/or clean-up of the pollutant) arising from or relating to contamination or pollution which results in whole or in part from:

(a) fire, blowout, cratering or Uncontrolled Flow or Reservoir Fluids regardless of cause;
(b) seepage of Reservoir Fluids from the seabed or surface of the land, or any other escape of Reservoir Fluids from any point upstream of the primary surface shut-off control valve of the well in question regardless of cause; and
(c) subject to Article 11.6.3, the possession, use or disposal by Other CONTRACTORs of Reservoir Fluids, Petroleum Products and other substances (including without limitation contaminated cuttings, and lost circulation and fish recovery materials and fluids) that are connected with the Work or wells to be drilled for COMPANY.

11.6.3 CONTRACTOR shall defend and indemnify COMPANY against all claims for loss, damage or expense (including cost of control and/or clean-up of the pollutant) arising from or relating to contamination or pollution which results in whole or in part from:
(a) any escape (other than an Uncontrolled Flow) of Reservoir Fluids from CONTRACTOR's Items at any point downstream of the primary surface shut-off valve of the well in question;
(b) subject to Article 11.6.3(c), any escape from CONTRACTOR's Items or from CONTRACTOR's or any Subcontractor's possession or control of any Petroleum Product, pipe dope, garbage, sewage, debris or other substance (excluding Reservoir Fluids) whether or not caused or contributed to by the negligence or breach of duty of COMPANY or of any Other CONTRACTOR; and
(c) any escape attributable to the negligence or breach of duty of CONTRACTOR or any Subcontractor of any oil emulsion, oil base or chemically treated drilling fluids or of lost circulation and fish recovery materials when such items are in the possession or control of CONTRACTOR or of any Subcontractor.

11.6.4 The provisions of this Article 11.6 apply only to contamination or pollution emanating from the Site or from the immediate vicinity of the Site that is connected with drilling and/or associated operations at the Site.

In the above contract extracts, risks are allocated without regard to the fault of the parties (whether it be sole or contributory, mere negligence or gross negligence). The basis of the risk allocation is the possession of equipment and facilities, and control of the operations that result in damage or loss. Unlike the Alternative sections in the AIPN Model, where gross negligence is a trigger, no carve-outs exist to trigger liability under the Nigerian regime for drilling contracts. The phrase 'without recourse to a fault' could be the reason for not defining gross negligence in any drilling contract between operators and contractors. As seen in these contracts, the indemnity clauses show that mutual indemnity is not subject to gross negligence. It creates no obligation for a party to prevent harm regarding a risk that has not been allocated to it. The practice suggests the existence of vertical integration between the operator and the driller. However, that is not the reality in practice. There is also no regulatory restriction against grossly negligent conduct, and the burden of the activity is not distributed according to the proportion of benefit to discourage wrongful conduct. The burden distribution accords with ownership and control. Thus, the practice does not align with the burden element of distributive justice, as discussed in Chapter 3 of this book.

The practice also allows a party to use the mutual indemnity agreement as a cover against liability for grossly negligent conduct. This practice eliminates the deterrence and liability underpinnings of public policy in contracts of this nature. The result will be the exercise of less care which can result in harm to people and the environment. The only area where gross negligence was evident as a liability trigger was in the contract between NNPC and Ideal Oil and Gas and two others, referred to above. This contract relates to the host government and an IOC, not a well operator and drilling contractor. Even the definition offers little help. It contains elements of intention and phrases such as 'reckless disregard and wanton indifference', which are pointers of wilful misconduct, as held in the BP case.

2.4.4 Indonesia

Indonesia was the first country to use the production-sharing model, and it still applies it with some modifications. Under its PSC, PERTAMINA, the state oil company, has a monopoly right over hydrocarbon. Thus, Concessions do not apply.[72] As a holder of the relevant right, the state uses the PSC to exercise control over hydrocarbons. Indonesia is an essential hydrocarbon producer and has tried several versions of the PSC to protect its interests in dealing with IOCs.[73] The contractor bears the costs and risks of exploration, while the ownership of the hydrocarbons remains with the state until the point of delivery. Again, the PSC is granted for thirty years with an option to apply for an extension.[74] The state-owned enterprise, SKK Migas, retains operational control of the hydrocarbon activities, including approval of work plans, budgets and field development plans, while the oil produced is shared as agreed in the PSC.[75] Under the Indonesian PSC model, a production split is based on specific percentages. The contractor, an IOC (which later becomes an operator of the well), can recover the operating expense through cost oil. It has the right to dispose of its share of hydrocarbon separately after the title has passed at delivery or export.[76]

[72] Tengku N Machmud, 'The Indonesia Production Sharing Contract: An Investor's Perspective' (2002) 20(3) Journal of Energy and Natural Resources Law 318.

[73] The pursuit of the interests of Indonesia may be connected with Article 33 of the Constitution of the Republic of Indonesia 1945, which provides for the use of the natural wealth of Indonesia found within its jurisdiction for the benefit and welfare of the people of Indonesia.

[74] Law No 22/2001, Petroleum and Natural Gas, art 14.

[75] Darrell R Johnson and Fransiscus Rodyanto, 'The Oil and Gas Law Review: Indonesia' (*The Law Reviews*, 17 November 2020) <thelawreviews.co.uk/title/the-oil-and-gas-law-review/indonesia> and <conventuslaw.com/report/oil-and-gas-law-review-indonesia> accessed 3 August 2021.

[76] PwC, 'Oil and Gas in Indonesia Investment and Taxation Guide 2020' (11th edn, May 2020) <www.pwc.com/id/en/pwc-publications/industries-publications/energy--utilities---mining-publications/oil-gas-guide-2020.html> accessed 12 October 2023, 45.

2.4.4.1 Regime for Risk Allocation in Indonesia

The Petroleum and Natural Gas Law of Indonesia, Law No 22/2001, regulates hydrocarbon activities in the country. It differentiates between upstream and downstream operations and requires executing upstream petroleum activities through a joint cooperation contract.[77] Joint cooperation contracts are predominantly PSCs. Law No 22/2001 sets out the framework for the exploration and production of oil and gas in Indonesia. Its main objective is the implementation of a populist economy for the welfare of all Indonesians.[78] It vests the ownership of hydrocarbon in the state and empowers it to control all petroleum activities. The state has the sole right to a mining concession for petroleum operations.[79] The law separates upstream operations from downstream petroleum activities.[80] It empowers the state to, among others things, protect the environment and ensure environmental management.[81] The Act does not provide for risk allocation or indemnification. Other national legislative acts deal with energy security, environmental conservation and environmental quality compliance before petroleum operations.[82] However, they do not mention risk allocation or indemnification.

Although the Indonesian regime does not expressly address risk allocation, local laws in Indonesia preclude the application of indemnity clauses as practised by the oil and gas industry, and this would presumably also apply to petroleum activities.[83] Thus, grossly negligent conduct may result in liability for the party at fault during offshore drilling activities.[84] The general law of contract influences freedom of contract in Indonesia, and non-compliance with relevant local laws can have severe implications.[85] Non-compliance can result in the revocation of a PSC due to breaches. However, regarding risk allocation, it has been asserted that indemnities and exclusion and limitation of liability clauses, when stated expressly under commercial contracts, are respected and recognised by the regime in Indonesia if there is no provision to the contrary.[86] In South and Southeast Asia, it is not unusual for contractors to be required to have specific cover for well control and to bear contractual liability where a contractor's acts or omissions occasion well pollution.[87]

77 Law No 22/2001 (n 74), art 6.
78 ibid art 2.
79 ibid art 4.
80 ibid art 5.
81 ibid art 42.
82 Environment Law No 32/2009 and Forest Law No 41/1999.
83 Cameron (n 17) 213.
84 ibid.
85 Toby Hewitt, 'An Asian Perspective on Model Oil and Gas Service Contracts' (2010) 28(3) Journal of Energy & Natural Resources Law 338.
86 DLA Piper, 'Guide to Going Global: Intellectual Property and Technology 2015' <www.lexology.com/library/detail.aspx?g=604c9bde-85c3-41e2-9179-5e0a982af8af> accessed 12 October 2023, 93.
87 Hewitt (n 85) 338.

Book III of the Civil Code governs contracts in Indonesia. The principle of freedom of contract is well established in this code. Article 1338 of the Indonesian Civil Code provides that all agreements legally made and not proscribed by law shall be applicable between the parties. There is one necessary condition: the contract should not be contrary to the provisions set out in the Act.[88] Under Article 1320 of the Indonesian Civil Code, an agreement is valid and binding if it includes, among other requirements, a legal cause, which shall constitute the substance of the contract. Such agreement may not be contrary to regulations, laws, public order and morality. Article 1337 of the Civil Code provides that a cause is proscribed by law if it is contrary to law, public order or good morals.[89] Articles 1365 and 1366 of the Indonesia Civil Code provide useful insights regarding risk allocation and indemnification. The Civil Code contains adapted definitions of recoverable contractual damages. However, parties may supersede these definitions in their contract, and in this respect, mutual indemnities would appear enforceable under Indonesian law.[90] However, it may be impossible to contract outside some strict liability provisions because it can result in fines and imprisonment of persons responsible for a polluting activity.[91]

Article 1365 of the Civil Code presents a tort perspective that any violation of law that leads to loss to another person would result in a cause of action to compensate the person who suffered the harm or damage. Under Article 1366, legal responsibility can arise for acts of omission or lack of prudence resulting in damages or losses. A broad interpretation of Article 1365 usually applies to embrace a wide range of claims regarding any violation of the law or negligent behaviour. This broad interpretation can provide grounds for liability for gross negligence arising from a drilling contract. This legal provision evidences the role of regulation in private contracts. It also strengthens the argument that regulators could exercise control through field approval agreements to prohibit contracts that allow gross negligence to pass as mere negligence.

In analysing Article 1365, Baker McKenzie[92] identify that the said clause sets the foundation for a responsible party to be liable to pay compensation for every unlawful act that causes losss to another. Although the Civil Code does not define the term 'unlawful act', we can deduce that an act is unlawful when it violates a

88 Irawan Soerodjo, 'The Development of Indonesian Civil Law' (2016) 4(9) Scientific Research Journal 32.

89 ibid 33.

90 Hewitt (n 85) 359.

91 ibid.

92 Baker and McKenzie, *International Arbitration Yearbook 2011–2012* (5th edn, JurisNet 2012) 260; Rosemary Rayfuse (ed), *ICSID Reports of Cases Decided under the Convention on the Settlement of Investment Disputes between States and Nationals of Other States* (vol 1, Grotius Publications Ltd 1993) 611. It was stated in this report that under Indonesian law, any damage or loss occasioned by the act of a wrongdoer shall be compensated by the wrongdoer.

statute or an unwritten norm such as reasonableness, custom and good morals. This provision of the Act is reproduced below to allow its better understanding.

> Article 1365 of the Civil Code states as follows:
> 'A party who commits an unlawful act which causes damage and/or loss to another party shall be obliged to compensate therefor.'
> Article 1366 provides as follows:
> 'An individual shall be responsible, not only for the damage which he has caused by his act, but also for that which was caused by his negligence or carelessness.'[93]

The above provisions are similar to the IADC forms, which suggest that drilling contractors operating in Indonesia may be members of the IADC,[94] but it is not clear whether the IADC risk allocation and indemnification model is applicable. This position is because a negligent party is obligated by law to pay compensation for a wrongful act that has led to damages or losses. However, it is worth noting that no specific Indonesian statute explicitly proscribes the exclusion of liability. Parties may limit their liability through carve-outs and liability caps in their contract.[95] Parties may also exclude certain contractual liabilities under the freedom of contract principle as contained in Article 1338 of the Civil Code. Exclusion clauses are subject to the doctrine of good faith[96] and must not be contrary to laws and regulations, customary practice and the principles of freedom of contract.[97] Although negligence is a critical term in tort law rather than in contract law, Article 1365 of the Civil Code, which covers negligence – where the wrongful act of a party that occasions damages gives rise to liability – does not differentiate between mere negligence and gross negligence. However, a look at the PSC forms of Indonesia may provide helpful answers.

2.4.4.2 Risk Allocation in Indonesian Production Sharing Contract Forms

This book evaluates two PSCs[98] from the public domain executed by PERTAMINA (representing the Indonesian government) and other contractors. The PSCs cover the contract terms, the work programme and the rights and obligations of the parties.

93 Indonesian Civil Code, arts 1365 and 1366.
94 See IADC, 'Membership' <www.iadc.org/membership> accessed 12 October 2023.
95 Iswahjudi A Karim and others, 'Contracts, Negotiation and Enforcement in Indonesia: Overview' (*Karim Syah Law Firm*, October 2016) <www.karimsyah.com/paper-publication/contracts-negotiation-and-enforcement-in-indonesia> accessed 12 October 2023.
96 Soerodjo (n 88) 34.
97 Karim and others (n 95).
98 These PSCs are between (1) PERTAMINA and Kerr McGee of Indonesia Inc (operator), Quintana Indonesia Ltd, Samedan Oil of Indonesia Inc and Wainoco International Inc, regarding the Bawean Block, signed in 1981; and (2) PERTAMINA and Apex (Bengara – II) Ltd for the Bengara II Block, signed in 1997.

They also provide for cost recovery and crude oil valuation, among other things, as stated in the contract. One provision of importance to the discussion about risk allocation is the issue of pollution containment. Under Section V of the PSC between PERTAMINA and Kerr McGee of Indonesia and others, which deals with parties' rights and obligations, the contractor (later a well operator) is obligated to prevent extensive pollution at sea, in rivers or in the contract area in question. It means that the well operator is responsible for ensuring a pollution-free operation. However, the PSC does not refer to negligence, gross negligence or risk allocation. Accordingly, the PSCs provide no valuable insight into risk allocation, which is the focus of this study. Nevertheless, private contracts offer some valuable insights into how operators and contractors allocate risk in Indonesia.

2.4.4.3 Risk Allocation in Operator and Contractor Private Drilling Contracts in Indonesia

In examining drilling contracts in Indonesia, this book uses an extract from a confidential private drilling contract. The clauses are set out below.

17.0 INDEMNIFICATION

17.1 CONTRACTOR shall be liable for, and shall indemnify (and promptly reimburse) and hold harmless the Indemnitees in respect of, Losses arising out of or in connection with:

17.1.1 injury to or death of any CONTRACTOR Personnel or loss of or damage to any property owned or used by CONTRACTOR, Affiliate of CONTRACTOR or subcontractor due to any cause whatsoever, regardless of any breach of the Contract or any negligent act or omission by the Indemnitee, notwithstanding Article 17.2;

17.1.2 injury to or death of any person other than CONTRACTOR Personnel or the Indemnitee (in this Article 17.0, a 'Third Party'), or loss of or damage to any property of a Third Party, due to CONTRACTOR's or the CONTRACTOR Personnel breach of duty or negligence, provided that if such Losses are attributable to the joint negligence of CONTRACTOR or the CONTRACTOR Personnel and COMPANY, each CONTRACTOR and COMPANY shall be responsible for such Loss to the extent of their respective negligence;

17.1.3 damage to the environment arising out of or in connection with CONTRACTOR's performance of the Contract including pollution or contamination which emanates from the equipment used by, or pollutants which are in the possession and control of or which are in transit arranged by, CONTRACTOR or any CONTRACTOR Personnel in the performance of the Contract, except to the extent such Losses are directly caused by the Gross Negligence of Company; and

17.1.4 CONTRACTOR's violation of or failure to comply with any applicable Laws or instructions given by COMPANY arising out of or in connection with CONTRACTOR's performance of the Contract.

17.2 Notwithstanding anything in the Contract to the contrary but subject to Article 17.1 and Article 17.3, COMPANY shall be responsible for, and shall indemnify (and promptly reimburse) and hold harmless CONTRACTOR in respect of Losses arising out or in connection with:

17.2.1 injury to or death of the Indemnity or loss of or damage to any property owned by the Indemnity due to any cause whatsoever;

17.2.2 injury to or death of any Third Party, or loss of or damage to any property of a Third Party, arising out of or in connection with COMPANY's breach of duty or negligence, provided that if such Loss is attributable to the joint negligence of CONTRACTOR and COMPANY, each of the CONTRACTOR and COMPANY shall be responsible for such Loss to the extent of their respective negligence;

17.2.3 pollution arising out of spills emanating from the equipment of COMPANY or its Affiliates provided such equipment is in the care, custody and control of COMPANY or Affiliate;

17.2.4 radiation damage, blowout, cratering or other uncontrolled well condition within the Area of Operations; and

17.2.5 loss of or damage to any underground reservoir or well or destruction of any property right in or to oil, gas or other mineral substance, water or geothermal resource, except, in relation to paragraph 17.2.3, 17.2.4 and 17.2.5 only, if such Loss is the result of the negligence of CONTRACTOR or the CONTRACTOR Personnel or an Affiliate of CONTRACTOR or employees, officers or agents of that Affiliate, in which case CONTRACTOR shall be responsible for and shall indemnify and hold harmless the Indemnitees for such Losses. The CONTRACTOR's liability under this Article 17.2 shall not exceed US$1,000,000.

17.3 It is expressly agreed that neither COMPANY nor CONTRACTOR shall be responsible to the other for loss of profits, loss of use of assets, *loss of revenue or similar indirect or consequential damages*.[99]

The highlighted contract is similar to the practice of risk allocation in other regimes examined. The operator and the contractor indemnify each other regarding losses arising out of, or in connection with, injury or death of personnel and property damage under their care, control and custody, notwithstanding the cause or any negligent act or omission. What is different is that, unlike in other regimes examined, an operator that causes pollution damage or loss from a piece of equipment under the care and control of the contractor shall be liable to indemnify the contractor where the pollution arises from the operator's gross negligence. A cap applies to the contractor's liability when the contractor's negligence results in subsurface pollution damage or loss. Again, the contractor's failure to comply with any applicable laws or instructions an operator gives could result in the contractor's liability. It means that where there is a legal requirement to perform a

[99] Emphasis added. This document was released on a confidential note.

specific activity in a particular manner, failure to comply with such law will result in the contractor's liability. An examination of the contract also reveals that parties cannot claim loss of profits or any other direct or indirect loss arising from the agreement. Third-party liability is also borne by the party that caused the damage, albeit where both parties jointly caused the damage, liability for the loss shall be to the extent of their negligence.

The practice of risk allocation regarding injury to or death of personnel and property damage does not align with public policy.[100] The contract provides that a party that causes loss or damage to another, injury or death of personnel and property damage shall be indemnified and held harmless for the loss, the cause, or any negligent act notwithstanding. It means that where the conduct leading to injury or property damage results from the gross negligence of the party at fault, the responsibility shall be borne by the party with control or custody of the personnel or property. This lack of regard to fault for injury to or death of personnel and damage to property is a disincentive for exercising care during drilling operations. There is a possibility that this contract may encourage parties to conduct their activities in a seriously wrongful manner, thereby causing injury, death or property damage. The contract attaches more concern to pollution damage and less to injury or death to personnel and damage to property. This position is so that the clauses dealing with pollution damage have an exception when a party's conduct results in liability, regardless of the responsibility of the party in control.

On pollution damage, the contract conforms to public policy and distributive justice. It provides that the gross negligence of an operator, resulting in pollution from a piece of equipment under the contractor's control, will result in the operator's liability. The contractor bears similar liability when its negligence results in pollution from the well. However, the contractor's liability is subject to a stated cap. This cap is in line with the proportionality element of distributive justice discussed in Chapter 3. The Indonesian risk allocation practice partially supports the tenets of public policy and distributive justice.

2.5 CHANGING PERCEPTIONS OF RISK ALLOCATION

The incident at Macondo resulted in a revised perception of risk exposure, especially for grossly negligent conduct. The oil spill led to notable litigations among various participants in the US and occasioned regulatory changes in several jurisdictions.[101]

[100] See Chapter 3 for discussion of public policy.

[101] Sergei Vinogradov, 'The Impact of the Deepwater Horizon: The Evolving International Legal Regime for Offshore Accidental Pollution Prevention, Preparedness, and Response' (2013) 44(4) Ocean Development and International Law 335, 336. The Macondo incident highlights the heightened challenge of hydrocarbon operation in extreme environment as regards drilling, well control and pollution management. Hydrocarbon exploration and production in remote environments and deepwater increases the likelihood of a higher aggregation of risk exposure.

It also brought about more onerous financial responsibility for offshore damages.[102] The heightened regulation has triggered operators' risk aversion and clamour for a change in the risk allocation regime. Evidence from individual contract negotiations suggests that operators generally seek to modify the traditional approach to allocating liability in oil and gas contracts.[103] The accident also presents a foundation for re-evaluating the industry practice, especially from a public policy perspective.[104] One issue debated in the Macondo litigation was the finding that the operator was grossly negligent in the accident. Although the findings of the National Commission on the BP Deepwater Horizon Oil Spill[105] show evidence of complicity by the drilling contractor, leading to the accident, the operator was held liable due to the contract entered by the parties, irrespective of fault.

On the other hand, contractors are opposed to the change because the operators negotiate with state regulators and commit to a well programme and other environmental and safety conditions.[106] They also argue that the operator benefits from the financial upside in the event of a successful operation. Contractors are not part of this financial upside as they do not operate as a vertically integrated company with operators. A vertically integrated company requires equity participation from a drilling contractor and a share in the statutory liability with an operator. Contractors further argue that significant and potentially adverse financial implications will result for them and for the long-term sustainability of the hydrocarbon industry if they take risks such as subsurface pollution.[107]

There is, however, a public policy and moral hazard dimension to risk allocation in the oil industry. When mutual indemnity does not apply against the party whose gross negligence caused the harm, it runs contrary to public interest. The industry practice takes away the incentive for a party to behave in ways that can prevent accidents. Thus, it creates harm for the public due to the absence of an obligation and making the other party to the contract bear the liability of

[102] Economist Intelligence Unit, 'Big Spenders: The Outlook for the Oil and Gas Industry in 2012' (*Economist Intelligence Unit*, 23 January 2012) <impact.economist.com/perspectives/sites/default/files/Big%20spenders%20-%20GLND_0.pdf> accessed 12 October 2023.

[103] Wan M Zulhafiz, 'Perception of Contractual Risk Allocation in the Oil and Gas Contracts in Malaysia' (2018) 11(1) International Journal of Trade and Global Markets 137.

[104] Wan M Zulhafiz, 'Recent Trends in Allocating of Risk Post-Macondo: The Growing Tension between Oil and Gas Standard Forms of Contract, and Contractual Practice' [2017] 5 International Energy Law Review 174, 180. Public policy is concerned with conduct which causes harm to society. It seeks to deter the occurrence of such harm and to punish people who occasion it. The essence is to protect society.

[105] The Commission noted that 'the oil spill could be seen as the embodiment of a long-lasting culture of complacency . . . the organisational culture allowed for missed warning signals . . . and poor perception of risks involved'. National Commission on the BP Deepwater Horizon Oil Spill and Offshore Drilling, *Deep Water: The Gulf Oil Disaster and the Future of Offshore Drilling* (Report to the President of the United States of America 2011).

[106] Cameron (n 17) 207.

[107] ibid.

severely wrongful conduct that was not the party's fault. Public policy is interested in deterring, and ensuring that a party assumes liability for harm or losses resulting from gross negligence.[108]

Public policy limits the freedom of contract when such freedom can lead to negative externalities,[109] particularly in gross negligence cases. Negative externalities refer to practices that encourage grossly negligent behaviour, resulting in harm/loss to society. Public policy could allow mere negligence to apply without regard to fault, giving the risk and reward underpinning, the 'market practice' of risk allocation and the utility of drilling activity to humans.[110] Restrictive contract practices are appropriate for disincentivising severely wrongful conduct[111] during petroleum operations.

2.6 RISK ALLOCATION TOOLS IN OIL AND GAS CONTRACTS

2.6.1 *Mutual Indemnity Agreements*

The oil and gas industry mainly uses indemnity clauses – or what are commonly known as knock-for-knock agreements, reciprocal indemnity or cross indemnity – to allocate risks. Indemnity clauses are also a common feature in fire insurance and maritime law and feature in construction contracts. According to *Black's Law Dictionary*, to indemnify means:

> (i) to restore the victim of a loss, in whole or in part, by payment, repair, or replacement; (ii) to save harmless; to secure against loss or damage, or to give security for the reimbursement of a person in case of an anticipated loss falling upon him; and (iii) to make good; to compensate, or to make reimbursement for a loss already incurred.[112]

An indemnity agreement relates to a promise by an indemnitor to protect or hold the indemnitee harmless regarding current or future liability or losses which result from third-party claims.[113] An indemnity could also be described as an agreement where an indemnitor accepts to protect an indemnitee against future damage or loss by paying the indemnitee when the latter suffers a loss in which the indemnitor

[108] S Kelleher, 'Public Policy Limitations on Indemnity for Sole or Partial Negligence' (*SmithCurrie*, 7 July 2014) <www.smithcurrie.com/publications/common-sense-contract-law/public-policy-limitations-on-indemnity-for-sole-or-partial-negligence> accessed 12 October 2023.

[109] Imran Naeemullah, 'Strong Headwinds: Statutes, Responsibility-Shifting, and Public Policy Continue to Frustrate Indemnity Agreements in the Offshore Oil and Gas Industry' (2013) 38 Tulane Maritime Law Journal 267.

[110] Smith I Azubuike, 'Rethinking Operator-Contractor Risk Allocation in a Post-Macondo Era' (PhD Thesis, University of Dundee 2019).

[111] Eric A Posner, 'Contract Law in the Welfare State: A Defense of the Unconscionability Doctrine, Usury Laws, and Related Limitations on the Freedom to Contract' (1995) 24 Journal of Legal Studies 283.

[112] *Black's Law Dictionary* (9th edn, West 2009) 769.

[113] Gerald F Slattery Jr. 'Indemnity and Insurance in the Texas Oil Patch' (2014) 10(1) Texas Journal of Oil, Gas and Energy Law 99.

agreed to protect the indemnitee.[114] An indemnity may be in the form of a claim for reimbursement whereby a party who has paid or may pay some money for liability claims against the other party to the agreement. In other cases, it could limit a party's liability to another party in the agreement.[115]

The above describes a simple indemnity that is purely one-sided. It is not reciprocal. On the other hand, a mutual indemnity is an essential tool to allocate risk in the oil and gas industry. Mutual indemnity describes an agreement where parties to the contract undertake to cover the loss, liability or damages suffered by the other party from some anticipated acts or damages arising from claims against such party. The essence of the agreement is to protect contractual parties against losses[116] with a control-based underpinning founded on care, custody and control to achieve efficiency.[117] In a mutual indemnity, both parties give and take protection regarding some species of loss, which must not be identical to what was given but should be related to it. This means that both the operator and contractor are simultaneously indemnifiers regarding one category of loss, and indemnified concerning a different but related type of loss.

The use of mutual indemnity as a tool for allocating risk in the oil and gas industry has received judicial approval. In the *London Bridge* case,[118] mutual indemnity was recognised as a 'market practice' created to address the unique nature of the oil and gas industry. However, courts tend to treat indemnity clauses with considerable suspicion because the stronger party may use them against the weaker party. In contractual interpretation, agreements entered into freely are recognised by courts, where a party, for a consideration, agrees to bear a risk that ordinarily would have been placed on another party by law.[119] The basis of this notion is the concept of freedom of contract. Nevertheless, in some jurisdictions, anti-indemnity statutes or public policy preclude a party from using a mutual indemnity agreement as a shield against certain kinds of negligence.[120]

In non-oil sectors, courts construe indemnity obligations in two ways. The first is where indemnity operates as an obligation on the indemnitor to prevent specific

114 Nick Kangles and others, 'Risk Allocation Provisions in Energy Industry Agreements: Are We Getting It Right?' (2011) 49(2) Alberta Law Review 341; Linda Richardson and others, 'Indemnities in Commonwealth Contracting' (*Legal Briefing*, 12 May 2015) <www.ags.gov.au/publications/legal-briefing/br105> accessed 10 October 2023.

115 Penny L Parker amd Slavich Slavich, 'Contractual Efforts to Allocate the Risk of Environmental Liability: Is There a Way to Make Indemnities Worth More Than the Paper They Are Written On?' (1991) 44 Southwestern Law Journal 1349.

116 David Peng, 'Mutual Indemnities in North Sea Contracts – Liability and Insurance Clauses' in David Peng (ed), *Insurance and Legal Issues in the Oil Industry* (Graham & Trotman 1993).

117 Smith and others (n 9).

118 *London Bridge* case (n 33).

119 *Tunkl v Regents of University of California* (1963) 60 Cal 2d 92. However, onerous or impracticable conditions may prevent a party from fulfilling their voluntary transaction.

120 Andrew A Beerworth, 'Emerging Trends in Construction Indemnity and Insurance Law' (2010) 58(5) Rhode Island Bar Journal 17; Kenneth Engerrand, 'Indemnity for Gross Negligence in Maritime Oilfield Contracts' (2012) 10 Loyola Maritime Journal 319; and Slattery (n 113).

wrongful acts from occurring, to protect the indemnitee against loss or damage.[121] The focus is on loss prevention; when construed in this regard, the indemnitor will be in breach of contract if the indemnitee suffers the stated loss. Accordingly, the remedy for the indemnitee will be to claim damages for breach of contract from the indemnitor. The second way is to construe the indemnity agreement as requiring an indemnitor to 'compensate or make good' an indemnitee for a loss that the indemnitee has suffered.[122] In this second construction, the focus is on how to 'make good'. Where this is the interpretation, the indemnitee can claim compensation under the contract against the indemnitor for the particular loss it has suffered.[123] The non-oil sector practice differs from the mutual indemnification practice by offshore oil and gas industry players.

2.6.2 Hold Harmless Clauses

The phrase 'to indemnify and hold harmless' is commonly used in allocating risk in the UK's oil and gas industry. The practice is for a party to agree to indemnify and hold another party harmless regarding death or injury to staff, property damage and pollution. Gordon highlights that scholars' view before the *Farstad Supply AS v Enviroco Ltd*[124] was that the inclusion of the phrase 'hold harmless' added little or nothing to the content of such clauses as they were simply indemnity clauses. This approach reflects the practice in the oil and gas industry as the words 'indemnify', 'hold harmless' and 'indemnify and hold harmless' were used interchangeably in allocating risks.[125] These phrases appear in the LOGIC standard contracts for the oil and gas industry, and the Mutual Hold Harmless Deed regulates the allocation of risk in the standard contract. This deed is often called the 'Deed of Adherence', by which parties become part of the scheme.[126] However, it applies only to parties who sign up for it.

However, it is essential to note that the UK Supreme Court in the *Farstad* case identified that the clause 'indemnify and hold harmless' in the agreement was not entirely an indemnity clause, but a mixed clause with elements of indemnity and exclusion. The court clarified that where a clause seeks to determine who bears liability for third-party exposure, it will operate as an indemnity. However, where the clause results in direct exposure to other contracting parties, it will operate as an exclusion. In the *Farstad* case, the court noted that the owner had suffered

121 *Firma C-Trade SA v Newcastle Protection and Indemnity Association* [1991] 2 AC 1.

122 *Caledonia North Sea Ltd v British Telecommunications Plc* [2002] 1 Lloyd's Rep 553, also known as the *Piper Alpha* case.

123 Rajdeep Choudhury, 'You Break It; I Buy It. The Curious Case of Knock-for-Knock Indemnities' (2018) 16(1) Oil, Gas & Energy Law Journal 2.

124 [2010] UKSC 18.

125 Gordon (n 29); David W Sharp, *Offshore Oil and Gas Insurance* (Witherby 1994); Toby Hewitt, 'Who Is to Blame? Allocating Liability in Upstream Project Contracts' (2008) 26(2) Journal of Energy and Natural Resources Law 177.

126 Gordon (n 29).

property damage and that the damage was a 'direct exposure'. Thus, the hold harmless clause operated as an exclusion of liability in the context of the contract.

2.6.3 *Mutual Indemnity and Hold Harmless Provisions in Context*

In the oil and gas industry, it is common for a party to offer the benefit of a simple indemnity or hold harmless provision to another party. This instance arises especially in a JOA where non-operators could, according to the extent of their various interests, agree to hold harmless and indemnify the operator against losses that the JV may incur, except for those arising from gross negligence or wilful misconduct.

In contracts involving an operator and a contractor, especially in well-related losses, an operator will typically indemnify and hold the contractor harmless against risk relating to any loss or damage to the hole, fire, blowout, damage to the reservoir, the underground strata and so on, regardless of the cause.[127] However, in the examples given above, it is evident that the indemnity or hold harmless provision is not mutual as neither the operator in a JV arrangement nor the contractor in the 'damage to the well' scenario is giving anything in return.

A mutual indemnity or hold harmless provision covers similar or related losses where parties undertake to indemnify or hold each other harmless on related categories of losses. However, neither of the parties takes sole responsibility for a category of loss; the responsibility for certain identified risks is shared among the parties. They identify the category of risk they are willing to accept and those they are not responsible for, and hold each other harmless regarding those specific elements of losses they have agreed on. In return, they both benefit from an indemnity or hold harmless clause relative to aspects of likely loss accepted. Where a party accepts responsibility for a particular risk, the party becomes liable for a downside even when it did not occasion the damage, irrespective of whether it arose from wilful misconduct, gross negligence or mere negligence during petroleum operations.

This practice applies to injury or death of the parties' staff, and pollution damage. Concerning the latter situation, the contractor accepts surface pollution damage, whereas the operator accepts subsurface or well pollution damage, notwithstanding the cause. Sometimes, the provision relating to pollution may be qualified, requiring the party in a better position to insure against the possible loss. There could also be carve-outs highlighting specific responsibilities, such as redrilling the hole when there is a downside or when damage arises from wilful misconduct or gross negligence. The essence is to protect the other party from deliberate acts of sabotage or conduct that falls below the standard of care expected in everyday petroleum operations. This practice presents a structure by which operators and contractors could allocate liability effectively.[128]

[127] ibid.

[128] Maria M Andrade, 'Knock for Knock Indemnities: Contract Practices and Enforceability Issues' (2011) 9(6) Oil, Gas & Energy Law Journal 3.

2.6.4 Exclusion and Limitation of Liability Clauses

2.6.4.1 Exclusion Clauses

At common law, a party to a contract can be absolved of liability where an exemption clause exists. An exemption clause could be in the form of an exclusion clause – where a party is excluded from liability such as responsibility arising from consequential losses. It has the effect of shifting liability from one party to another.[129] It can also be a clause limiting the party's liability at fault, thus reducing the compensation the party not at fault seeks to claim following a breach of contract due to negligence.[130] In commercial agreements, most exemption clauses exclude liability for consequential losses as well as losses arising from gross negligence and wilful misconduct. The reason for excluding the recovery of damages due to consequential losses is traceable to the case of *Hadley v Baxendale*.[131] The court considered the conditions under which a claimant can be awarded damages for loss suffered. It highlighted the difference between direct and indirect (consequential) losses. It noted that a party could recover damages that arise naturally from an alleged breach of contract or if the loss is presumed to be recoverable within the contemplation of the parties when they entered into the contract. Where the loss does not satisfy any of the conditions identified, it is considered consequential and not recoverable by the claimant.

Generally, in a contract, an exclusion clause seeks to exclude, restrict or modify a duty, liability or remedy meant to arise from a contractual relationship between the parties.[132] Exclusion clauses have three broad classifications. The first category involves clauses that exclude legal duties that should arise from the relationship between parties to a contract. The second category involves clauses limiting or excluding liability regarding a breach of duty. The last classification involves clauses that may be only procedural in approach and intend to modify the usual burden of proof by providing that an issue will be treated as conclusive of another or identifying a time limit within which to make a claim.[133] The clause operates as a release from responsibility regarding a particular risk in the contract. An exclusion clause differs from an indemnity clause in that it removes liability for the party seeking such exclusion. While the other party's financial position does not determine the efficacy of an exclusion clause,[134] the financial position of the indemnitor is a crucial factor in an indemnity agreement, especially in the oil and gas sector.

[129] The court in *Farstad* (n 125) identified that an exemption clause exculpates a party from assuming liability for loss.

[130] Wan M Zulhafiz, 'On the Contractual Risk Allocation in Oil and Gas Projects' (2017) The Law Review 168.

[131] *Hadley v Baxendale* (n 15).

[132] David Yates and Arthur Hawkins, *Standard Business Contracts: Exclusions and Related Devices* (Sweet & Maxwell 1986).

[133] Yates and Hawkins (n 133) 5.

[134] Laurence Koffman and Elizabeth Macdonald, *The Law of Contract* (OUP 2010).

2.6.4.2 Limitation of Liability Clauses

Limitation clauses are unlike exclusion clauses, given that they apply to limit or cap liability rather than eliminate a party's future liability. For example, in *Ailsa Craig Fishing Co Ltd v Malvern Fishing Co Ltd*, the House of Lords noted that

> clauses of limitation are not regarded by the courts with the same hostility as clauses of exclusion; this is because they must be related to other contractual terms, in particular to the risks to which the defending party may be exposed, the remuneration which he receives, and possibly also the opportunity to the party to insure.[135]

A party relying on a limitation clause can calculate the responsibility for remedying loss due to an act of the benefiting party and cap their possible liability up to a specific amount.[136] The cap could be based on a prearranged fixed sum or a portion. This type of limitation has commercial benefits when assuming liability, primarily in cases of indemnity and insurance; albeit a low limitation has been argued to have a similar effect as outright exclusion.[137]

In oil and gas contracts, clauses limiting a party's liability can also apply to cap the party's liability. The essence is to protect a party from the consequences of specific types of losses due to delays, loss of use, loss of profit, loss of production or some form of business interruption. Limitation of liability clauses apply due to how difficult it can sometimes be to calculate the quantum of a given loss in the present or future. These clauses apply to fill in the gap and can, for instance, apply to limit consequential loss in each petroleum operation. Remember that, according to the court in *Hadley v Baxendale*, for a loss to be consequential, it must arise naturally from the contract or be within the parties' contemplation.

A limitation of liability clause could also apply to generally cap or limit the liability of a party. In this regard, it is seen as a liability cap in a contract. This type of clause in a contract does not limit a party's liability by referring to a specific category of loss but by referring to a total amount payable. The amount could be a proportion or a fixed percentage, which is commonplace in the oil and gas industry contracting practice. A liability cap may not be necessary if the parties have already agreed to use the exclusion or indemnity clause to address consequential loss. However, a liability cap could still be useful to define what a contractor can bear. Again, some exclusion clauses may change over time, and a liability cap could be the best option for such future change. Thus, a liability cap is indispensable as it provides another layer of defence against indeterminate or disproportionate liability.[138]

135 *Ailsa Craig Fishing Co Ltd v Malvern Fishing Co Ltd* [1983] 1 WLR 964, 966.

136 Glenn D West and Benton W Lewis Jr, 'Contracting to Avoid Extra-Contractual Liability – Can Your Contractual Deal Ever Really Be the "Entire" Deal?' (2009) 64(4) The Business Lawyer 999.

137 Zulhafiz, 'On the Contractual Risk Allocation' (n 131).

138 Gordon (n 29).

2.7 RATIONALES FOR RISK ALLOCATION IN OIL AND GAS CONTRACTS

The risk allocation practice is based on two broad rationales: industry practice and economic/legal considerations.[139]

2.7.1 *Industry Practice Rationale*

The industry practice rationale relates to practices that the oil and gas industry has carried on for a long time or that inform the pattern of risk allocation. These practices are not borne out of written rules or agreements. Nevertheless, their global usage and acceptance support their existence and relevance. One can only say that the practice emanated from the philosophical underpinnings of the parties to a contract – there are various positions and perceptions. As a result, we can relate industry practice to the following concepts.

2.7.2 *Doctrine of Tradition*

This idea exists on the understanding that the risks for specific equipment, personnel and procedures are typically allocated to the contractor, leaving other risks open to parties for negotiation on how they should be distributed, while unallocated risks rest on the operator.[140] As such, this doctrine is supported by the concept of *custom*, under which terms emanating from the practice in a particular trade or from previous dealings could be implied in a contract.[141] Although no list of obligations falls within the doctrine of tradition, one can probably assume its existence through sustained practice by parties to a contract. For instance, it is customary in an oil and gas drilling operation for the contractor to provide the drilling unit and crew, while the operator provides the coring equipment, drilling mud, testing and completion services and other relevant equipment necessary for the operation.[142] As a result, the party that provides specific equipment or staff traditionally assumes its risk. This scenario may not be so all the time, but it represents the 'base case' of the practice in the drilling contract marketplace that regulates the operator and the contractor, just as the market forces of demand and supply regulate the price of products in the market.[143] It is therefore apparent that

[139] Kelechi Ofoegbu, 'How Contractual Risk Allocation Provisions of Oil and Gas Contracts Have Been or May Be interpreted by an English Court – A Case Study of Some Model Offshore Drilling Rig Contracts Developed in the United Kingdom, Canada and the United States of America' (PhD Thesis, University of Dundee 2018).

[140] MD Rankin and DR Richardson, 'The Offshore Drilling Contract-Operator and Contractor Perspectives' IADC/SPE 1983 Drilling Conference, New Orleans, Louisiana, 20–23 February 1983. Texas, USA: Society of Petroleum Engineers, 1.

[141] Richard Austen-Baker, *Implied Terms in English Contract Law* (Edward Elgar Publishing 2017).

[142] Owen L Anderson, 'The Anatomy of an Oil and Gas Drilling Contract' (1989) 25 Tulsa Law Journal 359.

[143] Rankin and Richardson (n 141).

the doctrine of tradition presents a default position in risk allocation that places liability based on care and control, not on fault.

2.7.3 Best Knowledge Doctrine

This doctrine specifies that risk allocation should be based on the contracting parties' knowledge of a particular risk and the party that is better positioned to avoid any legal action that may arise from it.[144] Kelechi Ofoegbu highlights that the doctrine of knowledge is functional in approach and emanates from 'experience relating to risk events, processes and procedures, geographical considerations and specificities'.[145] The gravamen of this doctrine is the prevention of legal claims that may result from a lack of knowledge regarding a particular subject-matter risk, thus mitigating the uncertainty that characterises such risk. Knowledge lessens the 'unknown' element in risk and controls the unpredictability that would otherwise arise. For instance, allocating the risk of damage to the drilling equipment or unit to the drilling contractor is in line with the doctrine of best knowledge, as the contractor has a better understanding of the unit than anyone else.

2.7.4 'Clay Feet' Doctrine

This doctrine advances that the party with the obligation under the contract to perform or refrain from executing an act should assume the economic outcomes resulting from the legal action.[146] This doctrine is based on the fact that legal obligations cannot be transferred. The obligation could arise, for instance, from statute, subsidiary legislation or a breach of a regulation. For example, the operator must execute the field development plan and work programme as approved by the government. Where there is a breach of this obligation, the doctrine presupposes that the operator should assume responsibility for non-compliance and not allocate the liability to the contractor. It also means that the party with the obligation cannot share liability arising from such risk and cannot allege contributory negligence arising from the legal duty.

The above concept appears to be in conflict with the practice of risk allocation, especially the use of mutual indemnity and exclusion clauses by participants in the offshore oil and gas industry to reallocate obligations. Even in cases of statutory breaches, courts have stated that parties to a contract can allocate these if they want to do so, and that the court will enforce the reallocation if the indemnity clauses are clear.[147]

144 Ofoegbu (n 140).
145 ibid.
146 ibid.
147 *Persimmon Homes Ltd v Ove Arup and Partners Ltd* [2017] EWCA Civ 373.

2.7.5 *Accountability Doctrine*

This doctrine focuses on the party controlling the process that could result in legal action. The doctrine emphasises that the party in control should be given the risk of the incidence of harmful activity arising from the process.[148] The gravamen of this doctrine highlights the difference between accountability and responsibility, as the two concepts may not always overlap in risk allocation. An instance is in offshore drilling operations where an operator controls the drilling of a well but is not responsible for physically engaging in the activity. In this instance, where there is a fire, blowout, uncontrolled well condition or cratering, the operator assumes liability for the downside, although the contractor is the one that does the actual drilling. The control issue could be resolved if we consider whether it is a contract of service or a contract for service. In the former, the operator is in control, while the contractor is in control in the latter. So, accountability will depend on the type of contract. In most drilling contracts, the contractor must comply with the legal instructions of the operator. Thus, this compliance with the operator's instruction puts the operator out as the directing entity, leaving it with more responsibilities while contractors assume the risk that they conventionally own and can acquire insurance.

2.7.6 *Rationale Founded on Legal/Economic Considerations*

Economic/legal considerations also constitute the main thrust under which certain risk allocation rationales are based. These factors focus on risk allocation optimality to allocate risks most effectively. The basis of these rationales is that risks can result in inefficiencies if allocated suboptimally, thus creating inefficiency in allocation.

2.7.7 *The Party in the Best Position to Bear the Risk*

This rationale hinges on the relative financial position of the parties, the benefit parties will derive from the activity, and how to achieve efficiency in the risk allocation process. An operator is believed to enjoy a long-term financial upside in a successful operation until the end of the well's life.[149] On the other hand, a contractor gets paid for services rendered and does not share in the long-term financial upside like the operator.

Richard Posner emphasises that the party in the best position to bear risk is the one who can bear it at the least cost.[150] The focus is on efficiency and cost, and the implication in our context involves placing the obligation to bear the economic consequences of the occurrence of a downside on the party that can deal with it cost-effectively. As such, parties to an oil and gas drilling contract usually allocate

[148] Rankin and Richardson (n 141).
[149] Cameron (n 17).
[150] Richard A Posner, *Economic Analysis of Law* (3rd edn, Little & Brown 1986).

risk based on who is better placed to secure insurance for a given risk. They also consider avoiding double insurance, where a party will require insurance coverage for its staff and equipment and the other party's staff and equipment. Apart from being cost-effective, a party is better placed to provide insurance for its own staff. Insurance, no doubt, increases the cost of the contract, and one way of ensuring the contract is cost-effective is to ensure that the party that can procure the lowest-cost insurance is allocated the relevant risk. This explains why contractors usually insist on the operator assuming well-related risks, as it is challenging for contractors to procure well insurance.[151]

2.7.8 Overall Efficiency Rationale

Certain factors are essential in facilitating efficiency in a transaction and serve as the basis for determining how to allocate risk between parties to a contract. Diversification and the party that can best avoid the cost of financial distress if a downside occurs are some of the factors.[152] The former entails evaluating the party that can best diversify risk cost-effectively by distributing risk into several undertakings to prevent exposure to the adverse effects of one of the endeavours. The efficiency rationale is based on the belief that a party with the capacity to mitigate risk volatility, due to the size of their assets or investment relative to the specific risk, should be allocated that contractual risk. Arising from this idea, a contractor assumes liability for the damage to its drilling rig, for instance. This is based on the understanding that the contractor owns several rigs and can obtain good insurance deals, the discount of which can be internalised in day rates. Also, contractors work for several clients simultaneously; as such, a contractor can leverage its entire contracts group, deploying people, materials and technology across the portfolio to boost individual contracts.

Sharing information about risk profiles, insurance and cooperation among parties can enhance overall efficiency and facilitate the process. However, information asymmetry or misinformation could create inefficiencies in communication and erode the potential of attaining optimality.[153] Evidence indicates that parties to a drilling contract sometimes engage in disinformation where market conditions and the balance of power are not in their favour. An instance is where a contractor misinforms the operator about their risk and insurance profile to get work. As a result, such a contractor could get the job and accept the risk that the operator allocates, despite their inability to assume liability if a downside occurs.[154]

151 Cary A Moomjian Jr, 'Contractual Insurance and Risk Allocation in the Offshore Drilling Industry' [1999] Drilling Contractor, March/April.

152 Ofoegbu (n 141).

153 Peter A Diamond, 'Posner's Economic Analysis of Law' (1974) 5(1) Bell Journal of Economics and Management Science 294.

154 Tessa Warren, 'The Operator-Contractor Relationship – Contract Changes, 1982 to 1984' (Paper Presented at the Society of Petroleum Engineers SPE/IADC Drilling Conference, New Orleans, March 1985).

In the long run, this could result in disputes and litigation should a downside occur, indicating economic inefficiency, given that resources are believed to have been allocated suboptimally. Note that the value that parties to a contract seek to achieve has an implication for how risk will be distributed and on the realisation of economic efficiency. For instance, a party's focus could be on what is fair and equitable when risks are being allocated, whereas the other party's focus could be on market conditions and how they can exploit the benefit to allocate risk in a particular way. Where an operator, for example, exploits the vulnerable rig market to allocate the risk of equipment or reservoir damage to a contractor, the latter could be put at a disadvantage as a driller, thus altering the overall efficiency of the contract.[155]

2.7.9 Economic Benefit Rationale

This rationale is premised on the grounds that parties who will partake in the upside of an activity should also participate in the downside risk. It stems from the *benefit principle* in taxation, where those who receive more benefit from government expenditure pay more tax to support the expenditure.[156] The rationale is underpinned by the fact that risk should follow reward and vice versa. It validates the position of contractors that operators should bear more risks given that they receive substantial financial upside from production in the oilfield in the event of commercial discovery and development. This argument is premised on the operator's proprietary interest in the oilfield after the contractor has finished drilling activities.

Again, when parties to a contract allocate consequential loss on a reciprocal indemnity basis, they validate the economic benefit principle. For instance, where the loss of profit, a consequential loss, is reciprocal, the economic benefit is validated as parties will bear their respective losses under the terms of the contract, just as they would have benefited had things gone well. The economic benefit rationale is similar to the business benefit logic. Risk allocation in the oil industry hinges on the 'business benefit'.

2.7.10 Foreseeability Rationale

This rationale advances that the allocation of risks should be based on the party that can best foresee the possibility of a downside and take steps to avoid its occurence.[157] It implies that risk allocation should be based on the ability of parties to take steps to prevent the economic consequences of a downside. The presumption here is that parties should have the economic capacity to prevent a risk from happening.

[155] Christopher E Houston, and Cass R Sunstein, 'Risk Assessment, Resource Allocation, and Fairness: Evidence from Law Students' (1998) 48 Journal of Legal Education 496.

[156] William H Oakland and William A Testa, 'State-Local Business Taxation and the Benefits Principle' (1996) 20 Economic Perspectives–Federal Reserve Bank of Chicago 2.

[157] Patrick Selim Atiyah, *Essays on Contract* (OUP 2012).

The absence of foreseeability could relieve a party from the consequences of a breach if the loss were unforeseen.[158] This rationale is based on the experience and knowledge of the subject matter protected by the allocated risk, primarily regarding procedures, likely pitfalls, resources and challenges.

It is essential to state that incentivising a party to mitigate foreseeable events is crucial and efficient. The incentive could be a liability for failing to act or a positive encouragement. Absent an incentive, a party may consider it more efficient not to act where the cost of preventing the consequence is higher than the liability if nothing is done about it. However, if both the foreseeability and likelihood of the event are high, the incentive to prevent it may be inevitable.[159] This emphasises the need to allocate foreseeable or anticipated risk. As Ofoegbu notes, parties always insert force majeure clauses in their contracts to deal with unforeseen situations and to allow the risk to lie where it falls. Each party bears the proportion of the resulting outcome attributable to them as losses.

2.7.11 *Other Rationales*

Another rationale behind industry practice is the certainty it provides. It gives parties to a contract an understanding of the nature and extent of their liability in a particular petroleum operation. Certainty of liability is critical for contractual parties in the offshore oil and gas sector who operate in an exceptional environment characterised by inherently hazardous conditions, high financial interests and the possibility for catastrophic outcomes if a downside occurs.[160] Where certainty is achieved, overlapping or double insurance cover may be prevented, reducing the overall project cost. Again, where a party assumes the risks associated with its property and personnel, such a party is better positioned to evaluate the risk and procure the necessary insurance coverage.[161]

Finally, an essential rationale is to avoid lengthy litigation while operations are ongoing. When an accident occurs on a platform, litigation is one way to determine causation and liability. This may take a long time, as the litigation may involve a 'multiparty donnybrook' with 'ambiguous-amphibious' workers.[162] It may also involve applying numerous principles of law to tort and contract claims, depending on the applicable law. Risks are therefore allocated between parties to avoid the long path of litigation.

[158] In *Hadley v Baxendale* (n 15), the court highlighted that the breach must be one that is foreseeable or contemplated by the parties for a claim of consequential loss to succeed.

[159] Posner (n 151).

[160] Pat Saraceni and Nick Summers, 'Reviewing Knock for Knock Indemnities: Risk Allocation in Maritime and Offshore Oil and Gas Contracts' (Clifford Chance, October 2015) <www.cliffordchance.com/content/dam/cliffordchance/briefings/2015/10/reviewing-knock-for-knock-indemnities-risk-allocation-in-maritime-and-offshore-oil-and-gas-contracts.pdf> accessed 12 October 2023.

[161] Choudhury (n 123).

[162] Kenneth Engerrand, 'Indemnity for Gross Negligence in Maritime Oilfield Contracts' (2012) 10 Loyola Maritime Journal 319.

2.8 REGULATORY INTERVENTIONS IN RISK ALLOCATION

2.8.1 Anti-Indemnity Legislation

The utility of the mutual indemnity clause has been highlighted. However, some statesy in the US[163] and some countries of the world view this tool with considerable suspicion. As such, they have adopted legislation limiting or excluding the use of mutual indemnity clauses, to protect allegedly vulnerable parties from contracts that may unfairly shift liability for damages onto them. The prohibition relates to injury, death and damages caused by an indemnitee's negligence or gross negligence. Thus, they explicitly void any agreement which intends to evade the prohibitive objective of the statute. An example is the Louisiana Oilfield Anti-Indemnity Act (LOAIA),[164] as stated below.

About forty-one states in the US have passed laws that prohibit construction contracts that provide that a subcontractor would indemnify another party for the party's negligence.[165] Notable among these anti-indemnity statutes are those of Texas and Louisiana. For example, the Louisiana statute explicitly states that

> Any provision contained in, collateral to, or affecting an agreement pertaining to a well for oil, gas, or water, or drilling for minerals which occur in a solid, liquid, gaseous, or other state, is void and unenforceable to the extent that it purports to or does provide for defense or indemnity, or either, to the indemnitee against loss or liability for damages arising out of or resulting from death or bodily injury to persons, which is caused by or results from the sole or concurrent negligence or fault (strict liability) of the indemnitee, or an agent, employee, or an independent Contractor who is directly responsible to the indemnitee.[166]

Although both Texas and Louisiana have passed anti-indemnity statutes, some marked differences exist between them. In Louisiana, contractual indemnity is outrightly void, while in Texas, contractual indemnity is permissible when supported with insurance and when it meets specific regulatory requirements. Public policy considerations have been the focal point of these anti-indemnity statutes. Some courts consider these statutes as the embodiment of public policy that would override the provisions of drilling contracts.

2.8.2 Indemnification in Texas

The state of Texas is central to early offshore petroleum activities in the US. As such, oil and gas activities occupy a prominent position in the Texas economy.

163 See for instance the Wyoming Act (Wyo Stat § 30-1-131 to 133 (1983)); the New Mexico Act (NM Stat Ann § 56-7-2 (1986)); the Louisiana Act (LA Rev Stat Ann § 9:2780(a) (West Supp 1989)); the Texas Act (Tex Civ Prac & Rem Code § 127.001 – 127.007).

164 ibid Louisiana Act 9:2780(g).

165 Foundation of the American Subcontractors Association Inc, 'Anti-Indemnity Statutes in the 50 States' (FASA 2013) <www.azfaircontracting.com/wp-content/uploads/2019/07/ASA-Anti-Indemnity-Chart-50-States.pdf> accessed 12 October 2023.

166 Louisiana Act (n 164) 9:2780(a).

The central role of petroleum in the state's economy accounts for the inclusion of anti-indemnity provisions in Texas's legal regime governing offshore petroleum operations. This inclusion provides the foundation for state authorities to implement the statute and on which the Supreme Court can base its judgments. Thus, where parties to a contract choose Texas law as the governing law, the mutual indemnity provisions must conform to the anti-indemnity statute[167] and the express negligence rule to be enforceable.[168]

2.8.2.1 *Texas Express Negligence Rule*

The express negligence test determines, to an extent, the enforceability of an indemnity provision under the law of Texas. The rule requires parties to state their intention in their contract expressly. The contract must identify that despite the sole or concurrent negligence of the indemnitee, the indemnitor will indemnify the indemnitee. Otherwise, the indemnity provision will be void. The Supreme Court of Texas indicated that a clause seeking to indemnify the indemnitee from the consequences of their own negligence must be stated in specific terms within the four corners of the contract.[169]

The express negligence rule is a doctrine of common law that applies when construing the validity of indemnity agreements. Note that the law of a state may include statutory and common law positions. This accounts for why some jurisdictions place common law restrictions on the enforceability of indemnity agreements. Another common law doctrine for deciding the enforceability of an indemnity provision is the 'clear and unequivocal' test, which is applicable in other jurisdictions. This test notes that the specific mention of the sole or concurrent negligence of the indemnitee is not required as long as the intention of the parties indicates their resolve to include all wrongs arising from their activity.[170] The court in *Dresser Industries Inc v Page Petroleum Inc*[171] adopted the above reasoning when it held that where a provision in a contract requires an indemnitee to be protected from its negligence, the threshold inquiry when construing such a provision is the fair notice requirement of conspicuousness. By this notice, a reasonable person's attention could be drawn to the contract's provisions. The decision encouraged parties, whose agreement is governed by Texas law, to provide for risk allocation expressly and to determine the nature and extent of the indemnity provisions in the contract. The contract must be clear for all to understand and explicitly emphasise the parties' intentions.[172]

[167] This is the Texas Oilfield Anti-Indemnity Act (TOAIA).

[168] Texas Civil Practice and Remedies Code 127.001.

[169] *Ethyl Corp v Daniel Construction Co* 725 SW 2d 705 (Tex 1987).

[170] *Metropolitan Paving Co v Gordon Herkenhoff & Assoc Inc* 341 P 2d 460 (NM 1959).

[171] 853 SW 2d 505 (Tex 1993); see also *Atlantic Richfield Co v Petroleum Personnel Inc* 768 SW 2d 724 (Tex 1989).

[172] Moomjian notes that the talismanic words to ensure enforceability should be drafted thus:

> It is the intent of the parties hereto that, where responsibility or liability is assumed by either party or where either of the parties agrees to release or indemnify the other party in respect

2.8.2.2 *Texas Anti-Indemnity Statute*

This statute is often called the Texas Oilfield Anti-Indemnity Act (TOAIA). It applies to petroleum, water and mineral wells.[173] TOAIA renders void any contractual provision which intends to indemnify a party against liability for damage or loss occasioned by or resulting from the indemnitee's concurrent or sole negligence, or his employee, agent or any person responsible to him.[174] Non-adherence to the law can render a service or drilling contract void. Besides the express negligence doctrine, the TOAIA must also be observed for an indemnity agreement to be enforceable in Texas. Introduced in 1973, the Act seeks to prevent operators from demanding contractors indemnify them for their negligence and that of third parties. Passing a party's negligence to another was adjudged unfair and stress-inducing on the contractual chain.[175] Section 127.003 of the TOAIA provides thus:

> (a) Except as otherwise provided by this chapter, a covenant, promise, agreement, or understanding contained in, collateral to, or affecting an agreement pertaining to a well for oil, gas, or water or to a mine for a mineral is void if it purports to indemnify a person against loss or liability for damage that:
>   (1) is caused by or results from the sole or concurrent negligence of the indemnitee, his agent or employee, or an individual contractor directly responsible to the indemnitee; and
>   (2) arises from: (A) personal injury or death; (B) property injury; or (C) any other loss, damage, or expense that arises from personal injury, death, or property injury.

The Act applies only to hydrocarbon, water or mine services for mineral wells, but it does not specify what range of activities constitute well and mineral services. The Texas Court of Appeal defined well and mine services by requiring a connection between the indemnity agreement and the well or mine service. In *Transworld Drilling Co v Levingston Shipbuilding Co*,[176] the court affirmed this

of any claim, demand or cause of action, unless it otherwise is expressly stated, such release, assumption of liability and/or indemnification shall apply notwithstanding the gross, sole, concurrent, active or passive negligence of any party hereto or any person, firm, or corporation for which such party is responsible (whether or not such negligence related to a pre-existing condition or defect), any breach of warranty or representation, unseaworthiness of any rig or vessel owned or hired by either party, or any other legal theory (including tort, strict or product liability) which otherwise may be applicable.

Cary A Moomjian Jr, 'Drilling Contract Historical Development and Future Trends Post-Macondo: Reflections on a 35 Year Industry Career' (*Drilling Contractor*, 7 March 2012) <www.drillingcontractor.org/wp-content/uploads/2012/04/Drilling-Contract-Historical-Development-and-Future-Trends-Post-Macondo.pdf> accessed 2 February 2024.

173 Tex Civ Prac & Rem Code § 127.001.

174 ibid § 127.003.

175 Tim Haidar, 'The Texas Anti-Indemnity Law – What Does It Mean for Your Business?' (*Oil and Gas IQ*, 3 December 2012) <www.oilandgasiq.com/legal-and-regulatory/articles/the-texas-anti-indemnity-law-what-does-it-mean-for> accessed 12 October 2023.

position by stating that the TOAIA would be inapplicable in an agreement to repair an offshore drilling rig that was performed in a shipyard. However, the Supreme Court of Texas has yet to define what well and mine services include. It is worth noting that where the indemnity agreement does not purport to indemnify a party for its negligence, the statute is inapplicable even if the services deal with wells or mineral mines. Accordingly, contracts relating to or dealing with transportation, purchasing, fixed facilities and JOAs are not covered by the TOAIA as they are not related to wells.

The statute precludes the indemnitee from receiving indemnification for its sole or concurrent negligence. However, an exception exists to the effect that if the parties agree in writing that the indemnitor will procure liability insurance to support the indemnity agreement, the indemnity will be enforceable.[177] This rule is, however, subject to some conditions.[178] The purchase of insurance for the benefit of another party makes mutual indemnity applicable. In 2012, Texas passed a law which voids clauses in construction contracts that require a party to an agreement to indemnify another party for claims occasioned by the fault or negligence of the indemnitee or a third party whom the indemnitee supervises or has control over.[179]

2.8.3 *Indemnification in Louisiana*

The general rule in Louisiana is that parties must explicitly state that indemnification applies in their contract for an indemnity clause to be enforceable.[180] Clarity of intention is a less rigorous test than the Texas express negligence rule. Although parties may not require an express reference to negligence in the contract, a strict interpretation is essential for indemnity provisions to deduce the parties' intention.[181] However, due to public policy considerations, the LOAIA has put some restrictions in place regarding the enforcement of an indemnity agreement by a negligent indemnitee.

The adoption of the LOAIA in 1981 was based on the consideration that unconscionable bargains were foisted on parties using indemnity clauses in drilling-related agreements.[182] The Louisiana Supreme Court identified this viewpoint in *Fontenot v Chevron USA Inc*,[183] wherein it observed that the unequal bargaining power of

[176] 693 SW 2d 19 (Tex Ct App 1985).
[177] TOAIA (n 174) § 127.005.
[178] ibid § 127.005.
[179] Texas Anti-Indemnity Act, Texas Ins Code § 151.001 (1 January 2012). See particularly Tex Ins Code § 151.002.
[180] Julia M Adams and Karen K Milhollin, 'Indemnity on the Outer Continental Shelf – A Practical Primer' (2002) 27 Tulane Maritime Law Journal 43, 82.
[181] Yates and Hawkins (n 133).
[182] G Roth Kehoe II, 'Louisiana Oilfield Indemnity Act: A Necessary Limit to Contract Freedom or Paternalism for Roughneck Contracts?' (1996) 70 Tulane Law Review 1097.
[183] 676 So 2d 557 (LA 1996).

parties and the need to avoid adhesion in contracts gave rise to the LOAIA. LOAIA proscribes any clause that shields or indemnifies an

> indemnitee against loss or liability for damages arising out of or resulting from death or bodily injury to persons, which is caused by or results from the sole or concurrent negligence or fault (strict liability) of the indemnitee, or an agent, employee, or an independent contractor who is directly responsible to the indemnitee.[184]

As used in this context, 'any agreement' relates to contracts governing exploration, development or transportation of hydrocarbons and minerals.[185]

Unlike the anti-indemnity statute of Texas, the LOAIA applies to death and personal injury only, excluding property damage and economic losses. Again, the LOAIA proscribes mutual indemnification clauses when the latter concerns death or bodily injury, even when the obligation is mutual and founded on adequate insurance. The author notes that the scope of the statute is not completely clear as this issue is still subject to litigation. The statute's language does not answer the question of whether any indemnity agreement is 'collateral to' or 'affects' an agreement that 'pertains to' a well or the drilling for minerals.[186]

After looking at the intent and history of the LOAIA, the Fifth Circuit concluded that the Louisiana and Texas statutes differ. The Texas statute defines agreements 'pertaining to a well' as requiring the contractor to render 'well or mine services'. On the other hand, the LOAIA provides that any agreement concerning oil and gas operations is 'pertaining to a well'. Generally, the Louisiana, Texas, Wyoming and New Mexico courts apply their Oilfield Anti-Indemnity Acts to agreements that have a slight connection with the operation, maintenance or repair of a separate hydrocarbon or mineral well but not to agreements for general oilfield work.[187] Also, the LOAIA proscribes insurance protection, contractual provisions, subrogation waivers and additional insured validations that would negate the statute's intent.[188] The Court of Appeal of the Fifth Circuit upheld this position when it stated that Section 2780G of the LOAIA means that the requirement of an additional insured clause in a contract is unenforceable.[189] However, the Supreme Court of Louisiana in *Fontenot*[190] held that Section 2780G would be enforceable for waivers of subrogation provisions in an indemnity

[184] LA RS 9:2780(b).

[185] ibid s 2780(c).

[186] The court in *Oliver Broussard v Conoco Inc v SHRM Catering Inc* 959 F 2d 42 (1993 AMC 2404) analysed this issue and provided a direction for future application as it affects the LOIA.

[187] R Redfearn Jr, 'Oilfield Anti-Indemnity Acts and Their Impact on Insurance Coverage: A Comparative Analysis' (*Insurance Journal Magazine*, 22 August 2005) <http://www.insurancejournal.com/magazines/features/2005/08/22/59608.htm> accessed 12 October 2023.

[188] LOIA s 2780G.

[189] *Babineaux v McBroom Rig Building Services Inc* 806 F. 2d 1282 (5th Cir 1987). This study posits that the proscription of additional insured in certain jurisdictions would impede the essence of indemnity clauses, especially as new risk dimensions have been noticed as a result of the Macondo litigation in the US.

contract where the clause does not negate or circumvent the LOAIA. Where a clause in an indemnity agreement purports to circumvent the intention of the LOAIA, such provision is unenforceable. The court further noted that a subrogation waiver is invalidated when it shifts liability: the shifting of liability is achieved in conjunction with an indemnity provision.

US courts have designated a 'judicial exception' to the LOIA for co-insurance, which allows an indemnitee to pay for the insurance coverage of the indemnitor. The court in *Marcel v Placid Oil Co* upheld this approach as it prevented shifting the economic burden to another party.[191] Thus, an indemnitee will benefit from the insurance it procured, rather than from an indemnity, which the statute prohibits.[192] The author considers this judicial exception innovative as it creates room for responsibility from both parties and creates a sense of burden on the indemnitee (contractor). As such, the indemnitor will be an additional insured in the indemnitee's insurance policy. While this practice may create a sense of burden on the indemnitee, it may not entirely discourage the indemnitee from moral hazard, especially as the risk shifts to an insurance company. However, there will be premium implications, and the insurance company can address this by stating in the policy that it will not cover gross negligence acts.[193] Concerning pollution risk, this could tackle moral hazard, incentivise pollution prevention and encourage environmental responsibility among parties. It could also indirectly facilitate applying the 'polluter pays' principle as the indemnitee will be paying for an act of negligence it solely or jointly commits.[194]

2.8.4 Unfair Contracts Terms Act 1977

The Unfair Contract Terms Act (UCTA 1977) of the UK is a regulation that seeks to protect the interests of businesses and individuals who transact as consumers. The essence is to prevent any injustice arising from a consumer's lack of understanding of the meaning and extent of a contractual provision or their weak bargaining position.[195] A weak bargaining position impacts the freedom to contract, notwithstanding that the party in question has read and understood the meaning and effect of the clause in the contract.[196] This form of protection is

190 *Fontenot* (n 184)
191 100 11 F 3d 563 [5th Cir 1994]. The procurement of insurance for personal liability will arise where the liability from a particular activity has been apportioned to parties.
192 Kehoe (n 183). However, where substantial part of the insurance coverage is to be borne by the indemnitee, the *Marcel* exception will not apply. See *Amoco v Lexington Ins Co* 745 So 2d 676 (LA App 1 Cir 1999), where Amoco paid $2,000 to get coverage of $11,000,000 and the court declared the indemnity unenforceable.
193 Michael Faure and Tom Hartlief, 'Remedies for Expanding Liability' (1998) 18 OJLS 699.
194 This reasoning is further strengthened by Articles 9 and 10 of Directive 2004/35/CE of the European Parliament and of the Council of 21 April 2004 on environmental liability regarding the prevention and remedying of environmental damage [2004] OJ L 143/0056.
195 Law Commission, *Law Commission's Second Report on Exemption Clauses* (Law Comm no 69, 1975).
196 Albert Choi and George Triantis, 'The Effect of Bargaining Power on Contract Design' (2012) 98(8) Virginia Law Review 1665.

also available to businesses that transact as consumers despite their size.[197] The question that comes to mind from the above position is whether an operator and a contractor who transact in the course of business fall within the contemplation of the Act as 'consumers'.

Courts have approached this question in the past. Initially, the position of some courts was that the UCTA applied only to consumer contracts, not general commercial ones.[198] This reasoning was based on the assumption that parties to a commercial agreement have equal power to bargain. As such, a court should not be seen to meddle in how parties allocate risks. However, this attitude has shifted following the principle that a party would not be

> 'dealing in the course of business' if it entered into a contract that was not in pursuit of its core business, or, if it was related to it, did not occur with frequency or regularity that could lead to the conclusion that it was 'dealing in the course of business'.[199]

This position aligns with Section 12 of the UCTA regarding transactions as a customer against a party who deals in the course of business. Despite that, the courts have progressed, using the test of reasonableness as a basis to intervene, notwithstanding that it is explicit that both parties are dealing in the course of business.

The court in *Salvage Association v CAP Financial Services Ltd*[200] applied the test of reasonableness even though both parties were dealing in the course of business. It has been noted that there is a possibility that this trend will continue, as a court may want to scrutinise and expand the reach of reasonableness.[201] As such, courts could extend the test of reasonableness under the Act to apply to offshore drilling contracts, especially as drilling companies such as Schlumberger appear more influential and wealthier than operators such as Tullow Oil Company. With this in mind, it is hard to contemplate that the parties would have the same bargaining power; hence the need to scrutinise the contract. The determination of reasonableness by a court is essentially a subjective process with the aid of possible guidelines, such as the bargaining power of parties to the contract. The test of reasonableness is a mechanism the Act uses to limit reliance on exemption clauses in certain circumstances. The focus is usually on contractual provisions limiting or excluding liability; however, parties can avoid the application of the Act through deliberate and careful drafting.

197 Steve Wilson and Sheila Bone, 'Businesses, Standard Terms and the Unfair Contract Terms Act 1977' (2002) 1 Journal of Obligations & Remedies 29.

198 Alison White, 'Caveat Vendor? A Review of the Court of Appeal Decision in St Albans City and District Council v International Computers Limited' [1997] 3 Journal of Information, Law and Technology.

199 ibid 4.

200 [1995] FSR 654. The test of reasonableness was also applied in *Edmund Murray Ltd v BSP International Foundations Ltd* [1992] Con LR 1, where the transaction was for the supply of a drilling rig, but the court held that the exclusion clauses were unreasonable after applying the test of reasonableness to them.

201 Saleem Sheikh and Susan Singleton, *Commercial Contracts: A Practical Guide to Standard Terms* (5th edn, Bloomsbury Professional 2019).

2.8.5 Contracts (Rights of Third Parties) Act 1999

Before the Contracts Act came into existence in the UK, third parties were precluded from claiming rights or benefits under a contract due to the common law doctrine of 'privity of contract': they could not sue or be sued as they were not parties to the agreement. Following the Law Commission's recommendation,[202] the Contracts (Rights of Third Parties) Act 1999 was enacted. The Act did not abolish the privity of contract doctrine but reformed it by creating a statutory exception that allows third parties to enforce their rights/benefits in a contract.[203]

The Act achieves the reform by providing circumstances under which third parties can legally sue a promisor and enforce the promise that benefits them under the contract. Note that the Act still preserves the rule that parties to a contract cannot impose obligations on third parties. The intention of the parties is crucial regarding third-party rights. This intention can be express or implied, especially as contracting parties, according to the Act, can expressly confer a right on third parties to enforce a benefit stated in the contract or suggest one through a provision in the contract.[204] Implied third-party rights are enforceable if there is nothing contrary in the agreement.

Regarding risk allocation, a third party can benefit from an exemption or limitation of liability clause only to the extent that the clause is included in the defences and set off.[205] This benefit applies where the intention of the provision granting the third party the right was expressed in the contract. Section 4 of the Act preserves the right of the promisor to seek the protection of a limitation of liability or exemption clause, even against third parties. Section 2 of the Act offers protection when a third party seeks to prevent the enforcement of the limitation of liability or exemption clause due to unreasonableness, as anticipated by the UCTA 1977. However, this protection is unavailable against the promisor in circumstances where negligence is suspected, as such negligence constitutes a breach of the promisor's obligation arising from the promise.[206]

No significant difference has been occasioned by the Act as far as risk allocation is concerned. The Act confers only benefits on third parties to enforce a promise, and not a right of action to enforce other clauses in the contract. The position would be different if the Act gave contracting parties the right to allocate risk to third parties claiming and enforcing a promise/benefit under the contract. This right would have changed the risk allocation dynamics and impacted the main parties' relationships with each other and the 'beneficiary' third parties. It

202 Law Commission, *Privity of Contract: Contracts for the Benefits of Third Parties* (HM Stationery Office 1991).

203 Tiong Min Yeo, 'When Do Third Party Rights Arise Under the Contracts (Rights of Third Parties) Act 1999 (UK)?' [2001] Singapore Academy of Law Journal 13, 34.

204 Contracts (Rights of Third Parties) Act 1999 s 1(1)(a) and (b).

205 ibid s 3(3).

206 ibid s 7(2). This protection applies to loss/damage arising other than from death or personal injury. Furthermore, the test of reasonableness in s 2(2) of the UCTA will not apply where the parties agree to exclude and/or limit a third-party's liability.

would require indemnity clauses to cover the appropriate third parties, which could also be considered as giving mutual indemnities to the key contracting parties by claiming a benefit under the contract. It is important to note that this position applies slightly differently to non-operators, who are co-venturers with the operator, a named agent. As such, it confers on non-operators the benefits stipulated under the Act.

2.9 CONCLUSION

The risk allocation practice and standard forms in Nigeria, Indonesia, the UK and the US are related, except for minor differences and the use of terms such as 'gross negligence' in the jurisdictions apart from the UK. An examination of the risk allocation practices in the above jurisdictions shows that risk is allocated without regard to negligence or gross negligence. In other words, negligence or gross negligence does not trigger liability on the part of the party at fault. The contract between the parties is based on the negotiation of the parties and the consideration of the party that is best able to manage the risk. This practice is based on the long-term financial upside of the operator and the short-term financial benefit of the drilling contractor. In risk allocation, a mutual indemnity clause is considered an essential risk allocation tool, used as a shield against liability for negligence and gross negligence. This is due to the range of actors involved and the risk and exposure during offshore operations. The industry practice of risk allocation applies based on the business benefit perception and the rationale that double insurance, lengthy litigation, the certainty of responsibility, custody and control, and so on, drive the risk allocation process.

Chapter 3

Conceptual Considerations in Risk Allocation in the Offshore Energy Industry

3.0 INTRODUCTION

Specific conceptual considerations come to mind when allocating risk in the oil industry. The concepts include freedom of contract, public policy, sustainability and distributive justice. This chapter will discuss these concepts to understand how they influence and shape risk allocation practice. It will assess how freedom of contract enables parties to determine the terms of their agreement and whether public policy limits the exercise of the freedom to contract. It will discuss the concept of justice and examine the various distributive justice considerations. Finally, it will explore the nexus between distributive justice and private law.

3.1 CONCEPT OF FREEDOM OF CONTRACT

Freedom of contract involves a process where persons or groups enter into an agreement without interference or restriction from the government. The concept of laissez-faire, an essential foundation of free-market libertarianism in economics, underpins the freedom of contract. This underpinning is so especially as the freedom to choose which term to contract is vital in a market-based economy. This freedom reflects the basic right of individuals to contract on terms mutually agreed by the parties.[1] The basic right to contract freely with one another received a judicial boost when the court in *Printing and Numerical Registering Company v Sampson* noted as follows:

> If there is one thing more than another which public policy requires, it is that men of full age and understanding shall have the utmost liberty of contracting and that their contracts, when entered into freely and voluntarily, shall be held sacred and shall be enforced by Courts of Justice.[2]

Indeed, freedom of contract places great emphasis on individual freedom and the belief that respect for personal independence is an essential complement to both a free-market economy and a liberal state. Liberal theorists believe that enforcing

[1] Sankalp Jain, 'Freedom of Contract – Concept, Postulations and Restrictions' (26 October 2020) <dx.doi.org/10.2139/ssrn.3896185> accessed 12 October 2023.

[2] [1875] LRCh 19 Eq 462, 465.

private contracts entered into freely by parties pursuing their business preserves individual liberty, safeguards equality of opportunity and maximises social wealth.[3] As such, the liberty to contract remains a fundamental right regularly applauded in our society and rightly receives primary credit for establishing a functional, market-based economy in which certainty is esteemed.[4] This idea highlights the importance of freedom of contract.

From the discussion presented, two limbs can be discerned. The first is that freedom of contract entails the liberty to choose the person you want to contract with, and the second highlights the freedom of parties to choose the terms of their agreement. This limb is ultimately underpinned by the intention of the parties. The first aspect – freedom to choose a contracting partner – is based on the fact that capitalism envisions free competition, an essential element of freedom of contract. However, welfare legislation and the acceptance of monopolies in some sectors of the economy have put constraints on the idea of free competition. The second aspect – the freedom of parties to choose the terms of their agreement – is vital where the terms of the agreement are fundamental to the contractual relationship. Nevertheless, the liberty to determine the terms of a contract is subject to the prevailing public interest and public policy, a constraint to freedom of contract.[5] However, a significant aspect of the agreement is still subject to the parties' free will. Nevertheless, the requirements of the law on illegal contract and public policy remain fundamental tools in contractual arrangements.[6]

The restraints from welfare legislation arise due to the interest of the public, especially in labour relations between employers and employees. Thus, any contract that runs contrary to a statute will be unenforceable. Some of these pieces of legislation regulate terms of employment, data protection, employee privacy, leave rights, compensation and so on. Apart from welfare legislation, standard form contracts can restrict parties' freedom to contract. This situation arises when a party has limited power to negotiate a term in a contract. The party is faced with a 'take it or leave it' contract, which occurs usually in insurance, thus compromising the idea of freedom of contract. A monopoly in transportation or the supply of electricity or water, for instance, could defeat contractual freedom. However, such monopolistic and restrictive trade systems can be controlled by legislation.

Furthermore, the utilitarian doctrine, as proposed by Jeremy Bentham, restricts freedom of contract. Betham advocated that the law must strive to achieve the maximum happiness of the maximum number of people. This argument arises from the understanding that the liberty to contract only favours a limited number of people and facilitates unparalleled discrepancies between differently situated

3 David Frisch, 'Contractual Choice of :aw and the Prudential Foundations of Appellate Review' (2003) 56 Vanderbilt Law Review 58.

4 David P Weber, 'Restricting the Freedom of Contract: A Fundamental Prohibition' (2013) 16 Yale Human Rights & Development Law Journal 51.

5 Roger Brownsword, 'Review: The Limits of Freedom of Vontract and the Limits of Contract Theory' (1995) 22(2) Journal of Law and Society 262.

6 Jain (n 1).

economic factors, thus necessitating reform for the benefit of all. These restrictions confirmed the words of Hughes CJ, who stated that, 'Freedom of contract is a qualified, and not an absolute, right.'[7]

3.2 LIMIT OF THE FREEDOM OF CONTRACT

The concept of freedom of contract, and its limits, have featured prominently in various areas of scholarship, including in the seminal work of Michael Trebilcock, *The Limits of Freedom of Contract*.[8] The foundation of freedom of contract in moral, economic and legal philosophy has also been evaluated to understand its application in private transactions.[9] There is a consensus in favour of contractual freedom on the grounds of economic liberalism and market economy,[10] which Trebilcock calls the *private ordering paradigm*. The theoretical underpinning of this consensus is that when people enter into private exchanges voluntarily, it is presumed that they might be better off in the exchange.

In his review of Trebilcock's work, Roger Brownsword notes that *The Limits of Freedom of Contract* focuses on the private ordering paradigm, which is based on an allocative system where what to produce and consume is determined by producers and consumers following individual preferences and incentives.[11] Brownsword notes that neoclassical economists' support for the private ordering paradigm is based on the justification that it can maximise welfare. At the same time, classical liberals believe it provides an opportunity for independent agents to be involved in pursuing what they think is good for them. The correlate of this idea in law is contract, which provides a system that allows parties to enter into agreements on terms that they consider beneficial. In a bid to maximise welfare, the state commits to maintaining the institution of the law of contract, to reduce transaction costs and facilitate utility-maximising transactions. On the other hand, a liberal system promotes opportunity for autonomous exchanges and underlines the essence of voluntarily accepted responsibilities.

In their discussion of the Coase theorem and its application to the freedom of contract, Daniel Muller and Patrick Schmitz note that restricting the freedom of parties to contract when there are no externalities on third parties will not enhance welfare.[12] The reason is that the freedom to contract will allow parties to maximise the total surplus arising from their relationship. As such, it will improve parties' welfare and promote efficiency, as advanced in the Coase theorem.

[7] *Chicago, Burlington & Quincy RR Co v McGuire* 219 US 549, 567 (1911).

[8] Michael J Trebilcock, *The Limits of Freedom of Contract* (Harvard University Press, 1997). See also Brownsword (n 5) 259.

[9] Peter Cserne, 'Reasons for Limiting Freedom of Contract: Questions of Philosophy and Policy' (undated) <jesz.ajk.elte.hu/cserne13.html> accessed 12 October 2023.

[10] Frisch (n 3).

[11] Brownsword (n 5).

[12] Daniel Muller and Patrick W Schmitz, 'The Right to Quit Work: An Efficiency Rationale for Restricting the Freedom of Contract' (2021) 184 Journal of Economic Behavior & Organization 653.

However, the Coase theorem holds that the freedom to contract should be allowed only when there are no transaction costs or externalities due to the contract. Moreover, transaction costs occur due to the contract between the parties, which could result in negative externalities or social costs for third parties,[13] such as oil pollution damage.

In the theory of contract, the moral hazard that results from actions that are not observed has been identified as an essential source of transaction cost.[14] Where the issue of moral hazard exists, there are circumstances under which welfare will not be enhanced if the terms of a contract are enforced as agreed by the parties. An instance is where the harm the contract will inflict is greater than the benefit it will result in for the parties. This transaction cost arising from moral hazard can limit the freedom of contract for welfare reasons. If enforcing a contractual term will result in unconscionability, a court will limit the freedom of contract by not ordering its enforcement.[15] These points explain the basis for the limits on the freedom of contract as advocated by Trebilcock, discussed below.

3.2.1 Commodification

Trebilcock identifies several limits to the freedom of contract. Among these limits are commodification and externalities, paternalism, symmetric information imperfections, discrimination and so on.[16] The focus here will be on commodification and externalities. Commodification relates to the nature of a commodity that can form the subject of a contract between parties. Examples include selling human organs, enforcing surrogacy contracts and so on. While this remains within the private ordering model, it overlooks the possibility for regulated markets to play an essential role in the contractual process unless certain checks are implemented. However, the law determines which terms or commodities can be contracted, and this control limits the freedom of contract. This makes the right of parties to enter into a contract qualified and not absolute.

3.2.2 Externalities

Externalities can limit term freedom in contract law. In economic terms, externalities are costs (negative)[17] or benefits (positive) imposed on non-consenting

[13] Ronald H Coase, 'The Problem of Social Cost' (1960) 3 Journal of Law and Economics 837.

[14] Oliver Hart and Bengt Holmström, 'The Theory of Contract', in T Bewley (ed), *Proceedings of the Advances in Economics and Econometrics, Econometric Society Monographs, Fifth World Congress* (CUP 1987) 71.

[15] Richard Craswell, 'Freedom of Contract' (University Of Chicago Law School Chicago Unbound, Coase-Sandor Working Paper Series in Law and Economics no. 33, 1995) <chicagounbound.uchicago.edu/cgi/viewcontent.cgi?article=1215&context=law_and_economics> accessed 12 October 2023.

[16] Trebilcock (n 8).

[17] Oil pollution is a negative externality due to the harm it imposes on man and the environment during offshore drilling operations.

third parties from an exchange transaction.[18] In everyday activities, we can say that it is rare for a transaction to avoid impacting third parties. In this respect, limiting parties' freedom of contract would undermine the private ordering model. However, specific third-party effects act as limiting factors on freedom of contract. This outcome is so whether one looks at the matter from the point of view of welfare economics or of autonomy-rights liberalism. A classic example is pollution risk allocation in gross negligence cases in the oil and gas industry.

In the oil and gas industry, participants exercise their freedom of contract in allocating risks. This freedom accounts for parties' use of mutual indemnity or exclusion clauses as a defence to liability arising from negligence and gross negligence. Scholars believe that transferring liability for negligence caused by one party to another is in line with the nature of oil and gas operations. However, doing the same for grossly negligent conduct is contrary to public policy, which seeks to protect the public's interest.[19] Moreover, the public in this context refers to non-consenting third parties. Thus, the public's interest is a ground on which the law could limit the freedom of contract. In a more critical examination of the concept, Holmes J noted thus: 'I confess that I think that the right to make contracts at will that has been derived from the word "liberty" in the [Constitutional] amendments has been stretched to its extreme by [these] decisions.'[20] This statement lends credence to the idea that using an exclusion clause as a defence for gross negligence stretches the limits of freedom of contract beyond the autonomous ideals of liberalism.

During offshore drilling operations, when oil pollution occurs due to a party's gross negligence, it damages the environment and affects people and their sources of livelihood. Nevertheless, the contract is usually between an operator and a contractor. Hence, to protect the environment and people's interest, contracts that allow for pollution risk to be allocated in gross negligence cases can be limited, thus reducing the scope of the parties' freedom to contract. The impact of the externalities on third parties becomes a reason for limiting the liberty to agree on terms that parties consider to be in their interest.

3.3 PUBLIC POLICY AND THE FREEDOM OF CONTRACT IN RISK ALLOCATION

3.3.1 What Is Public Policy?

The government exercises the primary duty of policy-making to protect its citizens from harm by mainstreaming the relevant legislation or policy to prevent or discourage conduct that could result in harm. Public policy is dynamic, primarily because its meaning depends on the needs of society at the time. However, the

[18] Brownsword (n 5).
[19] Smith I Azubuike, 'Rethinking Operator-Contractor Risk Allocation in a Post-Macondo Era' (PhD Thesis, University of Dundee 2019).
[20] *Lochner v New York* 198 US 45 (1905) 45.

conservative view of most courts is that public policy is determined by legislation and judicial decisions, not people's opinions. Because the meaning of public policy is dynamic, it has been described as 'an unruly horse', especially when interpreting contractual clauses.[21]

An agreement is considered contrary to public policy if it could harm society or the state or result in a breach of law. Where this happens, a court could hold against enforcing the agreement for being contrary to public policy. Although the traditional role of a court is to enforce contracts, agreements contrary to public policy provide an exception to the conventional function of a court. Thus, public policy consideration could act as a basis to invalidate a contract for being against the public good.

From a normative perspective, public policy can be viewed as the principles, primarily unwritten, on which social laws are established, or the principle that injury to the public good is a basis for refusing to enforce the legality of an agreement or transaction.[22] Public policy is a genuinely trans-substantive legal doctrine that exists in all legal systems as a ground for denying the enforcement of specific legal contracts.[23] It is discussed in the sense of policies pursued and enacted by governments,[24] as a rule that supersedes parties' contractual agreements, as a policy that limits the application of foreign law in the conflict of laws,[25] and as a bar on the enforcement of foreign arbitral awards or judgments.[26] An exact definition of public policy may not be possible due to its multidimensional character. However, Lord Truro's classical definition has been echoed in several courts in the US. In the notable case of *Egerton v Brownlow*, Lord Truro stated that, '[P]ublic policy is that principle of law which holds that no subject can lawfully do that which tended to be injurious to the public, or against the good of the public . . . in relation to the administration of the law'.[27] It has also been stated that public policy is a principle of judicial legislation or interpretation established on the community's present needs.[28] Farshad Ghadoosi categorised public policy into three aspects: public interest, public morality and public security.[29] This categorisation indicates that public policy seeks to achieve what is for the public's good. As such,it could

[21] David A Friedman, 'Bringing Order to Contracts Against Public Policy' (2012) 39 Florida State University Law Review 563.

[22] Oxford Lexico, 'Public Policy' (*Oxford Lexico*) <www.dictionary.com/browse/public-policy> accessed 12 October 2023.

[23] Farshad Ghodoosi, 'The Concept of Public Policy in Law: Revisiting the Role of the Public Policy Doctrine in the Enforcement of Private Legal Arrangements' (2016) 94(3) Nebraska Law Review 685, 713.

[24] Clarke E Cochran and others, *American Public Policy: An Introduction* (10th edn, Wadsworth 2012).

[25] Herbert F Goodrich, 'Public Policy in the Law of Conflicts' (1930) 36(2) West Virginia Law Quarterly and the Bar 152.

[26] Ghodoosi (n 23) 698.

[27] [1853] 4 HLC 1. In *Hornor v Graves* [1831] 131 Eng Rep 284, 287, the court provided a similar definition when it stated that 'whatever is injurious to the interest of the public is void, on grounds of public policy.'

[28] Percy H Winfield, 'Public Policy in the English Common Law' (1928) 42(1) Harvard Law Review 77.

[29] Ghodoosi (n 23) 685.

be seen as a practice, law or conduct that promotes the public's good and discourages harm to society.

Under common law, agreements incompatible with public policy are unenforceable.[30] The reason is expressed in the Latin phrase, *contra bonos mores*, which means contrary to public policy or morals.[31] *Ex ante*, public policy serves as a caution to private parties that a court will not endorse contracts prejudicial to public interests. Where parties have already entered into such an agreement, public policy then plays the anchor role in justifying an invalidation of the contract even where no evidence exists that a legal obligation has been contravened.[32] Courts do not enforce contracts that run contrary to public policy, to discourage contracting parties from bargains that are incompatible with public policy in the first place.[33]

Although the broad essence of public policy is not disputed, courts face challenges when implementing it. A case in point was when public policy violation was considered by Barbier J in the BP case. Barbier J noted that a party can only receive an indemnity for its gross negligence concerning compensatory damages, but not punitive damages, which could arise where a party was found grossly negligent.[34] Again, parties' bargaining power can present challenges to a court, especially where their bargaining power is roughly equal. This may affect a court's assessment, making it more likely to allow the indemnity clause on the freedom of contract policy as against public policy concerns. The court stated that

> [a]s to the 'freedom of contract' argument, Transocean and BP appear to have held 'roughly' equal bargaining power. Transocean and BP are sophisticated entities that engaged in a potentially lucrative and obviously risky endeavour. The Drilling Contract reflects that they attempted to allocate risk ahead of time, ostensibly in the hopes that some degree of certainty may be brought to the risks inherent in that undertaking. Given that their bargaining power was roughly equal, the 'freedom of contract' policy weighs in favour of upholding the indemnity.[35]

It is worthy of note that where a clause in an agreement conflicts with public policy, it does not necessarily render the entire contract unenforceable. The unenforceability will depend on whether the relevant clause is separable from the contract as a whole.[36] In both developed[37] and developing[38] countries, there

30 Restatement (Second) of Contracts § 195 (1979).
31 Jeanne Cilliers, 'When Contracts against Public Policy Are Void' (1994) 2(3) Juta's Business Law 139.
32 Zeeshan Mansoor, 'Contracts Contrary to Public Policy under English and Dutch Law: The Case of Agreements Commercialising the Human Body' [2014] 1 European Journal of Comparative Law and Governance 297.
33 Adam Badawi, 'Harm, Ambiguity, and the Regulation of Illegal Contracts' (2009) 17(2) George Mason Law Review 483.
34 *United States v BP Exploration & Production Inc (Re Oil Spill by the Oil Rig 'Deepwater Horizon' in the Gulf of Mexico, on April 20, 2010)* 21 F Supp 3d 657 (ED LA 2014) Phase 1 trial.
35 ibid.
36 Cilliers (n 31).
37 Mansoor (n 32) 297.
38 Matthew Kruger, 'The Role of Public Policy in the Law of Contract, Revisited' (2011) 128 South African Law Journal 712.

is convergence in recognition of public interest and the types of agreements considered as contravening public policy and good morals. Generally, an agreement that does not provide responsibility for a legal wrong will be unenforceable for being contrary to public policy, where such an agreement is likely to harm public interests.[39] In *Kalisch-Jarcho v City of New York*, it was held that an exculpatory agreement would not absolve a party from liability in all circumstances, no matter how flat and unqualified the terms are. The reason is that public policy will not apply to indemnity for grossly negligent acts.[40] Again, contracts intrinsically linked to the public interest have been declared unenforceable for violating public policy objectives.[41]

Additionally, a piece of legislation may be the basis for the non-enforcement of a contract on public policy considerations. This situation arises where a regulation prohibits the enforcement of certain agreements or where public policy outweighs the parties' interests in the contract. In this regard, determining whether a contract is unenforceable on the grounds of public policy depends on the context, which requires a consideration of the facts of a given situation and the applicable public policy concern.[42] The Restatement of Contract provides that public interest in enforcing a specific term, among other things, is a factor that should be taken into account in weighing the interest in enforcing a given provision. Again, in considering public policy against enforcement of a contractual term, it has been noted in the Restatement of Contract that regard should be to

> (a) the strength of that policy as manifested by legislation or judicial decisions, (b) the likelihood that a refusal to enforce the term will further that policy, (c) the seriousness of any misconduct involved and the extent to which it was deliberate, and (d) the directness of the connection between that misconduct and the term.[43]

From a broad perspective, the principle of public policy does not allow a person or government official to perform an act that tends to injure the public,[44] notwithstanding the nature of the transaction. The unenforceability of a contract does not arise from legally recognised vitiating elements of it but from factors that will infringe specific policies entirely independent of the parties' agreement. These factors may rest on the law or a court's initiative that such an agreement could harm the public.[45] This perception is based on social laws and founded on the principle

[39] William SM Knight, 'Public Policy in English Law' (1922) 38 LQR 207.

[40] *Kalisch-Jarcho v City of New York* 448 NE 2d 413 (NY 1983).

[41] *Maryland-National Capital Park & Planning Commission v Washington National Arena* 386 A 2d 1216 (MD 1978); *Wolf v Ford* 644 A 2d 522 (MD 1994).

[42] John Lillig, 'Magic or Misery: HBCUs, Guarantee Contracts, and Public Policy' (2009) 6 DePaul Journal of Sports Law & Contemporary Problems 41, 57.

[43] Restatement (Second) of Contracts § 178 (1981).

[44] The Free Dictionary, 'Public Policy' <legal-dictionary.thefreedictionary.com/Public+Policy> accessed 12 October 2023.

[45] Hugh G Beale and others, *Contract: Cases and Material* (5th edn, OUP 2008) 1069.

that the enforcement of a contract may be denied where it will cause injury to the public good[46] or where its harmful tendency is clear.[47] Nevertheless, the perceived economic efficiency or social utility of an activity may be a basis for allowing some degree of negligence against the public interest.[48] This exception is not absolute as a limit exists to which public policy would allow private legal acts of citizens (that is, freedom of contract), especially in cases of gross negligence. For instance, the economic efficiency consideration will not apply where a public policy outweighs the interest in a contract; such a contract will be unenforceable.[49]

3.3.2 *Public Policy – An Unruly Horse?*

The public policy doctrine appears unified and easy to apply. However, applying the doctrine to the parties' agreement is the real challenge. This challenge has led to its reference as an 'unruly horse'. This notion arises from the understanding that public policy provides an opportunity for judicial law-making and flexibility as society's perception of what constitutes 'public policy' changes.[50] Public policy is often critiqued since it involves using a particular set of values and policy considerations, including justice, fairness and equity. The reason for the critique is that it can result in contract uncertainty when applied without care.

The criticism against public policy has often been stated, quite illustratively, through the symbolic use of a horse. A long time ago, Burrough J observed:

> I, for one, protest, as my Lord has done, against arguing too strongly upon public policy. It is a very unruly horse, and when once you get astride it you never know where it will carry you. In *Driefontein Consolidated Mines Ltd v Jansen*, Smith MR carried the analogy further: 'This public policy is a high horse to mount and is difficult to ride when you have mounted it.' If I may be permitted to add to this equine analogy, frequently, as in the present case, this high horse attempts to stampede in opposite directions at the same time.[51]

In *Richardson v Mellish*,[52] the court called public policy 'a very unruly horse' because its application may extend to transactions not expressly prohibited by legislation. In this sense, some scholars argue that public policy lies in legislative and not judicial discretion.[53] It has been stated that the legislator, not a court or parties, should

[46] The Free Dictionary (n 44).
[47] Edwin Peel, *The Law of Contract* (13th edn, Sweet & Maxwell 2011) 485.
[48] Ghodoosi (n 23) 708.
[49] 'A Law and Economics Look at Contracts against Public Policy' (2006) 119(5) Harvard Law Review 1449.
[50] Sacha Judd, 'The Unruly Horse Put Out to Pasture: The Doctrine of Public Policy in the Modern Law Of Contract' (1998) 8 Auckland University Law Review 686.
[51] *Mabao v Nel's Melkery (Pty) Ltd* (1979) 4 SA 358 (W), 361–2, quoting *Driefontein* (1901) 17 TLR 604, 605.
[52] *Richardson v Mellish* (1824) 130 Eng Rep 294.
[53] John Shand, 'Unblinkering the Unruly Horse: Public Policy in the Law of Contract' (1972) 30(1) CLJ 144.

determine public policy.[54] However, enforcing private legal contracts could be prevented due to their conflict with a public policy deduced from legislation, rules made by a court,[55] or even a policy without a legislative foundation. Although understanding a public policy without a legislative source could seem like a common law adjudicative approach, it could even be broader than this.[56] Public policy could be considered under the law and economic approaches as protection for parties in the contract (paternalism), protection for third parties outside the contract (negative externalities) and as a means of wealth redistribution.[57]

Regardless of the observed judicial view, public policy has hitherto been accepted as a basis on which a court may decline to enforce the terms of an agreement, despite the parties having freely and voluntarily accepted these terms.[58] Indeed, public policy has now become firmly recognised as an instrument of judicial control over contractual enforcement. An old legal maxim, *nullus commodum capere potest de injuria sua propria*, provides that no one can benefit from their own wrongful act. In a modern context, this translates into whether it is expected for a person to be grossly negligent in their conduct and still use a mutual indemnity agreement as a protection against liability.

At its most basic level, public policy is the avenue by which society, through the courts, maintains some form of control over the contractual dealings of individuals; although, by the nature of the principle of freedom of contract, individuals are generally free to enter contracts with whom and on what terms they think fit, and courts will, by way of the principle of *pacta sunt servanda* ('agreements must be kept'), generally enforce these agreements. However, courts have thought it essential to retain a residual power to reject the enforcement of the terms of a contract when to do so would be contrary to public policy.

Public policy, by its standard nature, is dynamic and depends on the context it applies in. Its nature is unlike rules that may be static. Public policy has little or no practical meaning or content without context. Instead, it functions as an assemblage of broad principles and more specific rules of contract law. When courts examine these principles and rules of contract law, which they regard as policy considerations, they can give meaning and content to the concept of public policy. One of the essential features of public policy is that it is not a static concept: it is dynamic, and its content evolves as social conditions and basic freedoms advance. It is worth noting that the dynamic posture of public policy means that there is no closed list of considerations that a judge is limited to considering when discussing public policy.[59] This perspective means that a judge is armed with a 'basket' of policy concerns when faced with a public policy question. From this basket, the judge is obligated, in a particular case, to select those concerns that are significant

[54] ibid.
[55] Ghodoosi (n 23) 694.
[56] Friedman (n 21).
[57] Ghodoosi (n 23) 709.
[58] Kruger (n 38) 712.
[59] ibid 713.

to the facts of that case, and then balance these considerations against each other to determine whether a given contractual provision should be enforced or not. The result of this identification and balancing process is what courts refer to as public policy.

3.3.3 *Public Policy and the Exercise of the Freedom of Contract*

The sanctity of agreements occupies a fundamental position in contract law. Public policy generally supports this age-old position, especially when the contract was entered freely and voluntarily. The essence of this support is to preserve public morals and ensure that people respect their commitments and are bound by what they agree to do. This is the fundamental objective that modern contract law aims to achieve.[60] Even courts recognise this libertarian proposition and protect the choices of parties. Little wonder, Jeanne Cilliers notes that courts should not be in a hurry to interfere and declare a contract incompatible with public policy, except where the element of public harm is evident.[61]

The question may be whether the concepts of voluntary, informed consent and freedom from state interference are indeed symbols of the contemporary contract system. While contracts are enforceable based on freedom of contract, the doctrine is not absolute. Contracts could be declared unenforceable on the grounds of public policy where, for a 'promise or other terms of an agreement . . . the interest in its enforcement is outweighed in the circumstances by a public policy against the enforcement of such terms.'[62] This means that where the contracting of parties will corrupt public morals or harm the public, public policy will seek to protect the public's interest and ensure public safety.

Suppose we apply the above analysis to the oil and gas industry's risk allocation practice in gross negligence cases. In that case, contractual terms and practices that will negatively influence parties' behaviour or encourage bad oilfield practices that could harm society will be unenforceable due to public policy. This public policy objective has become a valuable tool when assessing mutual indemnity as a shield against liability for gross negligence. As the Chief Counsel noted in his report on the Macondo oil pollution, using mutual indemnity clauses as a shield against liability for pollution arising from gross negligence has created a culture of lack of responsibility.[63] The interest of the few in enforcing the use of mutual indemnity as a protection against liability for gross negligence under notions of freedom of contract is outweighed by the interest of the very many who are affected by oil pollution, property damage or death of personnel arising from a

[60] Daniel Kie Hart, 'Contract Law Now – Reality Meets Legal Fiction' (2011) 41(1) University of Baltimore Law Review 2.

[61] Cilliers (n 31).

[62] Myanna Dellinger, 'Trophy Hunting Contracts: Unenforceable for Reasons of Public Policy' (2016) 41(3) Columbia Journal of Environmental Law 395.

[63] National Commission on the BP Deepwater Horizon Oil Spill and Offshore Drilling, *Macondo: The Gulf Oil Disaster* (Chief Counsel Report, 2011).

party's gross negligence. Limiting the extreme use of a mutual indemnity contract is consistent with the precautionary principle in environmental law and public policy, primarily as the latter focuses on the substance of contractual terms and the nature of the outcomes.

Freedom of contract promotes welfare when it encourages an agreement that prevents harm as against a contract that facilitates harm. Allowing parties to a contract to use a mutual indemnity agreement as a shield against liability for gross negligence could lead to arbitrary conduct. If permitted in this regard, freedom of contract will conflict with public safety, moral and interest, which public policy seek to protect. Some judicial opinion suggests that a court has a role to play in protecting the public from contracts that violate the public policy of harm prevention. For example, in *Egerton v Brownlow*, Lord Pollock noted that if public welfare were to be removed from his thinking process, he would be abandoning the functions of his office. He further noted:

> It may be that judges are no better able to discern what is for the public good than other experienced and enlightened members of the community, but that is no reason for their refusing to entertain the question and declining to decide upon it. Is it, or is it not, a part of our common law, that is a new and unprecedented case, where the mere caprice of the testator is to be weighed against the public good, the public good should prevail? In my judgment, it is.[64]

In emphasising a court's role in applying public policy objectives in contracts, Walter Gellhorn notes that judges represent the community's conscience. As such, they should declare contracts against the public's interest unenforceable.[65] The reason is that aiding their enforcement incentivises practices and conduct against public welfare. Undesirable conduct could be discouraged, or anticipated results may be achieved by altering the practice or conditioning the enjoyment of privilege upon submitting some other privilege. Sometimes, the contract may not violate legislation; however, it should be invalidated if it runs against public policy. The use of judicial opinions is not rare and is accepted as suitable support in arriving at a related determination. In most jurisdictions, there may not be policies prohibiting certain conduct. In such a situation, reference could be made to the laws in other jurisdictions.[66] The essence of the reference to other laws is founded on the universal application of public policy for the interests of society. Legislative opinions could also be applied in a similar circumstance to enact laws that promote public interests.

A notable point of convergence when discussing public policy and contracts is that the focus is on contracts that are against public interest or may cause harm to the public.[67] The focus is context specific and relates to contracts where

[64] [1853] 4 HLC 1.

[65] Walter Gellhorn, 'Contracts and Public Policy' (1935) 35 Columbia Law Review 679.

[66] ibid.

[67] John Plattner, 'Contracts – Public Policy – Contracts against Liability for Negligence' (1960) 36 (2) North Dakota Law Review 141.

elements of public harm are evident. In such situations, a court will invalidate or refuse to give effect to any contract terms which invalidate liability for gross negligence. In the oil and gas industry, parties are free to allocate risks in a manner that suits them, including liability arising from gross negligence. However, the BP Deepwater Horizon accident and the report of the Presidential Committee on the BP oil spill highlighted issues of moral hazard in the risk allocation practice in the oil industry.[68] As noted by the Committee, moral hazard contributed to the accident and eventual damage that non-consenting third parties suffered in the BP oil spill. The BP oil spill shows that allowing contractual participants to use mutual indemnity as a shield against liability arising from gross negligence encourages moral hazard, affecting public interest since it harms society.

A pertinent question is whether the risk allocation practice prevents third parties from claiming compensation where they suffer damage. The practice does not prevent third-party claims but places the responsibility of actual payment on another party who may not have caused the damage. This could encourage conduct that causes harm to society and loss to a contracting party. The role of public policy is to mandate the avoidance of negative externalities through positive incentives – for example, good oilfield practices in the oil industry – to prevent harmful effects on the public.[69] Since public policy is against contracts that do not align with the public interest, it would not enforce a mutual indemnity contract that provides a shield against liability for gross negligence.

Regarding contracts that should protect third parties, some scholars believe that contracts that may result in oil pollution or prevent competition will negatively impact third parties and should not be enforceable.[70] While this view is debatable, it may be safe to say that the key phrase should be 'adverse negative impact' and not just a negative impact on third parties. This addition is so that there are contracts whose social utility benefits third parties but may still impact third parties. In this vein, contracts allowing the enforcement of indemnity clauses for mere negligence resulting in harm could be allowed due to the utility of hydrocarbons. However, where the contract allows a particular party to use specific provisions as a defence for its gross negligence, public policy would prevent the enforcement of such a clause. Moreover, as a general rule, the limitation of liability for gross negligence is not allowed under common law, the rationale being the protection of others against unreasonable risk of harm.[71]

[68] National Commission on the BP Deepwater Horizon Oil Spill and Offshore Drilling, *Deep Water: The Gulf Oil Disaster and the Future of Offshore Drilling* (Report to the President of the United States of America, 2011).

[69] Ghodoosi (n 23) 713.

[70] Frank H Easterbrook and Daniel R Fischel, *The Economic Structure of Corporate Law* (Harvard University Press 1996) 23.

[71] Imran Naeemullah, 'Strong Headwinds: Statutes, Responsibility-Shifting, and Public Policy Continue to Frustrate Indemnity Agreements in the Offshore Oil and Gas Industry' (2013) 38(1) Tulane Maritime Law Journal 281.

3.3.4 Public Policy and Risk Allocation behind the Veil of Ignorance

Behind the Rawlsian veil of ignorance, no one knows who would be responsible for severely wrongful acts. This lack of awareness puts parties in a situation where they would want to allocate risk in a manner that protects their interests.

3.3.4.1 Conceptual Understanding of the Veil of Ignorance

The veil of ignorance is an abstract concept which, like most experiments, may never be carried out in the ordinary sense of the phrase. Nevertheless, it can be applied when examining issues concerning fairness, to understand the idea of equity, justice, social status and morality in an organised pattern. As an aspect of the social contract theory, the veil of ignorance allows scholars to test ideas for fairness in society, just like the contractual practice of risk allocation in gross negligence cases used by participants in the oil industry. The idea of a veil of ignorance is espoused by John Rawls, who asks people to imagine that they are behind an imaginary veil – the veil of ignorance – and are therefore unaware of their own identity. They are unaware of their privileges, class, difficulties or even their personality.[72] Rawls highlights that exceptional features of people's psychology, such as their aversion to risk or liability and the circumstances of their society, are unknown to them. Their existence is analogous to an impartial group charged with designing a new practice or society with its concept of justice. The veil partially masks people's consciousness and knowledge of the consequences of their actions. This leaves them to make decisions without knowing how they will be affected.

Behind the veil of ignorance, the fact known to parties is that their society is subject to conditions of justice whose outcome should be fair and in the interest of everyone. Behind this imaginary veil, practices are agreed upon and decisions are made in the interests and for the happiness of society. As such, the veil of ignorance lays the foundation for a procedure that will be fair to all – operators, contractors, government and society. For this reason, specific circumstances which place people in a position where they are free to exploit social, contractual and natural situations to their advantage will not be chosen. For instance, where a clause exempts a party from liability arising from gross negligence, such a clause will not apply when parties are standing behind the veil of ignorance. The reason is simple: such a clause will give a party undue advantage over and above the interest of other parties and the non-consenting public. Therefore, parties will choose principles that will result in outcomes they are ready to live with, irrespective of the generation they belong to later.

As a cognitive test, the veil of ignorance is influential because people's views regarding what is just and unjust depend on their experiences and the situations they find themselves in. None of that situation exists on the other side of the veil

[72] John Rawls, 'Justice as Fairness' and 'A Theory of Justice', in Robert C Solomon and Mark C Murphy (eds), *What is Justice?: Classic and Contemporary Readings* (OUP 1990).

of ignorance. Strictly speaking, the subsequent society, idea or practice should be fair to all. Following this, scholars have provided valuable guides to understanding the test of fairness behind a veil of ignorance. For example, Michael Shermer describes '[t]he Fairness Principle: When contemplating a moral action, imagine that you do not know if you will be the moral doer or receiver, and when in doubt, err on the side of the other person.'[73] Similarly, Spencer J Maxcy notes:

> Imagine that you have set for yourself the task of developing a totally new social contract for today's society. How could you do so fairly? Although you could never actually eliminate all of your personal biases and prejudices, you would need to take steps at least to minimize them. Rawls suggests that you imagine yourself in an original position behind a veil of ignorance. Behind this veil, you know nothing of yourself and your natural abilities or your position in society. You know nothing of your sex, race, nationality, or individual tastes. Behind such a veil of ignorance, all individuals are simply specified as rational, free, and morally equal beings. You do know that in the 'real world,' however, there will be a wide variety in the natural distribution of natural assets and abilities, and that there will be differences of sex, race, and culture that will distinguish groups of people from each other.[74]

When people are unaware of the part of society they belong to, their ignorance will logically elicit an egalitarian and fair discussion, as no one wants to belong to a disadvantaged group. Cognitive prejudices fade behind the veil of ignorance and thought prejudices melt away. Those standing behind this imaginary veil are rational thinkers who use probabilistic thinking to assess the prospect that they may be affected by any preferred measure.[75] These fictional thinkers hold no opinions for which to require validation. They also do not have any newly learned information to focus their attention on. The only inducement they are biased towards is their survival, equivalent to protecting the entire group. They cannot disadvantage any group as they could be part of it.

As Rawls notes, the decision of those standing behind the imaginary veil of ignorance will be for everyone to possess rights and liberties, power and opportunity, income and wealth, and the conditions necessary for self-respect. They will want to agree that decisions regarding applicable principles and practices regulating public and private exchanges should be in the interest of all. Rawls further advances that, for these circumstances to take place, the people behind the veil of ignorance must find out how to attain the components of justice. These components are:

> everyone must have the best possible life which does not cause harm to others, everyone must be able to improve their position, and any inequalities must be present solely if they benefit everyone.[76]

[73] Michael Shermer, *The Moral Arc: How Science and Reason Lead Humanity Toward Truth, Justice, and Freedom* (Henry Holt and Co 2015).

[74] Spencer J Maxcy, *Ethical School Leadership* (Rowman & Littlefield Education 2002).

[75] Farnam Street, 'The Fairness Principle: How the Veil of Ignorance Helps Test Fairness' <fs.blog/2017/10/veil-ignorance> accessed 12 October 2023.

[76] Rawls (n 73) 181.

Although decisions behind the veil may sometimes be unfavourable, a cognitive experiment indicates that ignorance does not always affect society. However, in certain circumstances, it can lead to vigorous social structures.

Behind the veil of ignorance in risk allocation, not knowing where they might be – an operator, drilling contractor or part of the general public – parties would want to design a contract that protects the interest of everyone. As such, parties would not design contracts that allow the use of contractual terms or clauses to avoid liability, especially when the liability arises from gross negligence.

3.3.4.2 Hypothetical Risk Allocation behind the Veil of Ignorance in the Hydrocarbon Industry

As earlier stated, the veil of ignorance is an abstract concept, with people standing on both sides of the imaginary veil. In our context, these people include the government, the public, operators and drilling contractors, given our focus on the hydrocarbon industry. Although the veil does not reveal the identities of the parties to allow for a fair agreement in the interests of all, it highlights the unequal position of the parties – both contractual and non-consenting third parties. As such, an essential factor that needs to be considered when designing a risk allocation practice behind the veil of ignorance is the parties' positions and how the contract may affect them.

The position of the government behind this imaginary veil is crucial. The government's essential role emanates from its right to issue the required permit to an operator to search for, bore for and get hydrocarbon. The government's interest is for the operator to conduct its operations according to law, and to ensure an accident-free drilling activity with zero harm to people and the environment. Behind the veil, in issuing the permit, the government needs to consider the safety measures that must be observed in every phase of exploration and exploitation. It also needs to consider how the contract between the operator and the drilling contractor will protect people and the environment – non-consenting third parties. One way of doing this is to regulate how parties deal with clauses excluding liability arising from gross negligence.

Another group behind the veil is the operators' group, which is responsible under state law for conducting the operations as required by law and assuming liability when a downside occurs. The operator is responsible to the government as the holder of the permit or as the person in charge of the operation. The operator receives the long-term financial upside in the event of commercial discovery and continuous hydrocarbon exploitation. This factor gives the operator an advantage, hence its obligation to the government. In contracting behind the veil with the drilling contractor to drill a well, the operator needs to consider the possibility that the contract could encourage negative externalities to non-consenting third parties or result in transaction costs. As a result, the clause in their agreement should be a disincentive for moral hazard. An example is to make parties to the contract liable for gross negligence to the extent of the benefit they receive from the petroleum activity.

The contractor has no direct link to the government as they are answerable to the operator who hired them. The contractor's responsibility to the operator arises from the contract with the operator. This situation includes a spill or damage during petroleum operations. However, behind the veil of ignorance, transaction costs and externalities will be managed through the agreement by discouraging behaviours that could lead to damage and cost. An examples is making parties responsible for damages arising from gross negligence. In this case, the responsible party will be liable to the extent of the benefit they receive. The contractor will not take responsibility for the operator's grossly negligent conduct, thus reducing the contractor's exposure to cost. There is also the contractors' group, whose interest is in a successful drilling and a financial reward in the form of a day rate. Generally, contractors do not like to assume responsibility for certain risks when they are negligent or grossly negligent because they are not in charge of the operations and do not get any financial upside like the operator.

The last group, the public (non-consenting third parties), will be affected by the petroleum operation should a downside occur. Their interest is for the petroleum operations to be carried out in a manner that will not impact their livelihood or cause harm to them. They would not like the actors in the matrix to encourage practices that will affect them. Public policy protects their interest. As Rawls highlighted, the parties behind the veil are unaware of which position or group they will belong to when the veil is lifted and the law or practice that will apply. With this in mind, how will the parties design a risk allocation contract, taking into cognisance the interests of all the parties by ensuring that people live the lives they desire without harming others? How will those behind the veil ensure that everyone can improve their position and that, if inequality exists, it will be in the interests of all and not of a single group? In addressing the issue of using mutual indemnity as a shield against liability for gross negligence, the question is whether a person behind the veil of ignorance would design a contract that allows a party to walk away after that party's conduct has resulted in liability arising from gross negligence.

3.3.4.3 Assessing the Veil of Ignorance in Gross Negligence Cases

The veil of ignorance provides a theoretical foundation for critiquing the practice of risk allocation that the oil industry applies. However, it must be noted that this philosophical underpinning does not consider the parties' various positions in the oil industry, as it operates under the assumption that all the parties are equal. For instance, in the oil industry, the state stands behind the veil with sovereign power, the operator has the advantage of a long-term financial reward in the event of a commercial discovery, the drilling contractor benefits from the day rate it receives, while the public gets no direct benefit. However, from a public policy perspective, the veil of ignorance seeks to promote justice and disincentivise harm in the interests of participants and non-consenting third parties. Therefore, the veil of ignorance underpins the possible imbalance that will arise should a party impose the burden of gross negligence on another party that did not cause harm or loss.

It stands to reason that the industry practice of risk allocation provides a platform for imbalance to thrive, which can burden society in the form of harm or loss. To put a burden on society or a contracting party is to be unjust to society or the party. Being unjust is not in step with the theoretical allocation of risk behind the veil of ignorance. The allocation of risk behind the veil of ignorance would not encourage a party to use a mutual indemnity agreement as a shield against liability for gross negligence. Nevertheless, it will allow for the assumption of responsibility arising from grossly negligent conduct in line with the proportion of benefit the party receives.

Generally, it may be argued that a considerable upside balances an operator's risk upon successful drilling. However, the Macondo accident has shown otherwise. BP suffered losses in shares and paid over US$50 billion in compensation and cleanup costs when the accident occurred.[77] This financial burden arising from the Macondo accident emphasises that operators can suffer considerable losses in the event of a downside caused by a drilling contractor's gross negligence. Again, arguments may be advanced that a contract identifies who will pay compensation for damage and losses to members of society or fines to the government. Nevertheless, compensation does not mean a return to the status quo. It is only a palliative measure that often leaves society with untold hardship. A classic example of this soothing measure can be seen in the aftermath of the Gulf of Mexico oil spill, which forced businesses around the accident area to close and caused economic hardship for many fishing communities around the Gulf of Mexico.

The solution lies in preventive practices, not compensation – a proactive rather than a reactive approach. An allocation behind the veil of ignorance supports a proactive practice in risk allocation between participants where liability arises from a party's gross negligence. The proactive approach is one that makes a party aware that it will assume responsibility for its gross negligence in some way, shape or form, and not one that enables it to leave the entire responsibility to another party who did not cause the harm or loss. If the philosophical underpinning is correct, then we can say that the industry practice is incompatible with the Rawlsian veil of ignorance, which seeks to protect all parties behind the veil. The Rawlsian philosophy supports a distributive approach to liability and the assumption that the responsible party should assume liability arising from gross negligence, albeit to the extent of its benefit. This approach creates a disincentive for bad oilfield practices which could result in harm or loss to all concerned.

3.4 SUSTAINABILITY DIMENSIONS IN RISK ALLOCATION

Sustainability is linked with how we interact with the environment daily, how we use natural resources and the consequences that can arise from the adverse impact of our engagement with the environment. The consequences of our activities on

[77] Reuters, 'BP Reaches $18.7 Billion Settlement over Deadly 2010 Spill', *Reuters* (2 July 2015) <www.reuters.com/article/2015/07/03/us-bp-gulfmexico-settlement-idUSKCN0PC1BW20150703> accessed 12 October 2023.

the environment affect present and future generations since an impacted environment shapes our living patterns. People's activities revolve around the environment, and petroleum activities directly affect the marine and onshore environment when there is oil pollution on land or offshore.

3.4.1 Concept of Sustainability

Sustainability arises from the need to move from old practices into innovative ways of doing things with less impact on the ecosystem, in the interests of people and the environment. The transition of society towards sustainability depends on what it does and how it develops its activities, processes, practices and impact on the environment and social systems.[78] This understanding leads us to look at industry practices in the light of the following questions. The first question is whether the practice systematically degrades the environment and affects its ability to support human society. The second is whether the practice constitutes an increasing threat to the community and the business itself. These questions centre around business, society and the natural environment, and the answers to them provide a guide to the concept of sustainability.

This background leads us to the question of what sustainability means. The literature does not provide an exclusive meaning of the concept of sustainability. The reason is that the concept is still open to contest, with various opinions and perspectives.[79] The discussion around sustainable development by the United Nations World Commission on Environment and Development in 1987 helped shape the meaning of sustainability. The Commission noted that sustainable development is development that meets the needs of the current generation without compromising the future generation's ability to satisfy their needs.[80] This definition provides the foundation of a broad perspective on sustainability.

Some scholars see sustainability as 'any process that allows a business to create profit for its shareholders while safeguarding the environment and enhancing the lives of those with whom it interacts.'[81] A similar definition captures sustainability as 'the strategic inclusion and achievement of an organisation's social, environmental, and economic objectives in the methodical coordination of significant inter-organisational business processes for improving the long-term performance of the individual company and its supply chains.'[82] Other scholars see sustainability

78 Jesko Schulte and Soren Knuts, 'Sustainability Impact and Effects Analysis – A Risk Management Tool for Sustainable Product Development' (2022) 30 Sustainable Production and Consumption 737.

79 P Johnston and others, 'Reclaiming the definition of Sustainability' (2007) 14(1) Environmental Science and Pollution Research International 60; Robert O Vos, 'Defining Sustainability: A Conceptual Orientation' (2007) 82(2) Journal of Chemical Technology and Biotechnology 334.

80 World Commission on Environment and Development. *Our Common Future* (OUP 1987).

81 Andrew Savitz, *The Triple Bottom Line: How Today's Best-Run Companies are Achieving Economic, Social and Environmental Success – and How You Can Too* (John Wiley & Sons 2013).

82 Craig R Carter and Dale S Rogers, 'A Framework of Sustainable Supply Chain Management: Moving Towards New Theory' (2008) 38(5) International Journal of Physical Distribution & Logistics Management 360.

through a stakeholder lens. They view sustainability as the practices and objectives a company uses to meet the needs of its direct and indirect stakeholders without compromising its ability to meet future stakeholders' needs.[83] These stakeholders include employees, shareholders, clients, communities and pressure groups. Elkafi Hassini, Chirag Surti and Cory Searcy see sustainability in terms of how a company conducts its business. They note that sustainability relates to 'the ability to conduct business with a long-term goal of maintaining the wellbeing of the economy, environment and society'.[84] As earlier stated, the definition of sustainability encompasses a three-dimensional method that involves social, environmental and economic perspectives, which in turn comprise several notions and goals related to 'people', 'planet' and 'profit'.[85]

Despite the ubiquity of the concept and the variance in scale and contextual application of its definitions, there is some agreement about what constitutes sustainability. We can refer to sustainability as a concept which involves how we conserve the natural environment by avoiding practices that directly or indirectly impact our survival and the ecological, economic and social well-being of a community. Recent discussions about sustainability view it through the lens of environmental, social and governance perspectives (ESG).[86]

Aside from the definition, scholars have advanced methods to assess sustainability using the comcept of the 'triple bottom line' (TBL). This evaluation strategy has been expanded to cover environmental and social considerations beyond conventional investment return, profitability metrics and shareholder value.[87] Sustainability encompasses the crucial aspects of environmental, economic and social concerns. As such, it emphasises the need for economic, social and environmental performance to enhance the quality of human life. What this means is that a firm should not only focus on economic aspects but also on how to sustain the natural resources and the societies in which it operates.

The question of sustainability has been raised in offshore petroleum operations due to the possible environmental impacts of offshore drilling operations arising from drilling fluids, drill cuttings, offshore discharges, oil pollution and so on.[88] Scholars have identified a correlation between major oil and gas accidents and the

[83] Thomas Dyllick and Kai Hockerts, 'Beyond the Business Case for Corporate Sustainability' (2002) 11(2) Business Strategy and the Environment 130.

[84] Elkafi Hassini, Chirag Surti and Cory Searcy, 'A Literature Review and a Case Study of Sustainable Supply Chains with a Focus on Metrics' (2012) 140(1) International Journal of Production Economics 69.

[85] UNEP, *Protecting Our Planet Securing Our Future* (The World Bank 1998).

[86] Susanne Arvidsson and John Dumay, 'Corporate ESG Reporting Quantity, Quality and Performance: Where to Now for Environmental Policy and Practice?' (2022) 31(3), Business Strategy and the Environment 1091.

[87] Augustine Okeke, 'Towards Sustainability in the Global Oil and Gas Industry: Identifying Where the Emphasis Lies' (2021) 12 Environmental and Sustainability Indicators 100145.

[88] Paola Cardosode Almeida, Ofélia Fernandes-Araújo and José Luiz de Medeiros, 'Managing Offshore Drill Cuttings and Waste for Improved Sustainability' (2017) 165 Journal of Cleaner Production 143

absence of sustainable offshore petroleum practices.[89] The absence of consensus regarding the concept of sustainability makes it flexible and adaptable to many circumstances. In offshore petroleum operations, we can refer to sustainability as the practices and processes that participants in the industry apply to prevent the depletion of natural resources and mitigate damage to the environment. These practices consider the environmental and social dimensions necessary to maintain a balance so that the quality of human life does not decline.[90] The broad subject of sustainability encourages activities whose design is defined by social, human, and environmental dimensions for the long-term rather than on short-term gains. This long-term trajectory incorporates a TBL approach – people, planet and profit – and emphasises the need to explore petroleum sustainably. Thus, sustainability focuses on negotiating an effective compromise that addresses the social, economic and ecological objectives of competing interest groups.[91] The interest groups in this instance are the public and participants in offshore drilling operations. In the petroleum industry, sustainability assists in developing a framework that will enable oil and gas firms to frame decisions and practices regarding their environmental, social and human effects and ensure long-term value creation.

3.4.2 *Aspects of Sustainability*

In offshore petroleum operations, the environmental, social and economic dimensions of sustainability are evident in offshore oil pollution and other petroleum activities that adversely affect people and the marine environment. Each perspective incorporates offshore drilling-related concerns, highlighting how companies must conduct their operations to sustain society, the environment and the economy over several generations.

3.4.2.1 *Environmental Aspect*

Environmental sustainability relates to how we interact with nature, conserve natural resources and prevent deterioration of biodiversity, water, air and soil. This aspect is akin to sustainable development, which seeks to meet the needs of the present generation without compromising the ability of future generations to meet their own needs. It means that future generations will have the same opportunity to enjoy the earth's resources as the current generation. Inherent in environmental sustainability is the need to preserve the earth and return to a state of equilibrium

89 Mohamad Danish Anis and Tauseef Zia Siddiqui, 'Issues Impacting Sustainability in the Oil and Gas Industry' (2015) 5(4) Journal of Management and Sustainability 115, 116.

90 Smith I Azubuike, Susan Nakanwagi and Samuel C Dike, 'Utilizing Sustainability Assessment Framework to Obtain a Social License to Operate in Renewable Energy Projects' in Geoffrey Wood, J Górski and Gocke Mete (eds) *The Palgrave Handbook of Social License to Operate and Energy Transitions* (Palgrave Macmillan 2022).

91 Joerg Hartmann, 'Sustainability of Hydropower' in Jay H Lehr, Jack Keeley and Thomas B Kingery (eds) *Alternative Energy and Shale Gas Encyclopaedia* (John Wiley & Sons 2016).

after various shocks.[92] The objective of environmental sustainability is to maintain the balance of our planet within its boundaries and prevent global warming and loss of biodiversity and livelihood.

The environmental aspect of sustainability in offshore drilling operations focuses on the effects of drilling fluids, oil pollution, gas flaring and so on, on the health and well-being of coastal communities (for excample, air quality, respiratory allergies, asthma, water pollution) and the marine environment (for example, ecosystem damage, death of marine life). In particular, offshore drilling is a highly sensitive activity involving contact with the sea and the seabed to obtain oil and gas used for cooking, energy generation or powering machines. The complex drilling process involves using huge fixed or floating platforms to extract oil and natural gas reserves underneath the ocean. As such, offshore drilling can pose unacceptable risks to communities throughout the watershed, the economy, marine life and the environment, primarily when oil pollution occurs. An oil spill can also devastate beaches, wetlands and mudflats. In addition, it can result in the loss of heritage and fisheries and cause vast migration of sea creatures to other areas. This impact can affect the food system, agriculture and water quality in the area.[93]

The discharge of water-based and low-toxicity oil-based drilling muds and produced water can reach over two kilometres from the point of release. Consequently, the environmental impacts on neighbouring coastal communities can spread up to 320–480 kilometres from the discharge point. Moreover, the adverse effect of the discharge may persist in the sea for several years, and possibly longer for fragile ecosystems such as cold-water corals.[94] The situation is even worse for oil pollution. However, an effective strategy to reduce the risk of significant environmental harm typically encompasses regulation of the activity itself and a rethink of the industry practice of risk allocation, which encourages moral hazard. Although drilling an offshore oil well is arguably more challenging in deep-water environments, using a distributive risk allocation method will contribute to robust environmental management strategies for offshore oil and gas drilling operations. In general terms, it therefore means that environmental sustainability requires the exercise of a duty of care to avoid, minimize, maximize benefits of and assume responsibility for the adverse ecological effects of oil pollution.

Sustainability promotes objectives such as zero harm, which is necessary for offsetting adverse environmental impacts. Sustainable drilling operations lie at the heart of SDGs 3 (good health and well-being) and 6 (clean water and sanitation). They also connect with the 2030 UN Sustainable Development Agenda and the Paris Agreement for inclusive communities and greater protection from and resilience to climate change.[95]

[92] Alexey Cherepovitsyn, Anna Tsvetkova and Nadejda Komendantova, 'Approaches to Assessing the Strategic Sustainability of High-Risk Offshore Oil and Gas Projects' (2020) 8(12) Journal of Marine Science and Engineering 995.

[93] Azubuike, Nakanwagi and Dike (n 91).

[94] Erik E Cordes and others, 'Environmental Impacts of the Deep-Water Oil and Gas Industry: A Review to Guide Management Strategies' (2016) 4(58) Frontiers in Environmental Science 1.

[95] Azubuike, Nakanwagi and Dike (n 91).

3.4.2.2 Social Aspect

The social aspect of sustainability is connected to the impact of offshore drilling practices on the local community close to where the drilling operation is ongoing.[96] For example, this influence could relate to how the drilling activity impacts recreation, commercial fishing and tourism. Not much emphasis was laid on social sustainability previously, but the term is now gaining significant traction, especially in developing major projects.[97] Social sustainability considers how a project will affect people, and the need to develop policies and practices that prevent the occurrence of such an impact.

The social impact of offshore drilling operations can be multidimensional. It could be positive, negative, long term and short term. Hydrocarbon exploration supports energy generation, attracts people into an ongoing construction area and increases social relations. However, with this come issues about the project community's living standards and livelihoods, economic and physical displacement of community members and vulnerable groups, and concerns about safety, public health and living conditions.[98] In addition, the influx of people seeking employment on an offshore platform exerts pressure on community housing, lifestyle and healthcare and could result in a decline in social cohesion.[99]

Besides the social factors highlighted, oil pollution is a fundamental issue affecting social sustainability in offshore drilling projects. The oil discharged from drilling operations often affects communities' water bodies and their sources of recreation and livelihood. Oil pollution impacts their capacity for social engagement and existence. As such, a risk allocation practice that discourages moral hazard would mitigate the possibility of an offshore spill that might adversely affect local communities around the drilling site. Consideration of sustainability would require protecting public interests, vulnerable groups and individuals through drilling practices that place responsibility for gross negligence on the party at fault to forestall the likely occurrence of oil pollution.

3.4.2.3 Economic Aspect

Economic sustainability is connected to economic growth and how certain activities and practices assist the growth process in the long term without adversely affecting the environmental, social and cultural aspects of a community. It involves an assessment of the impact on economic activity and developing sustainable practices to create a more liveable future. Sustainability practices can mitigate the challenges brought about by humans' collective environmental footprint in several ways. For example, they can focus on reducing the depletion of the natural environment or advancing ways to reduce waste and limit oil pollution and

96 S Bathrinath and others, 'An Initiative towards Sustainability in the Petroleum Industry: A Review' (2021) 46 Materials Today: Proceedings 7798.
97 Cherepovitsyn, Tsvetkova and Komendantova (n 93).
98 Azubuike, Nakanwagi and Dike (n 91).
99 ibid.

carbon emissions. The crucial notion behind economic sustainability is promoting the planet's long-term well-being while discarding wasteful short-term processes in economic activities.

Petroleum operations are an economic activity that contribute to the growth of resource-rich nations, especially those that depend on petroleum revenue to fund development projects. Nevertheless, it has its flip side. The science available in 2023 is that petroleum activities contribute to global warming due to the release of carbon dioxide (CO_2).[100] If the science is correct, the oil industry must mainstream practices that promote the planet's long-term well-being and mitigate oil pollution. Furthermore, oil pollution affects economic activities such as commercial fishing, coastal businesses and the local economy, thus worsening the economic conditions of the local community near the spill site. For instance, the Gulf of Mexico oil pollution adversely impacted businesses, tariffs, incomes and profits, in addition to the struggles of the regional area at that time. The magnitude of the oil pollution can impair the functioning of the economy of certain areas. Besides the costs of the cleanup activities, the industries and individuals that depend on coastal resources can experience substantial economic losses.[101] Oil pollution can also hurt businesses due to disruption and loss of earnings because of a spill.

3.4.3 *Sustainability Risks*

The growing need for society to transition to low-carbon energy sources creates new requirements for sustainability approaches. This ever-increasing demand arises from evolving climate policies of several governments, environmental activism from the public and shareholders, and the changing investment strategy of oil majors to reduce carbon emissions.[102] Although hydrocarbon will likely remain an essential aspect of the global energy mix for the foreseeable future, the oil industry needs to develop proactive sustainability methods to contribute to the energy mix while identifying new pathways to transition to a low-carbon economy. As highlighted earlier, a distributive-style method of risk allocation in the oil and gas industry is one of the innovative ways of addressing the growing demand for sustainability requirements. In this line of thinking, David Branson states thus:

> To remain attractive to investors, oil and gas companies will need to develop and communicate proactive, integrated sustainability strategies that demonstrate continuously improving emissions performance, along with a clear position on diversification into low carbon forms of energy.[103]

[100] Intergovernmental Panel on Climate Change (IPCC), 'AR6 Climate Change 2022: Mitigation of Climate Change', (IPCC, Working Group III Contribution, 2022) <www.ipcc.ch/report/sixth-assessment-report-working-group-3> accessed 12 October 2023.

[101] Negar Dahi Taleghani and Mayank Tyagi, 'Impacts of Major Offshore Oil Spill Incidents on Petroleum Industry and Regional Economy' (2017) 139(2), Journal of Energy Resources Technology 022913.

[102] David Branson, 'Sustainability in the Oil and Gas Industry' (PwC, undated) <https://www.pwc.de/en/sustainability/sustainability-in-the-oil-and-gas-industry.html> accessed 13 October 2023.

[103] ibid.

The proactive strategy must also be attractive to the public and environmental activists, and those who will be impacted by oil pollution, either directly or indirectly. This requirement is akin to the Rawlsian veil of ignorance, where the final product of an agreement should reflect the interest of all – the government, oil industry participants and the public.

The above issues highlight specific challenges confronting the oil industry in the twenty-first century, commonly referred to as sustainability risks. These risks are either environmental or social in nature, and their occurrence significantly impacts the oil industry. It also comprises the possible opportunities a company has to adapt to the evolving environmental and social factors that confront its activities. As already highlighted, the oil and gas industry faces the challenges of climate change, oil pollution, safety risks, pressure from international organisations and governments, and community protest due to the impact of petroleum activities on the environment and livelihoods.[104] Changing this narrative requires the industry to develop a sustainability risk management strategy that aligns its objectives with its environmental trajectory. One strategy is repurposing the risk allocation practice for liability arising from gross negligence. This practice makes the responsible party bear liability for gross negligence in line with their benefit from the activity.

The pressure to boycott fossil fuels due to the impact of oil pollution and climate change is a risk confronting the petroleum industry. Innovative practice that prevents gas flaring and oil pollution is necessary to reduce the adverse impact of offshore petroleum operations on the environment and to combat the sustainability risk confronting the oil industry.

3.4.4 *Why Is Sustainability Essential to the Offshore Petroleum Industry?*

The traction sustainability has gained in the twenty-first century has made it a crucial survival issue for oil companies. This popularity is due to increasing pressure from environmental activists for more responsible practices during petroleum operations and new state regulations, which impact operations and costs. Again, the significance of sustainability lies in the need for the oil industry to match its sustainability goals with operational action.

Let us consider the importance of sustainability to the hydrocarbon industry.

3.4.4.1 *Reputation Risk Management*

Reputation risk is one of the several risks facing the oil and gas industry due to the complex and risky nature of petroleum operations, which sometimes result in oil pollution and environmental damage.[105] The hydrocarbon industry or a company

[104] Lyat Avidor Peleg, 'Where Is Sustainability on the Oil and Gas Agenda?' (*PRECOGNIZE*, 15 November 2021) <www.precog.co/blog/sustainability-challenges-oil-gas> accessed 14 October 2023.

[105] Evangelia Fragouli and Joseph Ekruka, 'Reputation Risk Management in the International Oil Companies' (2016) 8(2) International Journal of Information, Business and Management 245.

in the oil industry could be the focus of this type of risk. When it is the former, this risk tends to impact the activity of the oil industry positively or negatively, and could be called industry reputation risk. In the latter case, it relates to how a company's success or failure depends on society's perception of the company. When a company's reputation is good, it strengthens its market position and increases shareholder value. This generates great benefits for the company.[106] However, when a company's reputation is bad, it affects its share value and market presence. A good example is when BP's share value fell due to the Macondo oil spill in the Gulf of Mexico, which left the lives of cherished marine animals such as sea turtles and dolphins in danger.[107]

Oil pollution and environmental damage from petroleum activities give the oil industry negative publicity and a bad press image. In particular, the company involved in oil pollution is usually in the spotlight. For example, after the Macondo incident, BP was in the spotlight for a long time, and several claims against BP also gave the company a negative image in the eyes of the public. Aside from BP, major companies such as Shell and Exxon Mobil have suffered severe and, to some extent, irreparable damage from their operations due to oil pollution arising from their operations in places like Nigeria.[108] These incidents and the likes of them within the petroleum industry make reputation risk management essential, especially as pollution is an enabler of reputation damage in the industry.

Evangelia Fragouli and Joseph Ekruka advance that ensuring regulatory compliance, strong corporate governance and leadership, fulfilling corporate social responsibilities, meeting stakeholders' expectations and so on, can assist in managing a company's reputation.[109] Environmental and social disclosures have also been identified as a valuable tool for managing reputation risk.[110] Another effective way to manage reputation risk is adopting sustainable contracting practices as a long-term strategy in offshore drilling operations. This can be achieved through a risk allocation method that discourages using contractual clauses that protect a party against liability for gross negligence. A risk allocation practice that disincentivises oil pollution during offshore drilling activities can put the oil industry in a positive light. A positive image will arise from a risk allocation practice that mainstreams sustainability into its operational activities. Much of the agitation and public outcry stems from oil pollution by participants in the

106 Sergio Scandizzo, 'A Framework for the Analysis of Reputational Risk' (2011) 6(3) Journal of Operational Risk 41.

107 Fragouli and Ekruka (n 106).

108 John Vidal, 'Nigeria's Agony Dwarfs the Gulf Oil Spill, the US and Europe Ignore It' *The Guardian* (London, 30 May 2010) <www.theguardian.com/world/2010/may/30/oil-spills-nigeria-niger-delta-shell#:~:text=According%20to%20Nigerian%20federal%20government,been%20filed%20against%20Shell%20alone> accessed 13 October 2023.

109 Fragouli and Ekruka (n 106).

110 Mitali P Arora and Sumit Lodhia, 'The BP Gulf of Mexico Oil Spill: Exploring the Link between Social and Environmental Disclosures and Reputation Risk Management' (2017) 140(3) Journal of Cleaner Production 1287.

industry. This pollution is triggered by the risk allocation practice, which has been identified as an enabler of moral hazard. Not paying attention to risk allocation practice can damage corporate brands and reputations and trigger legal and regulatory penalties. The Macondo accident is a case in point.

3.4.4.2 A Way of Securing the Social Licence to Operate

Another importance of sustainability to the oil industry is that it can assist companies in obtaining a social licence to operate (SLO). The social licence to operate is a concept common in extractive industries and is now applied to renewable energy projects.[111] It emerged from discussion around the relationship between society and business.[112] 'Social licence' is a figurative term to explain the idea that, together with legal permits and licences, there is the often less quantifiable 'social acceptance' without which a business may face 'non-technical' risks such as workforce protests and community conflict.[113] It is an implied approval given by stakeholders, indicating their social acceptance of a project before or after the developers have met all the legal requirements to develop it.[114] It is not a formal agreement but involves general reliability, credibility and public acceptance of a project.[115] An SLO may arise from various places, such as informal relations or more formal, agreed 'impact-benefit agreements'.[116]

The SLO emerged as a concept to address mining operations' harmful social and environmental impacts and to obtain community approval for projects by building public trust to avoid social conflict. The key drivers of the term were the adverse impacts of the mining industry – like tailing dam accidents, chemical spills and disputes with local communities, especially indigenous people – which all damaged projects' reputations and bred societal contempt.[117] The absence of an SLO resulted in direct attacks and social unrest from the communities toward the resource projects, causing significant delays, financial loss and even abandonment of projects. The need for good relationships between project-affected communities and extractive companies, and the management of possible risks led to the SLO, which represents the general acceptance or approval by the local communities of energy, extractive or other natural resource projects in their area. An SLO

111 Azubuike, Nakanwagi and Dike (n 91).

112 Emma Wilson, 'What Is the Social Licence to Operate? Local Perceptions of Oil and Gas Projects in Russia's Komi Republic and Sakhalin Island' [2016] 3(1) Extractive Industries and Society 73.

113 Juliette Syn, 'The Social License: Empowering Communities and a Better Way Forward' (2014) 28(3–4) Social Epistemology 318; Leeora Black, *The Social License to Operate: Your Management Framework for Complex Times* (Routledge 2017).

114 Azubuike, Nakanwagi and Dike (n 91).

115 Govindan Kannan, Devika Kannan and Madan K Shankar, 'Evaluating the Drivers of Corporate Social Responsibility in the Mining Industry with Multi-Criteria Approach: A Multi-Stakeholder Perspective' (2014) 84(1) Journal of Cleaner Production 214.

116 Black (n 114).

117 Azubuike, Nakanwagi and Dike (n 91).

has since become a significant determinant of the success of critical projects in the mining and energy sectors.

We can distil from the above that concern for the environment due to the impact of mining is a significant contributor to various forms of protests. The same applies to the petroleum industry, where communities protest against petroleum operations due to the impact of these operations on their water sources, livelihoods and general well-being.[118] Moreover, oil pollution and environmental damage characterise offshore drilling operations in some cases, and affect community livelihoods and the ecosystem. As such, a sustainability approach to offshore drilling to prevent oil pollution will secure the SLO and save a company from incurring costs and damaging its reputation. Acceptance of a project comes from understanding the sustainability aspect of the project and the measures put in place by the company to handle oil pollution and other social and environmental damages that can arise from the activity. In other words, sustainability practice is a desideratum for a social licence to operate. Most communities protest because they fear the impact of petroleum operations on their livelihoods and environment. Despite that, sustainability practices that discourage oil pollution can result in a social licence to operate.

3.4.4.3 A Strategy to Maximise Environmental and Social Performance

Environmental performance refers to practices, measures or strategies a company uses to mitigate or manage the environmental impact of its activities or business. Environmental performance can be measured using indicators such as waste minimisation, pollution reduction, environmental conservation and emission reduction.[119] These indicators allow a company to understand how it is doing regarding environmental issues in its operations. On the other hand, social performance refers to effectively converting a company's mission to reality by following accepted social values. It is measured through actions, practices, outcomes and impact, and measures the company implements to attain its objectives. For instance, the company's activities could be evaluated to check how it has respected human rights, sustained the livelihoods of the community where it operates, and taken responsibility for its actions.[120]

[118] David Hill, 'Peru's Indigenous People Protest against Relicensing of Oil Concession' *The Guardian* (London, 2 February 2015) <www.theguardian.com/environment/2015/feb/02/perus-indigenous-people-protest-against-re-licensing-of-oil-concession> accessed 30 July 2022; Eromo Egbejule, 'Niger Delta Residents Protest against Month-Long Oil Spill' (*Aljazeera*, 7 December 2021) <www.aljazeera.com/news/2021/12/7/niger-delta-youths-protest-against-month-long-oil-spill> accessed 12 October 2023.

[119] Giovanni Azzone and others, 'Defining Environmental Performance Indicators: An Integrated Framework' (1996) 5(2) Business Strategy and the Environment 69.

[120] Ivo Hristov and Antonio Chirico, 'The Role of Sustainability Key Performance Indicators (KPIs) in Implementing Sustainable Strategies' (2019) 11 Sustainability 5742.

Most oil and gas companies have established environmental and social policies and trajectories as their core objectives. The realisation of these trajectories is dependent on, among other things, their sustainability practices during offshore petroleum operations. This position arises from sustainability, emphasising the need for social and environmental performance for societal and ecological preservation. These aspects consider the possible impact of petroleum operations on air, land, water, human health and livelihood, natural resources and how a company needs to respond to them, so that when sustainability is promoted in a company's business, it can actualise and maximise its environmental and social performance. This presents a win-win for the company and society to create sustainability value.

3.4.5 Sustainability in Risk Allocation in the Oil and Gas Industry

Sustainability in risk allocation in the hydrocarbon industry refers to industry practice that aligns its offshore drilling activities with environmental, social and economic policies and trajectories for the benefit of the public, the business and the environment. It involves framing the risk allocation practice in line with environmental, social and human effects and ensuring resilience and long-term value creation. Risk allocation is a non-technical tool for managing risk in the oil industry, and it can be used to drive sustainability in offshore drilling operations.

Earlier discussions have highlighted the meaning of sustainability, its components and its significance in the oil and gas industry. Strategic sustainability remains crucial in offshore drilling operations for long-term development. Given the impact of offshore drilling activities on the environment, the oil and gas industry must consider the environmental, economic, technological and social aspects of offshore drilling operations. The industry must also consider how its current practice of allocating risks fits into a long-term sustainability strategy, especially in gross negligence cases. This consideration requires rethinking the practice of risk allocation to incentivise good behaviour.

The sustainability objective can be mainstreamed into the risk allocation practice by using contracts which discourage behaviour that results in oil pollution or accidents during drilling operations. A good practice would be to adopt the distributive style of risk allocation in the event of liability for gross negligence. This risk allocation strategy places the liability for gross negligence on the party who caused the damage. Thus, it can make the parties more sensitive and responsive to environmental and social concerns arising from the moral hazard that characterises most drilling operations due to the absence of liability.

Flaws in the safety culture of most companies in the industry raises concerns about the risk allocation practice. This flawed safety culture is partly due to how risk is allocated among participants in the oil and gas industry, thus making a company's management pay less attention to safety issues, as liability will not arise even when a party is at fault. A downside raises sustainability concerns for people and the environment, leading to environmental protests, community agitation and project delays. Safety culture is an aspect of the overall culture that indicates general practice and approaches to safety and risk management.[121] Most often, dysfunctional safety cultures arise from a culture of denial, where accidents are seen as part of the drilling process instead of an opportunity to improve sustainability practices. The culture also contributes to the inability to learn from past accidents to prevent possible accidents in the future.[122]

Ultimately, incentives are required to change the safety culture to drive sustainability during offshore drilling operations. One of these incentives is a distributive practice of risk allocation to ensure sustainability in offshore drilling operations. The advantage of this type of incentive is that it can improve the sustainability trajectory of oil companies and ensure self-policing by oil and gas industry participants due to the need to exercise care during offshore drilling operations.

3.5 DISTRIBUTIVE JUSTICE IN RISK ALLOCATION

The concept of distributive justice received considerable attention in the seminal works of Rawls[123] and Robert Nozick.[124] Both authors, however, have divergent views on the subject. Rawls believes the concept involves a just way of distributing society's goods, including wealth, material goods, positions, offices and so on. He emphasises the fair manner in which things should be distributed. Nozick believes the concept involves a system where everyone is entitled to what they possess under a distribution.[125] His arguments stem from the entitlement theory of justice in holdings, which was advanced in his paper on distributive justice. Before advancing discussions on the idea of distributive justice, it is essential to understand the concept of justice, which forms the basis of the broad discussion.

3.5.1 *What Is Justice?*

Justice is the pivotal edifice upon which moral, legal and political philosophy stands. It is an essential virtue that guides how people interact with others and a primary virtue of social institutions.[126] Rawls believes that justice is the first of the four main virtues of social institutions.[127] However, this proposition is debatable.[128] To Plato and Aristotle, justice is the essential virtue, the summary virtue, the virtue most vital for humans as social animals who live together in a community, city or state.[129]

121 Nancy Leveson, 'Risk Management in the Oil and Gas Industry' (*MIT Energy Initiative*, 17 May 2011) <energy.mit.edu/news/risk-management-in-the-oil-and-gas-industry> accessed 13 October 2023.
122 ibid.
123 For further details see Rawls (n 73).
124 Robert Nozick, 'Distributive Justice' (1973) 3(1) Philosophy and Public Affairs 45.
125 ibid.
126 Brian Barry and Matt Matravers, 'Justice' (*Routledge Encyclopedia of Philosophy* 2011) <www.rep.routledge.com/articles/thematic/justice/v-2> accessed 14 October 2023.
127 Rawls (n 73).
128 David Miller, 'Justice' (*Stanford Encyclopedia of Philosophy* 2021) <plato.stanford.edu/entries/justice> accessed 14 October 2023.
129 Rawls (n 73).

Justice emphasises two crucial outcomes, rewards and punishments, which should be justly allocated to those who ought to have them. Nevertheless, where there are no claims, justice advocates equal treatment. This means that an aspect of justice asks for the payment of compensation for causing damages and the punishment for the commission of crimes, while another aspect involves just principles for the distribution of benefits and burdens.[130] This latter aspect underpins the conditions under which a particular distributive arrangement may be described as just or unjust. Justice does not vary in character in social and ethical parlance as it retains the same ethical underpinning. The moral idea of justice is not the same as the legal concept of justice, but they are connected.[131] This connection arises due to the ethical nuance to justice that can be seen in legal usage. An example is the allusion to the principles of natural justice, which acknowledges that the legal system should serve an ethical purpose and follow ethically accepted procedures.

Justice, viewed from the perspective of mutual advantage, is primarily a result of a fair bargain where two parties could be placed in a better position by engaging in an agreement. In this regard, it is a matter of fashioning rules to apportion or distribute the benefit and burden of cooperation. Justice can also be seen as reciprocity, which stems from a fair return or just price, capturing the idea of equal exchange. Finally, justice as impartiality relates to taking the points of view of other people, or putting oneself in their shoes.[132] As posited by Rawls, it is akin to ensuring the interests of everyone are protected when negotiating a contract behind the veil of ignorance. The reason is that no one knows who will belong to what side of the veil.

The term 'justice' is elusive, and defining it invites abstract philosophical speculation. In terms of its scope, the principle of justice applies in several forms depending on when it takes effect and the category of people or issues it covers. In society, we do not talk about justice for human beings alone, but also for animals.[133] Most times, the discussion is focused on relational versus non-relational justice. The former is the principle that applies among people engaged in a cooperative practice.[134] Another part of the scope extends to individuals versus institutions, and recognition versus redistribution in our everyday use of the term 'justice'.[135]

In discussing the concept of justice, there is an argument about what is just and unjust in international relations – that is, which rules or practices in society are just or unfair. This argument arises because justice represents one of the several virtues of social institutions. Some scholars believe that justice encompasses the fundamental idea of fairness[136] and varies according to its application to persons,

[130] Barry and Matravers (n 127).

[131] David Daiches Raphael, *Concepts of Justice* (Clarendon Press 2001).

[132] Jonathan Wolf, 'Models of Distributive Justice' (Novartis Foundation Symposium 2007) <www.ncbi.nlm.nih.gov/pubmed/17214316> accessed 14 October 2023.

[133] Martha Nussbaum, *Frontiers of Justice: Disability, Nationality, Species Membership* (Harvard University Press 2006); Robert Garner, *A Theory of Justice for Animals* (OUP 2013).

[134] Thomas Nagal, 'The Problem of Global Justice' (2005) 33 Philosophy and Public Affairs 113.

[135] Miller (n 129).

[136] Rawls (n 73) 305.

particular actions or practices. To Rawls, justice as fairness limits how practices define positions and accordingly apportion rights, duties and liabilities. Rawls believes that the fairness of a practice depends on how it apportions rights, duties and liabilities equally. If inequality exists, it will be arbitrary, unless it is reasonably expected to be for the benefit of all concerned. Inequalities are best understood not in terms of the differences between positions and offices of persons, but in terms of the benefits and burdens attached to them.

In the hydrocarbon industry, while inequalities of benefits and burdens exist, parties have rights, duties and obligations that affect their involvement in an activity. For this study, justice is conceived as the balance between benefits and burdens among people with rights and responsibilities within a particular practice. Justice, law and distribution depend on each other, and justice is a criterion, among others, to accomplish distribution in transactions.[137]

3.5.2 Distinctions in Justice

In the discussion of justice, certain conceptual contrasts are often made. These differences are discussed below.

3.5.2.1 Conservative versus Reformative Justice

Philosophy scholars observe that justice has two distinct faces. One face tends to conserve existing practices and rules, while the other seeks to reform these rules and practices. The former refers to conservative justice,[138] while the latter relates to reformative justice.[139] The conservative aspect of justice emphasises the primary function of law: preserving order and ensuring a functional society. This is achieved through punishment for crime and the payment of compensation. Punishment for crime is not victim focused (that is, not restorative) but state centred. The essence is to repair the violation of the social structure that arose due to breaking the rule that governs society. The payment of compensation is treated as the correction of a breach of an individual's right. The decision of a court to award damages is to preserve or restore an existing system of rights. In other words, conservative justice seeks to maintain an established order in civil and criminal proceedings.

The other face of justice serves a reformative function through laws that correct mischief in society. For example, this could occur through judge-made laws or laws made by the legislature to address an anomaly in a system. More often, new laws change the existing system and represent the reformative face of justice.[140] They reflect the dynamic nature of society and give effect to novel ideas of what

[137] Peter Cane, 'Distributive Justice and Tort Law' [2001] 4 New Zealand Law Review 404.
[138] Henry Sidgwick, *The Methods of Ethics* (Macmillan 1907).
[139] Raphael (n 132).
[140] ibid.

is fair and proper. They are primarily reflected in Acts of Parliament, case law and the judgments of superior courts. These analyses highlight the legal aspect of justice in its conservative and reformative roles.

Like law, social ethics also reflects conservative and reformative roles of justice. The conservative aspect of justice in social ethics seeks to retain the tradition of entitlements, provided the acquisition method is not immoral. Justice exists if a person is entitled to deal with their things as they choose. However, the reformative face of justice in social ethics seeks to change the existing entitlements method by considering merit and need. This same perspective could be applied in offshore drilling contracts in the hydrocarbon industry. The allocation of risks arose from contracts and established practices that the oil industry has held over time. Participants usually agree on this practice in the oil industry, and liability arising from gross negligence is not based on fault but on allocated responsibility in the contract.

From a conservative social ethics perspective, justice seeks to maintain the industry practice of risk allocation, especially when securing such a contract is not immoral or unconscionable. However, in reformative social ethics, justice requires a shift away from the traditional practice of risk allocation, allowing liability arising from gross negligence to exist without regard to fault. Justice from a reformative perspective follows the need to ensure that offshore drilling operations assume a pattern that ensures sustainability and discourages moral hazards in petroleum operations. In this regard, justice responds to the need for environmental protection and social well-being. The essence here is to address an anomaly that arises from the long tradition of allocating risks during offshore drilling operations. So, in this latter perspective, justice is given a reformative role in changing the existing risk allocation practice, considering society's needs.

A close look at both faces of justice reveals that they seek to fulfil various purposes. For example, the conservative face of justice operates on the assumption that a stable society is in the interests of everyone, despite its imperfection. Thus, it aims to maintain stability. As a result, it is a matter of justice to respect people's rights under extant laws, practices or moral rules or to fulfil their legitimate expectations obtained through past practice, agreements, social conventions and so on.[141] However, reformative justice supplements the argument for stability with another practice or rule to eliminate the flaws in the old system and redistribute rights to improve the social order.[142] This perspective is founded on the grounds that justice frequently gives us reason to fundamentally change laws, practices and conventions, thereby creating new entitlements and expectations. This is what a distributive risk allocation system in gross negligence cases seeks to achieve in offshore drilling operations, to address the sustainability challenge that the practice of risk allocation has brought about.

[141] Miller (n 129).
[142] Raphael (n 132).

3.5.2.2 Substantive versus Procedural Justice

Another distinction relates to the justice of the procedure used to determine how different benefits and burdens are shared with people, and the justice of the allocative outcome. The former is called procedural justice, while the latter is called substantive justice. A paper published in 2000 revealed that people are eager to accept decisions when they feel that the decisions result from a fair process.[143] Scholars of procedural justice judgements further suggest that people evaluate fairness using the criteria of participation, neutrality, respect and trust.[144] When these criteria are absent, people see the outcome as unjust, but when they are present, they accept the outcome due to the justice in the procedure.

Although these two types of justice are different, they tend to be connected. The question may be asked whether substantive justice is a function of procedural justice; that is, whether the justice that results from the outcome depends on the justice of the procedure. Some scholars, like David Miller, think otherwise: he believes there are times when an independently just outcome does not make sense.[145] This means that not all substantive outcomes can result in justice, even when the procedure is fair. However, Tom Tyler believes that later procedural justice research points to a more optimistic outcome about the value of social justice as a tool for resolving social conflicts than previous studies on distributive justice. According to Tyler, the outcome of procedural justice research indicates that social authorities are optimistic about the ability of procedural justice to assist in resolving conflicts in a manner that parties to a dispute will accept. Furthermore, using a cognitive appraisal model of emotion, some scholars note that the experience of procedural justice (or injustice) allows individuals to obtain meaning from favourable and unfavourable allocation decisions.[146]

When we evaluate these two distinct aspects of justice, we see a connecting thread with the Rawlsian veil of ignorance. The Rawlsian conception presents a fair outcome to all concerned, irrespective of where they will find themselves on the other side of the veil of ignorance. The decision-making process also considers the interests of everyone. Suppose we apply this analysis to the oil and gas industry practice of risk allocation. We can deduce that a risk allocation practice that seeks to protect the interests of all the parties (contractual and non-consenting third parties) aligns with the procedural justice perspective. That is to say that the allocation of risk discourages moral hazard by placing responsibility for gross negligence on the party at fault, subject to the proportion of their benefit. The outcome of such arrangements may be acceptable even when oil pollution occurs.

143 Tom R Tyler, 'Social Justice: Outcome and Procedure' (2000) 33(2) International Journal of Psychology 117.

144 John Thibaut and Laurens Walker, *Procedural Justice* (Lawrence Erlbaum Associates 1975).

145 Miller (n 129).

146 Patricia J Krehbiel and Russell Cropanzano, 'Procedural Justice, Outcome Favorability and Emotion' (2000) 13(4) Social Justice Research 339.

However, the outcome will be different when the process is unfair. As highlighted in the research of Patricia Krehbiel and Russell Cropanzano, sadness may result from an unfavourable outcome when a process is fair. Nevertheless, anger and frustration will result when an unfavourable outcome occurs due to an unfair procedure.[147]

3.5.2.3 *Comparative versus Non-Comparative Justice*

Justice assumes a comparative posture when we look at what one person can claim in relation to what other people should get. For instance, for a person to get a share from a pot of food, we need to know how many people need to eat the food and what possible sharing formula can be applied. On the other hand, justice assumes a non-comparative position when knowing relevant facts about a person assists in understanding what is due to them. For example, knowing a person's age helps determine how much food the person can consume. This is because an adult will consume more food than a child. In his seminal work, *Social Philosophy*, Joel Feinberg highlights that comparative justice requires similar issues to be treated similarly and that cases that are not similar should be treated differently. For non-comparative justice, Feinberg advances that this principle requires each person to be treated based on merit without regard to the treatment given to anyone else.[148]

There is an implied perception in certain ideas of justice that justice involves a comparative notion, such as the view that justice consists of the absence of arbitrary inequality. Other perceptions imply that justice is non-comparative. Both situations exist in society, as there are times when we do justice comparatively[149] and non-comparatively.[150] The core of the comparative justice principle is the comparison or contrast between how one person is treated and how another person is treated. After comparing treatment received, the principle evaluates each party's treatment to determine which one is unfair.[151] The non-comparative justice principle does not compare or contrast how one or more persons are treated. What it does is consider whether another person was treated justly or unjustly.

Comparative and non-comparative principles of justice are most common in the context of equal protection. Between the two types of justice, we can distil that a comparative form of justice is inclusive as it seeks to protect the interests of everyone who may be connected to the outcome of a particular thing. On the other hand, non-comparative justice is person centred. We can liken this situation to the practice of risk allocation that focuses on the interests of the parties to the

147 ibid.

148 Joel Feinberg, *Social Philosophy* (Prentice-Hall 1973).

149 ibid.

150 Phillip Montague, 'Comparative and Non-Comparative Justice' (1980) 30(119) Philosophical Quarterly 131.

151 Raleigh Hannah Levine and Russell Pannier, 'Comparative and Non-Comparative Justice: Some Guidelines for Constitutional Adjudication' (2005) 14(1) William & Mary Bill of Rights Journal 141.

contract or incorporates the interests of non-consenting third parties by adopting contractual strategies that will benefit everyone. In the oil and gas industry context, justice lies in how justly or unjustly the risk allocation practice treats stakeholders connected to petroleum activities. The argument could be advanced that compensating for damages is justice. However, most losses are irredeemable, and preventing them is the best way to manage them.

3.5.2.4 *Corrective versus Distributive Justice*

Another essential contrast is between justice as a basis for assigning distributable goods of various kinds to people, and justice as a remedial principle that applies when one person improperly interferes with another's legitimate interest.[152] The former is distributive justice, while the latter is corrective justice. Distributive justice assumes the role of an allocating agent and considers some persons with claims on what is being allocated. In a distributive arrangement, justice entails sharing the resources available to the distributor in line with essential criteria such as need, equality, desert and so on. Scholars like Aristotle note that distributive justice concerns how benefits and burdens are shared according to specific criteria. In contemporary debates, the elements of distributive justice are incorporated into discussions regarding tax systems, property and so on, which results in a distributive outcome in society.

On the other hand, corrective justice concerns a bilateral relationship between a wrongdoer and his victim. Miller notes that corrective justice requires that the fault be remedied by restoring the victim to their position if the wrongful behaviour had not occurred. Most times, it also requires the wrongdoer not to benefit from his wrong conduct. Similarly, Aristotle identified that corrective justice rests on the transactional nature of the wrongdoing, which imposes that transactional nature on the remedy for wrongdoing.[153] So, while corrective justice seeks to remedy wrongdoing, distributive justice allocates benefits and burdens with certain criteria. The former principle aligns with the tort of liability and promotes deterrence and compensation for wrongdoing. This outcome is related to distributive justice in some respect. The reason is that when burdens are allocated to people, depending on the nature of the burden, it can deter them from wrongdoing. This will be justice, whether from a corrective or distributive perspective.

As Miller notes, a wrongdoer should not benefit from their wrong, as benefiting from their wrong will be an injustice in the circumstance. So, the emphasis is on remedying the wrong and ensuring that the wrongdoer does not benefit from it. Suppose we juxtapose this situation with the practice of risk allocation in the oil industry. We can say that the way risks are allocated runs contrary to the corrective and distributive concepts of justice. The reason is that parties in an offshore drilling contract use mutual indemnity or exclusion clauses as a defence against

[152] Miller (n 129).

[153] Aristotle, *Nicomachean Ethics*, in J Barnes (trans) *Complete Works of Aristotle* (vol 2, Princeton University Press 2014).

liability for damages, even in gross negligence cases, thus making them entitled under the contract to benefit from their wrong, contrary to the justice perspectives discussed. Miller identifies that the value of corrective justice must lie in the notion that each person must be responsible for their conduct, and that if they fail to respect the legitimate interests of others by causing injury, they should remedy the harm. In that way, each person can plan their life knowing they will be protected against some external setbacks.

Jules Coleman's account of corrective justice agrees with Miller's position. Coleman talks about annulling wrongful gains and losses, and the need for the effect of a wrongful act to be reversed by the person who caused it.[154] From Coleman's account, we can distil that the concepts of wrongdoing and responsibility are placeholders, which aligns with several views about wrongful acts and the conditions under which someone can be held accountable for an outcome. The other discussion is on distributive justice, and further details will be discussed in Section 3.X.

3.5.3 *Types of Justice*

The concept of justice is broad, and does not lend itself to a steady definition due to the dynamic nature of society and the need to constantly expand rules to accommodate this dynamism. Several types of justice have been identified and discussed by scholars of repute. Some of these relate to energy and environmental law, including environmental justice, energy justice and climate justice. There can also be criminal justice, natural justice, social justice, poetic justice and so on. Nevertheless, the focus here will be on those types of justice most common in everyday interactions with others.

3.5.3.1 Distributive Justice

Distributive justice has been applied in politics,[155] contractual relationships[156] and tort law.[157] In simple terms, distributive justice concerns the fair allocation of the benefits and resources available to members of society. The fair allocation of justice is something that everyone agrees on, but the criteria for the distribution is where most scholars disagree. Some scholars believe the conditions for distributing economic resources should be based on equality, equity and need.[158] The conditions

[154] Jules L Coleman, *The Practice of Principle: In Defence of a Pragmatist Approach to Legal Theory* (OUP 2001).

[155] Christian Schnaudt, Caroline Hahn and Elias Heppner, 'Distributive and Procedural Justice and Political Trust in Europe' (2021) 3(3) Frontiers in Political Science 642232.

[156] Hugh Collins, 'Distributive Justice through Contracts' (1992) 45(2) Current Legal Problems 49.

[157] Lord Steyn, 'Perspectives of Corrective and Distributive Justice in Tort Law' (2002) 37 Irish Jurist 1; Gregory C Keating, 'Distributive and Corrective Justice in the Tort Law of Accidents' (2000) 74 Southern California Law Review 192.

[158] Marco Jimenez, 'Distributive Justice and Contract Law: A Hohfeldian Analysis' (2016) 43 Florida State University Law Review 1265.

of equality require everyone to receive the same resource or reward irrespective of their contribution. Rawls believes distributive justice involves the principles of justice dealing with the political process and socioeconomic structures that affect the distribution of benefits and burdens in societies. In other words, it focuses on the just way to distribute societal benefits and burdens. To Rawls, just principles of distribution would be the principles that we would all agree to if we were all in an equal bargaining position – principles that allow us all to look after ourselves, sit at the table, think about the proper way to divide the goods and agree to it. Nevertheless, scholars like Nozick believe this criterion should not be the basis for allocation as it will discourage hard work and will not reward merit. Nozick advocates for a distribution based on merit and not on equality. The equity criterion involves rewarding people based on their contribution to society. The need criterion of distribution emphasises that people who need more should be given more while people who need less should get less.

Distributive justice is essential to the stability of society and the well-being of its members, notwithstanding the school of thought. However, the various schools of thought reflect how we view what is fair in allocating resources. Distributive justice remains invaluable in society; and when its issues are not correctly addressed, and the interest in the allocation process is high, intractable disputes result.

It has been highlighted that distributive justice applies in several aspects of our daily engagements. However, scholars like Aristotle hold the view that its application in a contract is limited. In the context of contract law, Aristotle believes that distributive justice should focus on how the rules of corrective justice should be enforced to promote and rectify the just exchange of priorly allocated shares. It should not concern itself with how the share was distributed in the first instance.[159] In other words, Aristotle believes that corrective justice should drive distributive justice in contracts. However, other scholars believe that the apparent value-neutral rules of contract law are essentially distributive, and that to ignore these considerations is more than just bad policy – it is a misunderstanding of how the crucial building blocks of the law are arranged to form contract law in the first place.[160] Even in the courts, judges make distributive decisions when they administer the rules of contract law, which have strong roots deeply entrenched in distributive justice within their very structure.

3.5.3.2 Procedural Justice

Procedural justice concerns how decisions are made and implemented using a fair process that ensures a fair outcome. Essentially, procedural justice concentrates on the quality of the process through which a distributive decision is reached.[161] Of course, the outcome cannot be favourable to everyone, but the process from

159 Aristotle, *Nicomachean Ethics* vol V (trans WD Ross) (c 350 BCE), 3

160 Jimenez (n 159).

161 Schnaudt, Hahn and Heppner (n 156).

which the outcome emanates must be considered fair. Notable procedural justice models set out conditions for determining the procedural conditions of fair decision-making. One of the most basic conditions in these models is a person's control over the decision-making process or the actual decisions made.[162]

Procedural justice emphasises the need for rules to be impartially applied and consistently followed to achieve an unbiased decision. As highlighted earlier, procedural justice is founded on sacrosanct principles such as participation, neutrality, respect and trust. The neutrality principle emphasises the need for decision makers to be neutral in the process, while participation involves giving a voice to the people that will be affected by the outcome of a decision. These people must be represented in the decision-making process and should be allowed to speak up during it. Procedural justice also emphasises respect for the people that will be affected by the decision and the need for these people to trust the process.[163]

Six rules have been identified as essential in assessing the fairness of a distribution process. The first is that the process is regarded as fair if it applies consistently to everyone and over time, without bias, and is based on correct and detailed information. Again, procedural fairness provides an opportunity to rectify decisions, incorporate the interests of everyone in the affected group and respect moral values. It also considers a fair process to be a function of the valuable relationship between the authorities and people. This rule concerns the relational model of procedural justice. Some scholars have identified that this relational model uses the criteria highlighted earlier: trust, respect and neutrality.[164]

As Tyler notes, people's acceptance of a particular outcome depends on their perception of the fairness of the procedure leading to it, or through which the authorities exercised their authority to act.[165] This means that procedural justice is a desideratum for outcome acceptance, even when the outcome is unfavourable to them. Therefore, implementing fair procedures is essential to resolving disputes, and important in adjudication, negotiation, arbitration and mediation.[166]

3.5.3.3 *Retributive Justice*

This type of justice appeals to the idea of 'just deserts', which is the proper punishment for a wrong, or treating someone the same way they treat others. Retributive justice concerns how justice is achieved through the unilateral imposition of punishment.[167] This concept of justice is retroactive in approach as it validates punishment

[162] Thibaut and Walker (n 145).

[163] Michelle Maiese'Distributive Justice', *Beyond Intractability* (June 2013) <www.beyondintractability.org/essay/distributive_justice> accessed 12 October 2023.

[164] Schnaudt, Hahn and Heppner (n 156).

[165] Tom R Tyler, 'Procedural Justice, Legitimacy and the Effective Rule of Law' (2003) 30 Crime and Justice 283.

[166] Maiese (n 164).

[167] Michael Wenzel and others, 'Retributive and Restorative Justice' (2008) 32 Law and Human Behaviour 375.

as a response to previous wrongdoing or injustice. The core of retributive justice lies in the fact that the wrongdoer has gained an unjust advantage through their conduct and that punishment will correct the imbalance. In other words, the concept advances that those who do not abide by the rules should face the consequences of their wrongdoing. However, the punishment should be proportionate to the harm caused due to distorting the moral balance of society.

Retributive justice also incorporates the notion of deterrence as it envisages that punishment for misconduct will discourage people from engaging in illegal activities. This approach seeks to control behaviour to reduce the occurrence of wrong and to restore justice. The aim is to secure future compliance with a practice or rule using behavioural control, deterrence and incapacitation. These are all punitive means, but people often call for punishment to restore justice and not control behaviour. This is because the restoration of justice seeks to re-establish moral order and a sense of justice. However, the re-establishment of justice could still be punitive in some way, like unilaterally meting out punishment, which denotes just deserts or retributive justice.

Some scholars find the retributive approach to justice insufficient as it does not pay adequate attention to how people are supposed to reconstruct their lives. This inadequacy may be due to how victims of war crimes and other forms of wrongdoing are often left to bear their losses. Ultimately, retributive justice considers the distortion of society's moral balance rather than the victim's restoration. The reason is that the wrong is against the state, not the individual, and the state needs to punish people who do wrong to preserve law and order in society.

3.5.3.4 Restorative Justice

Restorative justice is the opposite of retributive justice. It seeks to achieve justice through reaffirming a shared value consensus in a bilateral process.[168] Restorative justice regards a wrong as a conflict that should be resolved by those involved. It conceives of misconduct as a wrong against an individual and not the state. It seeks to redress the wrong against an individual to heal the victim's hurt, repair harm done to interpersonal relationships and community, and restore wrongdoers to a life that conforms with the law. Restorative justice advocates an active involvement of the victim in the exchange process and in defining the obligations and responsibilities of the wrongdoer. This process allows wrongdoers to appreciate the harm they have caused their victims and to take responsibility for it. This perspective creates a bilateral relationship that can strengthen the community and forestall similar harms from occurring in the future.

Restorative justice provides a platform for affected parties to be directly involved in the justice process, creating an avenue for interaction. Thus, it enables victims to express their feelings, tell their side of the story, and come to terms with

[168] ibid.

the hurt the offence has caused, the offender's responsibility, and the necessary steps to achieve justice. This process involves measures such as direct compensation to the victim, and compensation or services to victims of similar offences or the larger community. Other measures include punishments to the offender that benefit the victim, the community and, through the facilitation of moral transformation, potentially the offender.[169] In all, we can say that restorative justice seeks to modify behaviour and rebuild a sense of justice through the victim healing and the offender owning up to their responsibility.

3.6 DISTRIBUTIVE JUSTICE: CONCEPT, DIMENSIONS AND ESSENCE

3.6.1 *Context*

Distributive justice refers to the principles of justice that deal with the political process and socioeconomic structures that affect the allocation of benefits and burdens in society.[170] As such, it concerns itself with the fair apportionment of benefits and burdens among members of a particular society. Fair distribution considers the quantity of what is to be distributed, the distribution process and the resulting allocation pattern.[171] Its principles indicate how some benefit or burden ought to be shared. Distributive justice is not limited to only economic issues but is also a normative principle that assists in apportioning the benefits and burdens of economic activities.[172] For example, petroleum operation is an essential economic activity that many hydrocarbon-rich nations depend on for income to fund development projects.

The concept of distributive justice is traceable to the discussions of Aristotle on justice in Book V of the *Nicomachean Ethics*, where he theorises that justice is concerned with the 'distribution of honour or money or other things that have to be shared among members of a political community.'[173] To John Finnis, distributive justice focuses on the challenge of distributing opportunities, resources, advantages, responsibilities and burdens among those who are members of a group or community.[174] Although some studies about distributive justice are centred on benefits and resources, Finnis includes burdens in his discussion.[175] Other scholars posit that distributive justice is concerned with sharing benefits and burdens that are 'communal' in some respect or, from a narrow perspective, the division by the state of benefits and burdens.[176]

169 ibid.

170 Julian Lamont and Christi Favor, 'Distributive Justice,' (Stanford Encyclopedia of Philosophy 2017) <plato.stanford.edu/entries/justice-distributive> accessed 12 October 2023.

171 Maiese (n 164).

172 Lamont and Favor (n 171).

173 Roger Crisp (ed) *Aristotle: Nicomachean Ethics* (CUP 2000) 85.

174 John Finnis, *Natural and Natural Rights* (2nd edn, OUP 2011) 166.

175 Cane, 'Distributive Justice' (n 138) 405.

176 David Bostock, *Aristotle's Ethics* (OUP 2000) 58.

3.6.2 Rawls's Distributive Justice Perspective

Besides Aristotle, Rawls, in his seminal work, *A Theory of Justice*, advances the concept of distributive justice and identifies two essential ideas as follows:

1. Each person is to have an equal right to the most extensive scheme of equal basic liberties compatible with a similar scheme of liberties;
2. Social and economic inequalities are to be arranged so that they are both reasonably expected to be to everyone's advantage and attached to positions and offices open to all.[177]

Rawls's ideas revolve around the just and fair way to distribute society's goods, material wealth, positions and so on. In other words, they are about the fair way to distribute societal benefits and burdens. Rawls's central idea is that justice involves fairness. This fairness underpins the two philosophical propositions stated above. Rawls identifies that the principles of justice are those that free and rational persons who want to further their interests would accept in an initial position of equity.[178] In other words, just principles of distribution are the principles that we would all agree to if we were all in the same bargaining position at the beginning – a position where people sit down to think about the right way to do a thing, and whatever they agree to is the principle of justice. If the principle of justice is the one that we would all accept from an initial position of equality, what would that position be? Rawls calls this the 'original position'. This position is hypothetical and not historical, as no one has been in it before except from an imaginary perspective.

Rawls believes this position provides a fair situation in which to agree on social arrangements, and that it helps us make rules that will not privilege one person and jeopardise the other because we do not even know if we will be in the jeopardised group. Rawls advances that because we do not know anything about ourselves, we will not agree to a social arrangement which privileges one person over another because it might end up hurting us. Rawls believes that putting ourselves in this original position enables us to think about what a genuinely equal social arrangement would be like. Then the real question is: what principles of justice would we agree to behind the veil of ignorance? Rawls thinks that, from that original position, we should all agree on the principle of equal rights for everyone. In this way, no one is limited, as allowing any limitation may impact us in the long run.

The second essential idea is about socioeconomic inequalities. Rawls posits that everyone should have equal opportunities despite socioeconomic disparities. He believes that despite our position in society, we should be able to grow to

[177] Rawls (n 73) 53. See also Erin Kelly (ed), *Justice as Fairness: A Restatement, John Rawls* (Harvard University Press 2001) 42; Thomas M Scanlon, 'Rawls' Theory of Justice' in Norman Daniel (ed), *Reading Rawls: Critical Studies on Rawls' A Theory of Justice* (Basil Blackwell 1975).

[178] Rawls (n 73).

the point where we can assume new leadership positions, notwithstanding our former position. This idea is more about equal rights and equal opportunities for everyone. Rawls's second principle of justice has two aspects. One is the ability to rise from one position to another, and the other is the 'difference principle' – how wealth and benefits are distributed in society. Scholars like Nozick consider this latter part of the principle controversial. This second aspect says that a distribution is just if it benefits the least disadvantaged in society. This suggests the need for a fundamental redistribution of wealth by the government or society. It involves taking from the wealthy and giving to the less privileged. This principle portrays a communist or socialist idea, which is different from Rawls's idea. Rawls merely seeks a redistribution that will benefit the least advantaged in society. He advocates a distribution practice that rewards those working hard while the most deprived are still okay.

3.6.3 *Nozick's Distributive Justice Perspective*

A notable political philosopher, Nozick advances a contrary opinion to Rawls's difference principle regarding how people will negotiate the core principles of society. Nozick is a hero of libertarianism.[179] His idea of justice stems from holdings, which he views as follows:

(1) A person who acquires a holding in accordance with the principle of justice in acquisition is entitled to that holding.
(2) A person who acquires a holding in accordance with the principle of justice in transfer from someone else entitled to the holding, is entitled to the holding.
(3) No one is entitled to a holding except by (repeated) applications of (1) and (2).[180]

Nozick's conception of justice in holdings stems from these three aspects: justice in the acquisition of holdings, justice in the transfer of holdings and rectification of injustice.[181] The first aspect relates to how a person originally acquired what they hold, which has never been held by anyone else. This involves how a person became entitled to a thing, the process through which the thing became held, what things can be held through that process, the extent of what can be held through that process and so on. The second part relates to transferring holdings from one person to another. It involves the process through which a person transfers a holding to another person. For instance, if a person gets money from another person, how did they get it? Was it a gift, or did they steal the money from another person? Nozick believes that if the acquisition and the process are right, the person is entitled to the holding, which is just.

179 Aaron R Powell, 'Robert Nozick and the Value of Liberty' (Cato Institute, 21 June 2011) <www.cato.org/blog/robert-nozick-value-liberty> accessed 12 October 2023.
180 Nozick (n 125) 45.
181 James S Coleman, 'Robert Nozick's Anarchy, State and Utopia' (1976) 3(3) Theory and Society 437.

Assuming this exists, it provides the basis for a theory of entitlement. The idea of entitlement is about who is entitled to hold what things they got. In other words, you are entitled to keep what you hold if you follow the principles of justice. Nozick's theory of distributive justice is engraved in the theory of entitlement. To Nozick, distributive justice is a just holding which results from an entitlement of a holding that a person possesses under the distribution. If you are entitled to something, then it is just for you to hold it.[182] He further posits that a distribution is just if it results legitimately from another distribution. This idea relates to the principle of justice in the transfer, where the transfer process accords with legitimate means. In other words, any holding resulting from a just situation through a just procedure is fair. This view resembles procedural and substantive justice, where people accept an outcome when the process is considered reliable.

In his discussion of distributive justice, Nozick further identifies the principle necessary to rectify injustice. He notes that a person is not entitled to a holding except through Processes 1 and 2 above. For instance, when someone steals something from another person, it is necessary to retrieve it to fix the injustice. The acquisition did not follow the proper process of holding, so keeping it will amount to injustice. Nozick does not like the idea of distributive justice. His 'Big Idea' is that justice in holdings is historical and depends on what happened. Nozick focuses on how the holding was acquired and not how it was distributed. To Rawls, what matters is not how the holding was acquired but whether the distribution benefits the least well-off. Rawls's position focuses on whether things are sorted in the right proportion. However, Nozick does not focus on equality or inequality but on how we acquired the holding. He believes that liberty upsets patterns of ideal distribution, and that to realise a patterned distributional principle of justice, you must interfere with people's lives. Therefore, it is not unjust if an inequality results from just acquisition and transfer rules.[183]

In the oil and gas industry context, the Rawlsian philosophical position could be used to examine the inequality between stakeholders. Again, it tends to look after everyone directly or indirectly connected to an offshore drilling contract, as it considers the least privileged – who, in this instance, are the non-consenting third parties. From a Rawlsian point of view, we could say that justice exists where a drilling contract protects the least well-off from possible pollution or environmental damage.

Let us consider Nozick's view about justice in oil and gas offshore drilling contracts. It means that parties to a contract can have their agreement implemented so long as it was not entered into under duress or undue influence, or through an unconscionable bargain. The operator and the contractor are entitled under the contract to allocate risk in whatever way they prefer, since their contract results from a legitimate process, and they can enjoy the benefit of the coverage

182 Nozick (n 125) 47.
183 ibid.

that a mutual indemnity clause provides, even when liability arises from gross negligence. If we followed Nozick's view in the oil and gas industry, we would be implementing anti-sustainability ideals, whereas, when we followed the Rawlsian position, we would enhance sustainability principles as drilling contracts would seek to protect the interest of all, resulting in justice for all.

Applying distributive justice between the operator and the contractor in gross negligence cases would require an allocation practice that protects the interests of non-consenting third parties. The distribution must also consider the rights and obligations of the operator and the contractor, who exist at different levels of economic advantage or strength. It should also apportion the liability according to the benefit reaped from the activity that has produced the burden, considering the economic advantage of the parties.

3.6.4 Keating's Distributive Justice Perspective

Aside from Rawls and Nozick, Gregory Keating addresses the issue of distributive justice in a way which aligns more with this study. Keating examines distributive and corrective justice in the tort law of accidents. The idea of corrective justice results from the justice conception of tort theory. The latter theory deals with harm and reparation, agency and responsibility as a matter of distributive justice to discourage negative behaviour.[184] Keating's idea of distributive justice provides a foundation upon which parties involved in a risky activity can share liability arising from that risky activity.

Keating advances that justice should be understood as how we fairly apportion the benefits and burdens of social life, and justice in tort law should be about the fair allocation of the benefits and burdens of risky but valuable activities. On a secondary note, it should be a matter of corrective justice.[185] Keating premises his concept of distributive justice on the argument that the benefits and burdens of harmful but mutually beneficial activities should be designed so that those who benefit from the activity also bear its burdens.[186] Bearing the burden of harm created is in line with corrective justice, which aligns with the economic conception of tort law.

Keating notes that it is unfair for an actor/party to impose the cost of its activity – physical harm or damage – on others when the party reaps the benefit from such activity. He argues that the burden of the activity that parties benefit from should be shared in accordance with the benefit (gains, profit and so on) reaped. That is to say, everyone benefiting from an activity must partake in its burden, and those who receive high rewards should bear an increased risk from the activity. Keating

184 Keating, 'Distributive and Corrective Justice' (n 158) 193.

185 To Keating, corrective justice is derived from the conception of justice which sees the tort law of accidents as being in line with the ordinary notion of harm and reparation, agency and responsibility, the rectification of losses for wrongful actions and so on.

186 One of the burdens of hydrocarbon exploration and production is oil pollution, which negatively impacts human and marine living resources in the case of offshore drilling.

identifies that it is unjust to fix the terms on which an activity is carried out so that some participants benefit from the activity while others bear its burdens. To him, the burden and benefit should be proportional, as fairness requires that the burdens of mutually beneficial but harmful activities should be allocated, preferably in proportion to the benefits reaped.

Keating's distributive justice idea forms the foundation for a party to share in the burden which results from their seriously wrongful conduct (in this case, gross negligence). Where, for instance, a party benefits from drilling operations, it should bear the burden, especially when the same party occasioned it. Distributive justice serves to justify the responsibility for an outcome, and this (outcome responsibility) imposes a duty to repair in proper situations.[187] It follows the logical pattern that where liability arises from a party's gross negligence, the responsible party or parties have to bear it, contrary to the long-time practice where fault does not count. This idea matches the underpinnings of public policy: deterrence, liability and protecting society from harm. The argument could be made that operators and contractors allocate surface and subsurface pollution between them and take responsibility for it. This practice can be accepted in negligence cases because oil pollution could result from a party's negligence during drilling activities. Despite that, it is difficult to make the same argument for liability arising from gross negligence: to sustain this argument is to impose the adverse impact of moral hazard on non-consenting third parties or impose the cost of their physical harm on society when participants reap the benefit from offshore drilling operations. Even between the contracting parties, the risk allocation practice of shielding liability resulting from gross negligence through mutual indemnity places the burden on another party, and Keating considers this unfair.[188] The petroleum industry practice is akin to imposing a strict liability regime on parties through a contract.

The point of convergence between the views of Rawls, Nozick and Keating is that they based their ideas of distribution on justice: what is fair, irrespective of where it is applied. Keating's distributive justice idea focuses on achieving justice when distributing benefits and burdens from a dangerous activity. This focus is crucial as this study has identified that protecting a party from liability arising from gross negligence is unfair and contrary to public policy. If gross negligence cannot be allocated the way the petroleum industry allocates negligence risks, what other way can parties adopt to ensure justice for everyone?[189] To achieve a just distributive outcome, Keating asks this vital question: 'What terms would free and equal persons concerned to cooperate fairly with each other agree upon to govern the risks of accidental injury created by beneficial activities?' Keating notes that this is a question about justice. It is about allocating the benefits and burdens of dangerous

[187] Tony Honoré, 'Causation in the Law' in Edward N Zalta (ed), *Stanford Encyclopaedia of Philosophy* (2010 edn) <plato.stanford.edu/archives/win2010/entries/causation-law> accessed 14 October 2023.

[188] Keating, 'Distributive and Corrective Justice' (n 158) 196.

[189] See Section 5.X on how the burden of gross negligence can be distributed between operators and contractors during risk allocation.

activities, partly because it highlights and seeks to protect the core interests of potential injurers and potential victims. The former represents operators and contractors, while the latter represents non-consenting third parties and the eco-system around the drilling site. Thus, the question seeks to ensure that the burden of a risky activity is distributed justly to ensure fairness for everyone.

In the Macondo case, BP and Transocean were direct beneficiaries of the drilling operations. BP was the operator, while Transocean was the drilling contractor. Both companies were determined to be involved to varying degrees in acts of negligence when the accident occurred.[190] For instance, the Commission for the Montara Oil Spill report indicates that the operator and the drilling contractor were both complicit in the spill.[191] However, only BP – the operator – was held liable for gross negligence. The operator's liability stemmed from its position as the party accountable to the government. The contractor had no obligation that could result in liability on its part. When a party has no responsibility to prevent damage, moral hazard will set in, to the disadvantage of the other contracting party and society, when a downside occurs.

Since public policy does not support contracts that absolve parties of their responsibility in cases of gross negligence, it is necessary to rethink the contractual strategy in gross negligence cases. The right to agree on contractual terms resides with the parties to a contract. However, this must be exercised within acceptable norms, rules and practices that provide a moral balance for society. Keating identifies that injurers have an interest in liberty just as possible victims of the harmful act have a fundamental interest in security. For example, in the petroleum industry, operators and contractors want to allocate risk in a manner that suits their needs during drilling operations. However, non-consenting third parties also have an interest in security. The absence of a substantial measure of the latter interest in preventing deaths and accidents jeopardises the opportunity to aspire throughout a regular and complete life span.[192]

According to Keating's distributive justice, the task of justice is to fairly and favourably reconcile these competing interests in liberty and security in terms that secure for each the most favourable conditions to pursue their ends, consistent with similar freedom for others. As such, Keating's distributive justice provides a foundation for, and a notable approach to, rethinking the oil industry strategy of allocating the risk of gross negligence. It advances a fair allocation method between parties involved in risky activities like petroleum operations.

[190] Bureau of Ocean Energy Management, Regulation and Enforcement (BOEMRE), 'Report Regarding the Cause of the April 20, 2010 Macondo Well Blowout' (*National Oceanic and Atmospheric Administration*, 14 September 2011) <www.dco.uscg.mil/Portals/9/OCSNCOE/OCS%20Investigation%20Reports/Macondo%20-%20DWH%20Reports/DWH%20DOI%20Vol%20II%20Final.pdf?ver=2017-10-05-072747-303> accessed 13 October 2023.

[191] Montara Commission of Inquiry, 'Report of the Montara Commission of Inquiry' (Commissioner David Borthwick AO PSM, June 2010) <www.iadc.org/wp-content/uploads/2016/02/201011-Montara-Report.pdf> accessed 13 October 2023.

[192] Keating, 'Distributive and Corrective Justice' (n 158) 197.

3.6.5 *Theoretical Elements of Keating's Distributive Justice*

From Keating's concept of distributive justice, three key elements can be distilled. These elements are *mutual benefit*, *proportionality*, and *fairness*. Keating's distributive justice is in line with the theory of enterprise liability, which advances that any activity that produces harm should internalise the cost of the harm, and the cost should be distributed among parties involved in the activities.[193]

3.6.5.1 Fairness

The principle of fairness is a fundamental element of distributive justice. From a public international law perspective, the requirements of legitimacy and distributive justice are embedded in fairness.[194] Iain Scobbie notes that legitimacy is concerned with process – ensuring that the right mechanisms are in place to make, interpret and apply the law. Legitimacy in this context has some similarities with procedural justice discussed earlier. However, legitimacy and distributive justice are distinct as the latter examines moral fairness while the former denotes fairness in the examination process.

Further to the international law perspective, Tom Franck identifies that fairness is the pivotal edifice that manages discursive tension.[195] He notes that the fairness discourse is the link bridge under which order and change are negotiated in society. To him, fairness is 'a human, subjective, contingent quality which merely captures in one word a process of discourse, reasoning, and negotiation leading, if successful, to an agreed formula located at a conceptual intersection between various plausible formulas for allocation.'[196] He asserts that fairness should satisfy participants' expectations of a justifiable distribution of burdens and benefits (costs).

Franck identifies the parameters of fairness – no trumping and maximum – and calls them the 'gatekeepers of fairness discourse'. Of the maximum parameter, he posits that the viability of the fairness discourse is justifiable 'if inequality has advantages, not only for those who benefit from that inequality but everyone else'.[197] This notion is in line with the Rawlsian justice position stated above. Rawls believes that the maximum parameter should be for the good of everyone and that, if inequality exists, it should be in the interests of all. The gatekeeper position sets out the broad contours of distributive justice. As can be distilled, the maximum principle follows Rawls's postulation – an unequal distribution is only justified if it does not widen the existing inequality. The maximum principle does not bring about a predetermined outcome but enables a variety of acceptable

193 Gregory C Keating, 'The Idea of Fairness in the Law of Enterprise Liability' (1997) 95(5) Michigan Law Review 1269.

194 Iain Scobbie, 'Tom Franck's Fairness' (2002) 13(4) European Journal of International Law 910.

195 Tom M Franck, *Fairness in International Law and Institutions* (OUP 1995) 7.

196 ibid 14.

197 ibid 18–22.

outcomes, leaving the choice of negotiation to the participants involved.[198] Rawls believes this could be achieved when laws are made or contracts are executed behind a veil of ignorance.

From a private law point of view, fairness relates to how parties to an agreement apply rules of practice to achieve a just outcome in their private transactions. From a distributive perspective, fairness highlights how the burdens of harmful activities should be fairly distributed among parties following their benefits from the activity. In other words, fairness highlights the procedure to adopt when sharing the burden. Keating advances a fairness-based conception of distributive justice with roots in the Kantian social contract,[199] by asking what condition persons concerned about fairly cooperating would accept to govern beneficial activities resulting in injury. This question is partly about justice/fairness (because it involves how the benefit and burden of risky activities are distributed) and partly about those whom the risk will affect. This question brings to light and seeks to protect fundamental interests.[200] Fortunately, the answer to this question is undoubtedly in the Rawlsian veil of ignorance.

From a public or private law perspective, fairness emphasises the need for a just process through acceptable rules, norms and practices. When we consider how fairness plays out in the allocation of risk in the oil and gas industry, we imagine that its application relates to private exchanges. The key question is how parties can allocate the risk associated with gross negligence in a manner that would be considered fair. The fairness solution underlies Keating's distributive idea. Fairness considers the parties' positions, the operator's long-term financial upside and the nature of the conduct of the party at fault – in this case, gross negligence.

Recall that the burden distribution is based on the benefits derived from the dangerous activity. However, the operator and the drilling contractor operate at different benefit levels. In other words, fairness here entails a reconciliation of the competing interests of the operator and the contractor under terms and conditions that are favourable and fair for the parties to pursue their aspirations.[201] Fairness considers the benefits of the activity in distributing the burdens to be borne by the parties. It should be about the fair distribution of the burdens from the activity in the interests of the parties. Fairness here is determined by the benefits, which result in the burdens. The benefits should be aligned with the burdens (which form the distribution parameter) so that those who profit the most from the activity bear more injury cost (liability).[202] The element of fairness also extends to the assumption of responsibility for gross negligence in some way, shape or form per the benefit reaped from the dangerous activity.

198 Scobbie (n 195) 912.
199 Keating, 'The Idea of Fairness' (n 194) 1266.
200 In this case, the interests to be protected would be that of humans and their marine environment that is being damaged. and that of the operator who is strictly liable by law for pollution damage occasioned by hydrocarbon exploration.
201 Keating, 'Distributive and Corrective Justice' (n 158) 197.
202 Keating 'The Idea of Fairness' (n 194) 1269.

The concept of fairness has been applied in judicial proceedings. In *Wright v Newman*,[203] the court applied the concepts of loss spreading and fairness in its decision. The court's reasoning was founded on the fact that those who profit from a venture should also partake in the cost of the harm that results. In accordance with Keating's view, when allocating risk through contracts, the nature and extent of the burden of risk would be based on the perceived benefit parties would gain from drilling hydrocarbon. That is to say that where gross negligence results from the conduct of both parties, their burdens should align with their benefits, whether in sole or joint fault.

Fairness lies at the centre of both private and public systems of law and forms the basis for managing discursive tension. Presumptively, fairness in the context of this book implies that those who impose risks on others should partake in the costs that arise from the risks they impose. Where a party, out of gross negligence, causes harm to society or loss to another party, fairness requires that the party also share in the ensuing liability. From the Rawlsian point of view, fairness in risk allocation entails designing a contract, behind the veil of ignorance, which will allocate responsibility for gross negligence for the benefit of everyone, irrespective of the inequalities that exist.

3.6.5.2 Proportionality

Proportionality in this book represents a compensatory balance wherein a burden reflects a person's benefit from an activity that occasioned damage. Distribution results in proportion, and proportion leads to more for some persons and less for others.[204] Proportionality is used loosely in this book as an element of distributive justice. The application of proportionality in a loose sense enables the comparison between the rewards and contributions[205] of one person or group and another.[206] When we compare rewards and contributions, we are dealing with the issue of distributive justice. It has been noted that, when applied in the context of causal uncertainty, proportional liability conforms to civil liability objectives and promotes compensation and deterrence.[207]

[203] 735 F 2d 1073 (8th Cir 1984). The court had held that the cost of injury from a defective product should be distributed to the seller as the seller also profits from the sale. See *Ira S Bushey & Sons Inc v United States* 398 F 2d 167 (2nd Cir 1968).

[204] John G Culhane, 'Tort, Compensation, and Two Kinds of Justice' (2003) 55 Rutgers Law Review 1064.

[205] This is akin to benefits and burdens, as rewards represent benefits while contributions represent duties, obligations performed or burdens borne. As a legal theory, it represents a balance between rights and duties, or benefits and burdens received. Rainhard Bengez and others, 'Proportionality and Quantitative Justice: An Introduction to Special Issue' (2011) 10 Law, Probability and Risk 164.

[206] Jerald Greenberg and Ronald L Cohen (eds), *Equity and Justice in Social Behaviour* (Academic Press Inc 1982) xiii.

[207] Giovani Comande and Luca Nocco, 'Proportional Liability in Uncertain Settings: Is it Precautionary?' in Israel Gilead and others (eds) *Proportional Liability: Analytical and Comparative Perspectives* (Walter de Gruyter GmbH 2013) 205.

In the broad context, the economic analysis of law[208] favours the *proportional liability rule* – liability based on the amount of damage an injurer contributed to a loss/risk – the application of which may be relevant to determine causal uncertainty in tort law.[209] However, proportionality in the context of this book concerns itself with the risk and reward derived. Thus, the risk and reward form the foundation for applying a liability cap between the parties when grossly negligent conduct results in a downside. It is essential to highlight that the proportional burden rule approach to liability distribution in tort may challenge environmental responsibility insurance.[210]

Justice as proportionality was first advanced as an idea in the *Nicomachean Ethics*, where a proportionate measure was used for distributive justice in Aristotle's schema.[211] Aristotle identifies distributive justice with 'proportionate equality', which involves a situation where goods should be allocated not precisely equally, like in 'arithmetic' justice, but in proportion to their worth or merit. This idea provides a perspective on proportionality which considers specific characteristics peculiar to the parties involved in a transaction. For example, in oil and gas drilling contracts, Aristotle's positions can be likened to considerations such as risk and reward and the parties' positions in a contract, thus providing a basis for applying proportionality between the parties when a downside occurs due to gross negligence.

Justice as the right ratio also forms the foundation of the proportionality inquiry. This means that proportionality is the nexus between a distributive principle and what is apportioned. In the context of distributive justice, proportionality emphasises that the benefit a person receives should equal the burden they bear. A classic example is the UK tax system, where those with higher incomes pay more tax than those with lower incomes. Similarly, in the risk allocation practice of the oil industry, proportionality means that the operator bears more liability than the drilling contractor, where gross negligence results from the fault of the drilling contractor. In the broad context of the principle of law, proportionality also applies as a criterion of fairness and justice in statutory interpretation.

Keating notes that a liability rule should distribute the burdens of risky activities in a manner proportionate to the benefits received from the activity.[212] He

208 Steven Shavell, *Foundations of Economic Analysis of Law* (Harvard University Press 2004) 174.

209 Michael Faure, 'Regulatory Strategies in Environmental Liability' in Fabrizio Cafaggi and Horatia M Watt (eds), *The Regulatory Function of European Private Law* (Edward Elgar Publishing 2009) 153.

210 ibid 154.

211 Eric Engle, 'The History of the General Principle of Proportionality: A Overview' (2012) 10(1) Dartmouth Law Journal 3. Proportionality has, however, evolved to gain acceptance in the fields of criminal law and human rights, where reference has been made to proportionality in self-defence. See Alec S Sweet and Jud Mathews, 'Proportionality, Balancing and Global Constitutionalism' (2008) 47 Columbia Journal of Transnational Law 96; MT Cicero, *Treatise on the Commonwealth in Francis Barham, Esq, The Political Works of Marcus Tullius Cicero: Comprising his Treatise on the Commonwealth; and his Treatise on the Laws*, (vol 1, trans Edmund Spettigue, 1841–2).

212 Keating, 'Distributive and Corrective Justice' (n 158) 209.

identifies that where benefits are equal in distribution, the burdens should also be equal. However, the burdens should also be unequal in distribution where benefits are unequal in distribution. To Keating, a party who receives a high reward should also receive a high risk in return. Keating's postulation aligns with Rawls's second principle of justice: if inequality exists, it should be in the interests of all. Presumptively, a proportionate distribution supports a practice where the burdens reflect the benefits obtained from the activity. Proportionality does not mean the absence of liability; it implies that responsibility should reflect benefit.

3.6.5.3 Mutual Benefit

Case law has established that a party who benefits from an activity or arrangement is bound by the corresponding burdens, even when they were not a party to the original agreement.[213] An obligation can result from an activity that grants the benefit of which a party may take advantage, but is not a condition for enjoying the benefit. The party would have to share in the corresponding burden arising from it.[214] Where parties to a contract benefit from an agreement, they are obligated to share in the burden arising from it, albeit in a manner that reflects their benefit.

Mutual benefit in distributive justice is akin to the equitable mutual benefit and burden principle in law. The equitable doctrine emphasises that obligation follows the enjoyment of a right. Courts have also applied this principle in certain areas of law[215] and developed conditions that should be satisfied for it to apply.[216] Mutual benefit and burden are sometimes expressed in the Latin maxim, *qui sentit commodum sentire debet et onus*[217] – a person cannot approbate and reprobate, or accept and reject, the same transaction. In this regard, a drilling contractor may not have executed any contract with the licensing authority but might share in the burden arising from its gross negligence. Mutual benefit in distributive justice advances the need for the burden to be distributed amongst persons who benefit from a given activity. In other words, mutual benefit obligates a contribution to enjoy a right (benefit).

After reviewing approaches to burden sharing, Edward Page concludes, among other things, that a principled reconciliation of parties' 'contribution to the problem' and 'beneficiary pays' is a crucial approach to burden distribution that will result in a satisfactory mix of practical application and theoretical coherence.[218]

213 *Goodman v Ellwood* [2013] EWCA Civ 1103; *Halsall v Brizell* [1957] Ch 169.

214 Christine J Davis, 'The Principle of Benefit and Burden' (1998) 57(3) CLJ 522.

215 ibid 522–3. The principle of benefit and burden finds it roots in the execution of deeds. See *Halsall v Brizell* (n 214).

216 The conditions are, to wit: that the benefit and burden must be conferred in, or by, the same transaction; the benefit must be conditional on, or reciprocal to, the burden; the party subject to the burden must have had the opportunity to reject the burden. See *Halsall v Brizell* (n 214).

217 RH Kersley, *Broom's Legal Maxims* (10th edn, Sweet & Maxwell 1939) 485; *Pickersgill v Rodger* [1876] 5 Ch D 163.

218 Edward A Page, 'Distributing the Burdens of Climate Change' (2008) 17(4) Environmental Politics 556.

He argues that those who have contributed to a harmful outcome and benefited in the process should also share in the burden as beneficiaries of the dangerous activity. This reasoning follows the requirement of public policy that a party at fault should bear responsibility for their wrong in some way or form. Moreover, it aligns with the idea of environmental responsibility, the core aspect of which involves guidance and accountability for harm done to the environment.[219] To Page, it will be unfair if a party contribute to a harm/consequence and benefits from the same and does not share in the burden – if you enjoy a benefit, you should share in the burden. The 'contribution to the problem' principle advocates that those who contributed to a problem and benefited from the contributing activity should contribute to the burden of managing the problem.[220] Following this, causal responsibility and connection become a foundation for burden distribution where the harm is connected to the operator and drilling contractor during offshore operations.

The enjoyment of a benefit goes with the acceptance of the resulting burden from the benefiting activity. This is applicable where the benefit and burden are relevant to each other.[221] This principle was developed by the court in *Halsall v Brizell* and emphasised in *Goodman v Ellwood*,[222] where the court held that the enjoyment of a right depends on compliance with an obligation and that, although a positive covenant by the original owner of the property does not bind successors-in-title, the obligation could be enforced against a successor-in-title where they enjoy the benefit of the associated rights. This position arises from the fact that the successor-in-title to the original owner of the land was obligated to contribute towards the maintenance of a road if he used it.[223] The discussion of mutual benefit does not suggest that the operator and the drilling contractor are equal. On the contrary, the operator's benefit far outweighs that of the driller as the operator enjoys a long-term financial upside upon commercial success. However, distributive justice and public policy tend to agree on liability for wrongful conduct.

3.6.6 Why Is Distributive Justice Essential in Risk Allocation?

An essential aspect of distributive justice identified in this book is that it provides a basis for how things can be distributed – opportunities, welfare, income, utility, wealth – who can benefit from the distribution and what criteria can be applied to achieve a fair outcome.[224] As such, distributive justice can help operators and drilling contractors understand how to allocate the risk of gross negligence to achieve a fair outcome.

219 Martin Reynold, 'Introduction to Environmental Responsibility' in Martin Reynold and others (eds), *The Environmental Responsibility Reader* (Zed Books 2009) 3.
220 Page (n 219) 557.
221 Davis (n 215) 523.
222 *Goodman v Ellwood* (n 214).
223 Davis (n 215) 523.
224 Lamont and Favor (n 171).

Again, distributive justice provides a basis for cooperation among people with competing needs. It specifies the weight that each competing interest can be allocated and provides an acceptable description of the standpoint from which judgments are formed.[225] Even the theory of mutual advantage contends that distributive principles can be derived from a rational bargain between participants in a cooperative venture, such as a contract, political community or market society. Furthermore, distributive justice provides a platform for evaluating the fairness of allocating desirable outcomes between parties to a contract. In this regard, Keating asks what principles ordinary people can agree on to achieve a fair outcome. The answer lies in distributive justice, which advocates just principles. When just principles are applied, the result is an outcome that fosters acceptance of the distributive share.[226]

In addition, distributive justice has relevance to environmental justice in offshore petroleum drilling operations. The principle is critical to environmental justice because it enables parties involved in the risky activity of petroleum drilling operations to equitably share the cost of ecological impacts and risks arising from gross negligence. The environmental justice framework assesses the distribution of the harmful impacts of petroleum operations.[227] Accordingly, justice is deemed to be achieved because the party at fault is also made to pay for their wrongful conduct in some manner, shape or form. This outcome makes distributive justice somewhat restorative. Similarly, distributive justice can lead to a change of behaviour because the allocation of outcomes places responsibility on a party at fault. As a result, most parties would exercise extra care to avoid liability arising from gross negligence. The result would be a win-win situation for the environment and the party, as the potential impact of pollution on the environment would be averted. At the same time, there would not be a need for a party to pay for damages.

Distribution is an essential aspect of justice, as identified by Rawls. His reference to how rights and duties are assigned, and the economic opportunities and social conditions of the sectors of society, is instructive. Rawls's reference to economic opportunities and social conditions tells us two things. The first is that distributive justice considers the economic prowess between parties in risk allocation. For example, in the oil and gas industry, the operator's long-term financial upside (economic advantage) is a vital factor to consider when risks are being allocated. The reference to social conditions resonates with the environmental justice movement.[228] The latter aspect aligns with the need to consider the social conditions that the

[225] Alexander Kaufman, 'Distributive Justice, Theories of' in Ruth Chadwick (ed) *Encyclopedia of Applied Ethics* (2nd edn, Academic Press 2012).

[226] Tyler, 'Social Justice' (n 144) 118. Tyler notes that people would be willing to accept fair outcomes instead of being angry if they did not receive everything they wanted. There is also a willingness to defer to justice due to a fair process and outcome, which shapes people's satisfaction.

[227] Dara O'Rourke and Sarah Connolly, 'Just Oil? The Distribution of Environmental and Social Impacts of Oil Production and Consumption' (2003) 28 Annual Review of Environment and Resources 587.

[228] Alice Kaswan, 'Distributive Justice and the Environment' (2003) 81(3) North Carolina Law Review 1056.

impact of oil pollution would bring to communities close to a drilling site. This consideration supports an allocative strategy where gross negligence is borne by a party at fault in proportion to the benefit from the activity. This allocative method is considered fair. As one scholar puts it, 'Justice consists in realising to the greatest possible extent a distribution that renders to each a fair share of the good (or evil) at issue.'[229] In essence, distributive justice protects against detrimental disparities and ensures that natural justice is mainstreamed in an allocation process.

It has been highlighted that distributive justice establishes principles of allocation that enable individuals to rightfully access what has been allocated to them. In this regard, distributive justice provides a moral foundation that guides social, contractual, economic and political processes and, essentially, each society's choices regarding whether to sustain, modify or reject abiding practices, policies, institutions and so on.[230] Therefore, justice requires equality unless a move away from it would result in more equity for everyone. Thus, a moral foundation facilitates a fair process and a just allocation outcome. This moral foundation often shapes society's legal rules and practices to achieve justice. It establishes the basis upon which a contractor would accept to bear liability for gross negligence to the extent of their benefit, and an operator would accept to bear any excess from a drilling contractor's liability, given that the operator receives a long-term financial upside in the event of a commercial discovery.

3.7 DISTRIBUTIVE JUSTICE AND PRIVATE LAW

3.7.1 Contract Law and Tort as Vehicles of Distribution

Generally, there seems to be a view that contract law does not seek to include a specific pattern of distributive justice as one of its aims. This point of view is based on the belief that contract law does not include the redistribution of wealth to achieve equality or inequality between parties. A further argument is that the test for forming a binding contract does not include consideration of a fair distribution pattern, but a fair procedure by which parties may reach an agreement.[231] This view advances the understanding that contract law is neutral on issues bordering on distributive outcomes. However, it has distributive consequences due to the rules of law that enhance a market transaction under which parties can be better off in the transaction process. Again, there is also the libertarian view that it is inappropriate to consider distributive considerations in a contract.[232] The reason

[229] Nicholas Rescher, *Distributive Justice: A Constructive Critique of the Utilitarian Theory of distribution* (Irvington Publication 1966).

[230] Sabastian Jindra-Cotilla, 'Distributive Justice' (*Berkeley*, undated) <live-mdp.pantheon.berkeley.edu/distributive-justice> accessed 15 October 2023.

[231] Hugh Collins, 'Distributive Justice through Contracts' (1992) 45(2) Current Legal Problems 49.

[232] Robert Nozick is the hero of the libertarian idea. He believes that the primary duty of the state is to protect against force, fraud and theft, enforce contracts and so on. This libertarian perspective has been extended to support arguments that governmental interference with a party's freedom to contract is inappropriate. In the context of this book, libertarians would think it an inappropriate

is that contractual freedom is an inviolable principle of contract law. Thus, when people freely enter into a contract, the court's duty is to enforce the agreement and not make a new contract for the parties. The libertarians believe that where a court does more than interpret the contract made by parties, it amounts to an impermissible interference that would infringe on the institution of contract law and individual liberty.[233]

Furthermore, differing perspectives regarding the connection between contract law and distributive justice have been expressed.[234] For instance, Richard Epstein[235] notes that the role of a contract is to ensure procedural fairness (that is, the absence of fraud, duress or undue influence) and not to make contracts distributionally fair.[236] He bases his argument on the utilitarian defence (so long as the agreement covers the parties, its enforcement will be for society's good) and on libertarian grounds (freedom to operate within the confines of the law). Public policy considerations impact the strength of Epstein's argument. Public policy would encourage contracts that protect third parties and not contracts that result in harm for compensation to be paid to third parties. Public policy influences societal practices and regulation, and parties must contract against a regulatory background of default rules reflecting unique distributive considerations. These distributive considerations are sometimes established by courts when they select, apply or interpret the default rules of an agreement.

Furthermore, Epstein's view is trumped by the fact that, by entering into an agreement and opting for express terms in place of default legal terms, parties are attempting to replace society's distributive arrangement with a distributive consideration of their choosing. As Marco Jimenez puts it, the role of distributive justice in contract law is inescapable. The reason is that in setting up the rules of contract law, the legislators and courts are setting up a meta-structure that distributes justice among the parties before they even contract with one another. Distributive justice does this by providing a background against which their actions will or will not be enforced, by which certain of their defences will or will not be allowed, or by which specific remedies will or will not be given in the case of breach by one of the parties.[237]

inference for the government to regulate how the risk of gross negligence should be allocated between parties in a contract. However, this book notes that shielding gross negligence through contract would be contrary to public policy.

233 Jimenez (n 159) 1265.

234 Aditi Bagchi and others affirm the essence of a fair bargain and the nexus between distributive justice and contract, while the likes of Richard A Epstein and Robert Nozick believe that contracts should not aim to be distributionally fair but procedurally fair.

235 RA Epstein, 'Unconscionability: A Critical Reappraisal' (1975) 18(2) Journal of Law and Economics 293.

236 Beale and others (n 45) 813.

237 Jimenez (n 159) 1270. For this book, distributive justice provides the background for a party whose conduct is grossly negligent to bear the burden of the gross negligence in proportion to their benefit.

Scholars such as Anthony Kronman propose that the legitimate function of a contract, among others, is to set out the rights (benefits) and duties (burdens) of parties as created by the agreement, and that contract law should be applied as a device for distributive justice. As earlier noted, distributive justice sets out the framework rules for these rights and duties in a contract. As such, distributive justice is the framework that allocates the rights and obligations between parties before they meet to agree on what rights and responsibilities should be amended and how. Kronman advances that the framers of contract rules – legislatures and courts – should do so with a mindset of fair distribution among parties.[238] Fair distribution takes into cognisance the nature of the risk exposure. To Kronman, considerations of distributive justice should influence contract rules as the situation dictates, and distributive concerns should not be excluded from a private exchange.[239] While a contract defines the rights and duties of parties in a transaction, distributive justice ensures the fair allocation of those rights and duties arising from the exchange.

In these discussions, there is a conventional view that contract/private law lies outside the realm of distributive justice principles.[240] Proponents of this view advance that the autonomy theory sees contract law as a separate body of law founded on a promise in the absence of procedural defects.[241] To autonomy theorists, the fairness or justice criteria upon which contracts are assessed are part of the contractual terms, given that the contract embodies the will of the parties. However, Richard Posner's concept of economic efficiency and Kronman's concept of distributive justice perceive contract law as having a specific social value.[242] This is because justice is considered the foremost virtue of social institutions, just as truth is of thought systems.[243] Some scholars posit that contractual rules are among the rules that determine resource allocation. Hence, on a Rawlsian account, contract law falls within the confines of distributive justice.[244]

These scholars note that fairness or justice in a contract should be assessed outside the will of the consenting parties by looking at standards such as distributive justice, utility and economic efficiency, as these principles impose duty even when the responsibility does not arise from the contracting parties' will. Again, philosophers and private law theorists argue that private law is partly a system of rights (benefits) and duties (burdens) and, as such, involves a means of distributing and maintaining the distribution of rights and obligations.[245] They further

238 Anthony T Kronman, 'Contract Law and Distributive Justice' (1980) 89(3) Yale Law Journal 472.

239 ibid 510.

240 Kevin A Kordana and David H Blankfein-Tabachnick, 'Rawls and Contract Law' (2005) 73(3) George Washington Law Review 598.

241 Charles Fried, *Contract as Promise: A Theory of Contractual Obligation* (Harvard University Press 1981) 17. Some recent philosophical thinking about contract has been within the promissory context.

242 Richard A Posner, *Catastrophe, Risk and Responses* (OUP 2004); Kronman (n 239) 510.

243 Rawls (n 73) 3.

244 Kordana and Blankfein-Tabachnick (n 241) 600.

245 Lucy William, *Philosophy of Private Law* (OUP 2006) 328.

note that a court's application of private law doctrines sometimes has distributive effects within and beyond the legal world, making private law a matter of distributive justice. Some authors contend that private law doctrines manifest concerns for loss distribution or fairness, focusing on cases such as legal liability,[246] thus inferring that private law embodies some conception of distributive justice.

In private law, such as contract and tort, the creation of a distribution pattern by courts is a burden from the defendant's viewpoint and a benefit and resource from the claimant's perspective.[247] When courts make rules regarding the circumstances under which the liability to repair harm arises in tort, they contribute to creating a form of distribution of benefits and burdens within society. Peter Cane believes that tort law has distributive outcomes that must be justified if tort law is to be adjudged a welcome legal and social institution.[248] This is so because distributive tasks involve making rules that define the bounds and grounds of liability in tort,[249] given that courts' decisions regarding who is liable in tort or contract are unavoidably issues of distributive justice. Given the allocative consequences, the nexus between private law and distributive justice is substantial.

The view in this book is that private law does not lie outside the bounds of distributive justice, as contract law must be viewed as subject to the concept of justice. Private law encourages distribution by allocating and maintaining a system of rights and duties.[250] This is partly because efficiency or distributive considerations will be used to evaluate the expected outcome of an agreement when a downside occurs. An example is in the hydrocarbon industry, where participants need to fashion ways of ensuring a balance between the benefits and burdens of the parties to a contract. It can also be understood from the discussions that proponents of distributive theories concentrate on legal liability as a distinct area ripe for the distribution of losses. Therefore, it is not out of place to apply the principle of distributive justice in drilling contracts to reflect a pattern of distribution that allocates the benefits and burdens of a particular activity amongst those who benefit from it.

Practices and concepts of legal responsibility are impossible to explain without reference to matters of distribution. In the hydrocarbon industry, harm and the resulting liability have prompted a repurposing of the contractual terms for liability.[251] This repurposing is an issue of liability distribution among parties. Cane suggests further that even agent-focused theories of responsibility are not distributionally neutral, as principles that limit the obligation to reckless conduct (gross negligence or wilful misconduct) also distribute duty, and that, in the principle

[246] ibid 333. See also Cane, 'Distributive Justice' (n 138) 401.
[247] Cane, 'Distributive Justice' (n 138) 404.
[248] ibid 404–5.
[249] William (n 246) 339.
[250] Peter Cane, *Responsibility in Law and Morality* (Hart Publishing 2002) 190.
[251] Cary A Moomjian Jr, 'Contractual Insurance and Risk Allocation in the Offshore Drilling Industry' [1999] Drilling Contractor, March/April.

of responsibility, an intentional act is a condition for responsibility distribution to discourage reckless conduct.[252] In his opinion, it is radically incomplete for a responsibility theory to fail to address distributional implications regarding protected interests and proscribed conduct.[253]

The concern for fairness/distributive justice in law and contract is an effort to induce and reward proper behaviour. Equity in contract law could invite parties to apply various considerations to ensure distributive justice. A redistributed burden to a party in a contract may be arbitrary when the core injustice is systemic, as correcting distribution through a contract may be futile.[254] This view has been refuted because background distribution forms the content and basis of private rights and obligations, even within contractual frameworks.[255] It is further identified that recognising distributive-sensitive constraints in the liability circumstances of contract law is not arbitrary. Consent does not prevent the allocation of economic losses from a contract for distributive ends, or the interpretation of vague agreements in line with distributive preferences.

In the oil industry, risks are allocated through contract by parties who consent to the terms and conditions of hypothetical risk situations without knowing the expected result of a particular negligent act. This method of reallocating risk between operators and contractors based on convenience is founded on distributive considerations.

Distributive justice originates from equity and morality, which may be incorporated into a binding contract when parties agree on terms and conditions. It must also be noted that moral responsibility may survive consent, even where consent renders risk-creating conduct blameless. There is a limit to making otherwise unacceptable conduct permissible. Consent may not prevent responsibility for outcomes that meet accountability conditions,[256] especially as an economic injury in shared contractual obligations may justify sharing losses.[257] One fundamental aspect of distributive justice seen in this book is the issue of responsibility. In both contract and tort, responsibility is vital in private exchanges. The responsibility practice of distributive justice supports causal attribution and ensures that the wrongdoer participates in their wrongful act rather than imposing it on others.[258] Therefore, in the hydrocarbon industry, distributive justice would not allow a party to indemnify

[252] Cane, *Responsibility* (n 251).

[253] ibid.

[254] The exclusion of distributive justice from contract law by some legal philosophers and economists is based on the morality of promising: that distributive justice has no effect on the substance of contract law.

[255] Aditi Bagchi, 'Distributive Justice and Contract' in Gregory Klass and others (eds), *Philosophical Foundations of Contract Law* (OUP 2014) 195.

[256] ibid 203.

[257] ibid 204.

[258] John Gardner, 'What Is Tort Law for? Part 2: The Place of Distributive Justice' in John Oberdiek (ed) *Philosophical Foundations of the Law of Torts* (OUP 2014) 347; Jeff McMahan, 'Self-Defence and the Problem of the Innocent Attacker' (1994) 104(2) Ethics 259.

against the gross negligence of another party who is causally or solely connected to the wrongful act. Distributive justice would instead facilitate the distribution of the resulting liability amongst parties, considering the proportion of the benefit received. This is the allocative function of distributive justice.[259]

3.8 DISTRIBUTIVE JUSTICE: A PRACTICAL ELEMENT IN ALLOCATING THE RISK OF GROSS NEGLIGENCE

Distributive justice provides the foundation upon which liability arising from gross negligence can be allocated. It provides a justice consideration based on the proportion of benefit, and aligns with public policy, which requires a party to partake in the outcome of their gross negligence. The justice consideration stems from the fact that the parties' positions differ, given that the allocation is structured around a risk-and-reward system supported by the oil industry. Ultimately, distributive justice considers these dynamics in advancing a portioning of liability that suits the parties' positions. Again, distributive justice aligns with the public policy consideration because it promotes an allocation system that makes a party bear the responsibility for their gross negligence. The essence is to discourage moral hazard and enhance environmental protection, so that parties are more careful during drilling operations.

Environmental sustainability remains a critical element in offshore petroleum operations due to the impact of oil pollution on coastal communities and the ecosystem. A practical way of promoting sustainability during drilling operations is to evoke the parties' consciousness of liability through contracts. Distributive justice provides the foundation for this consciousness of liability, because it supports a system of liability that attaches responsibility to grossly negligent conduct. It does not allow a party to impose on another party the economic cost of their harm when the party at fault reaps the benefit of the activity. In some way, this is corrective justice, as a party at fault becomes responsible for the harm/damage created. This practice places a duty on an injurer to repair wrongdoing, if the wrongdoing consists of harm that will yield distributive injustice unless it is rectified.[260] A party cannot wholly exempt themselves from liability for harm caused, either intentionally or recklessly, as doing so increases the risk that the general public will be harmed.

3.9 CONCLUSION

This chapter has advanced conceptual discussions that are essential to understanding risk allocation in the oil industry. At the centre of the discussion is the freedom of contract, which is not absolute but qualified. This means that specific underpinnings, like public policy, can limit the application of the freedom

[259] Hanoch Scheinman, 'Tort Law and Distributive Justice' in John Oberdiek (ed) *Philosophical Foundations of the Law of Torts* (OUP 2014) 364.

[260] Keating, 'Distributive and Corrective Justice' (n 158) 202.

of contract: public policy would not allow the enforcement of an agreement that would cause harm to the public. The reason the freedom to contract in the oil industry should be limited is for environmental sustainability to protect public interest. Distributive justice provides a foundation for addressing the problem of allocating the risk of gross negligence using the proportionality element, thus highlighting its necessity in offshore oil and gas drilling contracts and how it should apply in gross negligence cases. Ultimately, distributive justice considers the dynamics in advancing a liability proportion that suits the parties' positions, and aligns with public policy considerations because it promotes an allocation system that makes a party bear the responsibility for their gross negligence.

Chapter 4

Causation and Gross Negligence in Risk Allocation

4.0 INTRODUCTION

Responsibility for gross negligence arises from causation, and causation determines the extent of liability where parties are jointly liable for causing damage. As such, when we assess the oil industry's risk allocation practice, we refer to the cause of the downside and why the party at fault should be liable for gross negligence. This chapter will begin by considering the meaning and legal foundation of causation, to understand how liability can attach due to causation. It will also examine gross negligence in detail, its application in selected courts and the challenges associated with managing and allocating gross negligence risk. This chapter will provide a definition for gross negligence and identify how to prove it to enable the application of gross negligence as a term of art in the oil industry.

4.1 CAUSATION AND LIABILITY

4.1.1 Causation: Meaning and Legal Foundation

Causation is a fundamental driver in tort law as it gives rise to legal liability for the responsible party. It also indicates how liability between parties to an offshore drilling operation could be allocated when a downside occurs. This indication is possible as, through their contract, parties may agree to distribute the outcome of strict liability – such as responsibility for pollution damage, which is the operator's obligation due to government regulation. Nevertheless, a strict liability cannot be transferred to a party that is not strictly responsible. Therefore, although the size of a cheque for damage is of fundamental importance to the responsible party, the focus here is on liability for damage arising from gross negligence.

Causation means that the damage should emanate from the injurer's action, thus satisfying the requirement that remedies for damage should emanate from the person responsible for the harm.[1] Causation requires a link between the action and the harm suffered by the injured party.[2] It is, therefore, an essential condition for liability, as it explains the connection between a party's action and the outcome for which it is responsible.[3] Richard Wright notes that courts apply the

[1] 'Causation in Environmental Law: Lessons from Toxic Torts' (2015) 128 Harvard Law Review 2256.

[2] ibid.

[3] Steven Yannoulidis, 'Causation in the Law of Negligence' (2001) 27(2) Monash University Law Review 319.

causal rhetoric not only to determine whether a party's tortious action contributed to harm, but to ascertain whether a party should be held legally responsible since they contributed to the harm.[4] The causal connection of a party to harm goes in tandem with the attributive function of causation. This function is to fix the extent of a party's responsibility to the particular harmful outcome.[5]

In law, causal responsibility differs from legal responsibility, as a person's responsibility may arise because they are legally obligated to answer for particular harm they caused. This is legal causation. Factual causation relates to the cause of the harm and is not necessarily about the party legally responsible for it. This applies to the hydrocarbon industry, where a party may be causally responsible but not legally answerable for a harm. For instance, legal liability for pollution damage is strict, with the responsible party (the operator) bearing legal responsibility for any damage that may have arisen, irrespective of causation. The regulator enforces this position by holding the operator responsible for pollution damage. Pollution risk allocation in contracts in the hydrocarbon industry is driven along the lines that the responsible party is strictly liable. However, personal liability between parties still exists, as a party can, based on their contract, recover losses occasioned by a contracting party. In determining causation, there could be a factual connection that evidences the contributory negligence of parties to the contract. In risk allocation, causation is essential, and it can be checked by subjecting mutual indemnity to the gross negligence exception. This practice could discourage bad oilfield practices which result from the absence of an obligation to exercise care.

HLA Hart and Tony Honoré,[6] as well as Wright,[7] note that a fundamental condition of causation is that a party's action is a substantial factor in the resulting outcome or that their action contributed to the harm. As such, a party's role in the occurrence of a particular harm is sometimes a feature in offshore petroleum operations. According to several commissions of inquiry, the Macondo and Montara incidents resulted from causal contributions of the well operator and the drilling contractor.

It has been advanced that responsibility between parties may arise from causation or risk allocation.[8] Causation, accordingly, unsettles the responsible party when a downside occurs. The causal contribution referred to above is what Wright terms the NESS (necessary element of a sufficient set) condition.[9] In other words, the

[4] Richard W Wright, 'Causation in Tort Law' (1985) 73 California Law Review 1737.

[5] Tony Honoré, 'Causation in the Law' in Edward N Zalta (ed), *Stanford Encyclopaedia of Philosophy* (2010 edn) <plato.stanford.edu/archives/win2010/entries/causation-law> accessed 14 October 2023; Michael S Moore, *Causation and Responsibility: An Essay in Law, Morals, and Metaphysics* (OUP 2009).

[6] HLA Hart and Tony Honoré, *Causation in the Law* (2nd edn, Clarendon Press 1985).

[7] Wright, 'Causation in Tort Law' (n 4) 1738.

[8] Hart and Honoré (n 6).

[9] Wright, 'Causation in Tort Law' (n 4) 1788–803. For further explanations on the NESS condition see Euan West, 'The Utility of the NESS Test of Factual Causation in Scots Law' (2013) 4(3) Aberdeen Student Law Review 39; Desmond M Clarke, 'Causation and Liability in Tort Law' (2014) 5(2) Jurisprudence 217.

agent's negligent act, with other actions, resulted in the outcome under the NESS condition. Also, where actions contribute to an outcome, liability is expected to be shared between the parties following their causal connections. This causal connection arises from the theories of agent-focused responsibility, which are not neutral regarding distribution[10] but support distributional implications.[11] This implication results from a causal responsibility. Honoré calls it 'outcome responsibility' as it allocates outcomes or consequences for actions.[12]

4.1.2 Causation and Liability for Grossly Negligent Conduct

Causation gives rise to liability, which is the corrective result of causation. Whether the cause was factual or legal, liability attaches to negligent conduct. Causation is the underlying relationship between the defendant's conduct and the outcome, emphasising that the breach of duty should considerably contribute to the resulting damage. In tort, liability can apply in case of causation in fact or law. However, in a contract, where parties allocate risks among themselves, there can be factual causation, but the need for legal causation does not arise if the party is not contractually responsible for the damage. The reason is that legal causation follows a legal responsibility for harm or a breach of duty, whereas factual causation does not always give rise to liability, especially where liability has been reallocated, as is the practice in the oil industry. Factual causation only requires the other party to show that the defendant was the cause of, or contributed to, the damage that occurred.[13]

Although responsibility can be allocated in private agreements, this allocation must be within the confines of established law and policy. For instance, where public interest overrides parties' interest, such as in gross negligence situations, liability will attach to protect the society and deter the wrongdoer from engaging in similar conduct. On the other hand, where liability is not linked to wrongdoing, especially in gross negligence cases, moral hazard will set in, thus impacting society. As such, an objective of deterrence in the civil liability regime for offshore oil and gas drilling is to discourage harmful conduct and reduce the cost of accidents.[14] Without deterrence, parties may engage in riskier behaviour, resulting in more costly accidents than are socially desired.

In the context of gross negligence, it is necessary to determine causation in terms of the party's connection to the damage. This idea aligns the notions of causation and responsibility. The essence is for liability to attach to deter such conduct that will harm the public. In other words, a fundamental question is

10 Peter Cane, *Responsibility in Law and Morality* (Hart Publishing 2002) 190.

11 ibid.

12 Tony Honoré, *Responsibility and Fault* (Hart Publishing 1999) 15.

13 Clarence Morris, 'Duty, Negligence and Causation' (1952) 101 University of Pennsylvania Law Review 189.

14 Tamara Lotner Lev, 'Liability for Environmental Damages from the Offshore Petroleum Industry: Strict Liability Justifications and the Judgment-Proof Problem' (2016) 43 Ecology Law Quarterly 483.

whether the party is factually connected to the damage for which it seeks to use an exclusion or mutual indemnity clause to avoid liability. In gross negligence cases, where a party is factually connected to the harm, such connection places a duty on the wrongdoer(s) to compensate for their wrongful conduct following the proportion of their benefit in private arrangements. In this regard, public policy places an implied duty on contractual parties to prevent harm that will impact the public. Where such harm occurs due to gross negligence, the party has an implied responsibility to compensate for their wrong. For example, in the oil and gas industry, the duty arises from the need to protect people and the environment due to the nature of hydrocarbon activities, by discouraging conduct that will harm people and the ecosystem. In other words, where a party's gross negligence causes pollution damage, they have a duty to compensate for the damage caused by their gross negligence.

4.2 GROSS NEGLIGENCE: CONTEXT AND DIMENSIONS

4.2.1 *Gross Negligence – A* sui generis *Liability?*

Sui generis is a Latin phrase that means 'of its own kind'. It refers to anything peculiar to itself, of its kind or class. In legal parlance, *sui generis* represents an independent legal classification.[15] Why is gross negligence a unique type of liability? The unique nature of this type of liability arises from the fact that in most jurisdictions, like the US, gross negligence attracts a higher penalty or fine. Again, a classification of gross negligence is used to address harm or damage that is beyond the normal type of damage. It is usually used to express damage or wrongful conduct of monumental proportions.

4.2.2 *A Historical Perspective on Gross Negligence*

Gross negligence, as earlier identified, has an origin in Roman law. However, there are divergent opinions regarding negligence in Roman law. Despite these opinions, several degrees of negligence existed in the Justinian time.[16] In England, the concept of gross negligence is traceable to Henry de Bracton's *De Legibus et Consuetudinibus Angliae*, which incorporated much of the Roman theory of degrees of negligence.[17] Bracton's treatise contributed to the field of bailments, where courts used degrees of negligence in settling disputes. Bailment arises when a bailee takes possession of goods owned by a bailor.[18] Lord Holt, handing

[15] Cornell Law School, 'Sui Generis' (Legal Information Institute, August 2021) <www.law.cornell.edu/wex/sui_generis> accessed 15 October 2023.

[16] These degrees of negligence include *culpa lata* and *culpa levis*. See Section 1.X for more discussion about how gross negligence came about in Roman law.

[17] Frederick Green, 'High Care and Gross Negligence' (1928) 23(1) Illinois Law Review 12.

[18] Ben McFarlane, 'Bailment' in Peter Cane and Joanne Conaghan (eds), *The New Oxford Companion of Law* (OUP 2008).

down his opinion in *Coggs v Bernard*,[19] reviewed the degrees of negligence based on Bracton's treatise and outlined the liability and degree of care attached to each situation.[20] Bailment exists independent of contract, but arises mainly from a contractual relationship such as a hire or loan transaction.[21] It could be gratis or as a reward. The duty of care in bailment varies as the interest differs. In a bailment for the benefit of the bailor, the duty of care required of the bailee is slight. Where it is for bailee's benefit, extraordinary care is required, while an ordinary duty of care applies where the bailment is for the parties' mutual benefit.[22]

In an attempt to revise Lord Holt's opinion, Sir Williams Jones propounded negligence grouping, to wit:

> GROSS neglect, lata culpa . . . is in practice considered as equivalent to DOLUS or FRAUD, itself; and consists, according to the best interpreters, in the omission of that care, which even inattentive and thoughtless men never fail to take of their property . . . ORDINARY neglect, levis culpa, is the want of that diligence which the generality of mankind uses in their own concerns; that is, ordinary care. . . . SLIGHT neglect, levissima culpa, is the omission of that care which very attentive and vigilant persons take of their own goods, or in other words, of very exact diligence.[23]

The highlighted divisions of negligence became established in bailment before making inroads into tort law. For consistency in the law of torts, the contractual background of gross negligence and other identified degrees was overlooked. Bailment negligence in the field of torts appears to have been applied first in the early nineteenth century,[24] and in the US, Story J's commentaries on the law of bailments influenced the introduction of bailment into the legal system.[25] Apart from Roman contract and criminal law, gross negligence resurfaced in the English law of bailment in the eighteenth century before standing alone in torts in the early nineteenth century. In Roman and early English law, liability in bailment and torts was absolute but gradually became relative.

As a concept in bailment, gross negligence was still applicable as the primary contractual relationship whereby specific obligations could be ascertained. In contract, gross negligence applies to limit the application of indemnity clauses, where contracting parties identify that an indemnity clause does not cover gross

19 [1703] 2 Ld Raym 909. The defendant in this case undertook to transport some casks of brandy from one cellar to another without compensation. The defendant was negligent in handling the casks, and one of them broke and poured on the ground. The plaintiff sought to hold the gratuitous bailee (defendant) liable for the loss. The court then set out the liability and degree of care attached to each situation.

20 ibid; Green (n 17) 12; 'The Three Degrees of Negligence' (1874) 8 American Law Review 652.

21 McFarlane (n 18).

22 Richard H Helmholz, 'Theories and the Liability of Bailees: The Elusive Uniform Standard of Reasonable Care' (1992) 41 University of Kansas Law Review 97.

23 William Jones, *An Essay on the Law of Bailments* (2nd edn, 1804) 62.

24 Daniel O Howard, 'An Analysis of Gross Negligence' (1954) 37(4) Marquette Law Review 333, 338.

25 ibid.

negligence.[26] As a concept in tort, it became a labyrinth of complex definitions and reasoning. In English tort law, it has been abandoned.[27] However, other areas of English law, such as criminal law,[28] still apply gross negligence to determine liability, indicating that the concept is intelligible and its application is not entirely complex. In other areas of law, such as mortgages, where gross negligence is established in the conduct of a legal mortgagee, the mortgage will be postponed if it would be unjust to deprive a prior equitable incumbrancer of his priority.[29]

The application of gross negligence is even more complex in the US, as several states have the power to make laws. In states where gross negligence is considered a meaningful term, there is still the problem of whether the difference between gross negligence and ordinary negligence is one of degree or kind. Some courts hold that the difference is about kind, as ordinary negligence arises from inadvertence, while gross negligence falls within the area of actual or constructive intent to harm.[30] However, it must be noted that gross negligence, whether in tort or bailment, is conduct and not an intention.[31] Its origin is traceable to bailment and contracts rather than tort, and the focus is on the conduct of a party.

4.2.3 Varying the Standard of Care in Negligence

A fundamental question here is whether there have been instances where negligence was varied to achieve a particular purpose or underpinning, or whether we can vary gross negligence to achieve a specific objective. A different dimension is presented when we examine the degrees of negligence from a risk-utility perspective. These dimensions arise because the risk-utility formula suggests that some negligent conduct is worse than others. This perspective may invite bootless wrangling over questions about the objective test.[32] Nonetheless, there have been instances where courts and lawmakers have varied the requirement for negligent conduct by providing for a limited standard of care. Varying in this instance means

26 *Red Sea Tankers Ltd v Papachristidis (The Ardent)* [1997] 2 Lloyd's Rep 547.

27 Although gross negligence has been abandoned in English tort law, it remains applicable in cases where damages are claimed for the wrongful arrest of a vessel. The claim will succeed where gross negligence or bad faith is shown. See *Centro Latino Americano de Commercio Exterior SA v Owners of the Kommunar (The Kommunar No 3)* [1997] 1 Lloyd's Rep 22 (QBD).

28 A person's act of gross negligence could be used to establish manslaughter in English criminal law. See *Bawa-Garba v R* [2016] EWCA Crim 1841; *R v Sellu* [2016] EWCA Crim 1716; *R v Adomako* [1995] 1 AC 171; Corporate Manslaughter and Corporate Homicide Act 2007 s 1(1)(b).

29 *Northern Counties of England Fire Insurance Co v Whipp* (1884) 26 Ch D 482.

30 *Wedel v Klein* 229 Wis 419, 282 NW 606 (1938); *Wieczorek v Merskin* 208 Mich 145, 13 NW 2d 239 (1944).

31 In *Kastel v Stieber* 56 83 Cal Dec 249, 8 P 2d 474 (1932), the court held that: 'We should not confuse "gross negligence" with "wilful misconduct" because there is a clear distinction between the two terms . . . Whenever the element of knowledge and wilfulness enters into the act, it ceases to be negligence.'

32 Bryan ME McMahon and William Binchy, *Law of Torts* (3rd edn, Butterworths 2000) 160; Cf *O'Connell v CIE* (1954) 89 ILTR 95 (HC).

that for a person to be liable for a wrong, the negligence must be higher. This practice ensures that the negligent conduct does not go unpunished, so that public policy is not negated. Limiting the allowance of certain harmful conducts promotes public policy and discourages moral hazard in contractual transactions or where a legal duty exists.

This variation has been applied in cases where the statute provides that an operator of an emergency vehicle (fire engines, ambulances and so on) is only liable if the negligent conduct is of a higher degree.[33] Another example is where the conduct of a public officer is adjudged to be grossly negligent based on public policy decisions exercised in the performance of their public duty.[34] Other cases where the standard of care could be limited may include voluntary emergency assistance[35] or where parties agree in a contract that only a high degree of negligence should be the basis for liability. This variance could be due to the nature of the transaction and the benefit and burden of the parties.[36] Finally, there is evidence of the English courts applying a varied or limited standard of care in special circumstances. For example, a court applied a limited standard of care to show the obligation an occupier owes a trespasser and a non-visitor. The court's position was that, for an occupier to be liable to a trespasser, the injury must result from a reckless disregard for the trespasser's safety.[37]

Similarly, for public authorities, courts have applied a modified standard of care to enable the exercise of discretion by public officeholders. In *Home Office v Dorset Yacht Co Ltd*, the court held that negligence could only arise from the decision of a public authority when such a decision was so manifestly careless or unreasonable that it did not amount to an exercise of discretion granted by a statute.[38] The trustee's exemption clause also lends credence to the utility of the gross

33 *Saarinen v Kerr* 84 NY 2d 494, 644 NE 2d 988, 620 NYS 2d 297 (1994).

34 Elizabeth Carroll, 'Wednesbury Unreasonableness as a Limit to Civil Liability of Public Authorities' (2007) 15 Tort Law Review 77; *Calloway v Kinkelaar* 168 III 2d 312, 213 III Dec 675, 659 NE 2d 1322 (1995); Civil Liability Act 2002 (Western Australia); Civil Liability Act 2002 (New South Wales).

35 Kevin Williams, 'Medical Samaritans: Is There a Duty to Treat?' (2001) 21(3) OJLS 411; Emergency Medical Act 2000 (Alberta); Good Samaritan Act 1996 (British Columbia); Quebec Civil Code art 1471; Civil Liability Act 2002 pt 8A (Tasmania). The Irish Law Reform Commission in 2009, proposed a limited standard of care for volunteers. See Irish Law Reform Commission, *Civil Liability of Good Samaritans and Volunteers* (LRC 93, 2009). This limited standard of care for volunteers was however rejected by an English court in *Cattley v St John's Ambulance Brigade* (QBD 25 Nov 1998). However, the possibility of a legislative clarity was echoed in Lord Young's report: HM Government, *Common Sense, Common Safety* (Report by Lord Young of Graffham to the Prime Minister, October 2010), <assets.publishing.service.gov.uk/government/uploads/system/uploads/attachment_data/file/60905/402906_CommonSense_acc.pdf> accessed 15 October 2023.

36 In the oil and gas industry, parties (operator and contractor) sometimes agree that gross negligence will be a basis for a contractor to assume liability.

37 *Robert Addie & Sons (Collieries) Ltd v Dumbreck* [1929] AC 358. Although this limited application was abandoned in *British Railway Board v Herrington* [1972] AC 877, the court applied a lesser obligation of 'common humanity' as opposed to the standard of a reasonable man. This lesser duty later assumed a statutory strength in the Occupiers' Liability Act 1984.

38 [1970] UKHL 2.

negligence debate on the proper scope of the trustee's exemption, distinguishing between gross negligence, which is not allowed, and ordinary negligence, which is permitted.[39] The Trust Law Commission recognised the existence of the distinction between gross negligence and ordinary negligence. The Scottish Law Commission, in one of its discussion papers, concluded that gross negligence was a useful concept.[40] In all these situations, liability for a wrongful act applies to a high degree of negligence. The emphasis here is on the degree of carelessness, not just ordinary carelessness that would amount to negligence. This limited standard of care in particular cases makes the degree of negligence relevant in certain circumstances.

The variation of the standard of negligence arises from considering the social utility of the defendant's conduct,[41] the public authority in question or the parties' contractual relationship. In other words, to limit or modify the standard of care, a high degree of negligence, in the form of gross negligence, should occur in specific circumstances. This high standard is applied to protect the defendant's interest. A high standard for negligence affords public servants the protection they require to carry out their duty while preserving public policy and discouraging moral hazards. Moreover, liability only arises from a degree of harmful conduct and not the lack of ordinary care. As such, it is severely wrongful conduct that will determine liability.

4.2.4 Contextualising the Meaning of Gross Negligence

Gross negligence can result from special circumstances, but they attach liability when the conduct is wrongful beyond normal expectations. The following sections explore different jurisdictions' perspectives on gross negligence.

4.2.4.1 Regime of Gross Negligence in the United States

The term 'gross negligence' is essential in the US hydrocarbon contracting practice and tort law. Gross negligence can apply as a sword or as a shield. When used as a sword, it could be grounds for terminating a contract, a basis for indemnification or a reason for circumventing a waiver of liability. As a shield, it could act as grounds for a release from liability. However, the courts in the *City of Santa Barbara v Superior Courts*[42] and *Sommer v Federal Signal Corp*[43] cases held

[39] Trust Law Commission, *Trustees Exemption Clause* (Law Comm no 301, 2006) [A43]–[A48].

[40] Scottish Law Commission, *Breach of Trust* (Scot Law Comm DP no 123, 2003) [3.30].

[41] Richard W Wright, 'The Standard of Care in Negligence Law' in David G Owen (ed), *The Philosophical Foundations of Tort Law* (OUP 1995) 250.

[42] 161 P 3d 1095 (Cal 2007).

[43] 79 NY 2d 540 (NY 1992); David Shine, 'Contractual Application of Negligence/Gross Negligence Standards: Considerations under New York Law' (2005) 8(10) The M&A Lawyer 10. It must be noted that releases from gross negligence are not likely to be enforceable in New York.

[44] Page Keeton and William L Prosser, *Prosser and Keeton on the Law of Torts* (5th edn, West Publishing Co 1984) 210.

that advance releases of liability are unenforceable on the grounds of public policy consideration in cases of gross negligence. However, a liability release that employs negligence standards and other clauses may be enforceable. How a person's conduct, whether negligent or grossly negligent, is determined may depend on the circumstances.

Some scholars identify that gross negligence is vague, unrealistic in context and unfounded in principle and has no settled meaning.[44] They further argue that what makes a difference in most situations as a matter of law is not a particular degree of negligence or care but the fact that a different amount of care exists. In the case of *The Steamboat New World v King*,[45] the court noted that the applicability of the terms 'gross negligence' and 'wilful misconduct' is doubtful as their meaning is not fixed. The court also identified that when one degree is fixed, it confounds another and makes it impracticable to distinguish. This is because their significance differs according to the circumstances, and there are many exceptions. Hence, they are seen as not having general operation.[46] The court in the *Steamboat* case posited further that if the law provided no definition of gross negligence but left it to the jury to determine, the attempt to define that duty had better be abandoned. It has also been advanced that, historically, gross negligence is a fault-based moral judgment, and its usage in some areas of tort law has distortedly brought it into the concept of causation.

While gross negligence is not traditionally recognised as a separate concept in the UK and Australia,[47] the OPA 1990, through Congress, engraved the term 'gross negligence' in the US regime, albeit without a precise meaning. The OPA deals with oil pollution at sea in the US. The Clean Water Act, a federal law, does not define the term.[48] The intention of Congress may be for the term to operate as a moral basis for severe liability against a party for causing damage that would arise from negligence applicable under tort rules.[49] This perspective makes gross negligence a moral judgement rather than a legal judgment. In determining the extent of a responsible party's liability, the OPA limits the liability to US$75 million but states that the liability should be without limit if the responsible party is guilty of

[45] 57 US (16 How) 469 (1853).

[46] Patrick H Martin, 'The BP Spill and the Meaning of Gross Negligence or Willful Misconduct' (2011) 71(3) Louisiana Law Review 957, 959.

[47] *Tradigrain SA v Intertek Testing Services (ITS) Canada Ltd* [2007] EWCA Civ 154 [23] (Bick LJ); Carolyn Sappideen and Prue Vines, *Fleming's The Law of Torts* (10th edn, Lawbook Co 2011) [7.180].

[48] The OPA and the CWA both use the terms 'wilful misconduct' and 'gross negligence'. Before now, the standard for unlimited liability under the CWA was 'willful negligence or willful misconduct' 33 USC § 1321(b)(6)(B) (1988). This was, however, changed to gross negligence or willful misconduct by the OPA. Pub L 101-380 § 4301(b)(D) 104 Stat 484, 537 (1990). See also *Water Quality Insurance Syndicate v United States* 522 F Supp 2d 220 (DDC 2007) (relying on case law interpreting 'wilful misconduct' under the CWA to interpret that phrase under OPA); 82 CJS *Statutes* § 476 (2014) (statutes relating to the same subject matter 'generally should be read as together constituting one law and should be harmonized if possible').

[49] Martin (n 45) 991.

gross negligence.[50] This means that gross negligence is understood as negligent conduct beyond the normal level, which should be discouraged by making the party at fault pay a higher penalty. It must be noted that some mutual indemnity agreements carve out gross negligence as a liability trigger, except where parties agree to the contrary, as in the BP and Transocean contract case. The challenge before courts is to construe the meaning of gross negligence in the parties' contract. Notwithstanding this, the critical question is :what does the term 'gross negligence' mean under the US regime?

From the section of the OPA referred to above, we can understand gross negligence as a grade of negligence used as a heightened degree of fault to trigger responsibility for damage and impose severe liability on a responsible party. However, categorising the degree of negligence is difficult, hence the inability of courts to draw a coherent difference between gross negligence and ordinary negligence. In the US, however, this term is a vital part of the regulatory fabric of federal and state statutory schemes for deterrence and improving safety in high-risk activities such as hydrocarbon exploration and production.

The focus of gross negligence has always been about degree and not about kind. This perspective was identified by the Court of Appeal in *Sommer*, where it held that gross negligence must 'smack of intentional wrongdoing' and that the conduct must 'evince a reckless indifference to the right of others'.[51] In contrast to *Sommer*, the Supreme Court of California, in the *City of Santa Barbara* case, held that gross negligence 'has long been defined . . . as either a "want of even scant care" or an extreme departure from the ordinary standard conduct'.[52] The US Coast Guard's National Pollution Funds Center (NPFC) noted that a higher degree of care is required where more significant risk is apparent, and that a failure to exercise even slight care or an extreme departure from the care needed in a given circumstance would mean that the negligence is 'gross'.[53]

In trying to unravel the meaning of gross negligence used by parties in their contracts, courts have offered various definitions for the concept. The judicial perspective in some cases shows that gross negligence involves serious neglect for a palpable breach[54] and that conscious or intentional wrongdoing is not a component of gross negligence.[55] It also identifies that gross negligence appears to

[50] 33 USC s 2704(c)(1)(A).

[51] See *Sommer* (n 43) 554. This position was reiterated in the case of *Colnaghi USA Ltd v Jewellers Protection Services Ltd* 81 NY 2d 821 (1993), where the court stated that gross negligence differs 'in kind, not only degree, from claims of ordinary negligence' and that gross negligence is 'conduct that evinces a reckless disregard for the rights of others or "smacks" of intentional wrongdoing.'

[52] See *City of Santa Barbara* case (n 42) 1099.

[53] *Kuroshima Shipping SA Act of God Defense and Limit of Liability Analysis* 2003 AMC 1681 (2003). See also *Water Quality Insurance Syndicate* (n 48); Martin (n 45) 1017.

[54] Liam Brown, 'Gross Negligence in Exclusion Clauses: Is there an Intelligible Difference between Ordinary Negligence and Gross Negligence?' (2005) 16 Insurance Law Journal 9.

[55] *Armitage v Nurse* [1998] 1 WLR 270; *ANZ Banking Group Ltd v Intagro Projects Pty Ltd* [2004] NSWSC 1054 [28]–[29].

differ from mere negligence in degree and not kind. Gross negligence has been described as 'truly culpable or harmful' conduct[56] involving a high degree of careless or 'negligently egregious' conduct. Finally, there is also the perspective that gross negligence comprises a conscious choice of conduct that involves a palpable or high degree of risk with severe consequences. This perspective follows the reasoning that for conduct to constitute gross negligence, it must emanate from an objective determination.[57]

Black's Law Dictionary defines gross negligence as

> 1. A, lack of slight diligence or care. 2. A, conscious, voluntary act or omission in reckless disregard of a legal duty and of the consequences to another party, who may typically recover exemplary damages.[58]

The jurisprudence of gross negligence does not follow a definitive pattern. Rather, it focuses on case-specific facts, hence the challenge of contractually describing what conduct amounts to gross negligence. From an analytical perspective, different definitional streams emanate from the dictionary and judicial opinion regarding the meaning of gross negligence. The reference to 'lack of slight diligence or care', 'high degree of careless conduct' and so on portrays gross negligence as a wrongful act which does not incorporate a mental element.[59] This perspective requires a court to apply the 'reasonable man' test. Furthermore, the reference to the phrases 'want of or even scant care', 'reckless disregard' or 'reckless indifference' introduces the requirement of a mental element. It therefore invites a court to infer the party's state of mind that caused the wrong. When courts are left to decide whether gross negligence has occurred, there is a willingness to hold the operator grossly negligent or hold against an operator.[60] This reasoning, including the regulatory position, informed the finding that BP was grossly negligent in the Macondo disaster.

4.2.4.2 Regime of Gross Negligence in the United Kingdom

Gross negligence has no established legal foundation regarding its meaning in the UK. Therefore, it is subject to different interpretations, and a subject of dispute. In the UK, tort jurisprudence does not recognise degrees of negligence. However, negligence arising from the breach of a duty of care exists. In contract, the degrees of negligence must be made to distinguish one form of negligence from the other

[56] *Metro Life v Noble Lowndes* 84 NY 2d 430 (1994).

[57] *Lester v Atchison, Topeka and Santa Fe Railway Co* 272 F 2d 42 (1960).

[58] *Black's Law Dictionary* (9th edn, West 2009), *sub verbo* 'gross negligence'.

[59] The jurisprudence of criminal law, as advanced in *Fowler v Padget* (1798) 101 ER 1103, requires a concurrence of the intent and the act to constitute a crime.

[60] Miles Pittman, 'Gross Negligence in Canadian Energy Contracts' (2013) 52(2) Alberta Law Review 309; *Adeco Exploration Company Ltd v Hunt Oil Company of Canada Inc* [2008] ABCA 214.

to determine liability, especially in the oil industry. In law, a reference to negligence is clearly understood: a failure by a reasonable person to comply with the standard of care required by law.[61] However, this simple understanding is not so simple for gross negligence. For a contract to provide for gross negligence, the law must be clearly defined, and the conduct for which to be held responsible should be identified.

In the UK, the concept of gross negligence is often used in drafting contracts in the hydrocarbon industry, but the lack of clarity as to its meaning persists. It has also been posited that gross negligence is no different from negligence and that, under English law, 'negligence' is negligence. This view finds support in the cases of *Wilson v Brett*[62] and *Pentecost v London District Auditor*.[63] However, it may not stand the test of today's hydrocarbon industry, as the term 'gross negligence' is used often and deliberately. As will be seen, English court decisions have indicated a distinction between gross negligence and mere negligence. As a result, there is no basis for asserting that negligence and gross negligence are the same. The perspective exists that a separate and distinct meaning of gross negligence in the hydrocarbon industry is consistent with the fundamental principles in interpreting contracts. It is vital to note that, when contracts are interpreted, there should be reference to all background knowledge that would reasonably have been available to the contracting parties,[64] and an interpretation that is consistent with business common sense should be preferred.[65] Using the term 'gross negligence' in oil and gas contracts indicates that contracting parties intend to achieve a different outcome from mere negligence.

4.2.4.3 Gross Negligence: Perspective of the United Kingdom Courts

The term 'gross negligence' is commonly found in commercial agreements in the UK to represent a condition where a party at fault will not benefit from an exclusion clause or receive indemnity for their wrongful conduct. Although the meaning of gross negligence is not different from that of simple negligence in English civil law, English courts will usually interpret the term and give effect to it if it appears in a contract. As such, the interpretation of the term is left for a court to decide. Thus, its meaning usually results from the nature of the contract, the meaning parties ascribed to it on a case-by-case basis.

The court in *Camarata Property Inc v Credit Suisse Securities (Europe) Ltd*[66] attempted to explain the concept of gross negligence. However, the court's focus

[61] In law, for negligence to occur, a duty of care must exist; that duty must have been breached; and injury or damages must result. There appear to be no statutorily defined degrees of negligence in the UK.

[62] [1843] 11 M & W 113.

[63] [1951] 2 KB 759.

[64] *Investors Compensation Scheme Ltd v West Bromwich Building Society* [1997] UKHL 28.

[65] *Rainy Sky SA v Kookmin Bank* [2011] UKSC 50.

[66] [2011] EWHC 479 (Comm).

was not on the recognition or otherwise of the term 'gross negligence' under English law but on what it meant in the parties' contract. The court held the view that 'gross negligence' in the parties' contract was intended to represent 'something more fundamental than a simple failure to exercise proper skill and/or care to constitute negligence' and that, in plain language, it appeared to 'embrace not only conduct undertaken with an appreciation of the risk involved but also a serious disregard of or indifference to an obvious risk'.[67]

Ultimately, the court was descriptive, not definitive or precise, about the meaning of gross negligence. The wording and content of the party's contract must have driven the court's interpretation and decision. The court's perspective could have been so because the terms 'negligence' and 'gross negligence' were used in the contract, suggesting that the parties intended the degree of negligence to be fundamental in distinguishing mere negligence from gross negligence. However, under English contract law, gross negligence remains undefined.[68] Traditional arguments on gross negligence support the view that 'gross' adds little or nothing to negligence, given that gross negligence is negligence 'with the inclusion of a vituperative epithet'.[69] A modern view supports the argument that 'gross' does add something to negligence, with a difference in degree and not kind.[70] The Court of Appeal, per Beldam LJ, examined the meaning of gross negligence and held that

> [i]n the context of [this clause], the words 'gross negligence' . . . refer . . . to an act or omission not done deliberately, but which in the circumstances would be regarded by those familiar with the circumstances as a serious error. The likely consequences of the error are a significant factor. Thus, whether negligence is gross is a function of the nature of the error and the seriousness of the risk which results from it.[71]

The court did not mention what action(s) constitutes a serious error for gross negligence to arise, thus making gross negligence a subjective rather than an objective concept. Leaving the concept of gross negligence open to a subjective

[67] Per Smith J in *Camarata*. The conduct is unknown and the person whose office is tied to the conduct is also not stated. The question is what conduct(s) is defined or stated as gross negligence. This conduct must be clearly stated in the contract for precision. The court in *Camarata* followed the interpretation of gross negligence by the court in *The Ardent*, per Mance J, who stated:

> 'Gross' negligence is clearly intended to represent something more fundamental than failure to exercise proper skill and/or care constituting negligence. But, as a matter of ordinary language and general impression, the concept of gross negligence seems to me to be capable of embracing not only conduct undertaken with actual appreciation of the risks involved, but also serious disregard of or an indifference to an obvious risk.

[68] This position was advanced by the claimant in *Camarata*, who argued that no distinction exists under English law between negligence and gross negligence. The court in *Camarata* merely focused on its meaning as used in the contract and not on its application under English law.

[69] *Wilson v Brett* (n 62).

[70] *Camarata* (n 66).

[71] *Great Scottish & Western Railway Co Ltd v British Railway Board* (CA, 10 February 2000).

interpretation presents significant challenges in application. It means that parties will still approach a court to determine the meaning of gross negligence from the circumstances of their contract.

Affirming the interpretation in *Camarata* that gross negligence is about the degree of negligence, the Supreme Court of Ireland in *ICDL GCC Foundation FZ-LLC v European Computer Driving Licence Foundation Ltd* agreed with the reasoning of the lower court. It held that gross negligence meant 'a degree of negligence where whatever duty of care may be involved has not been met by a significant margin.'[72] From the court's interpretation of gross negligence, it is apparent that courts would interpret gross negligence as something more unusual and that involves greater wrong than ordinary negligence. However, no definitive ruling currently exists. This situation means that the interpretation of gross negligence is not based on earlier *dicta* but on the facts and context of each case. Moreover, 'gross negligence' as a tort that has no place under English law despite its continued use by parties in construction agreements.[73] However, in most cases in English law, the term 'wilful misconduct' is applicable.

4.3 WILFUL MISCONDUCT

The concept of wilful misconduct is another carve-out used in oil and gas contracts to attach liability to a party at fault when a downside occurs. Amongst co-venturers, their agreement sometimes reflects that indemnities, as stated in the agreement, will be inapplicable where wilful misconduct occurs. However, the challenge is that 'wilful misconduct' does not have a wholly settled meaning under English law.[74] As such, it is possible to improperly apply or misinterpret it to the detriment of another party to the contract. In an attempt to interpret the term 'wilful misconduct', the court in *Graham v Belfast and Northern Counties Railway Co*[75] posited that 'wilful misconduct . . . means misconduct to which the will is a party as contradistinguished from an accident, and is far beyond any negligence, even gross . . . negligence'. The court in *Forder v Great Railway Company*[76] adopted

[72] [2012] IESC 55 (SC)

[73] James Pickavance, 'Gross Negligence in Construction Contracts: Law and Practice' (Eversheds 2015) <www.lexology.com/library/detail.aspx?g=37573335-12ec-4f1b-bee9-0f8194fd9bb2> accessed 15 October 2023. Gross negligence is still viewed as simple negligence under English law.

[74] Greg Gordon, 'Risk Allocation in Oil and Gas Service Contracts' in Greg Gordon, John Paterson and Emre Usenmez (eds), *Oil and Gas Law: Current Practice and Emerging Trends: Volume II: Commercial and Contract Issues* (3rd edn, Edinburgh University Press 2018) 348.

[75] [1901] 2 IR 13.

[76] [1905] 2 KB 532; see also *Laceys Footwear Ltd v Bowler International Freight* [1997] EWCA Civ 1454, and *TNT Global v Denfleet International Ltd* [2007] EWCA Civ 405, where the Court of Appeal held that

> wilful misconduct is more than negligent misjudgement, and either an intention to do something which the actor knows to be wrong or reckless act in a sense that the actor is aware that loss may result from this act and yet does not care whether loss will result or not.

the position in *Graham* and added that wilful misconduct includes 'acting with reckless carelessness, not caring what the results of his carelessness may be'. The court in *De Beers UK Ltd v Atos Origin IT Services Ltd*[77] interpreted a contract that limited the defendant's liability but excluded the limit in the event of wilful misconduct or deliberate default. In arriving at its decision, the court held that 'wilful misconduct' was conduct by a person 'who knows that he is committing and intends to commit a breach of duty or is reckless in the sense of not caring whether or not he commits a breach of duty.'

A reckless disregard for stated duty is a question of fact based on the circumstances of each case. The interpretation of wilful misconduct by the court is subjective as it is based on a party's evaluation; hence, it is open to debate between parties. From the above, an element of knowledge of the wrongful act must exist in wilful misconduct. The knowledge of the wrongful act must also be subjective, with a deliberate action to proceed to take the risk. In other words, the party committing the wilful misconduct must be aware that they are committing or about to commit a reckless breach of duty but not care about it. In the UK, wilful misconduct appears more often in private contracts, and we can infer that wilful misconduct encompasses not knowing or not caring that a particular act is wrong under a contract.

4.4 CHALLENGES ASSOCIATED WITH MANAGING AND ALLOCATING GROSS NEGLIGENCE RISK

The discussion in the previous sections raises crucial questions about the factors that challenge the management and allocation of gross negligence risk. This section identifies and discusses those challenges, especially in the oil and gas industry.

4.4.1 Challenge of Defining Gross Negligence

In using 'gross negligence' as a term in law, reference is often made to a party's reckless conduct that leads to damages to another party. In the judicial circle, attempts have been made to define gross negligence as an egregious violation of a legal duty to protect the rights of others. In other cases, courts have defined the term using words such as 'intentional' and 'reckless'. Courts have also used other terms: for instance, in *Grill v General Iron Screw Collier Company*, Willes J remarked, '[G]ross negligence is ordinary negligence with a vituperative epithet.'[78] However, the Irish Supreme Court refused to follow the reasoning in *Grill* as an accurate interpretation of the term in contract law.[79] The Irish Supreme Court

[77] [2010] EWHC 3276 (TCC).

[78] (1866) LR 1 CP 600, 612. This position was also stated by Lord Cranworth in *Wilson v Brett* (n 62). English law has traditionally not distinguished between gross negligence and ordinary negligence, but English courts will always interpret contractual provisions that use gross negligence in a contract.

[79] The Irish case is *ICDL GCC Foundation FZ-LLC* (n 72).

instead concluded that gross negligence meant a degree of negligence involving a breach of the relevant duty of care by a significant margin, and that, for an exclusion cause to be effective, it is necessary to establish that the breach of contract arose from a significant degree of carelessness.

In *Grill*, the court's perspective was that gross negligence and negligence are the same, and that it is only a matter of semantics. However, in the Irish case, the court held that there is a difference between the two terms, and that the difference lies in a significant degree of carelessness. The Irish court further stated that the meaning of gross negligence should be derived from the context in which the parties had agreed to use it in the contract. This implies that the meaning of gross negligence is context specific, and not generally recognisable like ordinary negligence.

In the English case of *Camarata*, the court also emphasised that English courts will interpret contractual provisions referring to gross negligence by looking at what the parties to the contract intend the term to be. Nevertheless, in New York, for instance, a court will consider the degree of departure from the standard of care. This perspective is akin to the view of the English court in *Goodman v Harley*[80] and *Armitage v Nurse*.[81] In *Armitage*, the court identified that the difference between 'mere negligence' and 'gross negligence' is one of degree not kind and therefore is not easy to define or describe precisely. Again, gross negligence is considered by most courts as an intention, whereas other courts see it as conduct. These judicial perspectives present a challenge regarding the definition of gross negligence: the meaning of gross negligence is not settled, which is a challenge in tort and contract law.

Regardless of the position in English contract and tort, English criminal jurisprudence recognises the term 'gross negligence'. Outside the realm of contract, particularly in criminal jurisprudence, UK courts have had cause to determine guilt by reasoning along the lines of conduct that falls *far below* the required standard in gross negligence manslaughter. In determining whether a breach of duty amounted to gross negligence manslaughter, the court in *R v Sellu*[82] highlighted some things to consider. The court noted that the task before the jury was not just 'to decide whether [the defendant] fell below the standard of a reasonably competent consultant colorectal surgeon, but whether he did so in a way that was gross or severe'. On appeal, the defendant's appeal was allowed. The reason was that the trial judge failed to assist the jury in identifying the line that separates serious errors from conduct which was 'truly exceptionally bad and was such a departure from that standard [of a reasonably competent doctor] that it consequently amounted to being criminal'. For a person to be guilty of gross negligence

80 (1836) 4 A & E 870: 'But while we regard the difference between fraud on the one hand and mere negligence, however gross, on the other as a difference in kind, we regard the difference between negligence and gross negligence as merely one of degree.' Despite this distinction, the court did not attempt to define gross negligence.

81 *Armitage* (n 55).

82 *Sellu* (n 28).

manslaughter, their conduct must be severe. Mere negligence will not lead to a finding of guilt.

In a similar case where the conviction was upheld, the trial judge accurately brought to the jury's attention that the prosecution had to ensure that the defendant's conduct was 'truly, exceptionally bad' before they could find her guilty of gross negligence manslaughter.[83] These cases show the application of an interpretation akin to the definition by other English courts. Since gross negligence is still applicable in other areas of English law to demonstrate the degree of carelessness that will attract liability, it can safely be applied in contracts between parties in the oil and gas industry. The application will help to distinguish between conduct that will occasion liability and that which will not result in responsibility.

4.4.2 *Varied Standards of Proof for Gross Negligence Cases*

The question of the standard of care that courts will apply to determine if gross negligence has occurred is another challenge confronting the general use of gross negligence. In the case of ordinary negligence, the test is that of a reasonable person, in which the defendant's actions are evaluated against those of a person of normal intelligence who utilises average care, skill and judgment. Usually, a court will consider whether a reasonable person would foresee the damage in the circumstances. Additionally, a court will determine whether the defendant owes the plaintiff a duty of care, whether that duty has been breached, whether the breach caused the plaintiff harm and whether the defendant caused that harm. This standard of proof in negligence cases is immutable. Moreover, it has a global application and has remained a fundamental aspect of the law, applying to several types of claims, including defective product cases.

In cases where gross negligence is an issue, there must be a *marked departure* from the required standard of behaviour. A higher standard of proof is necessary to establish gross negligence, whereas, in negligence, the standard of proof is low. Despite this challenge, the standard of proof in gross negligence cases varies by jurisdiction. This variation presents another level of difficulty in proving gross negligence. In some states in the US, such as New York, for a plaintiff to prove gross negligence, the law requires the plaintiff to show that the defendant's conduct displays 'reckless indifference to the rights of others'.[84] The court noted that the conduct must show a failure to exercise the necessary care in the circumstances or demonstrate a total disregard for the rights and safety of others. The standard of proof highlighted by the court relates to the severity of a party's deviation from the required standard of care. The severity relates to the defendant's conduct instead of their intention.

In other instances, gross negligence is inferred from intention. A reference to intention presents gross negligence as a state of mind, which may give room for

[83] *Bawa-Garba* (n 28).

[84] ibid.

the argument that for a plaintiff to prove gross negligence, the test will be subjective as against an objective inference of the defendant's wrongdoing – the test of a reasonable person. Some scholars identify that to prove gross negligence, the plaintiff must establish that the defendant intentionally breached a duty of care or knowingly injured another person to whom they owe a duty of care.[85] This means that the plaintiff knew their actions were dangerous but proceeded anyway. The jurisprudence of gross negligence does not follow a definitive pattern; rather, it focuses on case-specific facts, hence the challenge of contractually describing what conduct amounts to gross negligence. The references to 'lack of slight diligence or care', 'high degree of careless conduct' and so on present gross negligence as a wrongful act which does not incorporate a mental element. This reference suggests the application of the reasonable person's test by courts.

On the other hand, the references to 'want of or even scant care', 'reckless disregard' or 'reckless indifference' introduce the mental element requirement. These references invite a court to infer the state of mind of the party that committed the wrong. Consequently, these references make the standard of proof challenging in gross negligence cases. In law, a finding of negligence is a question of fact for a jury in a given case, but it behoves the court to set the rules that will guide the jury in determining what negligence means. In cases where ordinary and gross negligence is alleged, the same element is needed to establish liability: a duty owed to a plaintiff by a defendant; a breach of that duty; a causal connection between the breach and the plaintiff's losses; and damages. The factor distinguishing the two causes of action is the defendant's degree of care, or lack thereof, in causing the supposed losses. The reason is that gross negligence requires a greater absence of care than is inferred by ordinary negligence. The standard for ordinary negligence is a failure to use the care that a reasonable person would use under the circumstances. Hence, to establish gross negligence, the conduct or omission must be severe, as distinguished from the failure to exercise ordinary care.[86] It does not involve a subjective state of mind.

4.4.3 *Limited Application of Gross Negligence: Not a Term of Art*

A crucial concern in managing and allocating gross negligence risk is that gross negligence is not a term of art. Its meaning is limited in application, unlike negligence, which has a universal application. As earlier identified, English civil law has no concept of gross negligence distinct from simple negligence. However, when this term appears in a contract, courts will interpret and give effect to it. The use of gross negligence is limited in practice in the UK.

[85] Contract Counsel, 'Gross Negligence' (Contract Counsel, 8 February 2022) <www.contractscounsel.com/b/gross-negligence> accessed 15 October 2023.

[86] Olga Voinarevich, 'An Overview of the Grossly Inconsistent Definitions of "Gross Negligence" in American Jurisprudence' (2015) 48 Journal of Marshal Law Review 471.

In US jurisprudence, gross negligence is recognised in most states as a type of negligence which can result in higher liability. However, the challenge in US jurisprudence lies not in recognition of the existence of gross negligence but in how it should be determined. For instance, courts in New York define negligence as conduct that touches on intentional wrongdoing. However, courts from other states in the US continue to recognise degrees of negligence and differentiate between various degrees of care. The result of these divergent perspectives is that some courts – in Illinois, for example – see gross negligence from the standpoint of recklessness, while others identify gross negligence as 'very great negligence'.[87] A scholar describes the imprecise definition of gross negligence thus: '[W]hen one attempts to define "gross negligence" the concept shatters into a kaleidoscopic disarray of terms, elements and subtle graduations of meaning. It is a legal Tower of Babel, where many voices are heard, but few are generally understood.'[88]

In Australia, gross negligence is limited in contractual application and not recognised as a separate tort. Nevertheless, the difference between negligence and gross negligence in Australia is assessed from the point of degree and not kind. In the case of *GR Engineering Services Ltd v Investment Ltd*,[89] Tottle J of the Supreme Court of Western Australia revisited the debate about the meaning of gross negligence, where the term is used as a carve-out from a no-liability clause. Tottle J identified that, when examining the common law meaning of 'gross negligence' in the context of exclusion and indemnity clauses, the Australian courts followed the approach of Mance J in *The Ardent*, in which his Lordship said:

> Gross negligence is clearly intended to represent something more fundamental than failure to exercise proper skill and/or care constituting negligence. But, as a matter of ordinary language and general impression, the concept of gross negligence seems to me to be capable of embracing not only conduct undertaken with actual appreciation of the risks involved, but also serious disregard of or an indifference to an obvious risk.[90]

In this jurisdiction, gross negligence extends beyond the failure to exercise proper care, but the context can determine additional dimensions.[91] This perspective highlights the imprecise meaning of the term 'gross negligence', as its meaning can only be derived from the context in which it was used. Under Australian contractual

[87] For details about the various definitions of gross negligence in the various courts in the US, see ibid.

[88] Howard (n 24) 334.

[89] [2019] WASC 439.

[90] *The Ardent* (n 26).

[91] *DIF III – Global Co-Investment Fund LP v Babcock & Brown International Pty Limited* [2019] NSWSC 52. In this case, Ball J identified that

> '[g]ross negligence' is not a term with a precise meaning; and its meaning is to be ascertained from the context in which it is used. In some cases, it has been held to encompass more than mere negligence . . . However, any distinction between gross negligence and mere negligence is one of degree and not of kind: *Armitage v Nurse* . . . at 254 per Millett LJ. In other cases, the word 'gross' has been found to add no additional meaning in the circumstances: see *Sucden Financial v Fluxo-Cane Overseas Ltd* [2010] EWHC 2133 (Comm) at [54] per Blair J.

jurisprudence, contracting parties can introduce a definition of gross negligence to guide their private exchange. However, where the definition concerns a type of conduct, judicial resolutions will be highly sensitive to the facts and, therefore, necessarily involve some degree of uncertainty. In addition, a plaintiff seeking to establish a defendant's gross negligence faces a higher bar regarding proof, due to the opinion of the Australian courts that gross negligence involves more than mere negligence.[92]

In South Africa, gross negligence seems to exist in contractual contexts. It applies as a sword to deny the parties protection under an exclusion of liability clause. That is, it prevents a party from benefiting from an exemption clause where liability for loss is attributable to the gross negligence of the party that seeks to rely on it.[93] The foundation of this regulatory position in South Africa arises from the public policy perspective that it is against public policy to uphold an exemption of liability for gross negligence.[94] Regarding the definition of gross negligence, only a few cases reference the imprecise term. In *Government of the Republic of South Africa (Department of Industries) v Fibre Spinners & Weavers (Pty) Ltd*,[95] the court, per Didcott J, referred to *Rosenthal v Marks*,[96] in which it was posited that 'gross negligence ... connotes recklessness, an entire failure to consider the consequences of one's actions, a total disregard of duty.' This South African perspective differs from most of the definitions given in the US. However, one thing we can deduce from the South African judicial perspective is that it considers gross negligence to be greater than negligence.

In the construction industry in Indonesia, contracting parties can limit liabilities, including for indirect or consequential damages, under the principle of freedom of contract. Despite that, the enforceability of such restrictions is subject to principles of fairness, customary practice, and laws and regulations set out under Article 1339 of the Indonesian Civil Code. A crucial point to note is that Indonesian courts can refuse to enforce a limitation of liability clause where the damage arises from gross negligence or wilful misconduct, due to public policy.[97] The challenge now lies with the meaning of gross negligence under the Indonesian regime, which has not been expressly provided.

A significant challenge with defining gross negligence has been how courts see this imprecise term. Some courts see it as the same thing as negligence, whereas others think it is different. However, most courts hold the opinion that

[92] *James Thane Pty Ltd v Conrad International Hotels Corp* [1999] QCA 516.

[93] See Consumer Protection Act 68 of 2008 s 51, which came into effect on 1 April 2011.

[94] Ian Chadwick, 'Contracting Out of Liability for Gross Negligence' [2012] De Rebus 34.

[95] 1977 (2) SA 324 (D) (on appeal 1978 (2) SA 794 (A)). See also *S v Dhlamini* 1988 (2) SA 302 (A); *Philotex (Pty) Ltd v Snyman* 1998 (2) SA 138 (SCA); *Transnet Ltd t/a Portnet v Owners of the MV 'Stella Tingas'* 2003 (2) SA 473 (SCA).

[96] [1944] TPD 172, 180.

[97] White & Case, 'Managing Construction Risks in Asia-Pacific: Indonesia' (17 November 2021) <www.whitecase.com/insight-our-thinking/managing-construction-risks-asia-pacific-indonesia> accessed 14 October 2023.

what prevails in most situations is that, as a matter of law, there exists no degree of negligence or care but that, as a matter of fact, different amounts of care exist. Some courts see gross negligence as conduct, whereas others believe it is an intention. This judicial inconsistency has further deepened the imprecise meaning of gross negligence. However, the definition in Section 4.X provides a pathway to solving the challenge.

4.4.4 Limited Statutory Provision for Gross Negligence in Petroleum Regulations

It is worth mentioning that the concept of gross negligence has imprecise and limited statutory provisions in petroleum regulations. While the term is not contained in most petroleum legislation, the ones referencing gross negligence offer little help. For instance, the OPA 1990 merely identified that the liability of a responsible party would not arise when the party seeking to rely on an exclusion clause is grossly negligent in their conduct, giving rise to the damage.[98] This provision means that gross negligence applies as a sword against a party seeking to rely on an exclusion of liability clause in a petroleum agreement. The OPA did not define gross negligence nor provide a direction for US courts to follow in determining conduct that can lead to gross negligence. In the petroleum regulations of several countries, gross negligence has received limited mention. It was mentioned in the OPA due to public policy considerations, and this direction has influenced the application of gross negligence in contracts globally.

4.4.5 Limited Insurance Coverage

The availability of insurance coverage is critical to participants in the oil and gas industry. As highlighted earlier, operators, drilling contractors and subcontractors procure insurance for their staff and group members to cover any downside. Usually, this coverage is for damages due to negligence leading to injury, death or property damage. However, insurance for pollution damage is specially procured. The reason is that standard-form business liability insurance policies exclude coverage of liability caused by pollution.[99] There is also a general exclusion of liability for the cost of cleanup and remediation. The exclusion of pollution arose from efforts by insurers to prevent moral hazard and circumvent sweeping liability for long-term releases of hazardous waste. However, an exception to this exclusion relates to discharges, releases or escapes which were sudden and accidental.[100]

[98] 33 USC 2703(b), OPA 1990, which highlights defences to liability.

[99] Kenneth S Abraham, 'Catastrophic Oil Spills and the Problem of Insurance' (2011) 64(6) Vanderbilt Law Review 1767.

[100] Eric McCabea, Alexander E Potente and Angela Probasco, 'Products Pollution Liability Insurance: Another Bridge Spanning the Pollution Exclusion Coverage Gap' (2021) 33(2) Environmental Claims Journal 149.

Most likely, spill defendants purchase customised insurance policies covering pollution liability and cleanup costs. The purchase of customised insurance often arises from the requirement of law, as evidence of financial responsibility is exemplified by obtaining liability insurance. However, parties that are not likely to be spill defendants do not purchase liability insurance. This is due to their contractual responsibility not extending to well pollution.

In the face of these challenges, providing insurance for gross negligence is even more challenging. For example, in the US, most states prohibit the use of mutual indemnity in gross negligence cases. The reason is that encouraging it would be contrary to public policy and would encourage moral hazard for conduct that is beyond ordinary negligence. A finding of gross negligence usually results in higher damages that may be beyond most insurance companies' capacity. Again, insurance companies are wary about providing coverage for liability arising from gross negligence, because no data exist to understand the probability of a liability arising from gross negligence. As such, the actuarially fair premium cannot be calculated, especially as few companies seek this type of insurance.

Furthermore, there is an insurance policy called 'operator's extra expense', which operators rely on to regain well control after damage. As the name suggests, it is only available to operators to cover the cost of control operations, redrilling the well and cleanup. However, coverage for pollution and other endorsements can be included in the policy.[101] However, this type of insurance is unavailable to drilling contractors due to the industry practice that does not allocate subsurface pollution to drilling contractors. Instead, drilling contractors procure surface pollution coverage for onboard fuel tanks and stores under commercial market liability policies or in non-poolable programmes of a Protection and Indemnity Club.[102]

4.5 A WORKING DEFINITION OF GROSS NEGLIGENCE IN OFFSHORE DRILLING CONTRACTS

As seen above, judicial interpretations of gross negligence have leaned towards the term being applied from a tortious perspective, with intention as a key element. However, examining the concept indicates that it did not emanate from tort but from bailment and was applied in contracts. A fundamental aspect of risk allocation in the oil industry is that liability is based on contract, not tort. Thus, the meaning and application of gross negligence ought to reflect the philosophical underpinnings of the law of contract. This contractual dimension enables a definition that will apply as a term of art in contracts. The historical evidence

[101] See International Risk Management Institute <www.irmi.com/term/insurance-definitions/operators-extra-expense-(oee)> accessed 15 October 2023.

[102] David Sharp and Andrew Rees, 'Drilling in Extreme Environments: Challenges and Implications for Energy Insurance Industry' (Lloyd's 2011) <docplayer.net/784935-Energy-drilling-in-extreme-environments-challenges-and-implications-for-the-energy-insurance-industry.html> accessed 12 October 2023.

from bailment and the contractual underpinning of gross negligence between operator and contractor in the oil and gas industry enables this study to define gross negligence as follows: *Gross negligence is conduct that falls far below the standard of a reasonable person in a given circumstance.*

In the definition above, the phrase 'the standard of a reasonable person' refers to, or could be used interchangeably with, the words 'good oilfield practice'. This practice is the required pattern for conducting oil and gas operations. Good oilfield practice is contained in the codes of practice of the oil industry, such as in the American Petroleum Institute (API) standards of practice. Good oilfield practice is referred to as those methods usually accepted as good and safe during petroleum exploitation or recovery operations.[103] With the 'far below' test, as provided in the definition, it will be easy for a reasonable person or a court to hold that the conduct of a party to a contract fell far below the required standard. Put differently, gross negligence is a 'major'[104] or 'marked departure'[105] from the expected standard of care. The difference between negligence and gross negligence does not lie in conscious risk-taking. They may overlap in a certain respect, but gross negligence cannot be equated with negligence, as the latter arises from a failure to comply with a particular standard of conduct. Gross negligence is also not a state of mind, as a person's conduct may amount to gross negligence committed in good faith, without wilfulness or dishonesty, while it is not their intention to be grossly negligent.[106]

Gross negligence is conduct evaluated without regard to the actor's particular state of mind; instead, reference is made to how unreasonably dangerous or severely wrongful the conduct was under a specific circumstance.[107] The person's mental features and qualities, abilities and habits, reactions and processes are not among the conditions to determine whether a person's conduct is reasonably safe.[108] The law sets up an external standard for protecting society, and this standard is from the ordinary reasonable person's perspective. The law seeks to protect society from conduct, not states of mind, which is unreasonably likely to cause harm. As a result, the specific mental state which causes gross negligence is not essential in determining liability.[109]

Although the difference between negligence and gross negligence lies in degree and not kind, the latter focuses on whether the conduct was a 'clear departure' from the reasonable person's standard in ways beyond the degree of departure.[110]

103 IADC, 'Good Oilfield Practice' (*Oil and Gas Drilling Glossary*, 29 October 2013) <http://www.iadclexicon.org/good-oilfield-practice/> accessed 15 October 2023; Michael Bunter; 'World-Wide Standards of Good Oilfield Practice – The Impact of the Blow-Out, Deaths and Spill at the BP Macondo Sell, MC 252/1-01, US Gulf of Mexico' [2013] Oil, Gas & Energy Law Journal 2.

104 Crimes Act 1961 (NZ) s 150A.

105 *McCulloch v Murray* [1942] SCR 141, 145 (Duff CJ).

106 *Spread Trustee Co Ltd v Hutcheson* [2011] UKPC 13.

107 Howard (n 24) 342.

108 Henry W Edgerton, 'Negligence, Inadvertence, and Indifference: The Relation of Mental States to Negligence' (1962) 39(7) Harvard Law Review 857.

109 ibid 856.

110 *Spread Trustee Co* (n 106).

The view advanced in this book is that where the conduct of a party to an offshore hydrocarbon contract falls *far below* the conduct of reasonable oil field practice, the party will be held liable for gross negligence. However, where it is a mere failure to comply with particular standards, the conduct shall be regarded as negligence and the party shall not be liable. This reasoning lies in the philosophical foundation of operator and contractor mutual indemnity contracts where carve-outs apply. Gross negligence could be grounds for terminating a contract, or a basis for indemnification by the other party. On the other hand, it could also be used to bypass a liability waiver or a cap on an indemnity which would have benefited the other party.[111]

Although negligence is the failure to conform to a required standard of behaviour, gross negligence is a 'marked departure' from the required standard. Gross negligence has a high standard of proof,[112] whereas, for negligence, the standard of proof is low. All the plaintiff needs to prove in negligence is that the defendant did not exercise care and, as a result, he has suffered harm/loss. In some states in the US, such as New York, for a plaintiff to prove gross negligence, the law requires that the plaintiff show that the defendant's conduct displays 'reckless indifference to the rights of others'.[113] The conduct must show a failure to exercise the necessary care in the circumstance or demonstrate a total disregard for the rights and safety of others. The gross negligence standard focuses on the severity of a party's deviation from the required standard of care instead of mere negligence.

In the oil industry, negligence is allowed in risk allocation practice because of the parties' positions and the complex nature of offshore drilling operations. However, it is essential to note that the difference between negligence and gross negligence exists in contract, not tort law. The reason is that, in tort law, a party's negligence or gross negligence does not exclude their liability. In oil and gas contracts, the reference to negligence and gross negligence is used to distinguish a situation when the responsible party will be liable for their conduct. Negligence does not result in liability, whereas gross negligence does. Often, gross negligence is used to represent severely wrongful conduct. It can be assumed that parties include gross negligence as a carve-out for liability in hydrocarbon contracts to check moral hazard, promote public policy and prevent deliberate acts of sabotage by non-risk-bearing parties in a contract. For gross negligence to apply in oil and gas contracts as a term of art, its meaning must be clear so that the purpose of its inclusion in contracts as a liability trigger will be achieved. Applying the definition proposed in this study will reflect the contractual underpinning and guide courts in determining what conduct amounts to gross negligence.

Gross negligence in the oil and gas industry should be understood by focusing on the seriously wrongful conduct of parties to a contract. The understanding of parties in the hydrocarbon industry is that gross negligence applies as a liability

[111] Ken Adams, 'Using the Terms 'Negligence and Gross Negligence' in a Contract' (Adams Drafting, 10 September 2012) <www.adamsdrafting.com/negligence-and-gross-negligence> accessed 15 October 2023.

[112] Shine (n 42) 10.

[113] ibid.

trigger, while mere negligence does not. The intention of parties is to share risks while also taking responsibility when liability results from certain conduct excluded in the contract. They intend that their contract will determine their liability, but tort law will not.

It should be pointed out that substantial financial liability in the oil industry applies when a party is found to be grossly negligent in their conduct. Scholars argue that if gross negligence leads to unlimited liability, it will fall under the second limb of the ruling in *Hadley v Baxendale*. The second arm of the case deals with damages 'as may reasonably be supposed to have been in the contemplation of both the parties at the time the contract was made'.[114] Losses under this limb are classified as indirect losses as they do not arise naturally from the contract but could be contemplated by both parties. This perspective means that pollution damage resulting from grossly negligent conduct could lead to unlimited financial liability. On the other hand, death or injury to personnel and property damage could be classified as direct losses as they naturally flow from the contract. Consequently, their occurrence does not lead to unlimited liability, even when a party's conduct is grossly negligent.

Unlimited liability results from a finding of gross negligence, as an indirect loss, and its focus is on the size of the cheque. The industry believes that substantial financial liability does not arise naturally from a contract, although it could be expected in pollution cases (indirect loss). This study notes that gross negligence is conduct; as such, it focuses on acts that fall *far below* the expectation of good oilfield practice. This study notes that gross negligence is corporate conduct carried out by a company employee. This definition of gross negligence is not dependent on the extent of liability or whether the damage caused losses that did not flow naturally from the contract. The degree of conduct is our guide.

4.6 GROSS NEGLIGENCE: EXAMINING THE TEST FOR CORPORATE RESPONSIBILITY IN OFFSHORE DRILLING OPERATIONS

In the corporate world and tort law, it is a basic understanding that an employer is vicariously liable for compensatory damages resulting from their employee's wrongful conduct within the scope of their employment. For example, in the oil and gas industry, petroleum operations are carried out by employees in the field who implement the will of the company's management. The company hires these employees; as such, the company is responsible for their wrongful acts. Although the company takes responsibility for the wrongful conduct of their employees, the question that comes to mind is, would the company still be punitively punished for the gross negligence of its employees? If we put the question differently, it would be thus: under what circumstances should the wrongful action of an employee be

[114] [1854] EWHC Exch J70.

attributed to the employer for a court to determine that the employer is liable for punitive damages based on an employee's conduct? What kind of defence can a company put forward in gross negligence cases?

The corporate test applies to determine the liability or otherwise of a corporation concerning grossly negligent conduct, thus allowing for a higher penalty on the company's part.[115] The finding of gross negligence in most jurisdictions serves the purposes of deterrence and liability[116] or to compensate for injuries or harm aggravated solely because of how they occurred.[117] In the context of a corporation, gross negligence is regarded as corporate conduct that causes damage or loss to the public. This explains why the conduct of an employee can be grossly negligent during drilling operations, but the responsibility for the act will be on the corporation or company where it ratifies or authorises the employee's conduct.[118] However, where an employee's conduct has caused harm which resulted from gross negligence, a court would not impute liability for higher damages to the employer where there is proof of some misconduct by high-level management staff.[119]

As a general rule, a company is not responsible for an employee's gross negligence unless it authorises or ratifies the conduct of the employee who caused it.[120] However, ratification or authorisation of the conduct could be indirect. For example, suppose a company employs a person unfit to do their job. The company is responsible for the employee's conduct due to its error of judgement in engaging the person.[121] Retaining an employee after they have occasioned a severely awful act has been held to be indirect ratification of the employee's action.[122] Where an employee is in a position of authority to act at the employer's behest, their abuse of authority is, by implication, abuse by the employer.[123] If a company's safety culture, practices and poor perception of risk encourage an employee to act grossly negligently, which endangers the public, the employer would be taken to have ratified the conduct. As such, the company bears the liability for such gross negligence to discourage bad results from its activity.

115 William T Curtis, 'Liability of Employers for Punitive Damages Resulting from Acts of Employees' (1978) 54 Chicago-Kent Law Review. 829.

116 *United Mine Workers v Patton* 211 F 2d 742 (4th Cir), cert. denied, 348 US 824 (1954).

117 *Lucas v Michigan Cent RR* 98 Mich 1, 56 NW 1039 (1893), and *Tenhopen v Walker* 96 Mich 236, 55 NW 657 (1893).

118 Curtis (n 115) 833.

119 Timothy J Moran, 'Punitive Damages in Fair Housing Litigation: Ending Unwise Restrictions on a Necessary Remedy' (2001) 36(2) Harvard Civil Rights–Civil Liberties Law Review 279.

120 Curtis (n 115).

121 As Kircher and Wiseman note, although the Restatement lists recklessness in employing or retaining an unfit employee as one of the circumstances in which punitive damages may be imposed vicariously, liability for punitive damages flows directly from the principal's recklessness. As such, the vicarious liability doctrine need not be invoked in this circumstance. See John J Kircher and Christine M Wiseman, *Punitive Damages: Law and Practice* (vol 2, West Group 2000).

122 *Coats v Construction & General Laborers Local* 185, 15 Cal App 3d 908, 93 Cal Rptr 639 (1971).

123 Curtis (n 115) 848.

The gross negligence of managerial employees of a company does not require ratification as the manager or person in a position already has the authority to act on behalf of the company. However, some courts have somehow altered the rule by removing the distinction between employees in a managerial capacity and supposed 'menial' employees in the case of corporate employers.[124] Accordingly, an employer may be liable if its employee's conduct is grossly negligent while they are within the scope of their employment,[125] notwithstanding any other attribution standard that may apply in 'traditional' common law.[126] In essence, where the gross negligence of a party to the contract results in property damage, death or injury to personnel, or pollution damage, the company whose staff has occasioned the damage or loss will be held responsible.

In summary, where an employee acts within the scope of their employment and for the employer's benefit, the company will be liable for the employee's acts of gross negligence. The emphasis is on deterrence, pressuring employers to exercise care in recruitment and employee supervision.[127] The underpinning is that gross negligence arises from poor perception of risk, employment of persons not fit to do the job, the company's poor safety and complacency culture, flawed managerial and organisational processes and so on. These could facilitate severely wrongful oilfield practices during operations that could result in harm or losses in the form of injury or death, property damage or pollution damage.

The Chief Counsel's report on the Macondo spill captured gross negligence as corporate conduct. The Chief Counsel identified that the underlying technical and management causes of the Macondo oil spill in the Gulf of Mexico revealed that management failures formed the foundation for all the technical shortcomings.[128] For instance, the report states:

> BP's decision to use a long string production casing increased the difficulty of achieving zonal isolation during the cement job. While the decision did not directly cause the blowout, it increased the risk of cementing failure. Again, BP's decisions to include rupture disks and omit a protective casing from its well design complicated post-blowout containment efforts.[129]

There is also evidence that workers were supervised poorly. They were allowed to do things as they wished. These are examples of a flawed organisational and

[124] *Stroud v Denny's Restaurant Inc* 532 P 2d 790 (OR 1975); Phase 1 trial in the BP case by Barbier J.

[125] *Stroud* (n 124) 793.

[126] See Phase 1 trial in the BP case where Barbier J stated that

> the court need not need not determine whether BPXP authorized or ratified the conduct, or whether Vidrine and Hafle (or any other BP employee) were 'managerial agents', or any other attribution standard that may apply under general maritime law, 'traditional' common law, or any other law or jurisdiction.

[127] Curtis (n 115) 847.

[128] National Commission on the BP Deepwater Horizon Oil Spill and Offshore Drilling, *Macondo: The Gulf Oil Disaster* (Chief Counsel Report 2011).

[129] ibid 35.

managerial process which resulted in death and injury, damage to property and pollution damage. The report also captures other serious management failures as opposed to common errors that contributed to the Macondo disaster. The serious nature and extent of management failures qualified the conduct as gross negligence, enabling the court to hold that gross negligence had occurred.[130] Depending on the situation, a company can argue that it is only negligent where the relevant elements of management misconduct are absent. However, this argument is based on facts and assessed case by case.

4.7 CONCLUSION

The meaning and nature of gross negligence have been the subject of interpretation before courts, especially in contract interpretation. Aside from the challenge of definition, the standard of proof for gross negligence varies between jurisdictions, especially as the term is not a term of art. In addition, the limited statutory provisions on gross negligence in several jurisdictions and limited insurance coverage make its usage complex. A pathway to solve the problem of defining gross negligence is by stating that gross negligence is conduct that *falls far below* a reasonable person's standard in a given context. The standard of proof for negligence applies in proving gross negligence, but the difference in the latter lies in failing to exercise a higher degree of care. With the definition above, courts can be properly guided when deciding whether a party's conduct falls far below good oilfield practice.

[130] Phase 1 trial of the of the BP case (n 34).

Chapter 5

Guiding Principles for Effective Risk Allocation in Gross Negligence Cases

5.0 INTRODUCTION

Risk allocation should not be undertaken in isolation; instead, it should be guided by established principles that support human existence and environmental protection, especially in the high risk sphere of offshore petroleum drilling operations. This chapter will explore guiding principles such as human rights, public policy, sustainability and distributive justice, and consider their potential role in allocating risk arising from gross negligence. It will then advance contractual and regulatory strategies that can help parties to an offshore drilling contract allocate risk arising from gross negligence, and also identify the implications of such strategies.

5.1 GUIDING PRINCIPLES

Guiding principles are ideas or moral values that influence people or governments when deciding or considering an issue. Ultimately, guiding principles establish a framework for how something should be done in the interests of those who will be affected by the outcome. These principles can be founded on established philosophies, norms, theories or laws. For instance, the principle of equality can be used to ensure that every group in a particular society (men, women, youths and so on) is represented in a decision-making process to achieve an acceptable outcome.

In the area of business and human rights, the United Nations advanced the guiding principles of 'Protect, Respect and Remedy' to ensure that states protect human rights while businesses respect and remedy any harm in breach of human rights.[1] The essence is to reduce the impact of businesses on people and the ecology, enhance standards and practices to achieve concrete outcomes for affected individuals and communities and contribute to a socially sustainable future. These principles are not obligatory, as they are regarded as nonbinding soft laws, but they provide a framework for sustainable business operation due to the heightened risk of communities being impacted by company activities. Companies could also develop specific policies and practices that would enable them to implement the duty to protect, respect and remedy human rights.[2]

[1] United Nations, *Guiding Principles on Business and Human Rights: Implementing the United Nations 'Protect, Respect and Remedy' Framework* (New York and Geneva 2011) <www.ohchr.org/sites/default/files/documents/publications/guidingprinciplesbusinesshr_en.pdf> accessed 15 October 2023.

[2] IPIECA, 'Putting the UN Guiding Principles at the Heart of the Oil and Gas Industry' (IPIECA, 10 December 2022) <www.ipieca.org/news/ungps-and-oil-and-gas> accessed 16 October 2023.

The oil and gas industry, especially through offshore petroleum drilling activities, carries the risk of negative environmental impact due to oil pollution. The risk allocation practice typically adopted by the industry for offshore petroleum drilling operations excludes liability for gross negligence, as discussed in Chapter 4. The chapter further noted that this practice has the potential to discourage the exercise of due care by the party not allocated the risk, as they will not bear the burden of a downside. The result of this is that necessary steps to prevent oil pollution may not be taken, resulting in oil pollution and environmental degradation. As discussed in the previous chapter, the industry risk allocation practice does not discourage oil pollution during drilling operations. Thus, it significantly affects the long-term sustainability of offshore petroleum drilling operations. Therefore, to promote environmental sustainability in petroleum drilling operations, certain principles should guide how the oil industry allocates liability arising from gross negligence, particularly pollution liability.

5.1.1 *Public Policy Principle*

As earlier noted, public policy encompasses the government's primary decisions, commitments and actions, informed by interactions with those who demand change, those who take the decisions and those who will be affected in the process.[3] It also emanates from laws and, sometimes, judicial pronouncements aimed at shaping conduct or solving societal problems.

The evolution of society defines acceptable and unacceptable conduct. This dynamic trend plays an essential role in shaping public policy to protect the interests of society. It does so by questioning how citizens, lobby groups and so on, who lie in the path of a given practice, will be affected by such practice. As such, it defines society's prevailing challenges/values and their solutions. Values predetermine public policies, although these vary from society to society. In other words, the public policy principle is the idea that drives a change in society to solve a problem identified in society using social laws. In a legal context, the public policy principle is the idea that enforcing an agreement or other transaction can be denied if it will cause injury to the public good.[4] This principle is built around public interest, safety and protection. Although the government is the primary agent of public policy, citizens are the prime focus of the policy.

The public policy principle revolves around the philosophy that there are certain things individuals cannot do for themselves.[5] Hence, government intervention through social laws is needed to protect the public interest and maximise welfare. A classic example is laws that protect consumers or the environment from business harm. These are laws that individuals cannot make for themselves.

[3] Larry N Gerston, *Public Policy Making: Process and Principles* (3rd edn, Routledge 2010).

[4] Michael Howlett and Ben Cashore, 'Conceptualizing Public Policy' [2014] Comparative Policy Studies 17.

[5] Dick Davies, 'Ten Principles of Sound Public Policy' (*Govloop*, 24 August 2013) <www.govloop.com/community/blog/ten-principles-of-sound-public-policy> accessed 15 October 2023.

Again, the public policy principle pursues the long-term interests of all instead of the short-term interests of a few. The short-term interests of some persons could be likened to the interests of the operator and drilling contractor in an offshore drilling operation. These interests do not include the public interest, as the focus is on their contract and how they will perform it. Nevertheless, the public policy principle seeks to mainstream practices that parties will include in their contract to protect society from harm.

Certain strategies are critical to mainstream the public policy principle, such as problem identification/definition, goal setting and policy instruments to achieve the goal.[6] These elements point to the involvement of public (government) and societal actors. The former's involvement relates to rule-making to solve the problem in society and achieve its objective. The latter's involvement relates to participating in the decision-making process, which corresponds with the basic idea of governance. In other words, public policy focuses on specific issues to address particular problems, such as oil pollution and environmental degradation,[7] that affect society. Where practices or norms are not in the interests of society, the government, through the problem identification process, puts in motion instruments that will address the challenge. This public policy philosophy applies in both public and private engagements.

Contractual arrangements in the offshore petroleum industry are private, and the public policy principle that an agreement or other transaction can be denied if it will cause injury to the public good applies to them. The conclusion presented in the previous chapter about gross negligence and exclusion of liability is that moral hazard arises from the practice of not holding a party liable for gross negligence, thus encouraging harm to people and the environment. Therefore, a public policy guide to excluding liability for gross negligence using mutual indemnity clauses would be for some part of the liability to attach to the party at fault when a downside occurs. This guiding principle would create a disincentive for moral hazard, thus protecting the public's long-term interests instead of the short-term interests of the operator and the contractor. As such, a guiding principle when allocating the risk of pollution arising from gross negligence would be to consider whether the risk allocation practice will be detrimental to society. If so, it will be a public policy principle to mainstream strategies to avoid harm to society.

5.1.2 Human Rights Principle

Human rights are inalienable rights, and include the right to a healthy environment.[8] Human rights principles are based on the understanding that people are

6 Melissa Mackay and Louise Shaxton, 'Understanding and Applying Basic Public Policy Concepts' (University of Guelph 2011) <www.politicipublice.ro/uploads/understanding_public_policy.pdf> accessed 15 October 2023.

7 Christoph Knill and Jale Tosun, *Public Policy: A New Introduction* (2nd edn, Bloomsbury Publishing 2020).

8 David R Boyd, 'The Right to a Healthy and Sustainable Environment' in Yann Aguila and Jorge E Viñuales (eds), *A Global Pact for the Environment – Legal Foundations* (CUP 2019).

entitled to certain basic privileges arising from their existence on earth.[9] Apart from a healthy environment, people have the right to life, the right to work and earn a living, the right to food, the right not to be discriminated against and so on.[10] The 1972 Stockholm Declaration is the catalyst for the recognition of the right to a healthy environment. As David Boyd, the UN Special Rapporteur, identified, the right to a healthy environment is included in some environmental and human rights treaties, enjoys constitutional protection in several states and is part of the environmental regulation of most countries. These forms of recognition establish the legal foundation of the right to a healthy and sustainable environment. However, environmental impacts, such as oil pollution, can affect how people enjoy these rights. For example, oil pollution can damage aquatic ecosystems and cause water pollution, groundwater contamination, destruction of wildlife and degradation of farmland, which constitute a significant source of social and economic existence for oil-bearing and coastal communities.

Ultimately, states, businesses and other duty-bearers are required to observe human rights as they interact with the environment. The human rights principle seeks to protect the interests of rights-holders, preserve their dignity and ensure accountability and the rule of law.[11] Achieving this objective requires integrating human rights standards into business practices, policies and frameworks. Nevertheless, the integration process must consider and assess the underlying and structural causes of human rights violations from its practices and set strategies to address the reasons for the rights violations.

Inherent in the human rights principle is the freedom to contract with anyone without restriction. However, the right to agree on terms is qualified and not absolute. Moreover, this qualified right to contract is curtailed because freedom of contract can impact the rights of non-consenting third parties and create externalities for them. This externality can affect a livelihood, thereby violating the human rights of an individual or community. Those whose human rights are violated are entitled to a healthy environment, and denying them this right through a contractual practice contradicts the human rights principle. A similar opinion has been identified in discussions about freedom and well-being.[12] Alan Gewirth highlights that the drive to exercise personal freedom also involves recognising and respecting the freedom and well-being of others. The reason is that, since everyone is in the same position and requires freedom and well-being, consistency requires those who may impact the rights of others to recognise and respect their claims to freedom and well-being. This opinion stems from the view that we all have equal rights to freedom and well-being and that no one should deny another person the enjoyment of this right.

[9] United Nations General Assembly Resolution 76/300, The Human Right to a Clean, Healthy and Sustainable Environment (UNGA, July 2022); Universal Declaration of Human Rights (UNGA Res 217 A(III).

[10] ibid Universal Declaration of Human Rights.

[11] United Nations Population Fund, 'Human Rights Principles' (UNPF, 2005) <www.unfpa.org/resources/human-rights-principles> accessed 14 October 2023.

[12] Alan Gewirth, *Human Rights: Essays on Justification and Application* (Chicago University Press 1982).

A close look at the UN Guiding Principles on human rights shows that the oil and gas industry has a responsibility to prevent human rights infringements in the areas where they operate. The guiding principles also place a duty on the industry to take steps, through due diligence, to identify their actual and potential impacts on rights and to address them using practices, policies and tools.[13] The due diligence involves asking questions, such as how the business practice harms society and which industry measures could be implemented to mitigate such harm. The human rights duty includes using practical measures during petroleum operations to discharge their responsibility to respect human rights. Inherent in this duty is the need to prevent adverse human rights impacts directly linked to their operations and services during their business activities. The guiding principles became necessary due to the adverse impact on human rights connected with the activities of transnational corporations and other business enterprises. They were instrumental in revising some international standards and instruments, such as the Organisation for Economic Co-Operation and Development (OECD) Guidelines for Multinational Enterprises ('OECD Guidelines') in 2011. This revision mainstreamed a chapter on human rights in line with the UN Guiding Principles.[14]

Oil and gas activities can affect the environment and, when this happens, people suffer. When people suffer due to environmental damage or oil pollution, it evidences a violation of their rights. As such, the oil and gas industry can utilise the human rights principle to reduce rights violations, especially in allocating the risk of gross negligence. This will guide the oil industry in mainstreaming practices and frameworks to ensure that the allocation of risks does not encourage moral hazard which violates human rights. One way of averting human rights violations through oil pollution is to make a party who causes damages from their gross negligence assume some liability for their conduct. This practice will deter parties from conduct that violates human rights. Achieving this goes beyond policy commitment but extends to binding contractual agreements such as excluding liability for gross negligence following parties' proportion of benefit during risk allocation. This type of contract delineates responsibilities for mitigating the risks of adverse human rights impacts.

In Gewirth's opinion, to mainstream contractual practices that discourage offshore oil pollution is to exercise the right to contractual freedom while also disincentivising moral hazard that can result in offshore oil pollution, thus respecting other people's well-being and freedom to live in a healthy environment, earn a living and live a healthy life, regardless of who they are or their station in life.

[13] Rae Lindsay and others, 'Human Rights Responsibilities in the Oil and Gas Sector: Applying the UN Guiding Principles' (2013) 6(1) Journal of World Energy Law and Business 2.

[14] ibid. The International Finance Corporation (IFC) Policy and Performance Standards on Environmental and Social Sustainability, which took effect as of 1 January 2012, refer to the 'private sector responsibility to respect human rights'. See IFC, 'IFC Performance Standards on Environmental and Social Sustainability' (IFC, 1 January 2012) <www.ifc.org/content/dam/ifc/doc/2010/2012-ifc-performance-standards-en.pdf> accessed 16 October 2023.

This respect for freedom and well-being is essential, especially as continuing to exclude liability for gross negligence in offshore contractual risk allocation in the oil industry would mean contracting away human rights principles. As such, human rights principles provide a vital guide for risk allocation in gross negligence cases, to discourage harm to human rights – a baseline expectation of all oil and gas companies.

5.1.3 *Sustainability Principle*

Sustainability remains a cardinal principle in today's society as it focuses on how business and economic activities can be conducted in a manner that caters to the needs of the present and future generations. Extensive discussions about sustainability have been presented in Chapter 3.X, from which we understand that the core elements of social, economic and environmental considerations drive the sustainability principle. Nevertheless, this book focuses on environmental sustainability and how offshore petroleum drilling activities can impact biodiversity and the natural environment due to oil pollution during drilling activities.

The subject of sustainability has given rise to divergent views regarding its approach. Opinions are divided between the strong and the weak sustainability approaches. The advocates of a strong sustainability approach believe that nature is the focus of sustainability. Thus, the priority is conserving its attributes in the most pristine state possible. This view resonates more with nature conservation movements. On the other hand, proponents of the weak sustainability approach believe that sustainability is centred on the sustainment of economic systems, relegating nature to the role of supplier of natural resources, ecosystem services and to absorb the residues generated by human activity.[15] The latter view sees nature as a means through which people can realise their aspirations. In both approaches, preserving the environment for the use and enjoyment of people is central, and this is the core focus of the sustainability principle.

What this means, in effect, is that the practice of humans in their natural environment should be geared towards protecting the environment rather than impacting it. The environment is critical to human survival, as human existence is mainly dependent on the state of the environment. In the context of the oil industry, this means that the industry's practices should promote environmental sustainability and not moral hazard that can lead to ecological damage. For example, moral hazard will arise where a party to a drilling contract is not responsible for liability resulting from their gross negligence. However, where a proportion of that liability is allocated to them, moral hazard will be discouraged, and environmental sustainability will be encouraged in the drilling process.

During offshore contractual risk allocation, a critical consideration is how an industry practice affects sustainability and how that practice can align with

[15] Carlos Alberto Ruggerio, 'Sustainability and Sustainable Development: A Review of Principles and Definitions' (2021) 786 Science of the Total Environment 147481.

environmental protection. This stems from the fact that the industry practice of risk allocation is connected with several offshore pollution cases; hence a sustainability perspective can guide future offshore oil and gas drilling contracts. Due to the immense public pressure on the oil and gas industry for environmental protection, there is a need to continuously reduce the extent of environmental damage caused by the industry during offshore petroleum operations,[16] and one way out of this situation is for industry practice to revolve around sustainability. Reconsidering the allocation of liability arising from gross negligence in the context of the oil industry and circular economy will result in changing conduct and values towards sustainability consistent with novel business goals.

Relatedly, corporate social responsibility arises from the oil industry's engagement with its business environment, especially as non-state actors. Therefore, a fundamental aspect of corporate responsibility is environmental sustainability, to enable their business environment to thrive in the interests of the present and future generations. Thus, sustainability is essential in allocating the risk of gross negligence, mainly as its design, implementation and consideration facilitate a balance between safeguarding public health and environmental concerns with technical and economic practicability. As such, the sustainability principle can be incorporated into the risk allocation practice of the oil and gas industry as a business model to reduce the impact of offshore drilling operations and promote sustainable development in oil-bearing and coastal communities.

5.1.4 Distributive Justice Principle

In Chapter 3.X, a discussion about distributive justice was presented. The underlying aspect of the analysis is that the distribution of liability in cases of gross negligence should be based on the proportion of benefit a party derive from an activity. In other words, the benefit should be the basis for the burden when a downside results from gross negligence. The principle establishes that it is fair that those who share in a benefit should take the burden. There is the view that the oil and gas industry practice already reflects the benefit-and-burden principle as participants allocate surface and subsurface pollution alike. However, the reverse side of this view is that the industry practice of risk allocation (as seen from the Macondo report) encourages moral hazard and creates externalities for third parties and costs for the other contracting party. Thus, it has a significant lasting impact on the environment and people, and applies beyond the limits of freedom of contract.

The distributive justice principle provides a basis or guide on how the liability arising from gross negligence can be distributed between an operator and a contractor when a downside occurs. The foundation of the method of liability

[16] Febrian Kwarto and others, 'The Potential Bias for Sustainability Reporting of Global Upstream Oil and Gas Companies: A Systematic Literature Review of the Evidence' (2022) 74 Management Review Quarterly 35.

distribution under this principle is proportionality. The distributive justice principle acts as a valuable tool when allocating liability arising from gross negligence in offshore petroleum drilling operations.

5.2 AN ADAPTABLE FRAMEWORK FOR RISK ALLOCATION IN GROSS NEGLIGENCE CASES: STRATEGIES FOR MAINSTREAMING LIABILITY

An adaptable framework will assist states in redesigning their oil and gas law or the model PSC/clause to reflect a new position regarding liability arising from gross negligence during petroleum activities involving the operator and the contractor.

5.2.1 *Regulatory Strategy*

Regulation can ensure that a party whose gross negligence caused liability bears the burden in an offshore petroleum drilling contract. As we have seen in the anti-indemnity statutes in some states in the US, only negligence is addressed, and not gross negligence. Some anti-indemnity laws in the US still allow exceptions that permit a party to benefit from gross negligence, while federal legislation is silent on this matter. Although Louisiana has passed anti-indemnity legislation, BP and Transocean contracted under Louisiana state laws, among others. That said, gross negligence was not a trigger for a responsible party to assume liability where a downside occurs during drilling operations. There is an apparent lacuna in the law, which calls for stronger regulatory support to qualify the use of gross negligence in indemnity agreements as a protection against liability.

Conversely, regulatory provisions against using indemnity clauses as an absolute shield for liability arising from gross negligence during offshore petroleum operations will be discouraged. This strategy could be incorporated in the award of licences or the petroleum regulation, making it explicit that mutual indemnity clauses are not absolute where liability arises from gross negligence.[17] The regulation could be oil and gas law, model clauses or model PSCs. When this is done, a court can uphold the regulation in case of violation, especially where vitiating elements in a contract are absent. For regulation to play its role in making mutual indemnity subject to gross negligence, the latter should apply as a sword and not a shield to the party who caused the wrong. As a sword, it will operate as a means through which a party at fault indemnifies the other party or circumvents a waiver of liability on the part of a party who seeks to take advantage of the indemnity agreement. Regulation could help public policy facilitate the use of gross negligence as a carve-out in indemnity agreements to prevent parties from causing harm to themselves or others through their wrongful conduct during drilling operations.

[17] Under s 133 of the Petroleum (Exploration, Development and Production) Act 2013 of Uganda, liability for pollution damage can arise where the conduct was wilful.

The regulation is implemented by the regulator, who approves the operator for field development when the relevant conditions for field development have been satisfied. Depending on the stage at which the field development plan is submitted (before or after the grant of licence), the regulator could require the operator to commit not to enter into certain agreements. In addition, an operator can be restricted by law or regulation from contracting either by itself, agents or group, with any person, contractor or subcontractor, directly or indirectly requiring any party to take responsibility for the gross negligence of another party during drilling operations.

In the UK, the licence granted to the operator incorporates the model clause by reference since it is a standard form agreement between the government and a well operator. As such, the model clause can include the proportionality element of distributive justice and guide the proportions of parties' respective stakes to influence how they negotiate liability arising from gross negligence in their agreements. When inserted in the model clause/model PSC between host government and well operator, the proportionality element effectively guides the desired behaviour to produce the necessary outcome. In the UK, for instance, to implement the strategy of maximising economic recovery (MER), every field development plan must show that it contains procedures on how MER could be achieved, among other things, before being granted field development approval. In addition, the well operator must show evidence of compliance with the strategy.[18] Similarly, gross negligence, as canvassed in this study, could be incorporated into model contracts or agreements to guide the relationship between a well operator and a drilling contractor.

In the UK, the regulator (the OGA, now the NSTA) implements the UK strategy by setting conditions for each licence in the regulation (model clause). Each licence, which takes the form of a deed, binds the licensee to obey the licence conditions.[19] In addition, the licensee must submit a field development plan (FDP) to get development and production consent from the NSTA. For the NSTA to give consent to the FDP, it must be satisfied that all the relevant guidelines and regulations have been followed.[20] This practice by the NSTA can apply to risk allocation in gross negligence situations. As part of the NSTA's strategy, gross negligence could be expressly qualified in offshore drilling contracts through its regulation. For example, the regulation could require the licensee to ensure that no person executes a contract or subcontract that purports to indemnify another for harm or loss arising from gross negligence during drilling operations without assuming

[18] North Sea Transition Authority, 'Exploration and Production: Field Development Plans' <www.nstauthority.co.uk/regulatory-information/exploration-and-production/development/field-development-plans> accessed 15 October 2023.

[19] ibid.

[20] North Sea Transition Authority, 'Requirements for the Planning of and Consent to UKCS Field Developments' (May 2018) <www.nstauthority.co.uk/media/7803/fdp_guidance_111021.pdf> accessed 12 August 2023.

some portion of the liability. In addition, the NSTA or the relevant authority could seek to know the driller and the nature and extent of the drilling agreement related to risk allocation. Anything done outside the licence would be in violation of the licensing condition and could result in the withdrawal of the licence. In this way, the contractual allocation practice of the operator and drilling contractor is guided by the regulatory strategy. This strategy will help to mainstream the exercise of care during drilling operations.

Every regime governing oil and gas production aims to prevent environmental damage and protect the public from the externalities of petroleum operations. One way to achieve this is for the party at fault to assume the burden of its gross negligence in order to discourage serious conduct resulting in harm, and to enforce public policy for societal protection. It is a viable way of implementing the gross negligence restriction without making a drilling contractor a duty holder, even though they carry out the actual drilling as the owner of the offshore installation for the operator. The operator is the duty holder of the offshore facility and the well operator, where they have been appointed to conduct the planning or execution of the well operations. Drilling contractors do not carry out this activity. As stated, the well operator is still the duty holder, while the drilling contractor is responsible, under the contract, to the operator. Suppose a drilling contractor is made responsible to the regulator or government in this situation; it will make the drilling contractor a duty holder or an equity partner. Even under the UK Offshore Petroleum Licensing (Offshore Safety Directive) Regulations 2015, the driller is not recognised as a well operator for purposes of the regulation, as they do not plan or execute well operations.[21] The drilling contractor is only contractually liable to the operator, not the regulator.

The regulatory strategy does not allow regulators to hold contractors liable for well pollution. Doing so would change the concept of a duty holder and shift from the long-held position that regulators look to the operator/licensee on liability issues.[22] The long-standing industry practice stems from operators negotiating with the regulators and pledging to particular well designs, well programmes and other safety/environmental conditions. The operator acts as the principally responsible party for selecting and approving contractors, exercising control of contractors' operations on the well site and ensuring that the contractors have duly accomplished the work plan results.[23]

From the above, one can see the underpinning for leaving the responsibility of well pollution on the operator, despite the other party's negligence. However, to allow gross negligence to thrive in drilling operations would run contrary to public policy and distributive justice principles. Public policy and distributive justice require a party to assume responsibility for its gross negligence, instead of

21 Offshore Petroleum Licensing (Offshore Safety Directive) Regulations 2015 s 2, 5 and 6.

22 Peter Cameron, 'Liability for Catastrophic Risk in the Oil and Gas Industry' (2012) 6 International Energy Law Review 207.

23 ibid.

the blanket application of a mutual indemnity agreement. The need for assuming liability is to promote good oilfield practices that could help prevent harm to third parties, deter negligent behaviour and distribute the burden of mutually beneficial but harmful activity according to the rewards of the activity. The emphasis here is not on 'mere' negligence, nor is this study proposing enforcement of a tortious act using a contract. What is being discouraged here is gross negligence.

Enforcing public policy and distributive justice in mutual indemnity contracts would create a deterrent effect, resulting in more effective care.[24] The social costs of gross negligence would be allocated to the causal source(s) of the risk, thereby creating precautionary incentives.[25] Sole liability is a disincentive for prevention. Borre Vanden identifies that a non-distributive liability is inefficient as it impacts the incentive for care when a single party assumes liability.[26] An efficient liability rule enables the allocation of risk among parties causally connected to the harm, in line with the principles of the Coase theorem.[27] The incentive to reduce harm only arises where the actors share the cost of the harm they caused,[28] and the incentive in cost-sharing lies in the proportion of the benefit received by each party to the contract.

This practice will create an incentive for parties to monitor the behaviour of each other during drilling operations.[29] As such, moral hazard will be discouraged, harm prevention will be incentivised and mutual monitoring will be promoted through risk distribution. A new standard of behaviour will apply to check and control conduct that *falls far below* the standard of a reasonable person. To put this in perspective, take driving, for instance. Driving at 35 miles per hour (mph) in a built-up area with a speed limit of 30mph is negligence. However, driving at 100mph in the same area is gross negligence. The emphasis is on the extent of conduct that falls far below what is reasonably expected in a built-up area. When we understand responsibility for gross negligence as a tool to discourage moral hazard in drilling operations, we can apply it as a carve-out for liability to attach to the party at fault. The application of liability will be subject to the proportion of the benefit from the activity.

[24] Guido Calabresi, 'Some Thoughts on Risk Distribution and the Law of Torts' (1961) 70(4) Yale Law Journal 499.

[25] Michael Faure, 'Environmental Liability' in Michael Faure (ed), *Tort Law and Economics* (Edward Elgar Publishing 2009) 231.

[26] Borre Vanden, 'Channelling of Liability: A Few Juridical and Economic Views on an Inadequate Legal Construction' in NLJT Horbach (ed), *Contemporary Development in Nuclear Energy Law: Harmonizing Legislation in CEE/NIS* (Kluwer Law International 1999) 13. When liability is applied to the operator alone and the operator becomes 'judgment-proof', victims are unable to sue other parties who were causally connected to the risk or who influenced the risk. Hence, the incentive for prevention will be diluted and victims may go uncompensated.

[27] Faure (n 25) 260.

[28] Giuseppe Dari-Mattiacci and Luigi A Franzoni, 'Innovation and Negligence Rules' (2014) 16(2) American Law and Economics Review 337.

[29] Kip W Viscusi and Richard J Zeckhauser, 'Deterring and Compensating Oil-Spill Catastrophes: The Need for Strict and Two-Tier Liability' (2011) 64 Vanderbilt Law Review 1742.

5.2.2 Contractual Strategy

An incentive-driven contract that distributes risk in a manner that could encourage safe drilling and mutual monitoring is essential to enhance environmental sustainability.

5.2.2.1 Liability Subject to the Proportion of Benefit

This book advances the idea that the burden of the liability for gross negligence should reflect the benefit gained from the harmful activity. This approach is consistent with the deterrence and liability philosophy in public policy, and accords with the proportionality element of distributive justice.

In some cases, there may be losses above the proportion of benefit. However, the party with control over the activity and associated risk will assume the excess liability above the benefit of the party at fault. Bearing losses above this proportion will make the risk allocation practice more consistent with distributive justice and reflect the liability underpinning of the oil industry. It is essential to emphasise that the scale of the loss or the size of the cheque does not determine gross negligence. The conduct of the party at fault, viewed through the lens of good oilfield practice, defines gross negligence.

Allocating the risk of gross negligence subject to the proportion of liability will create an obligation for a party at fault to bear responsibility for its wrongful conduct. The liability will only be up to the proportion of the benefit they enjoy. The proportion of the liability could be a stated amount, a stated percentage or derivable from the value of the contract to the drilling contractor. This approach can change the existing industry practice where the party at fault takes no responsibility for gross negligence but benefits from the mutual indemnity agreement, despite their gross negligence. This manner of allocating risk will make mutual indemnity subject to gross negligence and reflect the risk-and-reward system in petroleum operations, linked to the proportion of benefit and burden from the activity.

5.2.2.2 Indemnity

As stated earlier, mutual indemnity should apply as a sword, not a shield. That is, where a party's gross negligence results in damage or loss, that party indemnifies the other party for the loss caused to the innocent party, subject to their benefit. In other words, where an operator is grossly negligent, the operator will indemnify the contractor to the extent of the agreed proportion and vice versa. Mutual indemnification for injury, property damage and pollution damage would, in this way, be subject to gross negligence on behalf of the party that occasioned the harm. Standard mutual hold harmless clauses between contractors will also be subject to gross negligence under this proposed practice. It means that mutual indemnity clauses will no longer provide absolute protection for liability arising from gross negligence, but will provide qualified protection.

Risk sharing is an efficient liability principle that incentivises prevention as parties will act as checks to themselves, with a duty to report harmful oilfield practices. Some scholars note that 'a possible approach could be to obligate drilling contractors, well service contractors and other non-operators to assume some regulatory duty such as reporting unsafe practices to regulatory bodies'.[30] A contractual obligation such as this could complement safety regulations. For instance, in the UK, the Offshore Safety Directive requires an operator of a block, field or well to report safety and environmental concerns from any source relating to offshore oil and gas operations.[31]

In the corporate context, suppose that, in exercising authority, an employee acts grossly negligently, injuring a person, damaging property or causing pollution damage. In that case, the employer will be liable to indemnify the other party to the contract, albeit the indemnification will be to the extent of the benefit from the activity. This means that where, for instance, an operator's employee, out of their own gross negligence, causes damage to the contractor's property or injury to the latter's employee, the operator will be liable for the liability arising from the gross negligence of its employee. Although the employee is the contractor's employee, the operator will be responsible for whatever loss or injury the contractor or its employee suffered. The operator will not be allowed to use the mutual indemnity clause as a shield; neither will the operator be held harmless for the damage to the contractor's property. This practice will apply to situations involving operators and contractors similarly. In this manner, the deterrence and liability underpinning of public policy and distributive justice will be achieved. Corporate liability is based on the fact that the company's poor risk perception, inadequate supervision of employees, management failure or engaging an unfit person facilitated the employee's conduct which fell far below the required standard that could be exercised in the circumstance.

5.2.3 *Implications of Rethinking the Contractual Strategy*

The framework advanced in this book represents a dynamic repurposing of the traditional practice of risk allocation in the offshore energy industry. Adopting this new framework means that mutual indemnity clauses will no longer operate as an absolute shield for gross negligence, a situation which current industry practice supports. Instead, parties will be liable for severely wrongful conduct resulting in harm or loss during drilling operations, up to a stated proportion. This strategy will make mutual indemnity subject to gross negligence. However, the framework can awaken the need for specific contractual changes and similar stakeholder responses.

For instance, in 2015, post-Macondo activity saw operators shifting risks and liabilities to contractors, not in line with entrenched industry practices of risk

[30] Owen L Anderson and John S Lowe, 'Oil Spills' (2010) 3(2) OGEL Special Issue 2.

[31] Offshore Installations (Offshore Safety Directive) (Safety Case etc) Regulations 2015 s 31.

allocations. Operators sought to shift risk through carve-outs for some losses or types of behaviour, including gross negligence and breach of safety regulations and warranties. In addition to the carve-outs, operators have appealed for a minimum amount, between US$1–10 million, to be attached to contractors' liability for causing pollution damage arising from ordinary negligence, despite the pollution emanating from the reservoir.[32] The oil companies argue that this shift would incentivise contractors to avoid accidents. This view resonates with some of the discussions described in this book.

Contractors view this shift differently because they do not have access to the right insurance coverage like operators do. Contractors argue that putting aside the traditional knock-for-knock contractual division of liability will pose significant challenges for liability insurance. The reason is that most mobile offshore unit operators and practically all contractors in the offshore support vessel industry obtain liability insurance from the traditional marine liability insurance market – notably mutual protection and indemnity (P&I) clubs.[33] The applicable insurance conditions in this market are relatively standardised and assume that an insured contractor contracts on industry-standard terms. Contractors argue that since the meaning of gross negligence is unsettled, this might require contractual clarifications. One aspect dealt with in this book is the meaning and application of gross negligence in offshore petroleum drilling contracts. The discussion on the meaning and nature of gross negligence, as advanced in this book, will be helpful to operators and contractors alike. The argued-for shift by operators will elicit the demand by contractors for change to their advantage in some areas.

Another implication of adopting the strategy discussed in this book is that the public policy underpinning will be enforced through regulation. The enforcement of this underpinning will incentivise mutual monitoring and foster good offshore drilling practices that could prevent damage and losses in drilling operations. It will provide an optimal incentive for harm prevention to all parties in the risk matrix. Operators will monitor contractors, and contractors will monitor operators to maintain a suitable risk profile. Contractors will also monitor subcontractors, thus forestalling any negative distributional effect.[34] This will result in minimal accidents and reduce the sum of accident costs – the goal of every liability regime[35] – as gross negligence liability can constitute an *ex ante* incentive for prevention. The incentive effect is the result of controlling stochastic externalities in the offshore oil industry. The incentive effect motivates the need to take actions that will improve safety and reduce the possibility of an offshore accident.[36]

32 Torgeir Willumsen and Terje Holte, 'Contractors' Pollution Risk Gets Dirty' (*Offshore Engineer*, 14 April 2015) <www.oedigital.com/news/452942-contractors-pollution-risk-gets-dirty> accessed 9 October 2023.

33 ibid.

34 Richard A Posner, *Catastrophe, Risk and Responses* (OUP 2004).

35 Calabresi (n 24).

36 Kathleen Segerson, 'Risk-Sharing and Liability in the Control of Stochastic Externalities' (1987) 4(3) Marine Resources Economics 175.

A further implication of the strategy advanced in this book is that gross negligence will become a trigger for liability to apply in subcontracts during offshore drilling operations. Contractors and subcontractors would allocate the risk of injury, death or property damage subject to gross negligence. This new practice will apply because regulation would proscribe the indemnification of a party whose conduct is grossly negligent. Every development drilling contract leads to other subcontracts (such as cementing, wire logging and so on) to achieve the goal of drilling for production. In the UK, contractors enter into a mutual hold harmless agreement to indemnify each other when a downside occurs, despite the party's fault. The consequence is that a subcontractor will be liable for damages if their gross negligence results in damage or loss, albeit subject to the benefit reaped.

There is also an implication for day rates for operators and contractors. The day-rate charging method for offshore drilling is the primary method of costing drilling activities, although turnkeys and footage are sometimes used. The oil industry has carried on drilling offshore oil wells under the understanding that the long-term financial upside in the event of a commercial discovery belongs to the operator/licensee. The industry is also driven by the understanding that the operator designs the work programme and supervises the well.[37] As such, the operator exercises control over the well activities. Hence, the operator should solely bear any liability arising from oil pollution. However, suppose drilling contractors are made responsible for well pollution arising from gross negligence subject to a liability cap. The consequence could be an increase in the day-rate amount chargeable by drilling contractors.

Again, it is essential to highlight that this book has anchored its analytical lens on distributive justice – the distribution of the benefits and burden of mutually beneficial but harmful activities. Drilling contractors may argue that, since they are to bear a specific responsibility arising from gross negligence, despite not having control over the activity, they should benefit from the long-term financial upside of the operator. This burden-and-benefit idea relates to the oil industry's risk/reward system. Contractors may require the inclusion of clauses that confer benefits on them for sharing a burden they have hitherto believed belongs to the operator. This implication may arise because incentives and risk-sharing tools for reducing offshore accident costs prompt parties to employ measures towards better and safer offshore operations and risk reduction.[38] Contracting parties should reflect on the connection between gross negligence and safety regulations or drivers and the role of the operator or the contractor in the circumstance.

Furthermore, contractors may demand a change in the risk allocation regarding liability for redrilling a hole, loss of tools, wild well liability and so on, following a dynamic repurposing of the contractual risk allocation practice. The reason could be that risk-bearing leads to cost responsibility, as proposed by Keating's proportional benefit principle. A trade-off in cost-bearing comprises an incentive and

[37] Cameron (n 22) 208.

[38] Inho Kim, 'Introducing Oil Cargo Liability in the Oil Pollution Act of 1990' (2002) 33(2) Journal of Maritime Law and Commerce 185.

risk-sharing outcome and the individual sets of incentives and consequences on the responsible party. Although the distributive strategy advances that the party at fault should bear a proportion of the liability for pollution damage arising from gross negligence, contractors may request liability caps regarding well obligations such as loss of tools and redrilling.

5.3 CONCLUSION

The importance of the guiding principles lies in their public interest protection for sustainability. They further strengthen the qualified application of mutual indemnity clauses for liability arising from gross negligence. To achieve a qualified application of mutual indemnity in gross negligence situations, regulatory and contractual strategy are essential to implement a liability system that considers the wrong of the party at fault and aligns it with distributive justice. However, the liability should be subject to a cap to reflect the risk-and-reward system in drilling operations and the idea of distributive justice.

Chapter 6

Practical and Institutional Frameworks and Insurance Coverage for Implementing Risk Allocation in Gross Negligence Cases

6.0 INTRODUCTION

An institutional framework that will drive the successful implementation of a repurposed risk allocation in gross negligence cases is essential to mainstream the strategy. Besides this, the availability of insurance coverage and other financial assurance mechanisms will enable participants to secure the right insurance to cover gross negligence risk. This chapter will consider the necessary institutional framework and financial assurance mechanism to assist operators and contractors in managing a qualified gross negligence risk during offshore drilling operations.

6.1 INSTITUTIONAL FRAMEWORK

The institutional framework for managing risk allocation in gross negligence situations is critical for practically realising the regulatory objective of environmental sustainability in offshore drilling operations. This framework requires a regulatory foundation with support from competent and well-resourced authorities – this means an institution responsible for implementing the regulatory agenda in the oil and gas law or regulation. The institution's duty must be set out clearly, with regular assessment of its strategy to ensure that the goal of the regulation is achieved.

A classic example of an institutional framework is that of the OGA, now the NSTA, since March 2022. The NSTA is an agency of the Department for Business, Energy and Industrial Strategy, incorporated in 2016 as a government company. The NSTA is an economic regulator created to maximise oil and gas recovery in the UKCS. In 2022, upon becoming the NSTA, the authority took on responsibility for helping achieve the UK government's commitments to reach net zero emissions by 2050. It carries out this responsibility by setting guidelines for the industry to halve upstream emissions by 2030.[1] Before now, the responsibility of the NSTA has not included accelerating the energy transition. However, the imperative of the energy transition has led to the NSTA's evolving role in a net zero future in the North Sea.[2] Its new name encompasses the innovative context

[1] North Sea Transition Authority, 'Overview 2023' <www.nstauthority.co.uk/media/8846/a5l_a5overview-final-accessible-003.pdf> accessed 07 February 2023.

[2] Nermina Kulovic, 'UK Oil & Gas Regulator Rebrands to Reflect Role in Energy Transition (*Offshore Energy*, 21 March 2022) <www.offshore-energy.biz/uk-oil-gas-regulator-rebrands-to-reflect-role-in-energy-transition> accessed 07 February 2023.

and the NSTA's increasing role in energy transition, including as the carbon storage licence and permitting authority, monitoring emissions, assessing a net-zero test for new developments and supervising domestic production.

The governance of the petroleum activities lifecycle considers emissions reporting and ESG concerns. The latter concern includes environmental sustainability, which this book promotes by proposing a disincentive for liability arising from grossly negligent conduct. As such, specialised and existing institutions like the NSTA can be used to monitor and ensure compliance with the regulatory requirement that liability arising from gross negligence is distributed and not protected by a mutual indemnity clause. By way of reform, the NSTA's responsibility could extend to monitoring and assessing the level of compliance with the regulation and setting out guidelines for compliance. Other countries may use similar institutions to shape operators' and offshore drilling contractors' socioeconomic activity and behaviour during petroleum operations. This could be through a prescriptive or performance-based framework. The former highlights what the regulator expects a party to do and how it should be done; the latter highlights what a party needs to do but does not state how it should be done. It leaves the implementation to the party. However, the party needs to satisfy the regulator that the method of compliance with the regulation is adequate.

The practice of the NSTA is instructive, and its regulatory supervision of the North Sea provides useful insights to consider. The strategy document of the OGA[3] is produced pursuant to Section 9A(2) of the Petroleum Act 1998, from which the institution provides supporting obligations in governance, exploration, development, decommissioning and so on, and guidance on how to achieve each strategy. The strategy sets out a central obligation (which binds relevant persons), supporting obligations and required actions (which are as binding as the central obligation), and some safeguards. For instance, the governance guidance, a supporting obligation, sets out how the NSTA supervises the governance activities of oil and gas operators in the North Sea.[4] In particular:

> [t]he Central Obligation of the OGA Strategy includes that Licensees take appropriate steps to assist the Secretary of State in meeting the net zero target when securing the maximum value of economically recoverable petroleum. Furthermore, the Introduction to the OGA Strategy emphasises the importance of industry's continued social licence to operate and the need to develop and maintain good Environment, Social and Governance ('ESG') practices in their plans and daily operations.[5]

The institutional strategy enables the realisation of the regulatory objective. For example, regarding risk allocation, an additional responsibility of the NSTA could be to develop guidance on how operators and contractors for offshore drilling

[3] The OGA strategy was not renamed, despite the OGA's name changing to the NSTA in March 2022.
[4] Oil and Gas Authority, 'OGA Governance Guidance' (OGA, January 2022) <www.nstauthority.co.uk/media/7999/oga-governance-guidance_2022_feb22-1.pdf> accessed 10 October 2022.
[5] ibid 7.

operations enter into drilling contracts. The guidance could provide direction on the nature of risk and liability that parties can allocate in compliance with the regulation. It is easier for the NSTA to implement this novel regulatory proposal as it has the institutional structure to implement any regulatory objective. In addition, using existing institutions will strengthen coherence and coordination, avoid duplication of efforts and provide the opportunity to review progress in implementing the regulatory objective. For instance, the NSTA can require companies to show how they plan to meet the regulatory requirement that a mutual indemnity clause will not be used as a shield against liability for gross negligence. This type of framework accords with the performance-based framework highlighted earlier, which allows parties to design their contracts in any manner that suits them but per the direction of the regulation.

6.1.1 Coordination

The realisation of the regulatory goal depends on the coordination and implementation of the proposal advanced in this book. Coordination requires working in close partnership with the industry to deliver on the objective of the regulation. The regulatory authority provides leadership and coordination while the industry cooperates with the regulator to disincentivise mutual indemnity as a shield for liability arising from gross negligence.

Let us consider the NSTA, for instance. In addition to its strategy and key responsibility, it aims to deliver domestic energy security while driving down emissions from production to achieve the net zero target. To achieve the energy security objective, the NSTA, through its ESG taskforce, coordinates the ESG reporting to demonstrate a commitment to carbon reduction. As such, companies provide information connected to recommendations made by the NSTA's ESG taskforce in March 2021. There is also increased engagement of external specialists to verify data by companies to improve ESG-related disclosures. The essence is to secure funding for existing offshore production fields and related financing to ensure energy security for the UK.[6] Pursuing these objectives drives companies to upscale their emission reporting obligations to get the relevant funding for the exploration and development of oil fields, to keep up with the UK's energy security goal and maximise economic recovery.

A similar coordination framework could be adopted to implement the regulatory requirement when companies allocate risk during offshore drilling operations. The designated regulatory authority in a given country could require companies to design and publicise policies that qualify the application of mutual indemnity as a shield against liability arising from gross negligence. These policies should form part of the companies' environmental sustainability strategies for offshore

[6] Offshore, 'NSTA Urges Improved Coordination of UK Offshore ESG Reporting' (Offshore, 15 December 2022) <www.offshore-mag.com/regional-reports/north-sea-europe/article/14287181/nsta-urges-improved-coordination-of-uk-offshore-esg-reporting> accessed 10 June 2023.

petroleum operations. Regulatory agencies could use incentives such as giving points to companies that comply with the regulatory policies when they apply for field development, new licences or permits, to ensure compliance and ease coordination.

6.1.2 *Training and Capacity Building*

The importance of training and capacity building cannot be overemphasised. The regulatory authority that will implement the legal requirement needs training to understand the underpinning of the regulation and how best to achieve it. Training is an essential element of capacity building, and its core focus is on providing the skills necessary to engage with stakeholders and implement the regulatory requirements. Capacity building is broader, as it relates to a range of activities designed to enhance the capacity of the institution to implement the regulation. It includes an analysis of what type of guidelines will be suitable for the oil industry to ensure compliance with a qualified mutual indemnity clause, understanding the policy context, conducting policy research, creating awareness and repurposing institutions, and so on.

Capacity building also involves investment in further research to understand the dynamic nature of risk allocation and the new concerns in the industry during drilling operations. Essentially, it consists of new ways of implementing the regulatory requirement to ensure compliance with the law.

6.1.3 *Institutional Interoperability*

How institutions and agencies in a jurisdiction relate and interact with one another to implement a regulatory objective affects the objective's realisation. Institutional interoperability is incumbent on specific standards or guidelines that define institutional interaction. It is a crucial enabler of goal realisation in a government setting, representing the ability of government agencies to exchange information between themselves and businesses while ensuring that the objective of the information is maintained.

The NSTA provides an opportunity to understand interoperability. The NSTA regulates the UK oil and gas industry, with other regulatory authorities, to deliver its remit. Although independent, the NSTA works with the Department for Energy Security and Net Zero (DESNZ, previously known as the Department for Business, Energy and Industrial Strategy).[7] The NSTA also works with the industry to deliver its core objective. The Secretary of State for Energy Security and Net Zero, who heads DESNZ, sets the policy and legislative framework for the NSTA. The Secretary of State, who is answerable to Parliament on matters

[7] North Sea Transition Authority, 'Our Relationship with the UK Government' <www.nstauthority.co.uk/about-us/leadership-governance/our-relationship-with-the-uk-government> accessed 10 June 2023.

regarding the NSTA, must agree to extend the remit and any fundamental change to the NSTA's strategy when the agency decides to impose any fine above £1 million. The NSTA also works with the Permanent Secretary of DESNZ, as the Principal Accounting Officer advises the minister in charge on the appropriate budget and strategic objectives for the NSTA. A framework document sets out the relationship between the NSTA and the government institutions to ensure smooth institutional interoperability. [8] The NSTA also uses a memorandum of understanding to collaborate with other government agencies. For instance, it has executed a Memorandum of Understanding with the Secretary of State for Energy Security and Net Zero.

Some factors still affect interoperability. From a technical point of view, the incompatibility of information technology infrastructures and various data models and standards limit interoperability between and within organisations.[9] Aside from technical limitations, organisational and administrative fragmentation (including, for instance, organisational silos), slow pace of reform and legacy processes were identified as barriers to interoperability. There is also a lack of cooperation on, and shared governance of, interoperability initiatives among public administrations.

Suppose we contextualise interoperability within the confines of risk allocation. In that case, we will see that to actualise the regulatory objective of preventing an institution from using mutual indemnity clauses as a shield against liability for gross negligence, related government agencies must collaborate with the identified institution. Typical examples are the Minister for Petroleum and the Ministry of Natural Resources. In most petroleum regulations, the Minister is empowered to regulate the industry. As such, the Minister is responsible for setting out the policy and legislative framework within which the designated institution will operate. Again, a framework document must define the relationship between the various government agencies for effective synergy and identify interoperable frameworks that adhere to those relationships. The regulation made by the Minister for Petroleum should identify the ministry or agency responsible for coordinating and ensuring compliance with the applicable legal framework.

6.2 INSURANCE AND OTHER COVERAGE OPTIONS IN THE OIL AND GAS INDUSTRY

Insurance remains an essential aspect of implementing the qualification of the use of mutual indemnity agreements. However, given the oil industry's traditional practice of risk allocation in pollution cases, finding insurance cover for well pollution liability affects drilling contractors, since standard offshore marine insurance does not extend to contractors' well pollution liability.

[8] ibid.

[9] Alexandra Campmas, Nadina Iacob and Felice Simonelli, 'How Can Interoperability Stimulate the Use of Digital Public Services? An Analysis of National Interoperability Frameworks and E-Government in the European Union' [2022] 4 Data & Policy e19.

As already stated, well pollution liability is the responsibility of the operator/licensee, and it represents the primary source of offshore oil pollution from where a catastrophe may result, leading to colossal liability for the responsible party. The extant practice of pollution cover is only available for operators to cover liability arising from the cost of well control, blowouts, damage to underground resources and so on, during a drilling activity.[10] Operators in the offshore oil industry use the Operators' Extra Expense (OEE)[11] to insure against blowout and related well pollution liability. A drilling contractor would only require an OEE when the contractor carries out the drilling on a turnkey basis. Most contractors do not usually go for an OEE as the premiums are high, with low insured limits available. Post-Macondo, the maximum available capacity is US$500 million to cover well control, redrill and cleanup, which would be fundamentally inadequate to cover a Macondo-type blowout.[12]

This non-application of the traditional mutual indemnity clauses and liability division in gross negligence cases can pose challenges in liability insurance if a solution is not provided. Most mobile offshore unit operators, and nearly all contractors in the offshore support vessel industry, source liability insurance from the traditional marine liability insurance market – notably mutual P&I clubs.[13] Moreover, the applicable insurance conditions in the insurance market are relatively standardised and based on the premise that an insured contractor contracts on industry-standard terms.

6.2.1 *Insurance and Financial Coverage in the Oil and Gas Industry*

In the oil and gas industry, super majors such as BP and Shell often self-insure due to their deep pockets. Others sometimes obtain insurance from P&I clubs and other insurers who provide coverage for the offshore energy industry and offer extra coverage for certain non-standard or 'onerous' contractual terms. Although this extra 'comprehensive general liability' comes at an added cost and with lesser limits than those for standard cover, such extra insurance would, to some extent, cover the needs of support vessel contractors.[14] For mobile offshore unit operators working on live wells, limited insurance coverage is available for pollution liability

[10] Rawle O King, *Deepwater Horizon Oil Spill Disaster: Risk, Recovery, and Insurance Implications* (Diane Publishing 2010) 7.

[11] The International Risk Management Institute defines the OEE as a specialised policy available to well operators in the oil and gas industry that covers the cost of regaining control of a wild well. Through endorsement, the cover could be added for stuck drills, pollution, evacuation expense, and custody, care or control exposures. <www.irmi.com/online/insurance-glossary/terms/operators-extra-expense-oee.aspx> accessed 23 February 2023.

[12] Peter Cameron, 'Liability for Catastrophic Risk in the Oil and Gas Industry' (2012) 6 International Energy Law Review 207, 211.

[13] Torgeir Willumsen and Terje Holte, 'Contractors' Pollution Risk Gets Dirty' (*Offshore Engineer*, 14 April 2015) <www.oedigital.com/news/452942-contractors-pollution-risk-gets-dirty> accessed 9 October 2023.

[14] ibid.

from wells, holes and reservoirs. None of the usual extra insurance coverage available to the offshore contractor would cover the cost of controlling a wild well. The latter cost represents a considerable part of the loss from well accidents like the Gulf of Mexico oil pollution disaster. Oil companies can and do insure against pollution liability in the broad energy insurance market due to the capacity of the market to accommodate large-scale liability insurance. Nevertheless, this market is not readily available to most contractors.

6.2.2 *Liability Protection Schemes for the Offshore Oil Industry*

Depending on their jurisdiction of operation, offshore oil and gas firms rely on some coverage schemes for protection against liability for oil pollution. These specialised offshore liability protection schemes assist companies with liability coverage and enable them to meet the regulatory requirements for coverage in their jurisdictions. Some of these liability protection schemes are discussed below.

6.2.2.1 Offshore Pollution Liability Association Limited Scheme

The Offshore Pollution Liability Association Limited is an industry body in the oil sector, set up as a company limited to administer a voluntary but strict liability compensation scheme known as the Offshore Pollution Liability Agreement (OPOL).[15] OPOL has its origins in the UK. It entered into force on 1 May 1975 as an agreement between all offshore operators in the UK. However, its coverage was extended to offshore facilities within the jurisdiction of other states: Denmark, the Federal Republic of Germany, France, the Republic of Ireland, the Netherlands, Norway, the Isle of Man, the Faroe Islands and Greenland. OPOL is an agreement between several major oil companies to make funds available to compensate victims of oil pollution damage emanating from an offshore facility or reimburse public authorities for remedial measures after a spill. It was designed to fill the gap in the UK pending the ratification of the Convention on Civil Liability for Oil Pollution Damage Resulting from Exploration for and Exploitation of Seabed Mineral Resources (CLEE 1977).[16] However, the CLEE was never ratified, and OPOL remains the only instrument to address the issue of accidental pollution liability, not only in the North Sea and adjacent areas but globally.

The legal nature of OPOL is contractual, especially as it is an arrangement by offshore installation operators and is based on the principle of strict but limited

[15] Sergei Vinogradov and Smith I Azubuike, 'Arctic Hydrocarbon Exploration and Production: Evaluating the Legal Regime for Offshore Accidental Pollution Liability' in Lassi Heininen and Heather Exner-Pirot (eds.), *Arctic Yearbook 2018* (Northern Research Forum 2018).

[16] Julien Rochette and others, 'Seeing Beyond the Horizon for Deepwater Oil and Gas: Strengthening the International Regulation of Offshore Exploration and Exploitation' (IDDRI, 14 February 2014) <www.iddri.org/sites/default/files/import/publications/st0114_jr-et-al._offshoreen.pdf> accessed 10 October 2023.

liability. It is a licensing requirement that a company within the UK jurisdiction must be a member of OPOL. Outside the UK, OPOL membership has declined as there is no regulatory duty to be a member in states such as Germany, France or Denmark. The liability of an operator under OPOL is capped at US$250 million per incident, with a requirement for members to 'establish and maintain' financial responsibility to ensure that claims are met, which can be shown through insurance or self-insurance.[17] Claims to be considered admissible include offshore or onshore cleanup operations, property damage, disposal costs of collected material and other losses, which must be quantifiable and which must result directly from the contamination. OPOL does not take away a claimant's right to seek redress through the courts for losses exceeding the recoverable maximum or those beyond the scope of the agreement.

A commendable feature of the OPOL regime is that it demonstrates the industry's commitment to providing adequate coverage for pollution damage. If a member cannot meet its obligation due to insolvency, other members are obligated to contribute in proportion to the number of their offshore facilities at the time of the incident. This practice guarantees that funds are available to meet claims, thus ensuring expeditious settlement of claims and enhancing mutual risk sharing in the case of insolvency. Furthermore, the strict liability obligation means there is no need to prove fault, and the fact that liability is channelled to the operator removes the question of liability attribution when claims are lodged.

There are, however, limitations to OPOL. First, it is not a fund but a contractual arrangement to compensate for losses where a member fails to meet their obligation.[18] This means that OPOL will not intervene where there is no insolvency. Again, the scheme does not prevent a claimant from suing the operator for other damages. Further, OPOL's definition of direct loss or damage appears limited in scope. One such area is the definition of the nature of damages caused to the environment, which is still debatable.

Although OPOL's compensation limit is relatively high, it pales compared to the extent of damage occasioned by the Deepwater Horizon incident in the Gulf of Mexico.[19] However, it is unclear whether the industry will be willing to raise the limit to the point that assures adequate compensation. OPOL has not been tested, and the adequacy of its application in case of significant accidents is questionable. Nevertheless, OPOL demonstrates a potential governing option for liability and compensation for E&P activities in deep waters, if expanded or modelled adequately. This possibility exists due to it being established by operators. OPOL can be improved by increasing the limit of liability to cover Macondo-type damage and setting up a fund to address claims above the liability limit.

17 See the OPOL Agreement <www.opol.org.uk/agreement> accessed 14 October 2023.

18 Vinogradov and Azubuike (n 15) 317.

19 Marissa Smith, 'The Deepwater Horizon disaster: An Examination of the Spill's Impact on the Gap in International Regulation of Oil Pollution from Fixed Platforms' (2011) 25(3) Emory International Law Review 1477.

6.2.2.2 Oil Insurance Limited

Another notable protection scheme is the Oil Insurance Limited (OIL) scheme. The OIL scheme, unlike the OPOL, is a pooling scheme or mutual insurance arrangement that operates outside the North Sea. Although the OIL scheme provides global coverage, its primary market is the US.[20] Michael Faure and Jong Liu highlight that OIL was formed in 1972 by sixteen energy companies following two significant industrial accidents in the 1960s.[21] Membership of OIL (now called Everen as of 2022) stands at sixty-four, with 3.75 trillion globally insured assets. Its membership criteria have broadened to embrace mining, power and non-chemical petrochemical companies. However, there are no members in Africa, continental and northeast Europe, but the northwest of Europe.[22] They have members in other continents, such as North and South America and Australia. OIL offers cover for offshore and onshore assets, well control and pollution.

OIL identifies that its coverage for members includes pollution and terrorism cover, with an average credit rating of A–. Specifically, OIL provides coverage for loss of or physical damage to property owned by the assured and non-owned property covered by the policy. Under the OIL policy, replacement cost value is the basis of recovery, but the actual cost value is applied if the property is not replaced. The coverage capacity for this type of cover is US$400 million, including windstorm, terrorism, construction and cargo risks.[23] Another coverage category is well control, provided under the insurance agreement of OIL policy. This coverage applies to removal cost, restoration and redrilling, subject to the terms and conditions of the policy. The limit of US$400 million applies to cover each of these risks without a separate premium charge.

Furthermore, OIL covers third-party pollution liability, which applies to members' legal or contractual liability for personal injury, or damage to or loss of property resulting from pollution, seepage or contamination. Coverage is available on a non-continuing basis subject to a forty-day discovery/120-day reporting requirement, and the block coverage capacity is US$400 million.[24] One of the things operators desiring to acquire coverage under OIL must do is to fill out a premium indication request form which requires information about several things, including loss control measures by the operator. This loss control aligns with using incentives to reduce pollution harm.

[20] Michael Faure and Jing Liu, 'Pooling Mechanism for Offshore Liability' in M Faure (ed), *Civil Liability and Financial Security for Offshore Oil and Gas Activities* (CUP 2017) 200.

[21] The two accidents are the well blowout off the coast of Santa Barbara in southern California in 1969 and the refinery explosion in Lake Charles in 1967. OIL has rebranded itself and is now known as Everen. See Pete Carvill, 'Oil Insurance Limited Switches to Become Everen' (*Reinsurance News*, 29 June 2022) <www.reinsurancene.ws/oil-insurance-limited-switches-to-become-everen> accessed 14 October 2023.

[22] Everen, 'Brief Overview' <www.oil.bm/our-members> accessed 12 October 2023. Everen's global membership includes eleven members in Canada, thirty in the US, fifteen in Europe, one in Asia, three in Latin America and four in Australia.

[23] Faure and Liu (n 20) 212.

[24] ibid.

6.2.2.3 *Oil Casualty Insurance Limited*

Oil Casualty Insurance Limited (OCIL) was founded in 1986 as an industry-owned special-purpose vehicle to provide liability insurance for energy companies. It rebranded in 2022 to Everen Specialty Ltd. Like OIL, OCIL (Everen Specialty Ltd) is a mutual insurance arrangement operated by Everen and offers insured energy companies an opportunity to have a shareholding stake in the company[25] – albeit it is not necessary to become a shareholder; an energy company can choose to be a policyholder only. OCIL has members in Canada, the US, Australia, Africa, Europe and South America, and it is rated A– excellent by AM Best and BBB+ stable by Standard and Poor's.[26] OIL and OCIL provide an optional pooling model to OPOL to cover liability during offshore petroleum operations. Premium in OIL and OCIL is paid *ex ante*.

OCIL's insurance products include excess liability, property and reinsurance policies.[27] The core targets of the excess liability policy are energy, mining and metals, and transport companies. Although the policy conditions apply worldwide, the preferred place of arbitration is London or Bermuda, and the policy limit applies up to US$100 million.[28] On the property side, OCIL (Everen Specialty Ltd) provides direct and facultative property business (operational and construction risks) globally for energy companies and non-energy-targeted industries. The cover limit is US$50 million. It also provides reinsurance policies that support quota share, aggregate stop loss, excess of loss and industry loss warranty structures.

6.2.2.4 *Offshore Energy Insurance Cover*

Insurance is another option for energy companies to cover liability for pollution damage that may arise during drilling activities. However, before looking at the types of insurance available to energy companies, it must be highlighted that pre-1969, liability insurance was handled in-house by companies that owned shipping vessels and offshore oil rigs. The insurance of mobile offshore drilling units (MODUs) was not compulsory until the 1969 International Convention on Civil Liability for Oil Pollution Damage was introduced.[29] This requirement was triggered by the 1967 Torrey Canyon incident, after which the need for shipowners' liability insurance for oil pollution damage became obvious. Around that time, offshore energy insurance became necessary – hence, the development of a niche offshore oil and gas insurance market to offer insurance coverage for risks typically retained by the operator.

Following this new insurance market, international offshore energy underwriting syndicates began offering extended coverage for pollution liability resulting

[25] Everen, 'Specialty' <www.everenspecialty.bm> accessed 14 October 2023.
[26] ibid.
[27] ibid.
[28] ibid.
[29] International Convention on Civil Liability for Oil Pollution Damage 1969.

from blowouts, costs of well control and damage to underground resources. They also provided cover for liability to the operator's employees, loss or damage to equipment lost while actively in use, and loss to drilling and servicing equipment from corrosive elements.[30] In addition, in jurisdictions like the US, imposing strict liability for large-scale oil spills increased demand for offshore energy insurance cover. As a result, after the Macondo incident, the offshore energy insurance market has advanced, with insured losses spreading across a wide spectrum of global insurers and reinsurers based chiefly in London and Bermuda.

Although the insurance provided in the oil and gas industry covers a range of liabilities for offshore oil and gas exploration and production, the market is known as the offshore energy insurance market. In addition, the offshore energy insurance market is closely linked to the marine insurance market because offshore exploration activities are carried out on the water. The latter is a part of the offshore energy insurance market. Offshore oil and gas operators who use vessels and MODUs use marine insurance due to their multiple liability exposures during offshore petroleum operations. Marine insurance covers liability for injury, death, property damage and environmental damage resulting from oil pollution and other related incidents.

As already highlighted, operators of offshore energy facilities usually self-insure or purchase pollution liability coverage and excess liability limits in the surplus market or the international marine insurance market. This special arrangement enables operators to cover certain risks that could arise during offshore petroleum operations. However, despite the specialised nature of the offshore energy insurance market, more than one insurer needs to cover the risk exposure due to the limits being over US$1 billion in most cases.[31] As such, companies operating offshore drilling units, undersea pipelines, production platforms and so on usually insure their risk exposures on a subscription basis through specialised brokers who negotiate with underwriters in the energy industry. Most of these subscription transactions are bargained and placed in the London and Bermuda insurance markets by underwriters such as Lloyds of London and several global reinsurance firms and negotiators.

6.2.3 *Types of Offshore Energy Insurance*

Several types of insurance cover are available in the offshore energy market. Some of the notable ones are discussed below.

6.2.3.1 *Coverage for Damage to Offshore Facilities*

This type of insurance cover provides financing for any direct damage to or loss of property to a fixed offshore drilling unit, accommodation or production facility.

[30] King (n 10) 7.
[31] ibid 9.

These facilities include offshore energy drilling, accommodation facilities, subsea equipment, pipelines and facilities for offshore loading. Although this kind of insurance coverage extends to several types of physical damage, some risks covered in the OEE – such as regaining control of the well after a blowout and redrilling expenses – are excluded.

6.2.3.2 *Operator's Extra Expense*

OEE is designed to cover the cost of control operation, redrilling a well, taking care of any pollution and seepage from the well. Sometimes, OEE is called Cost of Control or Control of Well Insurance. OEE covers well blowout costs and indemnifies an offshore facility operator for claims arising from injuries to third parties or damage to and loss of third-party property, cleanup costs and attorney fees due to a blowout. This insurance type also covers evacuation expenses, wreckage removal, well safety and the safety of the property of others in the care, custody and control of the insured. The insurance coverage might include the redrilling of a well to the original depth after a blowout, and the legal expenses arising from oil pollution or rig sinking. The oil pollution must result from an accident or be sudden and unintended, and must have occurred during the subsistence of the insurance cover.[32] The operator is required to notify the insurance company of the incident within ninety days, and they must report the claim to the underwriter within 180 days.

OEE is sold as a 'Combined Single Limit of Liability; and covers actual costs or expenses incurred in regaining well control due to inadvertent subsurface pollution.[33] The operator's responsibility for subsurface pollution arises from the operator's risk allocation agreement with the drilling contractor, which lists the risks the operator will cover. Under traditional risk allocation practice, the drilling contractor usually is held harmless concerning pollution liability from the well and liability for damage to the operator's property or injury to the operator's staff arising out of the employee/employer relationship.

6.2.3.3 *Excess Liability Insurance*

Excess liability insurance coverage is an insurance type that provides cover when the limits of the underlying liability have been reached. In other words, coverage is purchased in layers that exceed a specific dollar limit, which extends the coverage of primary liability insurance when the limit has been reached. For instance, if an insured's liability is US$5.5 million, but the insured's liability limit is US$5 million, the insured can access the excess liability insurance to cover the remaining liability. Excess liability contracts are sometimes regarded

[32] David W Sharp, *A Brief Introduction to Energy Insurance* (Amazon Marketing Hub 2022) 29.
[33] ibid 11.

as catastrophic cover due to the insured obtaining excess insurance to shield themselves from rare catastrophic accidents.[34]

Although excess liability coverage is obtained as an extra layer of coverage above the OEE policy, it is subject to its terms and conditions. Thus, while OEE covers pollution, bodily injury to third parties, damage to or loss of property or loss of use on a strict liability basis, the excess liability insurance policy excludes pollution from wells. In addition, the excess liability insurance has a limited 'buyback', which requires the pollution event to be sudden, accidental, unintentional and subject to strict discovery and reporting requirements. As such, an operator needs to purchase specific 'pollution endorsements' that override the pollution exclusion provision in the excess liability policy. Note that pollution endorsements can impact coverage by reducing the general insurance capacity for well pollution cleanup, due to the insured's possible liability for higher levels of third-party liability on each policy.

6.2.3.4 Loss of Production Income Insurance

Loss of production income insurance is also known as business interruption insurance. It is used to indemnify an insured for lost net income that would have been earned had the damage not occurred, and to refund fixed expenses incurred during the period of damage. Under this insurance coverage, payment for damages is hinged on the loss of income due to damage to upstream facilities such as processing plants, trunklines and refineries owned by third parties but which the insured depends on for income.

The underwriting of this coverage goes with the coverage for offshore physical damage on standardised forms published by Insurance Services Office, Inc (ISO) or those that look like the ISO form.[35] Due to the standardised language of the contract, there appears to be more certainty in claim payments, thus reducing the likelihood of litigation over contractual interpretation. However, an insured who wants to claim under this policy must show that their business operation suffered a direct physical loss or their property was damaged. The absence of proof could result in a denial of the claim. The proof is essential because, for instance, the consequences of oil pollution can have far-reaching impacts without the oil reaching those impacted by the pollution. This situation could arise when businesses are affected due to an oil spill.

6.2.3.5 Protection and Indemnity Insurance Coverage

P&I coverage is an indemnity insurance under which the obligation to indemnify the insured only arises where the insured has paid for the damage.[36] It provides

[34] Scott M Seaman and Charlene Kittredge, 'Excess Liability Insurance: Law and Litigation' (1997) 32(2) Tort & Insurance Law Journal 653.

[35] King (n 10) 12.

[36] P&I insurance policies do not operate like regular insurance policies. To claim compensation for damages, the insured must have paid a third party before receiving monetary compensation from

third-party liability protection for owners and operators of vessels, and it is sold by P&I clubs, which are mutual associations of vessel owners. However, P&I policies offered by traditional insurance companies do not provide coverage to indemnify offshore energy facilities for oil pollution damages. Thus, supplemental pollution liability insurance is required under a separate policy. P&I clubs offer more than insurance coverage. They operate as a loss adjusters, insurance companies and law firms. Given their traditional risk-sharing arrangements, P&I clubs contribute to a risk pool in line with an *ex ante* agreement.

Apart from the coverage provided by P&I clubs, there is also the employers' liability insurance. This provides coverage for claims arising from employees' deaths or injuries sustained while working for the employer. In the coverage strategies and insurance types discussed above, the drilling contractor does not traditionally have any form of insurance coverage or pooling scheme that offers protection against liability for well pollution. As already discussed, this is because they do not assume liability for well pollution in the conventional industry agreement.

6.3 INSURANCE COVERAGE AND GROSS NEGLIGENCE

An issue that comes to mind is that insurance still protects parties whose conducts are grossly negligent. Some scholars believe providing liability insurance for harmful conduct defeats the incentive to exercise care since the party at fault can still access insurance coverage.[37] This is because insurance protection creates moral hazard, altering the insured's incentive to prevent loss or damage. As such, the insured will not appreciate the full benefit of taking steps to reduce risk. Christopher Parsons refers to this type of moral hazard as a 'policyholder hazard' because the policyholder will change their behaviour to produce undesirable outcomes due to the protection the coverage offers. As a result, the insured may become more careless. Parson identifies this moral hazard from an economist's perspective, which led early commentators to question the legality of liability insurance and attempt to suppress it on the grounds of public policy.

Under traditional insurance policies, an insurer is not allowed to assume responsibility for the conduct of an insured where such conduct arose from

the insurers. This means that an insured is only entitled to compensation for an amount they have spent due to an incident covered by their insurance. P&I insurance cover is sometimes called a 'pay to be paid' policy, which is part of the club's rule book. Although the practice is 'pay to be paid', the rule does not wholly apply in insolvency cases due to the introduction of international conventions which allow for direct action and for P&I clubs to intervene where there is a case of member insolvency. See Steven J Hazelwood and David Semark, *P&I Clubs: Law and Practice* (4th edn, Taylor and Francis 2013).

37 Christopher Parsons, 'Moral Hazard in Liability Insurance' (2003) 8(3) Geneva Papers on Risk and Insurance 448. See also Seth Blackledge, 'Knock-for-Knock Provisions and Maritime Law' (*Wilson Elser*, 24 August 2022) <www.wilsonelser.com/publications/knock-for-knock-provisions-and-maritime-law> accessed 13 October 2023.

gross negligence. Such coverage will be void.[38] However, the huge risk, financial involvement and risky environment of operation of the offshore energy industry put it in a peculiar situation.[39] Some insurance companies, mostly P&I clubs, provide additional liability insurance for specific non-standard contract terms.[40] It must be stated, however, that P&I clubs cover liabilities assumed under an agreement as long as the agreement assigns liability based on common law or contains a clean mutual indemnity provision.[41] The primary objective is to prevent claims for the damage to or loss of properties in the oilfield. Unbalanced mutual indemnity contracts are not poolable, as P&I clubs usually approve mutual indemnity clauses which are 'balanced' and do not expose members to wider liabilities. A P&I club will not approve a contract where the member has waived their right to limit liability under applicable law.[42]

[38] Nick Thomas, Jesus Velez and Alex Guillamont, 'Effects of Gross Negligence on Insurance Contracts' (Lexology, 13 July 2009) <www.lexology.com/library/detail.aspx?g=45f48f4f-b2a5-4962-bd7f-94a1580ef3d7> accessed 12 October 2023. Similarly, in some jurisdictions, an insured cannot claim against an insurer in marine insurance claims where the insured caused damage through gross negligence. See Thomas Miller Specialty, 'Shipowner's Liability Insurance Protection & Indemnity: Terms and Conditions for Policies Issued in Hamburg' (1 October 2020) <www.thomasmillerspecialty.com/fileadmin/uploads/tms/Documents/Policy_Wordings/P_I/TMS-PI_HH_OL_Terms_EN_2020-10-01.pdf> accessed 13 October 2023.

[39] *United States v BP Exploration & Production Inc (Re Oil Spill by the Oil Rig 'Deepwater Horizon' in the Gulf of Mexico, on April 20, 2010)* 21 F Supp 3d 657 (ED LA 2014). The court's summary judgment motion in the *Deepwater Horizon* litigation indicated that the pollution indemnity in the drilling contract, which was governed by US general maritime law, would be applicable even in the event of gross negligence. However, the court highlighted in a later order that public policy would not allow indemnification where fraud is involved because it involves wilful misconduct, which is more than gross negligence. This means that, depending on the statutory provision in the jurisdiction, insurance coverage for gross negligence may be allowed, since mutual indemnity provisions can be allowed under certain laws. The availability of insurance for gross negligence is essential in the offshore energy industry, given the peculiar nature of offshore petroleum operations.

[40] Although it is not likely to provide coverage for wilful misconduct on the legal principle that one is not permitted to profit from intentional wrongdoing, this position is less strict in gross negligence situations. What is essential is that the P&I club reviewed the contract in advance. As such, it may be feasible to cover more liabilities that fall outside the standard scope of cover under additional covers. This option must be discussed with an underwriter for everyone to be clear on the extent of the response that can be provided. See Lewis McDonald, 'Extending the boundaries of wilful misconduct and gross negligence?' (SKULD, March 2017) <www.skuld.com/topics/legal/pi-and-defence/extending-the-boundaries-of-wilful-misconduct-and-gross-negligence> accessed 13 October 2023. See also *Shell Oil Co v Winterthur Swiss Insurance* 12 Cal App 4th 715 (Cal 1993).

[41] Ozlem Giivses, 'The Role of Insurance in Offshore Oil and Gas Operations' in Gunther Handl and Kristoffer Svendsen (eds) *Managing the Risk of Offshore Oil and Gas Accidents the International Legal Dimension* (Edward Elgar Publishing 2019).

[42] Pat Saraceni and Nick Summers, 'Reviewing Knock for Knock Indemnities: Risk Allocation in Maritime and Offshore Oil and Gas Contracts' (Clifford Chance, October 2015) <www.cliffordchance.com/content/dam/cliffordchance/briefings/2015/10/reviewing-knock-for-knock-indemnities-risk-allocation-in-maritime-and-offshore-oil-and-gas-contracts.pdf> accessed 12 October 2023.

6.4 ALIGNING INSURANCE WITH THE PUBLIC POLICY AND DISTRIBUTIVE JUSTICE OBJECTIVES

It has been stated in this book that the risk allocation practice in the oil and gas industry, where a party uses a mutual indemnity contract as a shield for liability against gross negligence, is against public policy. On the other hand, distributive justice advocates the sharing of burdens between parties involved in the venture according to the proportion of their benefit. While insurance coverage might pass the burden of harmful conduct to another party, contrary to public policy and distributive justice, the premium payable by the party at fault is a form of distribution of the liability created. Although economists would argue that the premium cannot equal the liability burden that an insurer will bear, liability insurance is part of the oil and gas industry. The premium payable increases with negative behaviour, essentially to put the insured on a check. Despite that, economists argue that paying a higher premium is cheaper than bearing full liability for negative behaviour.

It could be asserted that liability insurance coverage is not entirely out of place in the offshore energy industry and indirectly aligns with the distributive agenda since the insured still needs to pay a yearly premium and must abide by the terms and conditions of the insurance policy. As such, insurance coverage does not entirely defeat the public policy agenda. However, due to the specialised nature of insurance required in the oil and gas industry, the premium payable is on the high side to cover the risk sought to be insured. Moreover, negative behaviour can result in higher insurance rates from underwriters, where future energy companies have to bear the cost of past misfortune. A classic example is the Deepwater disaster, which drove premiums up by 25–30% afterward.[43] Ultimately, there should be premiums for such risk, making a party find cover for their liability and pay a premium for what a mutual indemnity clause would have protected against under the oil industry practice of risk allocation.

6.5 APPLICABLE INSURANCE PRACTICE IN GROSS NEGLIGENCE CASES

There is a general notion that insurance should not be provided to cover gross negligence conduct due to the severity of this type of negligence.[44] However, special types of oil and gas industry coverage exist to protect against pollution liability during offshore operations due to the risky nature of operations and the possibility that the insured may not cover the financial claims arising from the damage. Therefore, a fundamental question is how insurance can be applied between the

[43] Julia Kollewe, 'Oil Industry Set For Surge In Insurance Premiums After Deepwater Disaster' *The Guardian* (London, 20 September 2010) <www.theguardian.com/business/2010/sep/20/deepwater-oil-rigs-insurance-costs> accessed 15 October 2023.

[44] De Castroverde Law Group, 'Does Insurance Cover Gross Negligence?' (3 May 2022) <www.dlg-team.com/blog/does-insurance-cover-gross-negligence> accessed 10 October 2023.

operator and the contractor in gross negligence cases so that both parties assume responsibility for the wrong and contribute towards it. The answer lies in adopting additional insured (AI) in insurance policies as a global practice.

6.5.1 An Additional Insured Provision in Insurance Policies

An AI is a party who receives insurance coverage for their liability under the insurance policy of a named insured. The policy covers the named insured's obligation to defend and indemnify the indemnitee under the indemnity agreement.[45] The liability for the AI is not borne by the named insured but by the insurance company of the named insured, which assumes such liability to the extent allowed under the 2013 ISO AI forms and manuscripts. An AI provision enables a party in a mutual indemnity scheme to be included as an AI in the other party's insurance policy. This inclusion ensures that liabilities that may arise are well covered by insurance, despite the standard insurance requirements.

AI clauses are operational in the US, but not without some restrictions. In Louisiana, the LOAIA proscribes insurance protection, contractual provisions, subrogation waivers and AI validations that would negate the intent of the LOAIA.[46] This position was upheld by the Court of Appeal of the Fifth Circuit in the US when it held that s 2780G of the LOAIA means that the requirement of an additional insured clause in a contract is unenforceable.[47] However, the Supreme Court of Louisiana in *Fontenot v Chevron USA*[48] said that Section 2780G would be enforceable for waivers of subrogation provisions in an indemnity contract where the clause does not negate or circumvent the LOAIA. Where parties tend to circumvent the intention of the LOAIA in an indemnity agreement, such provision will be unenforceable. The court further noted that a subrogation waiver is invalidated when it shifts liability.

However, the courts have created a 'judicial exception' to the LOAIA for co-insurance. This exception allows the use of indemnity clauses where the indemnitee pays for the insurance coverage of the indemnitor.[49] That is, the indemnitee pays for its coverage.[50] The court upheld this arrangement as it prevented shifting the economic burden of pollution to another party. In other words, the indemnitee receives the benefit of the insurance it procured, rather than an indemnity, which

[45] Stacy A Broman and Jenny L Sautter, 'Additional Insured Endorsements: Recent Efforts to Limit Coverage to the Additional Insured' [2006] FDCC Quarterly 81.

[46] Louisiana Oilfield Anti-Indemnity Act s 2780G.

[47] *Babineaux v McBroom Rig Building Services Inc* 806 E 2d 1282 (5th Cir 1987). This study posits that the proscription of additional insured in certain jurisdiction would impede the essence of indemnity clauses, especially as new risk dimensions has been noticed from the Macondo litigation in the US.

[48] 676 So 2d 557 (LA 1996).

[49] *Marcel v Placid Oil Co* 100 11 F 3d 563 (5th Cir 1994).

[50] Where a party is an AI to another party's insurance policy, the original holder of the policy pays for the AI. The procurement of insurance for personal liability will arise where the liability from a particular activity has been apportioned to parties.

the statute prohibits.[51] This study considers this judicial exception germane as it makes room for responsibility from both parties and creates a sense of burden on the indemnitee (operator or contractor). In this regard, the indemnitor will be an AI in the indemnitee's insurance policy.

Although this practice may create a sense of responsibility for the indemnitee, it may not entirely discourage them from moral hazard as the risk has been passed on to the insurance company. However, there will be implications for their premium, and the insurance company can address this by stating in the policy that deliberate acts of negligence will not be covered.[52] Concerning pollution risk, this could tackle moral hazards, incentivise pollution prevention and encourage environmental responsibility among parties. It could also indirectly facilitate applying the 'polluter pays' principle as the indemnitee will pay for an act of negligence it solely or jointly creates. This practice aligns with the principles of fairness and reasonableness.

In AI provisions in the energy industry, certain protections should be embedded in the contract. First, the operator should be named as an AI in all of the contractor's insurance policies, at least for the risks and liabilities undertaken by the contractor. AI status gives the operator direct rights against the contractor's insurer, possibly enhances the operator's rights to recover against the contractor's insurer for bad faith and increases the operator's 'moral authority' in a coverage dispute.[53] The standard AI provision also increases the pool of insurance protection available for a casualty and insulates the operator's insurance programme from reducing its limits. Moreover, the operator should consider requiring that the AI clause take a specific form – for instance, an accepted ISO form – to guard against the prospect of an excessively restrictive AI endorsement.

Ultimately, the operator should be named in the contractor's insurance policy, and the liability the operator seeks to be insured against should be stated in the relevant ISO form. When liability for gross negligence is distributed in proportions of benefit, it gives the operator a foundation to be named as an AI. For instance, in the BP and Transocean drilling contract, BP was named as an AI under Transocean's pollution insurance policy. However, in the case of *BP v Ranger Insurance*,[54] which arose from the Macondo litigation, BP could not recover as an AI under Transocean's insurance policy. BP's argument in that case was that, as an AI under Transocean's pollution policy, they should be able to recover for the pollution liability that BP assumed under the drilling contract. After the trial court ruled in

51 G Roth Kehoe II, 'Louisiana Oilfield Indemnity Act: A Necessary Limit to Contract Freedom or Paternalism for Roughneck Contracts?' (1996) 70 Tulane Law Review 1097. However, where substantial part of the insurance coverage is to be borne by the indemnitee, the *Marcel* exception will not apply. See *Amoco v Lexington Insurance Co* 745 So 2d 676 (LA App 1 Cir 1999), where Amoco paid US$2,000 to get coverage of $11 million and the court declared the indemnity unenforceable.

52 Michael Faure and Tom Hartlief, 'Remedies for Expanding Liability' (1998) 18 OJLS 685.

53 Lisa Bagley Brown, 'Drilling Contracts Post Macondo Considerations' (2016) 9(36) International In-House Counsel Journal 1.

54 Tex Sup Ct No 13-0670.

favour of the insurer, the Fifth Circuit, on appeal, ruled in BP's favour. Nevertheless, the Texas Supreme Court ruled that BP could not recover as an AI because the drilling contract provided that BP was an AI only as to liabilities assumed by Transocean. Had Transocean assumed a proportion of the liability from the well pollution, BP could have been able to claim from Transocean insurers. However, the contract stated that Transocean was shielded from liability arising from the well, irrespective of fault.

Besides naming the other party as an AI, the drilling contract should require a waiver of subrogation in all appropriate policies. The essence is to prevent the insurers from asserting a claim against the indemnified party for a share of the fault for a casualty. Of course, an insurance company can exercise the right of subrogation against an insured who negligently caused a loss covered by the insurance policy. In other words, to fully implement the indemnity scheme, parties to a drilling agreement must waive subrogation rights so that an insurance company cannot seek subrogation based on the common law of negligence. Lastly, the AI and subrogation protection should be designed to extend to all operator and contractor groups.

6.5.2 *Status of an Additional Insured*

Under an AI arrangement, the cover of the named insured is known as contractual indemnity coverage. This coverage applies to drilling contracts, determined by numerous definitions and exceptions. In a commercial general liability policy/scheme, a drilling contract falls within the meaning of an 'insured contract'. Accordingly, an AI is included as an insured in the insurance policy of a named insured under the insurance policy document.[55]

Before 2013, the position of the law regarding AI and indemnity agreements was that AI coverage had a wider application than contractual indemnity obligations and that the coverage was not voided by the sole or concurrent negligence of the AI.[56] The 2013 ISO AI forms, as released by the insurance industry, and the 2015 decision by the Texas Supreme Court in the *Transocean v BP* case[57] point towards a new approach to AI and liability coverage in indemnity agreements. The ISO forms CG 20 10 04 13 and CG 20 27 13, made available by the insurance industry, brought innovations that will have broad consequences for the status of

[55] Ellen Chapelle, 'Evolution of Additional Insured Endorsements' (2014) 23(1) Construction Litigation 10.

[56] *Evanston Insurance Company v Atofina Petrochemicals Inc* 256 SW 3d 660 (Tex 2008). The court held that Atofina is not barred from claiming payment for losses resulting from its own negligence even when the indemnity contract states so. According to the court, the reason is that the agreement that conferred upon Atofina the status of an AI is 'separate and independent' from the indemnity agreement. See also *Aubris Res LP v St Paul Fire & Marine Insurance Co* 566 F 3d 483 (5th Cir 2009); Laura J Thetford, 'In Re Deepwater Horizon: Texas to Revisit ATOFINA to Decide Scope of Additional-Insured Liability Coverage' (2014) Fall South Texas Law Review 2.

[57] *Re Deepwater Horizon* No. 13-0670, SW 3d (Tex 2015).

an AI. An analysis of the 2013 forms indicates that AI coverage is limited to what parties agreed to in their contract. This means that coverage under the policy is to the extent allowed by law and that coverage under the policy is limited to the amount required by the contract.[58] The decision of the Texas Supreme Court highlights that an AI is not limited only by policy terms but also by contractual terms as agreed by parties in the contract. The court identified that

> applying the only reasonable construction of that provision, we conclude that, as it pertains to the damages at issue, BP is an additional insured under the Transocean policies only to the extent of the liability Transocean assumed for above-surface pollution.[59]

BP and Transocean had agreed in their contract that

> [BP], its subsidiaries and affiliated companies, co-owners, and joint venturers, if any, and their employees, officers, and agents shall be named as additional insureds in each of [Transocean's] policies, except Workers' Compensation, *for liabilities assumed by* [Transocean] *under the terms of the Contract.*[60]

This contract informed the decision of the Supreme Court that BP was AI only to the extent of Transocean's liability under the agreement. The subsurface pollution was a responsibility BP agreed to assume under the contract without regard to fault. BP assumed it was insured under Transocean's insurance policy, hence its willingness to accept liabilities for subsurface pollution even in the face of the contractor's wilful misconduct or gross negligence. The AI status formed an aspect of BP's argument that coverage under applicable law is assessed exclusively by the insurance policy's wording and not the contract's indemnity portions. BP further argued that AI and indemnity provisions are 'separate and independent' under the law and that an indemnity provision does not limit the scope of additional insured coverage. BP's argument was supported by the case of *Evanston v ATOFINA*, which established that the insurance policy is separate and independent from the indemnity agreement for an AI. The Supreme of Texas did not uphold this argument.

The understanding from the insurance forms and Texas Supreme Court judgment is that coverage for an AI is not determined by the 'separate and independent' principle as established and believed by parties. However, coverage is determined by the extent of liability, as stated in the indemnity contract of the parties. Again, coverage applies only to the extent permitted by the law that governs the transaction[61]

[58] Chapelle (n 55) 2; Mark M Bell, '2013 ISO Additional Insured Endorsements: Putting the Changes into Context for the Construction Industry' (International Risk Management Institute Inc 2013) <www.irmi.com/articles/expert-commentary/history-of-iso-additional-insured-endorsements> accessed 10 October 2023.

[59] *Re Deepwater Horizon* (n 57).

[60] ibid, emphasis added.

[61] Roberta D Anderson, 'ISO's 2013 "Additional Insured" Endorsement Changes Merit Close Attention' (2013) 23(3) American Bar Association Section of Litigation, Insurance Coverage Litigation 2.

and, because the availability of coverage is a desideratum for risk acceptance, the scope of liability coverage for an AI will strengthen the willingness to accept a given risk during contractual negotiation.[62]

BP's assumption that it was an AI to Transocean's insurance policy appears erroneous, given that, from the contract document, Transocean had not assumed liability for well pollution in any manner. Again, anti-indemnity statutes and the new 2013 ISO insurance forms present concerns to parties in their choice of law since the clauses in the parties' contract must be in line with the applicable law.[63] BP contracted to bear Transocean's liability, notwithstanding the latter's fault. One way around this challenge lies in distributive responsibility, where the damage arises from a party's gross negligence. In this way, the emerging concern in the new insurance endorsements will be addressed.

A question that must be addressed is whether a named insured's insurance policy can provide coverage for an AI indemnity obligation proscribed by a statute. For example, in some states in the US, public policy considerations prevent a party from indemnifying another for negligence occasioned by the indemnitee.[64] However, procuring insurance for that negligence may not be against public policy. The 2013 new ISO endorsements, CG 20 10 04 13 and CG 20 27 04 13, seem to exclude coverage for liability for which an anti-indemnity statute proscribes indemnification.[65] Insurance coverage is a way of mitigating risk. Nevertheless, the judgment by the Texas Supreme Court judgment and the new ISO endorsements suggest that an operator solely bears the burden of well pollution without regard to any mitigating palliative. This issue remains to be clarified. Despite that, the *ATOFINA* case is instructive here: an analysis of it suggests that including an operator as an AI in a contractor's coverage would be an indirect way of distributing the burden of the liability the contractor would solely or jointly cause, and would facilitate the willingness to bear the said risk on the part of an operator.

6.6 FINANCIAL ASSURANCE MECHANISMS/STRATEGIES TO COVER POLLUTION LIABILITY

Financial assurance mechanisms are tools designed to show that the necessary funds to meet certain environmental protection needs and compensation requirements will be available when needed.[66] The mechanism could be a performance bond or bonding requirement, corporate guarantee, evidence of self-insurance or re-insurance, a risk-pooling scheme or financial protection from the capital market.

[62] Coverage in the form of insurance or self-insurance in the event of liability.

[63] Nicholas N Nierengarten, 'New ISO Additional Insured Endorsements' (2014) 44(1) Brief 33.

[64] Gerald F Slattery Jr, 'Indemnity and Insurance in the Texas Oil Patch' (2014) 10(1) Texas Journal of Oil, Gas and Energy Law 112.

[65] Chapelle (n 55) 3.

[66] Ohio Environmental Protection Agency, 'Financial Assurance Mechanisms' (EPA, July 2019) <epa.ohio.gov/static/Portals/34/document/guidance/FAMechanismsOverview.pdf> accessed 26 February 2023.

6.6.1 *Available Financial Assurance Tools*

6.6.1.1 *Pooling*

Pooling is an alternative source of insurance coverage that can be used to spread the financial risk from pollution or show evidence of financial capacity in the event of liability in the oil industry. As a risk transfer mechanism, it can be applied by operators (risk pooling or risk sharing) or insurers (fund pooling). For operators, it functions as a tool through which operators mutually agree to share one another's losses. Unlike insurance, it does not involve a third party (the insurance company), thus making operators the insured, insurers and financiers of the risk pool.[67] Pooling guarantees the availability of funds when a downside occurs because the resources come from other risk pool members.

As already highlighted, there exist pools that provide risk-sharing arrangements under P&I clubs.[68] Pooling, when applied by insurance companies, secures huge amounts of insurance capacity (funds) by spreading the uncertainties of the risk over many insurance companies. A good example is the American Nuclear Insurers, which underwrites nuclear liabilities as provided under the Price-Anderson Act[69] and makes available a large pool of funds in the event of a catastrophe.

When operators pool funds together, mutuality is created as members' contributions depend on the claims made by other members.[70] Low-risk claims by members promote mutual interest in risk minimisation. Mutuality incentivises risk differentiation among members, and the latter drives *ex ante* prevention as members' financial contributions are based on contribution to the risk. This practice motivates the exercise of care to avoid paying huge amounts toward the pool. It means that while risk pooling facilitates the availability of funds, contributions by members are based on the damage caused. The member involved in the damage will contribute more to enable the payment of compensation, cleanup and so on. Mutuality exists among members when they are faced with similar safety rules, liability levels and risk exposure, of which they have more knowledge than a third party.[71] Accordingly, they can evaluate each member's risk and monitor each other's behaviour.

An advantage of risk pooling is that members' contributions are agreed upon in advance, and payment is only made *ex post* when the risk materialises. This practice enables members to deal with uncertain, highly technical risks for which data may be rare or actuarially complicated. Again, differentiating members' risks becomes realistic as the *ex ante* premium charge is no longer necessary.[72] Unlike

67 Faure and Liu (n 20) 198.

68 These are non–profit making mutual insurance associations established by charterers and ship owners to cover third-party liabilities arising from ship operations.

69 CR Bardes, 'Role of Nuclear Insurance in US' (Sino-American Seminar on Nuclear Liability, China 2000) 379.

70 P Bennet, 'Mutual Risk: P&I Insurance Clubs and Maritime Safety and Environmental Performance' (2001) 25 Marine Policy 15.

71 Faure and Liu (n 20) 199.

72 ibid.

pooling, an insurer charges a premium for the risk they bear, which is not recoverable whether the risk occurs or not. Pooling is achievable in the offshore industry, given that players are few compared to a large membership group. A near-pool example in the oil and gas industry would be the OPOL, but the OPOL's practicability has not been tested.

6.6.1.2 *Insurance*

Insurance is the most common instrument to securitise risk in the oil and gas industry. As stated earlier, OEE is available to cover pollution and other related risks. However, only a finite amount of insurance capacity exists, even as insurers have increased premiums following the Macondo disaster. Oil majors are insurance-averse as they prefer to self-insure. A typical example is BP, which self-insured itself for the Macondo well.

An operator may be required to obtain insurance under a JOA or include other co-venturers in the insurance cover. Co-venturers could also take out personal insurance, but some super-majors may not seek market insurance as they prefer to self-insure or use a captive.[73] Other forms of offshore insurance coverage exist for offshore activities, covering physical damage, business interruption, workers' compensation and so on.

6.6.1.3 *Self-Insurance*

Majors in the oil industry use self-insurance as a mechanism for risk management by relying on their balance sheet as a guarantee/security for damages. Self-insurance works in two ways. The first is true pure self-insurance, and the other is captive insurance. For pure self-insurance, a reserve is held by the major for any future loss. In strict insurance terminology, the absence of risk distribution and loss spreading post-accident does not qualify as self-insurance.[74] It is merely a balance sheet guarantee. Self-insurance could also operate via a captive. A captive is an insurance company created by a major oil company to guarantee the payment of losses in the event of a downside during offshore operations. Risk is neither distributed nor loss shared, as the major owns the insurance company.

Using a captive enables the operator to retain profit and loss within the captive and operate at a lower cost than an insurance company in the real sense,

[73] PA Bawcut, *Captive Insurance Companies: Establishment, Operation and Management* (Woodhead-Faulkner 1991). See also T Dowding, *Global Development in Captive Insurance* (Pearson 1997). Captive insurers are in-house companies that insure the risk of a parent company. Their operation is similar to regular insurance companies as they charge premiums for designated risks and issue insurance policies. The financing of claims is entirely left to the captive, and they very rarely insure other companies' risk except for that of their parent company. Captives are used by super majors who are financially stable in the oil and gas industry.

[74] Michael Faure and Tom Hartlief (eds), *Insurance and Expanding System Risk, Policy Issues in Insurance, No 5* (OECD, 2003) 144.

thus making risk hedging attractive for majors. An insurance company can manage captives or a broker, as with BP, where Jupiter Insurance Ltd (a captive) was created by BP but managed by Willis, an insurance broker. Legally, a captive can underwrite risk as an insurance company. BP's captive, Jupiter Insurance, did the same for BP when BP was held responsible for the oil spill in the Gulf of Mexico.[75]

The converse side of self-insurance is that it may weaken the deterrent impact of pollution prevention since the low cost of self-insuring could lead to a reduced sense of risk prevention or responsibility.[76] It is also not a sure proof against insolvency, except that statutory requirements would preclude the usage of funds set apart as security for pollution liability. Besides, risk could be externalised in self-insurance due to insolvency and judgment-proof issues, especially for small companies. Therefore, it may not be suitable for medium-sized companies to self-insure.

6.6.1.4 *Capital Market*

Philip Bougen, in his work, identifies that the capital market is an efficient medium for securitising large pollution damage and establishing synergy with the market.[77] For example, before the Macondo incident, only natural catastrophes threatened and exceeded the capacity of individual insurance companies, and it even stretched the capacity limits of the insurance market. This situation threatened insurability, pushed the insurance market's limit and informed the idea of looking at the capital market for additional capacity to cover the risk of a natural catastrophe.[78] Similarly, offshore oil pollution risk could be hedged by using the capital market to securitise catastrophic pollution liability, which sometimes results from gross negligence.

The finite capacity of the energy insurance market and the limit of insurance regarding catastrophic risk inform the consideration of the capital market as a tool for securitising offshore pollution liability to provide additional capacity for higher liability.[79] Faure and Wang posit that the capital market has been mainly used to securitise environmental risk.[80] Fundamentally, the practice is to obtain catastrophe bonds at the stock exchange to transfer specific risks to investors in the capital market, especially for environmental risks.[81]

[75] Michael Faure and Hui Wang, 'The Use of Financial Market Instruments to Cover Liability Following a Major Offshore Accident' in Michael Faure (ed), *Civil Liability and Financial Security for Offshore Oil and Gas Activities* (CUP 2017), 236.

[76] BIO by Deloitte, *Civil Liability, Financial Security and Compensation Claims for Offshore Oil and Gas Activities in European Economic Area* (Final Report Prepared for the European Commission, DG Energy, Brussels, 14 August 2014) 129.

[77] Philip D Bougen, 'Catastrophe Risk' (2003) 32(2) Economy and Society 253, 271.

[78] F Wagner, 'Risk Securitization: An Alternative of Risk Transfer of Insurance Companies' (1998) 23(89) Geneva Papers on Risk and Insurance 574.

[79] ibid 575.

[80] See Faure and Wang (n 75) 242.

[81] V Bruggeman, 'Capital Market Instruments for Natural Catastrophe and Terrorism Risk: A Bright Future?' (2010) 40(2) Environmental Law Reporter 10136.

Catastrophe (CAT) bonds are also available in the capital market. These are insurance-linked securities (ILS) that transfer a set of specified risks from a sponsor(s) to investors in the capital market through a special-purpose vehicle (SPV). As insurance-linked high-yield debt instruments, they are used to raise money in the event of a catastrophe such as a hurricane or an earthquake and can be used for oil pollution catastrophes.[82] Rawle King posits that a CAT bond, as an alternative risk transfer mechanism, transforms a re-insurance contract into a financial security that could be passed on to capital market investors.[83] Thus, CAT bonds provide the capacity to cover higher liabilities in the offshore oil industry. CAT bonds act as a substitute for catastrophe re-insurance. Through an SPV, an insurance or a re-insurance company issues bonds to investors in the capital market to hedge catastrophic risk. When the risk occurs, the principal capital compensates for the loss, but when the risk does not happen, the investor(s) earns interest on the SPV.[84]

It has been noted, however, that CAT bonds are rarely used for offshore risks. The reason advanced is that the lifespan of a CAT bond is short. In contrast, offshore pollution accidents have a long tail,[85] and operators except insurers do not use CAT bonds.[86] This is expected as insurance and re-insurance companies use the capital market to transfer risk. However, the role of CAT bonds is still minor in the coverage of offshore risk. Therefore, its suitability to cover offshore oil pollution risks is doubtful as it cannot cover long-tail risks.[87]

6.6.2 *Are Financial Assurance Mechanisms Fulfilling Their Purpose?*

Financial assurance mechanisms assist in fostering cost internalisation by requiring prospective polluters to show the necessary financial resources to compensate for environmental damage that could arise during their operations. These tools

[82] M Edesess, 'Catastrophe Bonds: An Important New Financial Instrument' (Autumn 2015) <www.caia.org/sites/default/files/AIAR_Q4_2015-02_Edesses_CatBonds_0.pdf> accessed 21 February 2023.

[83] Rawle O King, *Deepwater Horizon Oil Spill Disaster: Risk, Recovery, and Insurance Implications* (Diane Publishing 2010). See also Darius Lakdawalla and George Zanjani, 'Catastrophe Bonds, Reinsurance, and the Optimal Collateralization of Risk Transfer' (2012) 79(2) Journal of Risk and Insurance 449.

[84] Qihao He, 'Climate Change and Effective Catastrophe Risk Management Mechanism: A Law and Economics Analysis of Insurance and Insurance-Linked Securities' (2015) 1(4) International Journal of Bonds and Derivatives 310.

[85] A long-tail exposure is the damage that occurs after the wrongful act has been committed. Faure and Hartlief posit that a solution to the long-tail problem is to examine the periods, to wit:

> 1. **The act-committed system**: in that case the wrongful act must have taken place during the period of insurance cover; 2. **The loss-occurrence system:** in that case the damage must have taken place within the period of insurance cover; 3. **The claims-made system:** in that case the claim for damages must have been received by the insured or his insurer during the period of insurance cover.

Faure and Hartlief (n 74), emphasis original.

[86] See Faure and Wang (n 75) 243.

[87] ibid.

complement liability rules and the obligation to restore the environment, and are essential to complying with regulatory requirements.[88] They enable policymakers to consider communities and their environment as of primary importance. Financial assurance tools, where possible, allow communities to use reclaimed land/area and effectively manage long-term environmental and other liabilities.[89] Most state agencies in the US demand financial assurance tools to restore public resources after they have been damaged. They are also required for use in offshore oil and gas activities in the US.

Financial assurance mechanisms benefit communities, their environment and underwriters. For communities, they enable quick and relatively low-cost access to compensation. They take away the usual delays and uncertainties linked to penalty collection, which can cause difficulties in transferring funds from a defendant to victims. The benefit can be greater when a quick response assists in minimising damages. For underwriters, assurance tools can harness the knowledge and scrutiny of private, third-party financial providers for the underwriter's commercial use. As such, the insurers, sureties and banks that provide the financial products use them to demonstrate compliance, and train and build the capacity of their staff on the financial and environmental risks presented by potential polluters.[90] This practice enables assurance to reflect a flexible, market-based approach to compliance and monitoring. Financial providers to firms that cannot self-insure are concerned that their clients' future liabilities will consume their capital. As such, they have a strong incentive as underwriters to monitor the environmental safety of firms they underwrite.

The safety behaviour of the firms a financial provider underwrites is used to base the cost of premiums on observable attributes. The afety behaviour observed during monitoring is an incentive offered to firms with meaningful risk management and safety programmes. Poor safety behaviour usually results in a high premium even before any accident, to indirectly discourage negative behaviour. Again, financial assurance helps ensure the polluter does not escape cost internalisation through dissolution or bankruptcy.

A question is whether financial assurance tools fulfil the purpose of their establishment or design.[91] This question arises due to the assurance level required, the conditions under which the bonds are released, and how assurance tools interact with other areas of law like bankruptcy. Nevertheless, of particular concern here is the coverage level. The level of assurance provided guarantees the performance of a stated obligation or internalisation of future financial responsibility. An exception

88 James Boyd, 'Financial Responsibility for Environmental Obligations: Are Bonding and Assurance Rules Fulfilling Their Promise?' (Resources for the Future Discussion Paper 01-42, August 2001) <media.rff.org/documents/RFF-DP-01-42.pdf> accessed 28 February 2023.

89 IGF, 'Global Review: Financial Assurance Governance for the Post-Mining Transition (*IISD*, August 2021) <www.iisd.org/system/files/2021-09/financial-assurance-governance-for-post-mining-transition.pdf> accessed 25 February 2023.

90 Boyd, 'Financial Responsibility' (n 88) 10.

91 ibid.

may be where the liability is beyond regulatory stipulation, like catastrophic liability arising from gross negligence or punitive damage.

Liabilities arising from these cases are usually difficult to calculate, such as in the Macondo oil pollution case. Aside from regulatory penalties/fines, third-party claims can exceed the assurance coverage. In that case, the assurance coverage may not be able to settle the entire claim, especially where the liability relates to oil pollution damage. Although coverage requirements are decided on a case-by-case basis, considering the risk in question that an operation poses, more procedural formality is imposed via established estimation methodologies. This situation poses uncertainty when determining the required assurance amount because of the method used to determine coverage requirements. James Boyd argues that coverage levels are not always adequate due to the relatively new assurance rules which cover responsibilities that arise over decades, making it difficult to draw firm conclusions regarding the adequacy of coverage levels.

The second concern relates to the bankruptcy or insolvency of the assurance provider. Under assurance rules, the possibility that a firm will not perform its environmental obligation due to insolvency is limited. Nonetheless, concerns exist where the assurance is imposed or a higher amount is involved while a firm is in bankruptcy. This legal situation creates a conflict between bankruptcy law and assurance requirements. For example, once a company is in bankruptcy in the US, environmental cleanup costs may be a dischargeable 'claim' under the bankruptcy code.[92] As a result, firms have attempted to evade assurance requirements with the bankruptcy code as protection, by claiming that assurance-related expenditures are dischargeable obligations. However, courts have held that assurance costs, required bond posting, and increased bond amounts to cover reclamation costs are not 'money judgments' under the bankruptcy code. Some courts also have identified that they fall within the 'police and regulatory powers' exception to the automatic stay.[93]

The underwriter can become insolvent, which can threaten the availability of the assurance fund. The challenge is that no insurance is available against an assuror's financial failure.[94] Although there are regulatory safeguards against likely

[92] A case in point is *Re Chateaugay Corp* 944 F 2d 997 (2nd Cir 1991), in which it was found that an injunction encountered in an environmental case, that does no more than impose an obligation entirely as an alternative to a payment right, is dischargeable. But see also *Ohio v Kovacs* 469 US 274, 105 S Ct 705 (1985): discharge ability is limited to situations where a cleanup order is converted into an obligation to pay money, and regulatory orders that demand performance and cannot be satisfied solely via a monetary payment are not dischargeable in bankruptcy. See also *In re Commonwealth Oil Refining Co*, 805 F.2d 1175 (5th Cir. 1986): a RCRA compliance order is not stayed by bankruptcy code even though compliance involved expenditure of money.

[93] *Commonwealth of PA Department of Environmental Resources v Peggs Run Coal Co* 55 PA Commw 312, 423 A 2d 765 (PA Commw Ct 1980): an injunction, including bond requirement, was a 'proceeding to enforce its police or regulatory power and as such is exempted from the stay provisions of Section 362 of the Bankruptcy Code'.

[94] In the US, for instance, the Federal Deposit Insurance Corporation does not insure letters of credit issued to governments, such as those that would be used as an environmental guarantee. Similarly, most states have an insurance guaranty fund to protect policyholders in the event of an insurer's

assuror's insolvency in the US, such as secure rating for insurers, US.Treasury certification of bond issuers or some form of licensing for financial institutions providing assurance, bankruptcy cases always occur. *The Economist* has highlighted that in the late 1990s and early 2000s, about eight insurance companies in the US failed,[95] while Boyd identifies that the annual failure rate for Federal Deposit Insurance Corporation–insured banks was 1.14%. The challenge of an assuror failure is that their customer must secure another assurance quickly. This may not be difficult for insured with a strong balance sheet, but those experiencing financial difficulties can have problems finding a replacement. Often, new assurances may not be available to meet the regulatory requirements for an activity.

An exception to the challenge of insolvency or bankruptcy is the capital market, where the market is the guaranteed source for the party requiring coverage. However, market failures could be a concern regarding the ability of the insured to cover their liability.

6.6.3 *Financial Assurance Tools and Gross Negligence Situations*

As stated earlier, financial assurance tools assist with the funding requirement when a downside occurs during petroleum operations. In addition, they help the assured comply with regulatory requirements and address compensation and third-party claims when needed. However, from the financial provider's perspective, steps must be taken to avoid a situation where the assured causes damage beyond the financial provider's ability. Thus, monitoring mechanisms are used to control the assured's behaviour, and positive conduct is rewarded with low premium charges. In contrast, negative behaviour is rewarded with a higher premium and the possibility that the assured may not get coverage in the future.

The monitoring mechanism used in financial assurance strategies aligns with the distributive philosophy in gross negligence cases. Monitoring by an assuror provides an incentive to exercise care, thus discouraging the likelihood of moral hazard. It creates a reason to mitigate damage and indirectly passes the burden of the risk created to the assured when a downside occurs, albeit not the totality of the financial obligation. The fact that an assured is made to bear the outcome of its behaviour via high premium or no coverage in the future is a negative reward for bad conduct. Although this type of negative reward for damage is for the future, it affects the overall conduct of the assured. Again, the monitoring provides an avenue for reassessing the insured's safety level with the finance provider

insolvency. However, most enabling statutes include a 'net worth exclusion' that eliminates governments as recipients of these funds. See Michigan, MCL 500.7925(3); and Illinois, 215 ILCS 5/534.3(b)(iv). Accordingly, government attempts to access such funds in environmental guarantee cases have not been successful. See *Attorney General ex rel Department of Natural Resources v Michigan Property and Casualty Guaranty Association*, 218 Mich App 342; 533 NW 2d 700 (1996).

95 *The Economist*, 'American Insurance: Bungee Jump' (*The Economist*, 14 September 2000) <www.economist.com/finance-and-economics/2000/09/14/bungee-jump> accessed 27 February 2023.

and discourages the likelihood of moral hazard. The denial of financial coverage due to unacceptable safety levels incentivises environmental sustainability, especially in the oil industry. Even the capital markets that arise to satisfy the demand for financial responsibility generate incentives to reduce environmental risks.[96]

Financial providers can use deductibles to mitigate moral hazard that could arise from having financial coverage.[97] The reason is that insurance or other financial coverage reduces the incentive to exercise care. Deductibles enhance liability distribution as the insured and the underwriter shares the risk arising from the insured's fault. As such, the deductible is a valuable strategy to discourage moral hazard and align with the distributive philosophy in petroleum operations. Furthermore, underwriters can specify a higher amount that an insured must pay should pollution damage arise from gross negligence during petroleum operations. This incentive can be complemented with policies with several preventative requirements, such as reduced premiums for undertaking systematic safety checks or upon passing specified safety inspections. In this way, financial assurance mechanisms can align with the distributive philosophy and indirectly fulfil the purpose in gross negligence cases, as these strategies provide an incentive to exercise care. This incentive can discourage grossly negligent conduct during petroleum operations.

6.7 REGULATORY REFORMS FOR EFFECTIVE ALLOCATION OF GROSS NEGLIGENCE RISK

An essential reform in most jurisdictions, such as the UK, would involve regulatory recognition of gross negligence as a trigger for liability in the offshore oil and gas industry. The concept of gross negligence is not novel in most jurisdictions where only wilful misconduct applies in oil and gas operations. In these jurisdictions, gross negligence is recognised in criminal jurisprudence, and the guiding principles of the term are well established. Again, since gross negligence is a *sui generis* type of negligence, and given the nature of oil and gas operations, a carrot-and-stick regulation which rewards good oilfield practices and places liability on a party at fault for damages arising from gross negligence is necessary to facilitate

[96] Goran Skogh, 'Insurance and the Institutional Economics of Financial Intermediation' (1991) 16(8) Geneva Papers on Risk and Insurance 59–72. The paper highlights the advantages of monitoring, especially when the assets of intermediate financial providers are exposed to liability claims of the companies they underwrite.

[97] Goran Skogh, 'Insurance Coverage of Accidental Damage to the Environment', Workshop Law and Economics of Environmental Policy (2000) <www.cserge.ucl.ac.uk/Skogh.pdf> accessed 27 February 2023. A deductible is an amount that an insured pays toward an insured loss when a downside occurs. For instance, if pollution damage occurs during offshore drilling operations, the deductible is subtracted from what the underwriter or insurance company pays toward pollution damage. What this means is that the insured will not get the full amount of the coverage. This practice can apply in gross negligence cases to discourage moral hazard and incentivize the exercise of care during drilling operations.

environmental sustainability. Gross negligence should receive the same regulatory and contractual attention as wilful misconduct.

In the oil and gas industry, regulatory reform needs to highlight the importance of proportionality in liability distribution between the contracting parties in gross negligence cases. As identified earlier, the rationale for the proportionality suggestion is the benefit that each party bears in the contractual relationship, following the long-term financial upside of the operator. Furthermore, the institutional framework to ensure compliance with the regulatory position is necessary to achieve the purpose of the regulation. The UK has an institutional set-up that can support regulatory reform, but other jurisdictions need to develop similar institutional arrangements.[98] In addition, regulations need to support financial assurance tools and their usage and provide an enabling environment for users in the oil and gas industry to access coverage for oil pollution. This reform, of course, should follow the requirement for compulsory liability insurance for offshore pollution.

6.8 CONCLUSION

An institutional framework is necessary to achieve the regulatory objective of allocating a qualified mutual indemnity clause for gross negligence risks and to define the insurance required for the operation of offshore oil and gas installations. It must be noted that the features of different types of insurance, as well as the interests that each covers, are different. Insurance and other financial assurance mechanisms are vital in risk allocation and securitisation. However, most of these tools and coverage are available to operators, not drilling contractors. Nevertheless, an OPOL-style pooling system for contractors, self-insurance, available financial assurance tools and the capital market provide options for contractors to explore. Besides these, the AI system of coverage for liability offers hope to offshore drilling participants.

98 See the earlier discussion on institutional arrangements.

Chapter 7

A Summary for Stakeholders

7.0 INTRODUCTION

This chapter summarises how mutual indemnity clauses can be qualified for liability arising from gross negligence during offshore drilling operations in the interest of stakeholders. It also considers strategies to overcome the limitations of allocating gross negligence risks.

7.1 A DYNAMIC APPROACH TO RISK ALLOCATION IN THE OIL INDUSTRY

The literature on pollution liability and indemnity considered in this book reveals that mutual indemnity provisions are used mainly to allocate risks in offshore petroleum contracts. Smith and others highlight an essential point about mutual indemnity clauses when they state that an indemnity clause is subject to ifs.[1] The business benefit of risk allocation is not universal in its application. For instance, in the deep waters of Brazil, liability is based on fault.[2] In the US and other notable jurisdictions, anti-indemnity statutes and public policy considerations still hinder the use of indemnity clauses. Again, the business benefit practice of the oil industry negates the 'polluter pays' principle and does not seem to support environmental sustainability by using mutual indemnity as a shield against liability for gross negligence.

The policy and contractual pathways identified in this book represent a dynamic repurposing of the traditional practice of risk allocation, especially for offshore petroleum drilling operations. The identified pathways highlight liability for grossly negligent conduct resulting in harm or loss during offshore drilling operations based on fault and the proportion of benefit. The implication is that mutual indemnity will be subject to gross negligence and no longer an absolute shield against liability between an operator and a drilling contractor. An obvious question would be to ask about the essence of the rule of effective risk allocation, given that parties allocate risk based on their ability to bear a given risk and secure the right insurance. This idea is a long-held notion in the oil industry. However, what purpose should a practice, law or rule serve: public interest or private interest?

[1] Ernest E Smith and others, *International Petroleum Transactions* (3rd edn, Rocky Mountain Mineral Law Foundation 2010).

[2] Peter Cameron, 'Liability for Catastrophic Risk in the Oil and Gas Industry' (2012) 6 International Energy Law Review 207, 213. Local laws in some jurisdictions like Indonesia, Brazil and some US states would not allow indemnity clauses to absolve a party of his negligence.

A contrary argument to the efficient risk allocation rule is that the industry risk allocation practice serves the interests of the contracting parties and not those of the public or the environment; and that the practice of using mutual indemnity clauses as a shield against gross negligence can result in externalities and losses to non-consenting third parties. In other words, from a public policy perspective, risk allocation should focus on creating a good deal for society. For private participants, risk allocation is about an attractive risk–return ratio. In any case, the suggested practice of risk allocation in gross negligence cases considers both private and public interests, as the benefit of the parties counts towards their level of liability.

The result of the practice identified in this book is a partial risk transfer, or a qualified use of mutual indemnity as a shield in gross negligence cases, to create a greater incentive for the exercise of care. This means that partial liability will arise on account of the gross negligence of the operator or the drilling contractor, irrespective of care custody or control of the negative event. The incentive is maximised when either party to the contract is allowed to share in the financial burden of the downside. Although it may seem outside of industry practice to require a party to bear a percentage of the liability for events over which they have no control, it often incentivises the party to engage in preventive risk mitigation or seek the most cost-efficient solutions. However, this sharing method should be capped, both per occurrence and overall. The concept of partial risk transfer is not new, especially as it applies to home or health insurance schemes, which usually require users to bear a small portion of the risk (the deductible) while insuring them against significant financial losses.[3] When users are required to bear a small amount of risk, it incentivises them to exercise care to prevent the risk from materialising. Public policy and distributive justice are the basis for this argument.

7.2 A DISTRIBUTIVE OUTCOME

The distributive philosophy of Gregory Keating can quell the concerns of operators and drilling contractors. According to Keating, the burden of mutually beneficial but harmful activities should be distributed among parties involved in an economic activity. As such, Keating believes that distributive justice focuses on the fair apportioning of the burden and benefits of risky yet valuable activities.[4] Inarguably, oil and gas exploration, particularly well drilling, is hazardous and comes with challenges to people and their environment. However, it has become a strategic tool in global energy politics and is a reliable source for powering the world and enabling machines to move. Therefore, it can be stated that offshore petroleum exploration is risky yet valuable.

[3] Pauline Hovy, 'Risk Allocation in Public-Private Partnerships: Maximizing value for money' (*IISD Discussion Paper*, August 2015) <https://www.iisd.org/system/files/publications/risk-allocation-ppp-maximizing-value-for-money-discussion-paper.pdf> accessed 15 October 2023.

[4] Gregory Keating, 'Distributive and Corrective Justice in the Tort Law of Accidents' (2000) 74 Southern California Law Review 192' 194.

Keating posits further that those who reap benefits should also bear the burden. To him, the justice concept of distribution is founded on a structured pattern that enables the responsibility for mutually beneficial but harmful activity to be apportioned to those who reap the benefit. Keating maintains that imposing on others the cost of an actor's harm is unfair in a social world when the actor reaps the benefit of the activity.[5] Therefore, designing the terms of a contract for some people to reap benefits while others bear the burden is unjust in gross negligence cases. In line with Keating's position, proportional benefit and burden is necessary as fairness requires that the burden of mutually beneficial but harmful activities be apportioned in a proportion that reflects the benefit derived from the activity.

When we assess the distributive philosophy in the context of the oil and gas industry, we see that well drilling operations involve an operator who designs the work programme and an independent contractor(s) who carries out the actual drilling activity. Although a contract of service is obtainable for day rates instead of a contract for service in turnkeys,[6] parties mutually benefit from the drilling contract. The contractor benefits from their day rate or turnkey, and the operator benefits from the oil extracted from the ground (in a Concession) or profit and cost oil (in a PSC).[7] As gleaned from this study, the liability for well pollution is the operator's responsibility even when the pollution is the sole or joint fault of the contractor. The contractor benefits from the well drilling operation but assumes no burden from any harm they solely or jointly caused.

A well-structured contractual agreement, which includes an allocation of risk that aligns the burden with the benefits derived from petroleum activities in gross negligence situations, satisfies Keating's distributive justice. The critical focus in distributive justice as applied by the oil industry is burden creation instead of control or ownership of property or personnel. Keating's distributive justice advocates a system where harm is borne by those who occasion it, albeit the burden of the harm should reflect the benefit reaped. In law, causation fixes liability, and the law abhors injustice and promotes justice in contract and tort. Because contractual justice facilitates execution and reduces strife or litigation when a downside occurs, pursuing a distributive outcome for pollution damage arising from gross negligence in offshore petroleum operations is essential. This distributive outcome will favourably and fairly reconcile the conflicting fundamental interests between operators and contractors, since liability for subsurface offshore pollution constitutes their primary area of disagreement in the post-Macondo era.[8]

The offshore oil industry practice of risk allocation is through contracts between participants, and such contracts mostly do not consider gross negligence

[5] ibid 195.

[6] Owen L Anderson, 'The Anatomy of an Oil and Gas Drilling Contract' (1989) 25 Tulsa Law Journal 359.

[7] It must be noted that the operator may not even benefit from the drilling where there is a dry hole or a hole that is not commercially viable.

[8] Cameron (n 2) 213.

as a trigger for liability or for situations where liability exceeds the stated statutory limit. Sometimes, gross negligence or wilful misconduct is a trigger to liability above statutory caps. Nevertheless, these triggers are often overlooked and not used as a carve-out to trigger liability between parties in risk allocation. Although the nature and extent of liability and the ability to control it determines how risks are allocated between parties, the change in risk exposure presented by the Macondo spill has opened more debates for carve-outs or exceptions to apply to industry practice. As stated earlier, operators seek to change the risk allocation regime so drilling contractors can be liable for gross negligence for well pollution and clean-up. Peter Cameron posits that this trend has characterised post-Macondo well drilling bargains between operators and contractors.[9] This trend can be regarded as risk-averse.

The aversion to risk stems from the need to make a profit, as the social responsibility of a business is to make a profit.[10] As a result, businesses would often not assume risk that may threaten their existence. Liability beyond the statutory cap can potentially place a company on the brink of bankruptcy. Aside from higher financial liabilities, post-Macondo negotiations during risk allocation have been focused on catastrophic loss and reputational damage in a globalised world.[11] The move away from traditional risk allocation by operators in the oil industry suggests a distributive outcome where liability is also borne by parties causally connected to it.

7.2.1 A Distributive Outcome through Capped Liability in Gross Negligence Cases

From a contractual perspective, a pollution liability clause subject to a financial cap supports a distributive outcome. The distributive outcome hinges on the benefit derived from the parties' activities. The operator receives the long-term financial upside while the contractor receives their day rate as a benefit. Both parties receive benefits that provide a foundation for assuming the burden when a downside occurs. The amount above the cap is then borne by the party that controls the source of pollution (that is, surface or subsurface pollution). It must be stated that there is no record of surface pollution resulting in liability beyond the statutory limit in the oil and gas industry known at the moment. In line with Keating's distributive justice, an operator should bear a substantial part of the burden of well pollution. The drilling contractor with a causal connection to the spill assumes a capped liability since they have no control or do not own the source of

[9] ibid.

[10] M Friedman, 'The Social Responsibility of Business is to Increase Profit' (*New York Times Magazine*, 13 September 1970) <www.nytimes.com/1970/09/13/archives/a-friedman-doctrine-the-social-responsibility-of-business-is-to.html?_r=0> accessed 15 October 2023.

[11] E O'Hara O'Connor, 'Organizational Apologies: BP as a Case Study' (2011) 64(6) Vanderbilt Law Review 1960. Immediately after the Macondo spill, BP share price plummeted as the world passed a moral judgement on BP for the spill at the Gulf of Mexico.

the spill or equipment. The capped liability could be a stated amount or percentage, or derivable from the value of the drilling contract.

This outcome supports Keating's principle[12] that it is unfair for a party to fix the terms of an activity so that they benefit from the activity while the other party bears the burden of the activity. In line with Keating's position, it would be unfair for a party who benefited through their day rate to pass on the entire burden of well pollution arising from their gross negligence to another party. Under tort law, the former party would be liable to the extent that they contributed to the damage, but under Keating's view, the contractor would be liable to the extent of the benefit received, as the burden should reflect the benefit obtained from the activity.

A distributive outcome in the form of a capped/limited liability will quell parties' concerns, promote the 'polluter pays' principle and foster environmental responsibility. To Keating, this serves the justice of the wrong and engenders responsible behaviour during drilling. In cases of subsurface pollution, distributive contractual well liability addresses the question of moral hazard as it ensures partial exposure to risk for the drilling contractor,[13] which will shape the contractor's behaviour to act in a preventive manner. This practice promotes the distribution of liability, reflects the risk valuation of the drilling contractor within the contractors' group, encourages the prevention of pollution and incentivises the care needed for offshore petroleum operations.

7.2.2 *Policy and Regulatory Direction for a Distributive Outcome*

A policy direction and/or regulation developed along the lines of distribution of burden can quell parties' concerns. The policy direction or regulation should be designed to involve parties that are causally responsible or whose responsibility arises from the law regarding pollution to achieve a distributive outcome and protect state interest. The interest of the public is the interest of the state since the state has a responsibility to protect the public interest. As such, the public interest is protected when the state uses policy and regulatory instruments to protect and preserve non-consenting third parties to a contract from practices that can result in harm to them and the environment.

The *sui generis* nature of gross negligence and its blanket application in offshore energy contracts requires regulatory direction to achieve a distributive outcome. This means that regulation has to lay the foundation for a distributive result by identifying, for instance, that liability for gross negligence will apply subject to a cap to reflect the benefit reaped from the risky activity. The government will drive the policy direction and, through regulation, support the application of an additional insured scheme to manage offshore pollution liability and prevent a situation where the liability outweighs the wrongdoer's assets or create a judgment-proof problem.[14]

[12] ibid.

[13] Michael Faure and Tom Hartlief, 'Remedies for Expanding Liability' (1998) 18 OJLS 684.

[14] Michael Faure, 'Private Liability and Critical Infrastructure' (2015) 6(2) European Journal of Risk Regulation 232.

An alternative to the AI scheme is a tiered insurance system with government oversight to settle pollution claims and cleanup costs. A tiered insurance system is used mostly to settle huge financial claims for large pollution damage. It enables the government to use its apparatus to establish insurance and a claims process that ensures adequate compensation. In a tiered system, the government sets a liability threshold subject to inflation and review by a private risk assessor, requiring those who need it to demonstrate the ability to meet the threshold when a downside occurs. Those requiring insurance demonstrate their ability through private insurance and insurance pool. Where liability exceeds the threshold, their retrospective premium is triggered, and payments are added to the threshold to fund the catastrophe. At this point, the contractually agreed amount between the operator and contractor is also brought in. The contribution towards the retrospective premium would be based on risk differentiation.[15] The efficiency goal behind risk differentiation is to incentivise pollution prevention, reduce risk or mitigate damages, and forestall the moral hazard issue among participants.

Although a tiered insurance system applies mostly to operators, regulation can also ensure an OPOL-styled association for drilling contractors to have access to financing. Just as the regulatory authorities in the UK have made OPOL membership an *ex ante* licensing requirement, regulatory guidance could require operators to hire only registered members of the drilling contractors' association within the state-controlled offshore waters. This regulatory requirement will create an incentive for membership since operators will not engage non-members in drilling activities. Operators would be made to satisfy this requirement *ex post* licence. In addition, the regulator, like the NSTA, can support the association of drillers by engaging them in safety awareness and providing guidelines for reporting unsafe practices and other environmental risks and hazards during drilling activities. The regulation could also facilitate a contractors' pooling system by ensuring a minimum level of safety through safety regulations to guide drilling contractors' operations.[16]

More, draft guidelines could be drawn up to assist drillers in bringing a well under control through a relief well drilling. In the UK, the NSTA has developed guidelines for relief well planning,[17] considering how factors such as well depth, water depth, location and geographical environment can affect a relief well. Under the pooling system, contractors contribute to funding the pool under the same framework that differentiates risk, forestalls moral hazard, promotes mutual monitoring and incentivises pollution prevention. This practice can enhance safety regulations and reduce the possibility of well pollution damage. The duty to contribute to the operator through the pool is based on the contractual agreement.

15 Risk differentiation in this regard means that members' contributions would be on the basis of their safety behaviour. Members whose safety behaviour poses a higher risk pay more, while members who possess lower risk pay a lower premium.

16 Under the US nuclear regime, the NRC enforces minimum safety standards for nuclear operators.

17 Offshore Energies UK, 'Guidelines on Relief Well Planning – Issue 2' <oeuk.org.uk/product/guidelines-on-relief-well-planning-issue-2> accessed 14 October 2023.

Designing an OPOL-style or pooling association for contractors may seem like transferring the statutory responsibility for pollution damage to drilling contractors. However, regulation will only provide a platform for contractual responsibility and availability of funds to facilitate contractors' share of a distributive outcome in the drilling agreement to cover for pollution damage, while the operator still retains statutory liability. Nevertheless, of importance is the fact that the regulatory requirement of an OPOL-style association for drilling contractors will affect moral hazard: efficiency is created, the social cost of an accident is minimised and pollution accidents can be prevented because of the requirement that the drilling association contribute to members' pollution damages. In addition, this practice will promote the desire to exercise care, which is the goal of every pollution liability regime. This policy direction supports a distributive outcome, which is also in line with the efficient liability rule, requiring the distribution of liability to parties that contribute to the risk.[18] Conversely, a non-distributive outcome is inefficient as it will impact the incentive for care by applying liability to one party despite another party causing harm.[19]

The model presented does not distort the statutory position of pollution liability, nor does it bring about double insurance. It allocates the risk of offshore pollution following the benefit reaped from the harmful activity while discouraging moral hazard. The policy/regulatory direction is fundamental as it seeks to promote the development of other sources of insurance capacity for distributing the financial risk of offshore oil pollution.[20] It also facilitates the availability of security necessary in the offshore oil industry to address pollution liability. A distributive outcome is built on Keating's fairness element, where the party that receives the greater benefit assumes the greater burden from the hazardous economic activity. The idea of liability distribution in gross negligence cases makes wrongdoers internalise cost, and cost internalisation breeds innovation and incentives for safety and risk reduction. The incentive to reduce harm arises when the actors share in the cost of the harm or risk.[21]

Guido Calabresi notes that the economic objective of a liability regime is to prevent accidents and to minimise the total of the accident cost.[22] The goal is

[18] See Faure (n 15) 232.

[19] B Vanden, 'Channelling of Liability: A Few Juridical and Economic Views on an Inadequate Legal Construction', in NLJT Horbach (ed), *Contemporary Development in Nuclear Energy Law: Harmonizing Legislation in CEE/NIS* (Kluwer Law International 1999) 13. When liability is applied to the operator alone, and the operator becomes 'judgment proof', victims cannot sue other parties causally connected to the risk or influenced the risk. Hence the incentive for prevention will be diluted, and victims may go uncompensated.

[20] Rawle O King, *Deepwater Horizon Oil Spill Disaster: Risk, Recovery, and Insurance Implications* (Diane Publishing 2010). These alternative risk transfer mechanisms include catastrophe bonds, reinsurance sidecars, and financial derivative instruments such as futures, options and swaps that securitise catastrophic risk.

[21] Giuseppe Dari-Mattiacci and Luigi A Franzoni, 'Innovation and Negligence Rules' (2014) 16(2), American Law and Economics Review, 337. See also Giuseppe Dari-Mattiacci and Luigi A Franzoni, 'Innovation and Liability Law 4' (14 January 14 2011) <economix.fr/pdf/seminaires/lien/franzoni.pdf> accessed 25 February 2023.

[22] Guido Calabresi, *The Costs of Accidents. A Legal and Economic Analysis* (Yale University Press 1970) 131.

risk control, hence the apportionment of risk to create the relevant sets of efficient incentives. An incentive is efficient if it provides a duty to contribute to the risk produced.[23] Distributing the liability of oil pollution costs arising from gross negligence is founded on economics and justice. Drilling contractors are obliged to contribute to well pollution liability as they may be solely or jointly connected to the cause of the spill during drilling activities. Shared liability is necessary for an equitable distribution of offshore oil pollution liability, as only operators are made to internalise the cost of well pollution liability. Sharing liability is an equitable and acceptable compromise for joint involvement in the harmful business of oil extraction.

A critical assessment of mutual indemnity clauses as a shield against liability for gross negligence in risk allocation shows that it does not incentivise pollution prevention. It focuses on a compensatory approach to oil pollution damage, rather than the preventive approach of a more incentive-oriented regime for pollution damage. A distributive outcome is incentive oriented and achievable through shared liability and mutual monitoring, thus encouraging good practices for oil pollution prevention during drilling activities. Risk sharing is an efficient liability principle that incentivises prevention, as parties will act as checks to themselves, with a duty to report bad oilfield practices. According to Owen Anderson and John Lowe, the duty can arise from regulation. They note that 'a possible approach could be to obligate drilling contractors, well service contractors and other non-operators to assume some regulatory duty, such as reporting unsafe practices to regulatory bodies.'[24]

For appropriate incentives and efficient risk distribution to apply, a contractual provision for allocating risk is essential, with regulatory support for a distributive outcome in gross negligence cases for offshore drilling contracts. The regulation sets the platform for operating a distributive outcome, while the parties' agreement enables the implementation of the outcome to ensure environmental sustainability. Distributive justice is achieved as the parties' financial burden is based on the proportion of benefit from the risky activity. As such, no party's gross negligence is left for another to bear entirely – which would be a distributive injustice in the industry practice of risk allocation.

7.3 A STRATEGY TO OVERCOME THE LIMITATIONS IN ALLOCATING GROSS NEGLIGENCE RISK

The general principle of contractual freedom must be balanced against public policy concerns that a party should not be absolved of their wrong, where it caused harm to non-consenting third parties arising from the party's gross negligence. Some strategies to balance the freedom of contract are stated below.

[23] KD Smedt, H Wang and M Faure, 'Towards Optimal Liability and Compensation for Offshore Oil and Gas Activities' in Michael Faure (ed), *Civil Liability and Financial Security for Offshore Oil and Gas Activities* (CUP 2016).

[24] Owen L Anderson and John S Lowe, 'Oil Spills' (2010) 3(2) OGEL Special Issue 2.

7.3.1 Statutory Control

Apart from selected states in the US identified in this book, where anti-indemnity statutes expressly prohibit the use of an indemnity clause as a shield against liability, most jurisdictions worldwide are yet to develop a regulation to address its application to contracts in the energy industry. In the UK, the UCTA 1977 as amended and the Unfair Terms in Consumer Contracts Regulations 1999 as amended are the most significant regulatory control dealing with negligence in business. They impose germane restrictions, but the 1999 Regulations apply only to consumer contracts and thus cannot apply to offshore energy contracts. Regulation 3(1) of the 1999 Regulations defines a 'Consumer' as 'any natural person who, in contracts covered by these Regulations, is acting for purposes which are outside his trade, business or profession'. For this regulation to apply to an operator or a drilling contractor, they must operate outside their trade, business or profession.[25] For the UCTA, the limitations against using indemnity clauses apply when the indemnifying party deals as a consumer. A party deals as a consumer when they do not contract in the course of a business, but the other party to the contract does.[26] This situation does not apply to operators' and contractors' drilling contracts where pollution damage arises from a party's gross negligence, in which they usually seek to protect themselves from liability by relying on mutual indemnity provisions.

The above UK regulations control business relations and consumer contracts, and businesses must operate within the confines of the law when it relates to negligence and other subjects. From them, we can glean that statutes can play a role in wholly or partially qualifying how gross negligence applies to offshore energy drilling contracts. Statutory control can be introduced to qualify the use of mutual indemnity clauses in gross negligence and not to make it an absolute shield against liability. Again, regulatory recognition of gross negligence in the oil industry can provide the foundation for gross negligence to become a term of art, thereby enlarging its application.

7.3.2 Statutory Harmonisation

Regulatory harmony is essential to overcoming the limitations of applying gross negligence. However, this harmonisation must come from federal law, especially in jurisdictions like the US, where multiple state laws provide different meanings and applications of indemnity and gross negligence to contracts. The essence is

[25] Greg Gordon, basing his argument on the decision of *Fastad v Enviroco*, identifies that indemnity clauses could operate as exclusions when they apply in the context of 'direct exposure' to the other contracting party. Details of this position are highlighted in *Fastad v Enviroco* per Lord Mance [2010] UKSC 18 [59]. On the basis of this, an argument could be made that the UCTA could apply in some aspects of offshore energy contracts, depending on the subject at stake.

[26] S 4 (for the law of England, Wales and Northern Ireland) and s 18 (for Scots law). A party deals as a consumer when they do not contract in the course of a business, but when the other party does.

to avoid numerous regulatory meanings of gross negligence, as this will continue to make gross negligence an ambiguous term. A harmonised statutory direction will enhance the application of gross negligence as a term of art, like negligence. Since gross negligence is recognised in criminal jurisprudence, it is also vital that it should receive broad regulatory inclusion in civil jurisprudence, to overcome the challenge of limited statutory inclusion in some petroleum regulations.

7.3.3 *Judicial Decisions and Harmonisation*

Judicial decisions are critical in clarifying legal grey areas. They enable the application of law and expand the frontiers of private and public exchanges. Moreover, as society evolves, judicial decisions help to construe law and practice to accommodate the dynamic nature of society and its changing norms. For example, although there have been conflicting decisions about the meaning of gross negligence, especially from US courts, judicial decisions can clarify the subject of gross negligence and lay the foundation for the requirements and means of proof to establish gross negligence. In the past, notable case law has set the stage to resolve some legal issues.

Let us consider two cases in point that significantly contributed to tort law. The first is *Ryland v Fletcher*,which established a strict liability regime for private nuisance. The rule developed by the House of Lords, per Lord Cranworth, established that

> [i]f a person brings, or accumulates, on his land anything which, if it should escape, may cause damage to his neighbour, he does so at his peril. If it does escape and cause damage, he is responsible, however careful he may have been, and whatever precautions he may have taken to prevent the damage.[27]

This case clarified a defendant's liability resulting from an abnormal or non-natural use of their land which causes harm to another person. The second case is *Donoghue v Stephenson*,[28] which shaped the negligence doctrine in tort law. In this case, a core question for the House of Lords was whether, contrary to established case law, the beer manufacturer Stephenson owed Donoghue a duty of care in the absence of a contractual relationship. The law of negligence at the time was not fully developed and was invoked only where there was some established contractual relationship.

These cases demonstrate that courts can shape practices and doctrines by providing clarity on their usage. Similarly, courts can clarify the meaning of gross negligence and the standard of proof required to establish gross negligence, especially when the term is understood as conduct, and the *far below* test, highlighted in this book, is applied. This pathway is essential to clarifying and understanding gross negligence and its application as a carve-out in offshore energy drilling contracts. In Chapter 4, an extensive discussion was presented on how gross negligence should be defined. This understanding provides a foundation for a

[27] [1868] UKHL 1.
[28] [1932] UKHL 100.

court to set the standard of proof required in gross negligence cases, just like in ordinary negligence.

Judicial harmonisation is essential in addressing conflicting opinions on the meaning and nature of gross negligence in offshore drilling operations. As stated earlier, the meaning of gross negligence has confounded courts, giving rise to a litany of conflicting definitions, especially in the US. Barbier J's opinion in the BP case is an instance of contradictory judgment. While Barbier J accepted the meaning of gross negligence as offered by the Fifth Circuit in *United States v Citgo Petroleum Co*, in his view, the definition offered no assistance as it was vague and contradictory. It means that courts are still unable to lay a clearly defined legal standard for determining gross negligence. An opportunity arose to resolve the meaning of gross negligence and develop a clear legal standard in the Supreme Court case of *Exxon Shipping Co v Baker*,[29] but it was missed as the court was divided evenly. The BP case presented another opportunity to provide a legal pathway for the meaning of gross negligence, but BP opted for a rather political settlement to avoid damaging further its corporate image.

7.4 CONCLUSION

The allocation of risk in the offshore petroleum industry has been carried out with absolute freedom by parties on terms that they consider to be in their best interests, despite the interests of all the parties (including third parties) connected to the outcome of the contract. This practice is underpinned by the business benefit of the industry to provide energy. The global argument about energy security and the need to benefit from resource wealth, especially in the Global South, drives new licensing rounds and petroleum development. However, there is no substantial evidence that suggests an end to petroleum exploration. Thus, we are left to reflect on better ways of making offshore drilling operations environmentally sustainable in the meantime.

This book calls for a qualified approach to mutual indemnity provisions for liability arising from gross negligence to promote sustainability through drilling contracts. However, this call opens up a research agenda to advance scholarly understanding and debate and eventually improve practice for insurance coverage for participants in the offshore energy industry. In all of these, there is a need for legislative and judicial harmonisation, especially on the meaning of gross negligence and how it should apply in risk allocation. Thankfully, this book provides a guide to achieving this objective.

[29] 554 US 471, 484 (2008).

Bibliography

BOOKS

Aguilar FJ, *Scanning the Business Environment* (Macmillan 1967)

Anderson BF and others, *Concepts in Judgement and Decision Research: Definitions, Sources, Interrelations, Comments* (Praeger 1981)

Aristotle, *Nicomachean Ethics* vol V (trans WD Ross) (c 350 BCE)

—— *Nicomachean Ethics*, in J Barnes (trans) *Complete Works of Aristotle* (vol 2, Princeton University Press 2014)

Armstrong C, *Global Distributive Justice: An Introduction* (CUP 2012)

Atiyah PS, *Essays on Contract* (OUP 2012)

Arinaitwe PW, *Risk Allocation in Oil and Gas Service Contracts: A Comparative Analysis of US Outer Continental Shelf and UK Continental Shelf Jurisdictions* (Lap Lambert Academic Publishing 2014)

Austen-Baker R, *Implied Terms in English Contract Law* (Edward Elgar Publishing 2017)

Baker McKenzie, *International Arbitration Yearbook 2011–2012* (5th edn, JurisNet, 2012)

Banks E, *Catastrophic Risk: Analysis and Management* (John Wiley & Sons Ltd 2005)

Bawcut PA, *Captive Insurance Companies: Establishment, Operation and Management* (Woodhead-Faulkner 1991)

Beale HG and others, *Contract: Cases and Material* (5th edn, OUP 2008)

Bernoulli J, *Ars Conjectandi* (Thurnheysen 1731)

Bigelow MM, *The Law of Torts* (8th edn, Little, Brown and Company 1907)

Black L, *The Social Licence to Operate: Your Management Framework for Complex Times* (Routledge 2017)

Bostock D, *Aristotle's Ethics* (OUP 2000)

Cane P, *Responsibility in Law and Morality* (Hart Publishing 2002)

Cibinic J, RC Nash and JF Nagle, *Administration of Government Contracts* (5th edn, Wolters Kluwer 2016)

Cicero MT, *Treatise on the Commonwealth in Francis Barham, Esq, The Political Works of Marcus Tullius Cicero: Comprising his Treatise on the Commonwealth; and his Treatise on the Laws* (vol 1, trans E Spettigue, 1841–42)

Cochran CE and others, *American Public Policy: An Introduction* (10th edn, Wadsworth 2012)

Coleman JL, *The Practice of Principle: In Defence of a Pragmatist Approach to Legal Theory* (OUP 2001)

Cooper R and AA John, *Theory and Applications of Economics* (McGraw-Hill Education 2012)

Crisp R (ed) *Aristotle: Nicomachean Ethics* (CUP 2000)

Dobbs DB, *The Law of Torts: Practitioner Treatise Series* (vol 1, West Group 2001)

Dowding T, *Global Development in Captive Insurance* (Pearson 1997)

Duval C and others, *Internaitonal Petroleum Exploration and Exploitation Agreements: Legal, Economic & Policy Aspects* (Barrows 2009)

Dye T, *Understanding Public Policy* (15th edn, Pearson 2016)

Easterbrook FH and DR Fischel, *The Economic Structure of Corporate Law* (Harvard University Press 1996)

Faruque AA, *Petroleum Contracts: Stability and Risk Management in Developing Countries* (Bangladesh Institute of Law and International Affairs 2011)

Faure M and T Hartlief (eds), *Insurance and Expanding System Risk, Policy Issues in Insurance, No.5* (OECD 2003)

Feinberg J, *Social Philosophy* (Prentice-Hall 1973)

Finnis J, *Natural and Natural Rights* (2nd edn, OUP 2011)

Fischhoff B and others, *Acceptable Risk* (CUP 1984)

Franck TM, *Fairness in International Law and Institutions* (OUP 1995)

Fried C, *Contract as Promise: A Theory of Contractual Obligation* (Harvard University Press 1981)

Gao Z, *International Petroleum Contracts: Current Trends and New Directions* (Graham & Trotman Ltd 1994)

Garner R, *A Theory of Justice for Animals* (OUP 2013)

Gerston LN, *Public Policy Making: Process and Principles* (3rd edn, Routledge 2010).

Gewirth A, *Human Rights: Essays on Justification and Application* (Chicago University Press 1982).

Greenberg J and RL Cohen (eds), *Equity and Justice in Social Behaviour* (Academic Press Inc 1982)

Harrison FE, *The Managerial Decision-Making Process* (5th edn, South-Western College 1998)

Hazelwood SJ and D Semark, *P&I Clubs: Law and Practice* (4th edn, Taylor and Francis 2013)

Heuston RFV and RA Buckley, *Salmond and Heuston on the Law of Torts* (21st edn, Sweet & Maxwell 1996)

Hart HLA and T Honoré, *Causation in the Law* (2nd edn, Clarendon Press 1985)

Hillson D and P Simon, *Practical Project Risk Management: The ATOM Methodology* (2nd edn, Berret-Koehler Publishers 2012)

Holmes P, *Investment Appraisal* (International Thomson Business Press 1998)

Honoré T, *Responsibility and Fault* (Hart Publishing 1999)

Jones W, *An Essay on the Law of Bailments* (2nd edn, 1804)

Kaiser MJ, *Decommissioning Forecasting and Operating Cost Estimation: Gulf of Mexico Well Trends, Structure Inventory and Forecast Models* (Gulf Professional Publishing 2019)

Keeton P and WL Prosser, *Prosser and Keeton on the Law of Torts* (5th edn, West Publishing Co 1984)

Kelly E (ed), *Justice as Fairness: A Restatement, John Rawls* (Harvard University Press 2001)
Kersley RH, *Broom's Legal Maxims* (10th edn, Sweet & Maxwell 1939)
Keynes JM, *A Treatise on Probability, The Collected Writings of John Maynard Keynes* (vol VIII, Macmillan 1921)
Kircher JJ and CM Wiseman *Punitive Damages: Law and Practice* (vol 2, West Group 2000)
Knight FH, *Risk, Uncertainty and Profit* (Dover Publications 2006)
Knill C and J Tosun, *Public Policy: A New Introduction* (2nd edn, Bloomsbury Publishing 2020)
Koffman L and E Macdonald, *The Law of Contract* (OUP 2010)
Lam J, *Enterprise Risk Management: From Incentives to Controls* (2nd edn, John Wiley & Sons 2014)
Lupton D, *Risk* (2nd edn, Routledge 2013)
Maldonato M and Dell'Orco S, *Natural Logic: Exploring Decision & Intuition* (Sussex Academic Press 2011)
Maxcy SJ, *Ethical School Leadership* (Rowman & Littlefield Education 2002)
McCormick R, *Legal Risk in the Financial Markets* (OUP on Demand 2010)
McMahon BME and W Binchy, *Law of Torts* (3rd edn, Butterworths 2000)
Mian MA, *Project Economics and Decision Analysis: Deterministic Models* (Pennwell Books 2011)
Moore MS, *Causation and Responsibility: An Essay in Law, Morals, and Metaphysics* (OUP 2009)
Nussbaum M, *Frontiers of Justice: Disability, Nationality, Species Membership* (Harvard University Press 2006)
Peel E, *The Law of Contract* (13th edn, Sweet & Maxwell 2011)
Posner RA, *Catastrophe, Risk and Responses* (OUP 2004)
—— *Economic Analysis of Law* (3d edn, Little & Brown 1986)
Raphael DD, *Concepts of Justice* (Clarendon Press 2001)
Rescher N, *Distributive Justice: A Constructive Critique of the Utilitarian Theory of Distribution* (Irvington Publication 1966)
Sappideen C and P Vines, Fleming's *The Law of Torts* (10th edn, Lawbook Co 2011)
Savitz A, *The Triple Bottom Line: How Today's Best-Run Companies Are Achieving Economic, Social and Environmental Success – and How You Can Too* (John Wiley & Sons 2013)
Shapiro S and R Glicksman, *Risk Regulation At Risk: Restoring a Pragmatic Approach* (Stanford University Press 2002)
Sharp DW, *A Brief Introduction to Energy Insurance* (Amazon Marketing Hub 2022)
—— *Offshore Oil and Gas Insurance* (Witherby 1994)
Sheikh S and S Singleton, *Commercial Contracts: A Practical Guide to Standard Terms* (5th edn, Bloomsbury Professional 2019)
Shermer M, *The Moral Arc: How Science and Reason Lead Humanity Toward Truth, Justice, and Freedom* (Henry Holt and Co 2015)
Sidgwick H, *The Methods of Ethics* (Macmillan 1907)

Smith EE and others, *International Petroleum Transactions* (3rd edn, Rocky Mountain Mineral Law Foundation 2010)

Thibaut JW and L Walker, *Procedural Justice: A Psychological Analysis* (Lawrence Erlbaum Associates 1975)

Trebilcock MJ, *The Limits of Freedom of Contract* (Harvard University Press 1997)

UNEP, *Protecting Our Planet Securing Our Future* (The World Bank 1998)

Vaughan EJ and T Vaughan, *Fundamentals of Risk and Insurance* (10th edn, John Wiley & Sons 2007)

William L, *Philosophy of Private Law* (OUP 2006)

World Commission on Environment and Development, *Our Common Future* (OUP 1987)

Yates D and A Hawkins, *Standard Business Contracts: Exclusions and Related Devises* (Sweet & Maxwell 1986)

BOOK CHAPTERS

Aven T and O Renn, 'Risk Perspectives' in T Aven and O Renn (eds) *Risk Management and Governance Concepts, Guidelines and Applications* (Springer 2010)

Azubuike SI, S Nakanwagi and SC Dike, 'Utilizing Sustainability Assessment Framework to Obtain a Social License to Operate in Renewable Energy Projects' in G Wood, J Górski and G Mete (eds), *The Palgrave Handbook of Social License to Operate and Energy Transitions* (Palgrave Macmillan 2022)

Bagchi A, 'Distributive Justice and Contract' in G Klass and others (eds), *Philosophical Foundations of Contract Law* (OUP 2014)

Boyd DR, 'The Right to a Healthy and Sustainable Environment' in Y Aguila and JE Viñuales (eds), *A Global Pact for the Environment – Legal Foundations* (CUP 2019)

Comande G and L Nocco, 'Proportional Liability in Uncertain Settings: Is it Precautionary?' in I Gilead and others (eds) *Proportional Liability: Analytical and Comparative Perspectives* (Walter de Gruyter GmbH 2013)

Ewald F, 'Insurance and Risk' in G Burchell, C Gordon and P Miller (eds) *The Foucault Effect: Studies in Governmentality* (University of Chicago Press 1991)

Faure M, 'Environmental Liability' in M Faure (ed), *Tort Law and Economics* (Edward Elgar Publishing 2009)

—— 'Regulatory Strategies in Environmental Liability' in F Cafaggi and HM Watt (eds), *The Regulatory Function of European Private Law* (Edward Elgar Publishing 2009)

—— and J Liu, 'Pooling Mechanism for Offshore Liability' in M Faure (ed), *Civil Liability and Financial Security for Offshore Oil and Gas Activities* (CUP 2017)

—— and H Wang, 'The Use of Financial Market Instruments to Cover Liability Following a Major Offshore Accident' in M Faure (ed), *Civil Liability and Financial Security for Offshore Oil and Gas Activities* (CUP 2017)

Gardner J, 'What is Tort Law for? Part 2: The Place of Distributive Justice' in J Oberdiek (ed) *Philosophical Foundations of the Law of Torts* (OUP 2014)

Giivses O, 'The Role of Insurance in Offshore Oil and Gas Operations' in G Handl and K Svendsen (eds), *Managing the Risk of Offshore Oil and Gas Accidents the International Legal Dimension* (Edward Elgar Publishing 2019)

Gordon G, 'Risk Allocation in Oil and Gas Service Contracts' in G Gordon, J Paterson and E Usenmez (eds), *Oil and Gas Law: Current Practice and Emerging Trends: Volume II: Commercial and Contract Issues* (3rd edn, Edinburgh University Press 2018)

Hart O and B Holmström, 'The Theory of Contract', in T Bewley (ed), *Proceedings of the Advances in Economics and Econometrics, Econometric Society Monographs, Fifth World Congress* (CUP 1987)

Hartmann, J, 'Sustainability of Hydropower' in JH Lehr, J Keeley and TB Kingery (eds) *Alternative Energy and Shale Gas Encyclopaedia* (John Wiley & Sons 2016)

Kaufman A, 'Theories of Distributive Justice' in R Chadwick (ed) *Encyclopedia of Applied Ethics* (2nd edn, Academic Press 2012)

Masham D, 'What Are Risk Management and Insurance?' in JE Besant-Wones and L Hyln (eds) *Managing Risks of Investments in Developing Countries* (World Bank 1992)

McFarlane B, 'Bailment' in P Cane and J Conaghan (eds), *The New Oxford Companion of Law* (OUP 2008)

Ortwin R, 'Concepts of Risk: A Classification' in S Krimsky and D Golding (eds), *Social Theories of Risk* (Praeger Publishers 1992)

Peng D, 'Mutual Indemnities in North Sea Contracts – Liability and Insurance Clauses' in D Peng (ed), *Insurance and Legal Issues in the Oil Industry* (Graham & Trotman 1993)

Rawls J, 'Justice as Fairness' and A Theory of Justice, in RC Solomon and MC Murphy (eds), *What is Justice?: Classic and Contemporary Readings* (OUP 1990)

Renn O, 'Concepts of Risk: A Classification' in S Krimsky and D Golding (eds) *Social Theories of Risk* (Praeger Publishers 1992)

Reynold M, 'Introduction to Environmental Responsibility' in M Reynold and others (eds), *The Environmental Responsibility Reader* (Zed Books 2009)

Scanlon TM, 'Rawls' Theory of Justice' in N Daniel (ed), *Reading Rawls: Critical Studies on Rawls' A Theory of Justice* (Basil Blackwell 1975)

Scheinman H, 'Tort Law and Distributive Justice' in J Oberdiek (ed) *Philosophical Foundations of the Law of Torts* (OUP 2014)

Smedt KD, H Wang and M Faure, 'Towards Optimal Liability and Compensation for Offshore Oil and Gas Activities' in M Faure (ed), *Civil Liability and Financial Security for Offshore Oil and Gas Activities* (CUP 2016)

Vanden B, 'Channelling of Liability: A Few Juridical and Economic Views on an Inadequate Legal Construction' in NLJT Horbach (ed), *Contemporary Development in Nuclear Energy Law: Harmonizing Legislation in CEE/NIS* (Kluwer Law International 1999)

Vinogradov S and SI Azubuike, 'Arctic Hydrocarbon Exploration and Production: Evaluating the Legal Regime for Offshore Accidental Pollution Liability'

in L Heininen and H Exner-Pirot (eds), *Arctic Yearbook* (Northern Research Forum 2018)
Wright RW, 'The Standard of Care in Negligence Law' in DG Owen (ed), *The Philosophical Foundations of Tort Law* (OUP 1995)

JOURNAL ARTICLES

'A Law and Economics Look at Contracts against Public Policy' (2006) 119(5) Harvard Law Review 1449
Abraham KS, 'Catastrophic Oil Spills and the Problem of Insurance' (2011) 64(6) Vanderbilt Law Review 1767
Adams JM and KK Milhollin, 'Indemnity on the Outer Continental Shelf – A Practical Primer' (2002) 27 Tulane Maritime Law Journal 43
Adepetun S, 'Production Sharing Contracts: The Nigerian Experience' (1995) 13(1) Journal of Energy and Natural Resources Law 21
Almeida PC, O Fernandes-Araújo and JL de Medeiros, 'Managing Offshore Drill Cuttings and Waste for Improved Sustainability' (2017) 165 Journal of Cleaner Production 143
Althaus CE, 'A Disciplinary Perspective on the Epistemological Status of Risk' (2005) 25(3) Risk Analysis: An International Journal 567
Anderson OL, 'The Anatomy of an Oil and Gas Drilling Contract' (1990) 25(3) Tulsa Law Review 359
—— and JS Lowe, 'Oil Spills' (2010) 3(2) Oil, Gas & Energy Law Review Special Issue 2
Anderson RD, 'ISO's 2013 "Additional Insured" Endorsement Changes Merit Close Attention' (2013) 23(3) American Bar Association Section of Litigation, Insurance Coverage Litigation 2
Andrade MM, 'Knock for Knock Indemnities: Contract Practices and Enforceability Issues' (2011) 9(6) Oil, Gas & Energy Law Journal 3
Anis MD and TZ Siddiqui, 'Issues Impacting Sustainability in the Oil and Gas Industry' (2015) 5(4) Journal of Management and Sustainability 115
Arora MP and S Lodhia, 'The BP Gulf of Mexico Oil Spill: Exploring the Link between Social and Environmental Disclosures and Reputation Risk Management' (2017) 140(3) Journal of Cleaner Production 1287
Arvidsson M and J Dumay, 'Corporate ESG Reporting Quantity, Quality and Performance: Where To Now for Environmental Policy and Practice? (2022) 31(3) Business Strategy and the Environment 1091
Aven T and BS Krohn, 'A New Perspective on How To Understand, Assess and Manage Risk and the Unforeseen' (2014) 121 Reliability Engineering & System Safety 1
Aven T and V Kristensen, 'Perspectives on Risk: Review and Discussion of the Basis for Establishing a Unified and Holistic Approach' (2005) 90(1) Reliability Engineering & System Safety 1

Azubuike SI and O Songi, 'A Rights-Based Approach to Oil Spill Investigations: A Case Study of the Bodo Community Oil Spill in Nigeria' (2020) 1(1) Global Energy Law & Sustainability 28
Azubuike VC, 'The Energy Transition and Energy Security Nexus: An Outlook for the United Kingdom' (2023) Journal of Energy and Natural Resources Law, 503
Azzone G and others, 'Defining Environmental Performance Indicators: An Integrated Framework' (1996) 5(2) Business Strategy and the Environment 69
Badawi A, 'Harm, Ambiguity, and the Regulation of Illegal Contracts' (2009) 17(2) George Mason Law Review 483
Bathrinath S and others, 'An Initiative Towards Sustainability in the Petroleum Industry: A Review' (2021) 46 Materials Today: Proceedings 7798
Beerworth AA, 'Emerging Trends in Construction Indemnity and Insurance Law' (2010) 58(5) Rhode Island Bar Journal 17
Bengez R and others, 'Proportionality and Quantitative Justice: An Introduction to Special Issue' (2011) 10 Law, Probability and Risk 164
Bennet P, 'Mutual Risk: P&I Insurance Clubs and Maritime Safety and Environmental Performance' (2001) 25 Marine Policy 15
Bougen PD, 'Catastrophe Risk' (2003) 32(2) Economy and Society 253
Broman SA and JL Sautter, 'Additional Insured Endorsements: Recent Efforts to Limit Coverage to the Additional Insured' [2006] FDCC Quarterly 81
Brown L, 'Gross Negligence in Exclusion Clauses: Is There an Intelligible Difference between Ordinary Negligence and Gross Negligence' (2005) 16 Insurance Law Journal 9
Brown LB, 'Drilling Contracts Post Macondo Considerations' (2016) 9(36) International In-House Counsel Journal 1
Brownsword R, 'The Limits of Freedom of Contract and the Limits of Contract Theory' (1995) 22(2) Journal of Law and Society 259
Bruggeman, V, 'Capital Market Instruments for Natural Catastrophe and Terrorism Risk: A Bright Future?' (2010) 40(2) Environmental Law Reporter 10136
Bunter M, 'World-Wide Standards of Good Oilfield Practice – The Impact of the Blow-Out, Deaths and Spill at the BP Macondo Well, MC 252/1-01, US Gulf of Mexico' [2013] Oil, Gas & Energy Law Journal 2
Calabresi G, 'Some Thoughts on Risk Distribution and the Law of Torts' (1961) 70(4) Yale Law Journal 499
Cameron P, 'Liability for Catastrophic Risk in the Oil and Gas Industry' (2012) 6 International Energy Law Review 207
Campmas A, N Iacob and F Simonelli, 'How Can Interoperability Stimulate the Use of Digital Public Services? An Analysis of National Interoperability Frameworks and e-Government in the European Union' [2022] 4 Data & Policy e19
Cane P, 'Distributive Justice and Tort Law' [2001] 4 New Zealand Law Review 401
Carroll E, 'Wednesbury Unreasonableness as a Limit to Civil Liability of Public Authorities' (2007) 15 Tort Law Review 77

Carter CR and DS Rogers, 'A Framework of Sustainable Supply Chain Management: Moving Towards New Theory' (2008) 38(5) International Journal of Physical Distribution & Logistics Management 360
'Causation in Environmental Law: Lessons from Toxic Torts' (2015) 128 Harvard Law Review 2256
Chadwick I, 'Contracting Out of Liability for Gross Negligence' [2012] De Rebus 34
Chapelle E, 'Evolution of Additional Insured Endorsements' (2014) 23(1) Construction Litigation 10
Cherepovitsyn A, A Tsvetkova and N Komendantova, 'Approaches to Assessing the Strategic Sustainability of High-Risk Offshore Oil and Gas Projects' (2020) 8(12) Journal of Marine Science and Engineering 995
Choi A and G Triantis, 'The Effect of Bargaining Power on Contract Design' (2012) 98(8) Virginia Law Review 1665
Choudhury R, 'You Break It; I Buy It. The Curious Case of Knock-for-Knock Indemnities' (2018) 16(1) Oil, Gas & Energy Law Journal 2
Cilliers J, 'When Contracts against Public Policy Are Void' (1994) 2(3) Juta's Business Law 139
Clarke DM, 'Causation and Liability in Tort Law' (2014) 5(2) Jurisprudence 217
Coase RH, 'The Problem of Social Cost' (1960) 3 Journal of Law and Economics 837
Cole BM, 'Misrepresentation in Public Contracts: Allocating the Risk of Loss' (1970) 21 Syracuse Law Review 1004
Coleman JS, 'Robert Nozick's Anarchy, State and Utopia' (1976) 3(3) Theory and Society 437
Collins H, 'Distributive Justice through Contracts' (1992) 45(2) Current Legal Problems 49
Cordes EE and others, 'Environmental Impacts of the Deep-Water Oil and Gas Industry: A Review to Guide Management Strategies' (2016) 4(58) Frontiers in Environmental Science 1
Culhane JG, 'Tort, Compensation, and Two Kinds of Justice' (2003) 55 Rutgers Law Review 1064
Curtis WT, 'Liability of Employers for Punitive Damages Resulting from Acts of Employees' (1978) 54 Chicago-Kent Law Review 829
Dari-Mattiacci G and LA Franzoni, 'Innovation and Negligence Rules' (2014) 16(2) American Law and Economics Review 337
Davis CJ, 'The Principle of Benefit and Burden' (1998) 57(3) CLJ 522
Dellinger M, 'Trophy Hunting Contracts: Unenforceable for Reasons of Public Policy' (2016) 41(3) Columbia Journal of Environmental Law 395
Diamond PA, 'Posner's Economic Analysis of Law' (1974) 5(1) Bell Journal of Economics and Management Science 294
Dyllick T and K Hockerts, 'Beyond the Business Case for Corporate Sustainability' (2002) 11(2) Business Strategy and the Environment 130
Edgerton HW, 'Negligence, Inadvertence, and Indifference: The Relation of Mental States to Negligence' (1962) 39(7) Harvard Law Review 857
Egbochue C, 'Reviewing Knock for Knock Indemnities Following the Macondo Well Blowout' (2013) 7(4) Construction Law International 9

Eisenberg MA, 'Probability and Chance in Contract Law' (1997) 45 UCLA Law Review 1005
Elliot SD, 'Degrees of Negligence' (1933) 6(2) Southern California Law Review 99
Engerrand K, 'Indemnity for Gross Negligence in Maritime Oilfield Contracts' (2012) 10 Loyola Maritime Journal 319
Engle E, 'The History of the General Principle of Proportionality: A Overview' (2012) 10(1) Dartmouth Law Journal 3
Epstein RA, 'Unconscionability: A Critical Reappraisal' (1975) 18(2) Journal of Law and Economics 293
Farber DA, 'Legal Pragmatism, and the Constitution' (1987) 72 Minnesota Law Review 1331
Faure M, 'Private Liability and Critical Infrastructure' (2015) 6(2) European Journal of Risk Regulation 232
—— and T Hartlief, 'Remedies for Expanding Liability'(1998) 18 OJLS 684
Fragouli E and J Ekruka, 'Reputation Risk Management in the International Oil Companies' (2016) 8(2) International Journal of Information, Business and Management 245
Friedman DA, 'Bringing Order to Contracts Against Public Policy' (2012) 39 Florida State University Law Review 563
Frisch D, 'Contractual Choice of Law and the Prudential Foundations of Appellate Review' (2003) 56 Vanderbilt Law Review 58
Gellhorn W, 'Contracts and Public Policy' (1935) 35 Columbia Law Review 679
Ghodoosi F, 'The Concept of Public Policy in Law: Revisiting the Role of the Public Policy Doctrine in the Enforcement of Private Legal Arrangements' (2016) 94(3) Nebraska Law Review 685
Goodrich HF, 'Public Policy in the Law of Conflicts' (1930) 36(2) West Virginia Law Quarterly and the Bar 152
Green F, 'High Care and Gross Negligence' (1928) 23(1) Illinois Law Review 12
Hart DK, 'Contract Law Now – Reality Meets Legal Fiction' (2011) 41(1) University of Baltimore Law Review 2
Hassini E, C Surti and C Searcy, 'A Literature Review and a Case Study of Sustainable Supply Chains with a Focus on Metrics' (2012) 140(1) International Journal of Production Economics 69
He Q, 'Climate Change and Effective Catastrophe Risk Management Mechanism: A Law and Economics Analysis of Insurance and Insurance-Linked Securities' (2015) 1(4) International Journal of Bonds and Derivatives 310
Helmholz RH, 'Theories and the Liability of Bailees: The Elusive Uniform Standard of Reasonable Care' (1992) 41 University of Kansas Law Review 97
Hewitt T, 'Who Is to Blame? Allocating Liability in Upstream Project Contracts' (2008) 26(2) Journal of Energy and Natural Resources Law 177
Holdway DA, 'The Acute and Chronic Effect of Waste associated with Offshore Oil and Gas Production in Temperate Marine Ecological Process' (2002) 44(3) Marine Pollution Bulletin 185
Houston CE and CR Sunstein, 'Risk Assessment, Resource Allocation, and Fairness: Evidence from Law Students' (1998) 48 Journal of Legal Education 496

Howard DO, 'An Analysis of Gross Negligence' (1954) 37(4) Marquette Law Review 333
Howlett M and B Cashore, 'Conceptualizing Public Policy' [2014] Comparative Policy Studies 17
Hristov I and A Chirico, 'The Role of Sustainability Key Performance Indicators (KPIs) in Implementing Sustainable Strategies' (2019) 11 Sustainability 5742
Jamali D and M Ramez, 'Corporate Social Responsibility (CSR): Theory and Practice in a Developing Country Context' (2007) 72(3) Journal of Business Ethics 243
Jimenez M, 'Distributive Justice and Contract Law: A Hohfeldian Analysis' (2016) 43 Florida State University Law Review 1265
Johnston P and others, 'Reclaiming the Definition of Sustainability' (2007) 14(1) Environmental Science and Pollution Research International 60
Judd S, 'The Unruly Horse Put Out To Pasture: The Doctrine of Public Policy in the Modern Law of Contract' (1998) 8 Auckland University Law Review 686
Kaiser MJ and B Snyder, 'A Primer on the Offshore Drilling Industry' (2013) 44(3) Ocean Development and International Law 287
Kangles N and others, 'Risk Allocation Provisions in Energy Industry Agreements: Are We Getting It Right?' (2011) 49(2) Alberta Law Review 341
Kannan G, D Kannan and MK Shankar, 'Evaluating the Drivers of Corporate Social Responsibility in the Mining Industry with Multi-Criteria Approach: A Multi-Stakeholder Perspective' (2014) 84(1) Journal of Cleaner Production 214
Kaswan A, 'Distributive Justice and the Environment' (2003) 81(3) North Carolina Law Review 1056
Keating GC, 'Distributive and Corrective Justice in the Tort Law of Accidents' (2000) 74 Southern California Law Review 192
—— 'The Idea of Fairness in the Law of Enterprise Liability' (1997) 95(5) Michigan Law Review 1269
Kehoe II GR, 'Louisiana Oilfield Indemnity Act: A Necessary Limit to Contract Freedom or Paternalism for Roughneck Contracts?' (1996) 70 Tulane Law Review 1097
Kim I, 'Introducing Oil Cargo Liability in the Oil Pollution Act of 1990' (2002) 33(2) Journal of Maritime Law and Commerce 185
Kinna JC, 'Investing in Developing Countries: Minimisation of Political Risk' (1983) 1(2) Journal of Energy & Natural Resources Law 89
Knight WSM, 'Public Policy in English Law' (1922) 38 LQR 207
Kordana KA and DH Blankfein-Tabachnick, 'Rawls and Contract Law' (2005) 73(3) George Washington Law Review 598
Krehbiel PJ and R Cropanzano, 'Procedural Justice, Outcome Favorability and Emotion' (2000) 13(4) Social Justice Research 339
Kronman AT, 'Contract Law and Distributive Justice' (1980) 89(3) Yale Law Journal 472
Kruger M, 'The Role of Public Policy in the Law of Contract, Revisited' (2011) 128 South African Law Journal 712

Kuhlman T and J Farrington, 'What is Sustainability' (2010) 2 Sustainability 3436
Kwarto F and others, 'The Potential Bias for Sustainability Reporting of Global Upstream Oil and Gas Companies: A Systematic Literature Review of the Evidence' (2022) 74 Management Review Quarterly 35
Lakdawalla D and G Zanjani, 'Catastrophe Bonds, Reinsurance, and the Optimal Collateralization of Risk Transfer' (2012) 79(2) Journal of Risk and Insurance 449
Lam CK and others, 'Modelling Risk Allocation Decision in Construction Contracts' (2007) 25(5) International Journal of Project Management 485
Lev TL, 'Liability for Environmental Damages from the Offshore Petroleum Industry: Strict Liability Justifications and the Judgment-Proof Problem' (2016) 43 Ecology Law Quarterly 483
Levine RH and R Pannier, 'Comparative and Non-Comparative Justice: Some Guidelines for Constitutional Adjudication' (2005) 14(1) William & Mary Bill of Rights Journal 141
Lillig J, 'Magic or Misery: HBCUs, Guarantee Contracts, and Public Policy' (2009) 6 DePaul Journal of Sports Law & Contemporary Problems 41
Lindsay R and others, 'Human Rights Responsibilities in the Oil and Gas Sector: Applying the UN Guiding Principles' (2013) 6(1) Journal of World Energy Law and Business 2
Loosemore M and CS McCarthy, 'Perceptions of Contractual Risk Allocation in Construction Supply Chains' (2008) 134(1) Journal of Professional Issues in Engineering Education and Practice 95
Machmud TN, 'The Indonesia Production Sharing Contract: An Investor's Perspective' (2002) 20(3) Journal of Energy and Natural Resources Law 318
Mansoor Z, 'Contracts Contrary to Public Policy under English and Dutch Law: The Case of Agreements Commercialising the Human Body' [2014] 1 European Journal of Comparative Law and Governance 297
March JG and Z Shapira, 'Managerial Perspectives on Risk and Risk Taking' (1987) 33(11) Management Science 1404
Marshal Jr CD, 'Liability for Oil and Gas Operations: An Operator's Perspective' (1993) 39 Annual Institute on Mineral Law 211
Marshall JB, 'Joint Operating Agreements in the Oil and Gas Industry: The Consequence of Sole Risk and Non-Consent Clauses to Joint Operations' (2016) 6(10) Journal of Asian Business Strategy 251
Martin A and TA Martin, 'Model Contracts: A Survey of the Global Petroleum Industry' (2004) 22(3) Journal of Energy & Natural Resources Law 281
Martin PH, 'The BP Spill and the Meaning of Gross Negligence or Willful Misconduct' (2011) 71(3) Louisiana Law Review 957
Martin T, 'Decommissioning of International Petroleum Facilities: Evolving Standards and Key Issues' [2003] Oil, Gas & Energy Law Journal 5
Martin TA, 'Model Contracts: A Survey of Global Petroleum Industry' (2004) 22(3) Journal of Energy and Natural Resources Law 282

McCabea E, AE Potente and A Probasco, 'Products Pollution Liability Insurance: Another Bridge Spanning the Pollution Exclusion Coverage Gap' (2021) 33(2) Environmental Claims Journal 149

McMahan J, 'Self-Defence and the Problem of the Innocent Attacker' (1994) 104(2) Ethics 259

Megens P, 'Different Perspective of Construction Risk – How Should It Be Allocated?' (1996) 15(4) AMPLA Bulletin 179

Mills DG and others, 'Exploring the Balance of Power in the Operator/Non-Operator Relationship under the CAPL Operating Procedure' (2010) 48(2) Alberta Law Review 378

Montague P, 'Comparative and Non-Comparative Justice' (1980) 30(119) Philosophical Quarterly 131

Moomjian Jr CA, 'Contractual Insurance and Risk Allocation in the Offshore Drilling Industry' [1999] Drilling Contractor, March/April

—— 'Drilling Contract Historical Development and Future Trends Post-Macondo: Reflections on a 35 Year Industry Career' (*Drilling Contractor*, 7 March 2012) <www.drillingcontractor.org/wp-content/uploads/2012/04/Drilling-Contract-Historical-Development-and-Future-Trends-Post-Macondo.pdf> accessed 2 February 2024

Moran TJ, 'Punitive Damages in Fair Housing Litigation: Ending Unwise Restrictions on a Necessary Remedy' (2001) 36(2) Harvard Civil Rights–Civil Liberties Law Review 279

Morris C, 'Duty, Negligence and Causation' (1952) 101 University of Pennsylvania Law Review 189

Muller D and PW Schmitz, 'The Right to Quit Work: An Efficiency Rationale for Restricting the Freedom of Contract' (2021) 184 Journal of Economic Behavior & Organization 653

Naeemullah I, 'Strong Headwinds: Statutes, Responsibility-Shifting, and Public Policy Continue to Frustrate Indemnity Agreements in the Offshore Oil and Gas Industry' (2013) 38(1) Tulane Maritime Law Journal 281

Nagal T, 'The Problem of Global Justice' (2005) 33 Philosophy and Public Affairs 113

Nierengarten NN, 'New ISO Additional Insured Endorsements' (2014) 44(1) Brief 33

Nozick R, 'Distributive Justice' (1973) 3(1) Philosophy and Public Affairs 45

Nwaokoro J, 'Beyond Legislation: A Contractual Alternative to Legislating Local Content in Nigeria' (2009) 18 Current International Trade Law Journal 42

O'Connor N, 'Whose Autonomy is it Anyway? Freedom of Contract, the Right to Work and the General Principles of EU Law' (2020) 49(3) Industrial Law Journal 285

O'Hara EO, 'Organizational Apologies: BP as a Case Study' (2011) 64(6) Vanderbilt Law Review 1960

O'Reilly DI and others, 'Productivity Determination for Cyclic Production Using Steady State Harmonic Theory – Application to Artificial Lift Wells' [2019] Journal of Petroleum Science and Engineering 787

O'Rourke D and S Connolly, 'Just Oil? The Distribution of Environmental and Social Impacts of Oil Production and Consumption' (2003) 28 Annual Review of Environment and Resources 587
Oakland WH and WA Testa, 'State-Local Business Taxation and the Benefits Principle' (1996) 20 Economic Perspectives–Federal Reserve Bank of Chicago 2
Ogunleye TA, 'A Legal Analysis of Production Sharing Contract Arrangements in the Nigerian Petroleum Industry' (2015) 5(8) Journal of Energy Technologies and Policy 2
Okeke A, 'Towards Sustainability in the Global Oil and Gas Industry: Identifying Where the Emphasis Lies' (2021) 12 Environmental and Sustainability Indicators 100145
Omorogbe Y, 'The Legal Framework for the Production of Petroleum in Nigeria' (1987) 5(4) Journal of Energy and Natural Resources 273
O'Regan PW and TW Taylor, 'Joint Ventures and Operating Agreements' (1984) 14(1) Victoria University of Wellington Law Review 85
Osmundsen P, T Sørenes and A Toft, 'Drilling Contracts and Incentives' (2008) 36(8) Energy Policy 3138
——, 'Offshore Oil Service Contracts New Incentive Schemes to Promote Drilling Efficiency' (2010) 72(3) Journal of Petroleum Science and Engineering 220
Page EA, 'Distributing the Burdens of Climate Change' (2008) 17(4) Environmental Politics 556
Parker PL and S Slavich, 'Contractual Efforts to Allocate the Risk of Environmental Liability: Is There a Way to Make Indemnities Worth More Than the Paper They Are Written On?' (1991) 44 Southwestern Law Journal 1349
Parsons C, 'Moral Hazard in Liability Insurance' (2003) 8(3), Geneva Papers on Risk and Insurance 448
Peters MS and M Kumar, 'Why International Oil Companies Choose to Enter into Joint Operating Agreement' (2012) 53(2) Acta Juridica Hungarica 179
Pittman M, 'Gross Negligence in Canadian Energy Contracts' (2013) 52(2) Alberta Law Review 309
Plattner J, 'Contracts – Public Policy – Contracts against Liability for Negligence' (1960) 36(2) North Dakota Law Review 141
Posner EA, 'Contract Law in the Welfare State: A Defense of the Unconscionability Doctrine, Usury Laws, and Related Limitations on the Freedom to Contract' (1995) 24 Journal of Legal Studies 283
Rankin MD and DR Richardson, 'The Offshore Drilling Contract-Operator and Contractor Perspectives' IADC/SPE 1983 Drilling Conference, New Orleans, Louisiana, 20–23 February 1983. Texas, USA: Society of Petroleum Engineers 1
Renn O and others, 'Systemic Risks from Different Perspectives' [2020] Risk Analysis 1
Ruggerio CA, 'Sustainability and Sustainable Development: A Review of Principles and Definitions' (2021) 786 Science of the Total Environment 147481
Scandizzo S, 'A Framework for the Analysis of Reputational Risk' (2011) 6(3) Journal of Operational Risk 41

Schnaudt C, C Hahn and E Heppner, 'Distributive and Procedural Justice and Political Trust in Europe' (2021) 3(3) Frontiers in Political Science 642232

Schulte J and S Knuts, 'Sustainability Impact and Effects Analysis – A Risk Management Tool for Sustainable Product Development' (2022) 30 Sustainable Production and Consumption 737

Scobbie I, 'Tom Franck's Fairness' (2002) 13(4) European Journal of International Law 910

Seaman SM and C Kittredge, 'Excess Liability Insurance: Law and Litigation' (1997) 32(2) Tort & Insurance Law Journal 653

Segerson K, 'Risk-Sharing and Liability in the Control of Stochastic Externalities' (1987) 4(3) Marine Resources Economics 175

Seita AY, 'Uncertainty and Contract Law' (1984) 46 University of Pittsburgh Law Review 75

Shand J, 'Unblinkering the Unruly Horse: Public Policy in the Law of Contract' (1972) 30(1) CLJ 144

Shine D, 'Contractual Application of Negligence/Gross Negligence Standards: Considerations under New York Law' (2005) 8(10) The M&A Lawyer 10

Short Jr JF, The Social Fabric at Risk – Towards the Social Transformation of Risk Analysis (1984) 49(6) American Sociological Review 711

Silvestre BS, FAP Gimenes and RS Neto, 'A Sustainability Paradox? Sustainable Operations in the Offshore Oil and Gas Industry: The Case of Petrobras' (2017) 142 Journal of Cleaner Production 360

Skogh G, 'Insurance and the Institutional Economics of Financial Intermediation' (1991) 16(8) Geneva Papers on Risk and Insurance 5

Slattery Jr GF, 'Indemnity and Insurance in the Texas Oil Patch' (2014) 10(1) Texas Journal of Oil, Gas and Energy Law 99

Smith M, 'The Deepwater Horizon Disaster: An Examination of the Spill's Impact on the Gap in International Regulation of Oil Pollution from Fixed Platforms' (2011) 25(3) Emory International Law Review 1477

Soerodjo I, 'The Development of Indonesian Civil Law' (2016) 4(9) Scientific Research Journal 32

Srivastava A and A Srivastava, 'Economic Analysis of Accident Law: A New Liability Rule that Induces Socially Optimal Behaviour in Case of Limited Information' (2021) 17(1) Review of Law & Economics 119

Steyn L, 'Perspectives of Corrective and Distributive Justice in Tort Law' (2002) 37 Irish Jurist 1

Sweet AS and J Mathews, 'Proportionality, Balancing and Global Constitutionalism' (2008) 47 Columbia Journal of Transnational Law 96

Syahrir MS, 'Liability and Risk Control through Effective Clauses in Oil and Gas Service Contracts' [2004] Oil, Gas & Energy Law Journal 2

Syn J, 'The Social License: Empowering Communities and a Better Way Forward' (2014) 28(3–4) Social Epistemology 318

Taleghani ND and M Tyagi, 'Impacts of Major Offshore Oil Spill Incidents on Petroleum Industry and Regional Economy' (2017) 139(2) Journal of Energy Resources Technology 022913

'The Three Degrees of Negligence' (1874) 8 American Law Review 652

Thetford LJ, 'In Re Deepwater Horizon: Texas to Revisit ATOFINA to Decide Scope of Additional-Insured Liability Coverage' (2014) Fall South Texas Law Review 2

Tyler TR, 'Procedural Justice, Legitimacy and the Effective Rule of Law' (2003) 30 Crime and Justice 283

—— 'Social Justice: Outcome and Procedure' (2000) 33(2) International Journal of Psychology 117

Vinogradov S, 'The Impact of the Deepwater Horizon: The Evolving International Legal Regime for Offshore Accidental Pollution Prevention, Preparedness, and Response' (2013) 44(4) Ocean Development and International Law 335

Viscusi KW, 'How Do Judges Think about Risk?' 1(1) American Law and Economics Review 26

—— and RJ Zeckhauser, 'Deterring and Compensating Oil-Spill Catastrophes: The Need for Strict and Two-Tier Liability' (2011) 64 Vanderbilt Law Review 1742

Voinarevich O, 'An Overview of the Grossly Inconsistent Definitions of "Gross Negligence" in American Jurisprudence' (2015) 48 Journal of Marshal Law Review 471

Vos RO, 'Defining Sustainability: A Conceptual Orientation' (2007) 82(2) Journal of Chemical Technology and Biotechnology 334

Wagner F, 'Risk Securitization: An Alternative of Risk Transfer of Insurance Companies' (1998) 23(89) Geneva Papers on Risk and Insurance 574

Weber DP, 'Restricting the Freedom of Contract: A Fundamental Prohibition' (2013) 16(1) Yale Human Rights and Development Law Journal 51

Wenzel M and others, 'Retributive and Restorative Justice' (2008) 32 Law and Human Behaviour 375

West E, 'The Utility of the NESS Test of Factual Causation in Scots Law' (2013) 4(3) Aberdeen Student Law Review 39

West GD and BW Lewis, 'Contracting to Avoid Extra-Contractual Liability – Can Your Contractual Deal Ever Really Be the "Entire" Deal?', (2009) 64(4) The Business Lawyer 999

Williams K, 'Medical Samaritans: Is There a Duty to Treat?' (2001) 21(3) OJLS 411

Wilson E, 'What Is the Social Licence to Operate? Local Perceptions of Oil and Gas Projects in Russia's Komi Republic and Sakhalin Island' [2016] 3(1) Extractive Industries and Society 73

Wilson S, 'Contractual Allocation of Risk in Upstream Oil and Gas Projects' (2008) 3 Energy Source 3

—— and S Bone, 'Businesses, Standard Terms and the Unfair Contract Terms Act 1977' (2002) 1 Journal of Obligations & Remedies 29

White A, "Caveat Vendor? A Review of the Court of Appeal Decision in St Albans City and District Council v International Computers Limited' [1997] 3 Journal of Information, Law and Technology

Winfield PH, 'Public Policy in the English Common Law' (1928) 42(1) Harvard Law Review 77

Wright RW, 'Causation in Tort Law' (1985) 73 California Law Review 1737

Yablon C, 'The Meaning of Probability Judgments: An Essay on the Use and Misuse of Behavioral Economics' (2004) University of Illinois Law Review 899

Yannoulidis S, 'Causation in the Law of Negligence' (2001) 27(2) Monash University Law Review 319

Yeo TM, 'When Do Third Party Rights Arise Under the Contracts (Rights of Third Parties) Act 1999 (UK)?' [2001] Singapore Academy of Law Journal 13

Zulhafiz WM, 'On the Contractual Risk Allocation in Oil and Gas Projects' (2017), The Law Review, 168

—— 'Perception of Contractual Risk Allocation in the Oil and Gas Contracts in Malaysia' (2018) 11(1) International Journal of Trade and Global Markets 137

—— 'Recent Trends in Allocating of Risk Post-Macondo: The Growing Tension between Oil and Gas Standard Forms of Contract, and Contractual Practice' [2017] 5 International Energy Law Review 174

REPORTS

BIO by Deloitte, *Civil Liability, Financial Security and Compensation Claims for Offshore Oil and Gas Activities in European Economic Area* (Final Report Prepared for the European Commission, DG Energy, Brussels, 14 August 2014) 129

HM Government, *Common Sense, Common Safety* (Report by Lord Young of Graffham to the Prime Minister, October 2010), <assets.publishing.service.gov.uk/government/uploads/system/uploads/attachment_data/file/60905/402906_CommonSense_acc.pdf> accessed 15 October 2023.

Michael Latham, *Constructing the Team: Joint Review of Procurement and Continental Arrangement in the United Kingdom Construction Industry* (Final Report, July 1994) <constructingexcellence.org.uk/wp-content/uploads/2014/10/Constructing-the-team-The-Latham-Report.pdf> accessed 12 October 2023

National Commission on the BP Deepwater Horizon Oil Spill and Offshore Drilling, *Deep Water: The Gulf Oil Disaster and the Future of Offshore Drilling* (Report to the President of the United States of America 2011)

National Commission on the BP Deepwater Horizon Oil Spill and Offshore Drilling, *Macondo: The Gulf Oil Disaster* (Chief Counsel Report, 2011)

Rayfuse R (ed), *ICSID Reports of Cases Decided under the Convention on the Settlement of Investment Disputes between States and Nationals of other States* (vol 1, Grotius Publications Ltd 1993) 611

The Royal Society, *Risk: Analysis, Perception and Management – Report of a Royal Society Study Group* (The Royal Society, 1992)

LAW COMMISSION REPORTS

Irish Law Reform Commission, *Civil Liability of Good Samaritans and Volunteers* (LRC 93, 2009)

Law Commission, *Law Commission's Second Report on Exemption Clauses* (Law Comm no 69, 1975)

Law Commission, *Privity of Contract: Contracts for the Benefits of Third Parties* (HM Stationery Office 1991)
Scottish Law Commission, *Breach of Trust* (Scot Law Comm DP no 123, 2003)
Trust Law Commission, *Trustees Exemption Clause* (Law Comm no 301, 2006)

THESES

Azubuike SI, 'Rethinking Operator-Contractor Risk Allocation in a post-Macondo Era', (PhD Thesis, University of Dundee 2019)
Macmillan, F, 'Risk, Uncertainty and Investment Decision-Making in the Upstream Oil and Gas Industry' (PhD Thesis, University of Aberdeen 2000)
Ofoegbu, K, 'How Contractual Risk Allocation Provisions of Oil and Gas Contracts Have Been or May Be Interpreted by an English Court – A Case Study of Some Model Offshore Drilling Rig Contracts Developed in the United Kingdom, Canada and the United States of America' (PhD Thesis, University of Dundee 2018)

DICTIONARIES

Black's Law Dictionary (9th edn, West 2009)
Compact Oxford English Dictionary (OUP 2006)
The Free Dictionary, 'Public Policy' <legal-dictionary.thefreedictionary.com/Public+Policy> accessed 12 October 2023

WEB PAGES

Adams K, 'Using the Terms 'Negligence and Gross Negligence' in a Contract' (Adams Drafting, 10 September 2012) <www.adamsdrafting.com/negligence-and-gross-negligence> accessed 12 October 2023
Akinjide-Balogun O, 'Nigeria: Legal Framework of the Nigerian Petroleum Industry' (Mondaq, 3 April 2001) <www.mondaq.com/nigeria/corporatecommercial-law/10726/legal-framework-of-the-nigerian-petroleum-industry> accessed 12 October 2023
Arinaitwe PW, 'Risk Allocation in Oil and Gas Service Contracts: A Comparative Analysis of U.S. Outer Continental Shelf and U.K. Continental Shelf Jurisdictions' (Admiralty and Maritime Law Committee Newsletter, Winter 2014) <www.sebalulule.co.ug/wpcontent/uploads/2014/02/Risk_allocation_in_oil_and_Gas.pdf> accessed 12 October 2023
Association of International Energy Negotiators, 'Service Contracts (2002)' <www.aien.org/forms/store/ProductFormPublic/service-contracts-2002> accessed 12 August 2023
Barry B and M Matravers, 'Justice' (Routledge Encyclopedia of Philosophy 2011) <www.rep.routledge.com/articles/thematic/justice/v-2> accessed 12 October 2023.

Bell MM, '2013 ISO Additional Insured Endorsements: Putting the Changes into Context for the Construction Industry' (International Risk Management Institute Inc 2013) <www.irmi.com/articles/expert-commentary/history-of-iso-additional-insured-endorsements> accessed 12 October 2023

Bindemann K, 'Production Sharing Agreements: An Economic Analysis' (Oxford Institute for Energy Study WPM, October 1999) <ora.ox.ac.uk/objects/uuid:3ba0589f-8c3a-43b9-b034-24f7dae7e0c5> accessed 12 October 2023

Blackledge S, 'Knock-for-Knock Provisions and Maritime Law' (*Wilson Elser*, 24 August 2022) <www.wilsonelser.com/publications/knock-for-knock-provisions-and-maritime-law> accessed 13 October 2023

Boyd J, 'Financial Responsibility for Environmental Obligations: Are Bonding and Assurance Rules Fulfilling Their Promise?' (Resources for the Future Discussion Paper 01-42, August 2001) <media.rff.org/documents/RFF-DP-01-42.pdf> accessed 28 February 2023

Branson D, 'Sustainability in the Oil and Gas Industry' (PWC, undated). <www.pwc.de/en/sustainability/sustainability-in-the-oil-and-gas-industry.html> accessed 12 October 2023.

British Petroleum, 'BP ANZ Health and Safety Policy' (BP, 29 July 2019) <www.bp.com/content/dam/bp/country-sites/en_au/australia/home/products-services/fuels/health-safety-policy.pdf> accessed 12 October 2023.

Bureau of Ocean Energy Management, Regulation and Enforcement (BOEMRE), 'Report Regarding the Cause of the April 20, 2010 Macondo Well Blowout' (*National Oceanic and Atmospheric Administration*, 14 September 2011) <docs.lib.noaa.gov/noaa_documents/DWH_IR/reports/dwhfinal.pdf> accessed 12 October 2023

Carvill P, 'Oil Insurance Limited switches to become Everen' (Reinsurance News, 29 June 2022) <www.reinsurancene.ws/oil-insurance-limited-switches-to-become-everen> accessed 15 February 2023.

Cavcic M, 'UK's First Licensing Round Since 2019 Brings 115 Bids from 76 Oil & Gas Firms' (OFFSHORE ENERGY, 17 January 2023) <www.offshore-energy.biz/uks-first-licensing-round-since-2019-brings-115-bids-from-76-oil-gas-firms> accessed 02 March 2023

CNA, 'Risk Transfer: A Strategy to Help Protect Your Business' (CNA Risk Control, 2006) <www.cna.com/web/wcm/connect/b7bacbf0-b432-4e0c-97face8730b329d5/RC_Guide_RiskTransferStrategytoHelpProtectYou+Business_CNA.pdf?MOD=AJPERES> accessed 20 May 2023

Contract Counsel, 'Gross Negligence' (Contract Counsel, 8 February 2022) <www.contractscounsel.com/b/gross-negligence> accessed 12 October 2023

Cornell Law School, 'Sui Generis' (Legal Information Institute, August 2021) <www.law.cornell.edu/wex/sui_generis> accessed 12 October 2023

Crovelli MR, 'Why the Definition of Probability Matters (Mises Institute, 26 January 2011) <mises.org/library/why-definition-probability-matters> accessed 12 October 2023

Cserne P, 'Reasons for Limiting Freedom of Contract: Questions of Philosophy and Policy' (undated) <jesz.ajk.elte.hu/cserne13.html> accessed on 12 October 2023

Dari-Mattiacci D and LA Franzoni, 'Innovation and Liability Law 4' (14 January 2011) <economix.fr/pdf/seminaires/lien/franzoni.pdf> accessed 25 February 2023.

Davies D, 'Ten Principles of Sound Public Policy' (*Govloop*, 24 August 2013) <www.govloop.com/community/blog/ten-principles-of-sound-public-policy> accessed 12 October 2023

De Castroverde Law Group, 'Does Insurance Cover Gross Negligence?' (3 May 2022) <www.dlgteam.com/blog/does-insurance-cover-gross-negligence> accessed 12 October 2023

DLA Piper, 'Guide to Going Global: Intellectual Property and Technology 2015' <www.lexology.com/library/detail.aspx?g=604c9bde-85c3-41e2-9179-5e0a982af8af> accessed 12 October 2023

Drilling Contractor, 'Nurturing Growth in Africa' <www.drillingcontractor.org/nurturing-growth-in-africa-30580> accessed 12 October 2023

Economist Intelligence Unit, 'Big Spenders: The Outlook for Oil and Gas Industry in 2012' (*Economist Intelligence Unit*, 23 January 2012) <https://eiuperspectives.economist.com/energy/big-spenders/white-paper/big-spenders> accessed 12 October 2023

Edesess, M, 'Catastrophe Bonds: An Important New Financial Instrument' (Autumn 2015) <www.caia.org/sites/default/files/AIAR_Q4_2015-02_Edesses_CatBonds_0.pdf> accessed 21 February 2023

Egbejule E, 'Niger Delta Residents Protest against Month-Long Oil Spill' (*Aljazeera*, 7 December 2021) <www.aljazeera.com/news/2021/12/7/niger-delta-youths-protest-against-month-long-oil-spill> accessed 12 October 2023

Elser W, 'Knock-for-Knock Provisions and Maritime Law' (Wilson Elser, 24 August 2022) <www.wilsonelser.com/writable/files/Attorney_Articles_PDFs/knock-for-knock_provisions_and_maritime_law.pdf> accessed 12 October 2023.

Everen, 'Brief Overview' <www.oil.bm/our-members > accessed 15 February 2023

—— 'Specialty' <www.everenspecialty.bm> accessed 15 February 2023

Faria J, 'Main Oil Producing Countries in Africa 2020 (*Statista*, 29 July 2021) <www.statista.com/statistics/1178514/main-oil-producing-countries-in-africa> accessed 12 October 2023

Farnam Street, 'The Fairness Principle: How the Veil of Ignorance Helps Test Fairness' <fs.blog/2017/10/veil-ignorance> accessed 12 October 2023

Foundation of the American Subcontractors Association, Inc, 'Anti-Indemnity Statutes in the 50 States' (FASA, 2013) <www.azfaircontracting.com/wp-content/uploads/2019/07/ASA-Anti-Indemnity-Chart-50-States.pdf> accessed 12 October 2023

Future Learn, 'Decision Making in a Complex and Uncertain World: Risk and Uncertainty' (University of Groningen) <www.futurelearn.com/courses/complexity-and-uncertainty/0/steps/1824> accessed 12 October 2023

Haidar T, 'The Texas Anti-Indemnity Law – What Does it Mean for Your Business?' (*Oil and Gas IQ*, 3 December 2012) <www.oilandgasiq.com/legal-and-regulatory/articles/the-texas-anti-indemnity-law-what-does-it-mean-for> accessed 12 October 2023

Hill D, 'Peru's indigenous people protest against relicensing of oil concession' *The Guardian* (London, 2 February 2015) <www.theguardian.com/environment/2015/feb/02/perus-indigenous-people-protest-against-re-licensing-of-oil-concession> accessed 12 October 2023

Honoré T, 'Causation in the Law', in Edward N Zalta (ed), *Stanford Encyclopaedia of Philosophy* (2010 edn) <plato.stanford.edu/archives/win2010/entries/causation-law> accessed 12 October 2023

IADC, 'Drilling Lexicon' (*Oil and Gas Drilling Glossary*, 29 October 2013) <www.iadclexicon.org/good-oilfield-practice> accessed 12 October 2023

—— 'Good Oilfield Practice' (*Oil and Gas Drilling Glossary*, 29 October 2013) <http://www.iadclexicon.org/good-oilfield-practice/> accessed 15 October 2023

—— 'IADC International Daywork Drilling Contract Offshore' (*IADC*, revised 2007) <store.iadc.org/product/iadc-international-daywork-drilling-contract-offshore> accessed 12 October 2023

—— 'Membership' <www.iadc.org/membership> accessed 12 October 2023

—— 'Nigeria Chapter' <www.iadc.org/chapters/nigeria> accessed 12 October 2023

IFC, 'IFC Performance Standards on Environmental and Social Sustainability' (*IFC*, 1 January 2012) <www.ifc.org/content/dam/ifc/doc/2010/2012-ifc-performance-standards-en.pdf> accessed 12 October 2023

IGF, 'Global Review: Financial Assurance Governance for the Post-Mining Transition (*IISD*, August 2021) <www.iisd.org/system/files/2021-09/financial-assurance-governance-for-post-mining-transition.pdf> accessed 25 February 2023

Intergovernmental Panel on Climate Change, 'Climate Change 2022: Mitigation of Climate Change' (*IPCC*, Working Group III Contribution, 2022) <https://www.ipcc.ch/report/sixth-assessment-report-working-group-3> accessed 12 October 2023

International Maritime Organisation, 'International Convention on Civil Liability for Oil Pollution Damage, 1969' <www.imo.org/en/About/Conventions/Pages/International-Convention-on-Civil-Liability-for-Oil-Pollution-Damage-(CLC).aspx> accessed 20 February 2023

International Risk Management, 'Institute Operators Extra Expense (OEE)' <www.irmi.com/online/insurance-glossary/terms/operators-extra-expense-oee.aspx> accessed 12 October 2023

IPIECA, 'Sustainability Reporting Guidance for the Oil and Gas Industry' (IPIECA, March 2020) <www.ipieca.org/resources/sustainability-reporting-guidance> accessed 12 October 2023

—— 'Putting the UN Guiding Principles at the Heart of the Oil and Gas Industry' (IPIECA, 10 December 2022) <www.ipieca.org/news/ungps-and-oil-and-gas> accessed 12 October 2023

Jain S, 'Freedom of Contract – Concept, Postulations and Restrictions' (26 October 2020) <dx.doi.org/10.2139/ssrn.3896185> accessed 12 October 2023

Jindra-Cotilla S, 'Distributive Justice' (*Berkeley*, undated) <live-mdp.berkeley.edu/distributive-justice> accessed 12 October 2023

Johnson DR and F Rodyanto, 'The Oil and Gas Law Review: Indonesia' (*The Law Reviews*, 17 November 2020) <thelawreviews.co.uk/title/the-oil-and-gas-law-review/indonesia> accessed 12 October 2023

Jones MS, 'Offshore and Onshore Drilling Contracts' (*Energy Symposium* 27 July 2011) <cdn.ymaws.com/www.iiah.org/resource/resmgr/imported/Offshore%20%20and%20Onshore%20Drilling-%20Part%201%20Contr.pdf> accessed 12 October 2023

Karim IA and others, 'Contracts, Negotiation and Enforcement in Indonesia: Overview' (Karim Syah Law Firm, October 2016) <us.practicallaw.com/8-634-4686?q=&qp=&qo=&qe> accessed 12 October 2023

Kelleher S, 'Public Policy limitations on Indemnity for Sole or Partial Negligence' (*SmithCurrie*, 7 July 2014) <www.smithcurrie.com/publications/common-sense-contract-law/public-policy-limitations-on-indemnity-for-sole-or-partial-negligence> accessed 12 October 2023

Kollewe J, 'Oil Industry Set for Surge in Insurance Premiums after Deepwater Disaster' *The Guardian* (London, 20 September 2010) <www.theguardian.com/business/2010/sep/20/deepwater-oil-rigs-insurance-costs> accessed 12 October 2023

Kulovic N, 'UK Oil & Gas Regulator Rebrands to Reflect Role in Energy Transition' (*Offshore Energy*, 21 March 2022) <www.offshore-energy.biz/uk-oil-gas-regulator-rebrands-to-reflect-role-in-energy-transition> accessed 7 February 2023

Lamont J and C Favor, 'Distributive Justice' (*Stanford Encyclopaedia of Philosophy*, 1996) <plato.stanford.edu/entries/justice-distributive> accessed 12 October 2023

—— 'Distributive Justice', (*Stanford Encyclopedia of Philosophy*, 26 September 2017) <plato.stanford.edu/archives/win2017/entries/justice-distributive> accessed 12 October 2023

Lawson A, 'UK Offers New North Sea Oil and Gas Licences Despite Climate Concerns' *The Guardian* (London, 7 October 2022) <www.theguardian.com/business/2022/oct/07/uk-offers-new-north-sea-oil-and-gas-licences-despite-climate-concerns> accessed 2 March 2023

Leveson N, 'Risk Management in the Oil and Gas Industry' (*MIT Energy Initiative*, 17 May 2011) <energy.mit.edu/news/risk-management-in-the-oil-and-gas-industry> accessed 12 October 2023

LOGIC, 'IMHH General Guidance' <logic-energy.org/imhh/guidance> accessed 12 October 2023

—— 'Signatory Withdrawals – IMHH 2012 Scheme' (LOGIC 2018) <logic-energy.org/imhh/2012-2/signatory-withdrawals> accessed 12 October 2023

—— *General Conditions of Contract for Supply of Major items of Plant and Equipment* (2nd edn, LOGIC 2005) <jimdo-storage.global.ssl.fastly.net/file/8adbb68e-23e7-44c2-9f53-c0e9ee20cc67/SCA%20T&C.pdf> accessed 12 October 2023

—— '2022 Mutual Indemnity and Hold Harmless Deed' (21 October 2021) <app.logic-energy.org/imhh/documents/download/3> accessed 12 October 2023

Mace P and others, 'Oil and Gas Regulation in the UK: Overview' (*Thomson Reuters Practical Law*, 1 October 2017) <uk.practicallaw.thomsonreuters.com/5-524-5349?transitionType=Default&contextData=(sc.Default)&firstPage=true&bhcp=1> accessed 12 October 2023

Mackay M and L Shaxton, 'Understanding and Applying Basic Public Policy Concepts' (University of Guelph 2011) <www.politicipublice.ro/uploads/understanding_public_policy.pdf> accessed 12 October 2023

Maiese M, 'Distributive Justice', *Beyond Intractability* (June 2013) < www.beyondintractability.org/essay/distributive_justice> accessed 12 October 2023

McDonald L, 'Extending the boundaries of wilful misconduct and gross negligence' (SKULD, March 2017) <www.skuld.com/topics/legal/pi-and-defence/extending-the-boundaries-of-wilful-misconduct-and-gross-negligence> accessed 12 October 2023

Miller D, 'Justice' (*Stanford Encyclopedia of Philosophy* 2021) <plato.stanford.edu/cgi-bin/encyclopedia/archinfo.cgi?entry=justice> accessed 12 October 2023

Montara Commission of Inquiry, 'Report of the Montara Commission of Inquiry' (Commissioner David Borthwick AO PSM, June 2010) <www.iadc.org/wp-content/uploads/2016/02/201011-Montara-Report.pdf> accessed 12 October 2023

Natural Gas Intelligence, 'Anadarko: BP-Mitsui Settlement a Positive Step' (*Natural Gas Intelligence*, 23 May 2011) <www.naturalgasintel.com/anadarko-bp-mitsui-settlement-a-positive-step-2> accessed 12 October 2023

North Sea Transition Authority, 'Our Relationship with the UK Government' <www.nstauthority.co.uk/about-us/leadership-governance/our-relationship-with-the-uk-government> accessed 12 October 2023

—— 'Overview 2023' <www.nstauthority.co.uk/media/8846/a5l_a5overview-final-accessible-003.pdf> accessed 7 February 2023

—— 'Exploration and Production: Field Development Plans' <www.nstauthority.co.uk/regulatory-information/exploration-and-production/development/field-development-plans/> accessed 15 October 2023

—— 'Licensing and Consents: Overview' <www.nstauthority.co.uk/regulatory-information/licensing-and-consents> accessed 23 September 2023

—— 'Requirements for the Planning of and Consent to UKCS Field Developments' (May 2018) <www.nstauthority.co.uk/media/7803/fdp_guidance_111021.pdf> accessed 12 October 2023

Offshore Energies UK, 'Guidelines on Relief Well Planning for Offshore Wells' (OEUK, Issue 2, March 2013) <oeuk.org.uk/product/guidelines-on-relief-well-planning-issue-2> accessed 23 March 2023

Offshore, 'NSTA Urges Improved Coordination of UK Offshore ESG Reporting' (Offshore, 15 December 2022) <www.offshore-mag.com/regional-reports/north-sea-europe/article/14287181/nsta-urges-improved-coordination-of-uk-offshore-esg-reporting> accessed 8 February 2023

Ohio Environmental Protection Agency, 'Financial Assurance Mechanisms' (EPA, July 2019) <epa.ohio.gov/static/Portals/34/document/guidance/FAMechanisms Overview.pdf> accessed 26 February 2023

Oil & Gas Authority, 'OGA Governance Guidance' (January 2022) <www.nst-authority.co.uk/media/7999/oga-governance-guidance_2022_feb22-1.pdf> accessed 12 October 2023

OPOL Agreement < https://www.opol.org.uk/agreement > accessed 12 October 2023.

Oxford Lexico, 'Public Policy' (*Oxford Lexico*) <www.lexico.com/definition/public_policy> accessed 12 October 2023

Peleg LA, 'Where Is Sustainability on the Oil and Gas Agenda?' (*PRECOGNIZE*, 15 November 2021) <www.precog.co/blog/sustainability-challenges-oil-gas> accessed 12 October 2023

Pickavance J, 'Gross Negligence in Construction Contracts: Law and Practice' (Eversheds, 2015) <www.eversheds.com/documents/services/construction/04369%20-%20Construction%20Article%20-%20Jan%202015_v4.pdf> accessed 12 October 2023

Powell AR, 'Robert Nozick and the Value of Liberty' (Cato Institute, 21 June 2011) <www.cato.org/blog/robert-nozick-value-liberty> accessed 12 October 2023

PwC, 'Oil and Gas in Indonesia Investment and Taxation Guide 2020' (11th edn, PWC 2020) <www.pwc.com/id/en/pwc-publications/industries-publications/energy--utilities---mining-publications/oil-gas-guide-2020.html> accessed 12 October 2023

Redfearn Jr R, 'Anti-Indemnity Acts and their Impacts on Insurance Coverage: A Comparative Analysis' (*Insurance Journal Magazine*, 22 August 2005) <www.insurancejournal.com/magazines/features/2005/08/22/59608.htm> accessed 12 October 2023

Reuters, 'BP Reaches $18.7 Billion Settlement over Deadly 2010 Spill', *Reuters* (2 July 2015) <www.reuters.com/article/2015/07/03/us-bp-gulfmexico-settlement-idUSKCN0PC1BW20150703> accessed 12 October 2023

Richardson L and others, 'Indemnities in Commonwealth Contracting' (Legal Briefing, 19 August 2011) <www.ags.gov.au/publications/legal-briefing/br93.pdf> accessed 12 October 2023

Rochette J and others, 'Seeing Beyond the Horizon for Deepwater Oil and Gas: Strengthening the International Regulation of Offshore Exploration and Exploitation' (IDDRI, 14 February 2014) <www.iddri.org/sites/default/files/import/publications/st0114_jr-et-al._offshoreen.pdf> accessed 10 October 2023.

Saraceni P and N Summers, Reviewing Knock for Knock Indemnities: Risk Allocation in Maritime and Offshore Oil and Gas Contracts (Clifford Chance, October 2015) <www.cliffordchance.com/content/dam/cliffordchance/briefings/2015/10/reviewing-knock-for-knock-indemnities-risk-allocation-in-maritime-and-offshore-oil-and-gas-contracts.pdf> accessed 12 October 2023

Sharp D and R Andrew, 'Drilling in Extreme Environments: Challenges and Implications for Energy Insurance Industry' (Lloyd's 2011) <docplayer.net/784935-Energy-drilling-in-extreme-environments-challenges-and-implications-for-the-energy-insurance-industry.html> accessed 12 October 2023

Skogh G, 'Insurance Coverage of Accidental Damage to the Environment', Worshop Law and Economics of Environmental Policy (2000) <www.cserge.ucl.ac.uk/Skogh.pdf> accessed 27 February 2023

Solli TE, 'Workover/Well Intervention and Regulatory Challenges', (OnePetro, 4 October 2011) <onepetro.org/OTCBRASIL/proceedings-abstract/11OBRA/All-11OBRA/OTC-22586-MS/37021> accessed 12 October 2023

Street F, 'The Fairness Principle: How the Veil of Ignorance Helps Test Fairness' <fs.blog/2017/10/veil-ignorance> accessed 12 October 2023

Surbhi S, 'Difference between Risk and Uncertainty' (*Key Differences*, 15 June 2017) <keydifferences.com/difference-between-risk-and-uncertainty.html> accessed 12 October 2023

The Economist, 'American Insurance: Bungee Jump', (*The Economist*, 14 September 2000) <www.economist.com/finance-and-economics/2000/09/14/bungee-jump> accessed 12 October 2023

Thomas Miller Specialty, 'Shipowner's Liability Insurance Protection & Indemnity: Terms and Conditions for Policies Issued in Hamburg' (1 October 2020) <www.thomasmillerspecialty.com/fileadmin/uploads/tms/Documents/Policy_Wordings/P_I/TMS-PI_HH_OL_Terms_EN_2020-10-01.pdf> accessed 12 October 2023

Thomas N, J Velez and A Guillamont, 'Effects of Gross Negligence on Insurance Contracts' (Lexology, 13 July 2009) <www.lexology.com/library/detail.aspx?g=45f48f4f-b2a5-4962-bd7f-94a1580ef3d7> accessed 20 February 2023

United Nations Population Fund, 'Human Rights Princples' (UNPF, 2005) <https://www.unfpa.org/resources/human-rights-principles> accessed 12 October 2023. United Nations Population Fund, 'Human Rights Principles' (UNPF, 2005) <https://www.unfpa.org/resources/human-rights-principles> accessed 12 October 2023.

United Nations, *Guiding Principles on Business and Human Rights: Implementing the United Nations 'Protect, Respect and Remedy' Framework* (New York and Geneva 2011) <www.ohchr.org/sites/default/files/documents/publications/guidingprinciplesbusinesshr_en.pdf> accessed 12 October 2023.

Vidal J, 'Nigeria's Agony Dwarfs the Gulf Oil Spill, the US and Europe Ignore It' *The Guardian* (London, 30 May 2010) <www.theguardian.com/world/2010/may/30/oil-spills-nigeria-niger-delta-shell#:~:text=According%20to%20Nigerian%20federal%20government,been%20filed%20against%20Shell%20alone> accessed 12 October 2023

White & Case, 'Managing Construction Risks in Asia-Pacific: Indonesia' (17 November 2021) <www.whitecase.com/insight-our-thinking/managing-construction-risks-asia-pacific-indonesia> accessed 12 October 2023

Willumsen T and T Holte, 'Contractors' pollution risk gets dirty' (*Offshore Engineer*, 14 April 2015) <www.oedigital.com/news/452942-contractors-pollution-risk-gets-dirty> accessed 9 October 2023

Wolf J, 'Models of Distributive Justice' (Novartis Foundation Symposium, 2007) <www.ncbi.nlm.nih.gov/pubmed/17214316> accessed 12 October 2023

WHITE PAPERS

Anderson OL, *Drilling for Black Gold under the Model Form Drilling Contracts* (White Paper, Energy and Mineral Law Foundation 1994) <emlf.org/product/drilling-for-black-gold-under-the-model-form-drilling-contracts> accessed 12 October 2023

Zigrand JP, H Song Shin and J Danielsson, *Risk Appetite and Endogenous Risk* (Financial Markets Group AXA Working Paper Series No 2 Discussion Paper No 647, 2010)

WORKING PAPERS

Bindeman K, 'Production Sharing Agreements: An Economic Analysis' (Oxford Institute for Energy Study WPM, 30 October 1999) <https://ora.ox.ac.uk/objects/uuid:3ba0589f-8c3a-43b9-b034-24f7dae7e0c5> accessed 12 October 2023

Craswell R, 'Freedom of Contract' (University of Chicago Law School Chicago Unbound, Coase-Sandor Working Paper Series in Law and Economics no 33, 1995) <chicagounbound.uchicago.edu/cgi/viewcontent.cgi?article=1215&context=law_and_economics> accessed 12 October 2023

He Q, 'Climate Change and Effective Catastrophe Risk Management Mechanism: A Law and Economics Analysis of Insurance and Alternative Approaches' (Working Paper for the Seminar on Market Integration: The EU Experience and Implications for Regulatory Reform in China, May 2014, and the Workshop in Rutgers School of Law-Camden, September 2014)

Hovy P, 'Risk Allocation in Public-Private Partnerships: Maximizing Value for Money' (IISD Discussion Paper, August 2015) <www.iisd.org/system/files/publications/risk-allocation-ppp-maximizing-value-for-money-discussion-paper.pdf> accessed 3 March 2023

CONFERENCE PAPERS

Bardes CR, 'Role of Nuclear Insurance in US' (Sino-American Seminar on Nuclear Liability, China 2000)

Cole JC, 'Replacement Cost Economics of Offshore Drilling Rigs' (SPE/IADC Drilling Conference Paper, 28 February–2 March 1995) <onepetro.org/SPEDC/proceedings-abstract/95DC/All-95DC/SPE-28197-MS/57115> accessed 12 October 2023

Warren T, 'The Operator-Contractor Relationship – Contract Changes, 1982 to 1984' (Paper Presented at the Society of Petroleum Engineers SPE/IADC Drilling Conference, New Orleans, March 1985)

UNPUBLISHED WORKS

Mildwaters K, 'Oil and Gas: Commercial Contracts Matrix' (University of Dundee 2016)

MODEL FORMS

AIPN Well Services Model Form 2002

Standard Contracts for UK Offshore Oil and Gas Industry: General Conditions of Contracts for Service On- and Off-shore, LOGIC Edition 4, 2019, <extension://ngphehpfehdmjellohmlojkplilekadg/pages/pdf/web/viewer.html?file=file%3A%2F%2F%2FC%3A%2FUsers%2Fcex%2FDownloads%2FThe%2520current%2520version%2520Attachment%2520No.%25206%2520-%252011.03.2022.pdf> accessed 12 October 2023.

Index